Francis Espinasse

Literary Recollections and Sketches

Francis Espinasse

Literary Recollections and Sketches

ISBN/EAN: 9783337011635

Printed in Europe, USA, Canada, Australia, Japan

Cover: Foto ©ninafisch / pixelio.de

More available books at **www.hansebooks.com**

LITERARY
RECOLLECTIONS

AND SKETCHES

BY

FRANCIS ESPINASSE

LONDON
HODDER AND STOUGHTON
27 PATERNOSTER ROW
1893

CONTENTS

I. SOME EARLY REMINISCENCES

IN the days of my boyhood there may have been several denizens of Edinburgh, my native city, who knew and remembered Burns ; but I was aware of the existence of only two such, and both of them belonged to the gentler sex. One of them played a prominent part in the poet's biography, being no other than the Clarinda of his fervid love-letters, the 'Nancy' of several of his songs and other poems, especially of the exquisite and impassioned 'Ae fond kiss, and then we sever!' When I was a boy and first heard of her as alive and in Edinburgh, the Clarinda of Burns's rapturous prose and verse was an old and invalid lady of eighty, living in solitude and seclusion in a quiet little street just round the south-western corner of the Calton Hill. There a short walk would take her to the monument erected, opposite the southern boundary of the High School of Edinburgh, to the poet whose memory she appears to have cherished to the last. She was the widow of a husband who was unworthy of her and whose name, M'Lehose, she has made familiar to all worshippers of Burns. Among these, in a boyish way, I might then be reckoned. Often as I wended my way homewards from the High School, where I received my early education, I turned into that little street and looked wistfully at the words 'Mrs. M'Lehose' on the door-bell of the flat in

A

which was her modest domicile.   How I wished that I
could master audacity enough to ring and ask to see the
old lady who in earlier life had inspired Burns with a
passionate love which, as the wife of another, she could not
return as he desired it to be returned !   But the audacity
never came, and I never caught even a glimpse of the
aged gentlewoman, whose infirmities seldom allowed her
to take her walks abroad.   She was eighty-two when
she died.   An authentic edition of Burns's letters to her,
with an interesting biographical notice of herself, was
published not many years ago by one of her descendants.

The other Edinburgh lady who in her youth knew Burns
and had been made by the admiring poet the heroine of
a well-known song was a friend of my family and showed
herself kindly disposed towards me as a boy.   This was
Mrs. Cumming of Logie, a very genial elderly dame of
the old Scottish school, who in age retained traces of the
beauty which, added to a peculiar maidenly charm, threw
the susceptible Burns into raptures.   When Burns knew
her she was Miss Lesley Baillie, one of the two daughters of
Mr. Baillie, an Ayrshire gentleman of good family, and her
father, sister, and herself, on their way to England, called
at Dumfries on Burns, of whom Scotland was proud, and
who was an Ayrshire man to boot.   Burns was so struck
by Miss Lesley Baillie that, when the visit was over, he
mounted on horseback and accompanied the party fourteen or fifteen miles on their way southward.   As he rode
home he bethought him of the old Scotch ballad :

> ' My bonnie Lizzie Baillie
> I 'll rowe thee in my plaidie, etc.'

Still on horseback, he composed in memory of his young

and beautiful visitor, the song so flattering to her, which begins

> 'Oh ! saw ye bonnie Lesley
>   As she gaed o'er the Border ?
> She 's gane, like Alexander,
>   To spread her conquests farther.'

A few days afterwards, writing to his friend Mrs. Dunlop, who was also an acquaintance and a neighbour of ' Bonnie Lesley,' he spoke of his heroine of a few hours in language of the most glowing admiration. He compared her to ' a messenger of Heaven appearing in the unspotted purity of her celestial home, among the coarse, polluted, far inferior sons of men.' This and still more ardent laudation, almost amounting to rhapsody, Burns poured forth while engaged in the prosaic task at ' Annan Water Foot,' as he told Mrs. Dunlop, of 'discharging a vessel of rum from Antigua !' Mrs. Cumming was proud of the song, and almost as much so of an emendation of her own which she suggested in his touching effusion of too exaggerated gratitude, the ' Lament for James Earl of Glencairn.' In the first draft of the poem Burns had made the last stanza run thus :

> ' The mother may forget the child
>   That smiles sae sweetly on her knee ;
> But I 'll remember gude Glencairn,
>   And a' that he has done for me !'

Some member of the Earl's family appears to have thought the epithet 'gude' not strong enough, and wished to have 'great' substituted for it, but this Burns in his turn thought *too* strong. Miss Lesley Baillie suggested that neither epithet should be used and that Glencairn should be apostrophised. Burns adopted her suggestion, and printed in the edition of his poems which was published in

1773, the stanza as it has ever since appeared, thanks to the young lady's very happy emendation of more than a hundred years ago,

> ' The mother may forget the child
> That smiles sae sweetly on her knee ;
> But I 'll remember thee, Glencairn,
> And a' that thou hast done for me ! '

The other sister of the party whom Burns accompanied on their way to England never married. I remember her as Miss Baillie, a rather severe-looking elderly spinster. She wore that now, for British ladies at least, long obsolete head-dress, a turban, which aided in impressing my youthful mind with a certain awe of her. Both sisters died long ago. Mrs. Cumming's only daughter married the late Sir James Coxe, who became head of the Lunacy Board, whose acquaintance I made in Edinburgh many years after I knew his mother-in-law, and who cherished the remembrance of her very happy emendation of the last lines of Burns's lament for Lord Glencairn. Dead also is her only son, the late Dr. W. F. Cumming, who accompanied the present Duke of Argyll on a continental tour when his Grace was a young man.

My earliest personal recollection of a great author is a very slight one of Sir Walter Scott. *Virgilium vidi tantum* is all that I can say of the most famous of Scotchmen, yet perhaps there are not many persons living who can say even that. My solitary glimpse of him was when, though a little boy, I was old enough to have read with delight the *Tales of a Grandfather*. They were as familiar to me as the fairy tales of childhood and the hymns of the revered Dr. Watts, when I was sent to a preparatory school at Melrose, which, as everybody knows,

is not far from Abbotsford. One day I was out walking
with a governess or other female guardian, when an open
carriage, with an elderly gentleman sitting in it reading,
and a boy on a pony trotting by its side, was seen coming
along a bend of the road, so that we had them in full view.
'Look,' said my companion, 'that is Sir Walter Scott
and his grandson.' Look I did at the author of my
favourite *Tales of a Grandfather*, and especially at the
enviable boy for whom they were written, to whom they
were addressed, and who seemed to me more or less
deformed. The carriage with its illustrious inmate, the
pony with Hugh Littlejohn on its back, passed by, and
I never saw either of them again. In a very few years
both of them were in their graves ; the death of the
grandson at ten preceding by some nine months that of
his sexagenarian grandfather.

My next reminiscence, a little less slight, is of another
Scottish literary celebrity, though one far inferior to Sir
Walter. Thomas, familiarly known as 'Tom' Campbell, I
not only saw, but heard. At the time of which I am writing
Campbell had ceased to produce any verse that added to
his poetic fame. 'Theodric' was adjudged rather a poor
sequel to the 'Pleasures of Hope,' to 'Gertrude of Wyo-
ming,' and to some of the most spirit-stirring lyrics in the
language. But on the visit which he paid to Scotland,
and during which I saw him, he was received with as
much enthusiasm as if his poetic genius had never waned.
In Glasgow especially, the city of his *alma mater*, which
had thrice elected him its Rector, once when Sir Walter
himself was a candidate, his reception was one of boundless welcome. He was fêted and caressed in Edinburgh
too, where he was the guest of Mr. (afterwards Sir Archi-

bald) Alison, and the hero of any number of dinner
parties given in his honour by the best people there. It
was not however under the roof of an Amphitryon of the
upper class that I saw Campbell and listened to his talk.
The chief public honour paid him in Edinburgh was by
the Town Council, which conferred on him the freedom
of the city. One of the members of the Council who
had been most active in procuring him this distinction
was a Bailie (the Scottish analogue of Alderman) who
was intimate with my family. The Bailie asked Campbell to dinner, and, as a boy of supposed intelligence and
enthusiasm for poetry and poets, I was asked to put in
an appearance with the dessert, that I might gaze on the
Bard of Hope. The guests were chiefly Edinburgh
ministers of the Kirk, one of them being the long-headed,
pawky Dr. Lee, then in charge of one of the most important city churches, and afterwards Principal of the University of Edinburgh. Among them, and a striking contrast
to his clerical fellow-guests, sat the poet, a spruce little
gentleman, with finely cut features, in a gay and talkative
mood, which became more so as he made an end of glass
upon glass of brandy and water. He told amusing story
after story, to the great delectation of his listeners. Young
as I was, I noticed that some of the poet's anecdotes verged
on the improper, and that in these cases, Dr. Lee's countenance wore an embarrassed expression, as if, while
bound to smile, he as a cleric felt it to be his duty to look
grave. So the evening wore on until Campbell had told
his last story, finished his last glass of brandy and water,
and it was time for seniors, much more for juniors, to take
their homeward way.

Lord Jeffrey was an old friend of my father, and had a

high opinion of him in his professional capacity. A few years before Jeffrey became a judge of the Court of Session —he had long before resigned the editorship of the *Edinburgh Review*—my father, seeing him in his carriage, which was standing before an Edinburgh door, asked permission to present to him the writer of these pages, then a stripling. Whatever he may have been in criticism, Lord Jeffrey was in private life one of the most amiable of men. He good-naturedly assented, and invited father and son to breakfast on the following Sunday at Craigcrook, his summer residence near Edinburgh. On a fine summer morning we wended our way to the baronial-looking pile (familiar enough to me from without) into which Jeffrey had converted a solitary old tower, and which nestled delectably at the foot of the beautifully-wooded Corstorphine Hill. In the drawing-room we found ourselves alone. There was only one book visible. With youthful curiosity I took it up, and found it to be Carlyle's *French Revolution*, a presentation copy, with the brief inscription: 'To Lord Jeffrey, from T.C.' Strange to say, in spite of Jeffrey's fastidiousness in regard to style in general, and frequent censures of Carlyle's in particular, he was a warm admirer of the *French Revolution*. Summoned to the breakfast-room, we found in it our host, his wife, his daughter (the 'Charlie' of his correspondence), with her husband, not long married to her, Mr. Empson, who succeeded Macvey Napier (himself Jeffrey's successor) in the editorship of the *Edinburgh Review*. What struck me most in Lord Jeffrey's physiognomy was the piercing brilliancy of his eyes, which I have never since seen equalled. Mrs. Jeffrey was afflicted with a twitching movement in her face and arms. It never ceased, and made one nervous to look at her, inducing an expectation that some disaster would befall the tea equipage, which, however, she handled with unfailing dexterity.   Mrs. Empson, a tall young lady, with cheeks like peonies, and a remarkably erect carriage, never opened her mouth, at least to speak.   Her husband was very quiet and gentlemanlike.   Lord Jeffrey had a long chat with my father about old times.   Now and then in the intervals of conversation he glanced at the *Times*, which lay beside him on the table, and expressed satisfaction with the progress of the Municipal Corporations Bill (it abolished the hole-and-corner municipalities of the olden time), which was making its way through the House of Commons.   Asking some question as to what my father intended me to be, and receiving a rather ambitious reply, he gave me one glance with those piercing eyes of his and said, ' Make a doctor of him ! '   Breakfast over, we accompanied our host and Mr. Empson to the gardens, luxuriant with summer blossoms.   There, with his own judicial hands, Lord Jeffrey culled and cut a pretty nosegay for my mother, went with us to the entrance, and with Mr. Empson bade us goodbye, leaving on me the pleasant impression of a very courteous and amiable old gentleman.

The last of these early reminiscences is one of Wordsworth, whom Jeffrey in the *Edinburgh Review* had done his best, and his worst, to depreciate and keep down.   But for myself and the friends among my coevals, Jeffrey's harsh criticisms had been superseded by Christopher North's glowing praises of Wordsworth in *Blackwood's Magazine*, and we learned to revere the poet of ' Tintern Abbey ' and the ' Excursion.'   I was visiting during school holiday-time some relatives at Kendal, when another at a distance, thinking to do me a kindness, and without informing me of his intention, wrote to Wordsworth to the effect that a young admirer of his was sojourning at Kendal, and would be overjoyed to be allowed to visit him. To my great surprise I received an amiable note from the poet, saying that he would be visible at Rydal up to a certain date. There was no Kendal and Windermere Railway in those days (nor even a steam-boat on Windermere itself), and, if I remember rightly, no stage-coach or anything of the kind. By the well-to-do the journey between the town and the lake was made in post-chaises, which in that region of steep acclivities and declivities rattled down hill, the impetus thus given them aiding them to rattle up hill again, in a fashion unknown to me elsewhere. I started on foot one fine autumn day, at an hour rather too late for a walk of fifteen or sixteen miles, through an unfamiliar region in which there was so much that was picturesque, beautiful, and grand to make a pedestrian with eyes in his head linger lovingly on the way. Evening was coming on when, after a happy, happy day—for Windermere and its surrounding scenery was new to me—I reached the quaint old building known as Rydal Mount, which was the goal of my pilgrimage. There was light enough without, but the sitting-room on the ground-floor, into which I was ushered without the conventional announcement, was darkened by the ivy and shrubs which enshrouded the windows. I found the poet and his wife dozing in their chairs. My entrance roused them, and after the due greetings the poet proposed to show me his grounds. He donned a Tam-o'-Shanter bonnet, threw a plaid round his shoulders, and forth we sallied. He must then have been not far off seventy, but he looked remarkably hale and erect. Of his features, that which struck me most was his nose, one massive enough to have satisfied Mr. Walter Shandy himself. His countenance had not to my mind that refinement which is visible in his portraits. Altogether, if I had not known that a great poet was by my side, I might have taken him for a Lowland farmer of the better class. As we wandered in the evening sunshine, along terraces (the work of his own hands) and garden walks, among trees and shrubs and flowers, mountains behind us, mountains in front of us, with occasional glimpses of Windermere, he pointed out the beauties of the changeful view, and questioned me about my parentage, upbringing, and prospects. Though a walk of sixteen miles would have been a trifle to him at my age, he seemed pleased that a town-bred youth should have trudged all the way from Kendal to visit him. Once only was the subject of his poetry touched on, and then by me, not by himself. It was when he pointed out the chapel which owed its existence to one of the Châtelaines of Rydal Hall. I said that I remembered the grateful lines which he had addressed to her on the completion of her pious work, and this reminiscence, too, seemed to please him. Before we parted, something that I said may have betrayed a hankering after a literary life. At any rate, he warned me against it, and spoke of what he had known of suffering among friends of his drudging for, and dependent on, 'booksellers.' He advised me to be 'a surgeon.' As nothing came of Lord Jeffrey's monition to my father and of Wordsworth to myself, probably some lives have been saved to the world and some limbs spared to their owners.[1]

[1] Of the primitive simplicity to be found in the Lake District half a century ago I can furnish from my own experience an illustration. A year or two after my visit to Wordsworth I was making with a young friend a walking tour through the Lake country. When from Windermere we reached the placid vale of Grasmere we partook of a modest refection of bread and cheese and ale at what was then the little inn there—it has, I daresay, long since disappeared, and instead of it large hotels invite the traveller. The meal being finished, and our small change being exhausted, I tendered the landlord a sovereign. But he, too, had no small change, and he declared himself unable to procure any. Here was a slight financial dilemma. After some reflection and scrutiny of his guests, the landlord said: 'Where are you young gentlemen going?' 'We are walking to Carlisle,' was the reply. 'Well,' he rejoined, 'if you will call at the carrier's there, naming street and house, and pay him, he will be coming here on such and such a day, and will bring me the money.' On reaching Carlisle we did as he had suggested, and no doubt our host of Grasmere found no reason to regret his trustfulness.

II. THE BRITISH MUSEUM LIBRARY FIFTY YEARS AGO, AND AFTER

M ANY are the changes, within and without, which the British Museum has undergone during the last half-century. Fifty years ago it was still Montague House —an extensive red-brick mansion, fronted by a high brick wall, through an aperture in which intending visitors, passing a French-looking lodge, were surveyed by the obesest of porters, who might have been evolved from the Fat Boy in *Pickwick*. Montague House has disappeared, and it is needless to say what a different aspect the frontage of the Museum now presents, with its gilt railings, Ionic columns, and other stately Greek architecture. It is, however, with the Library of the Museum that I am now mainly concerned. Numerous and important have been, since 1843, the structural alterations and expansions of the Library. But the greatest of them all is the transformation of the spacious grass plot which was enclosed by the four wings of Montague House. It was pleasant in summer to steal away to it from the gloom of the Library proper, and in stillness and solitude look up at the blue sky. Such an escape is impossible now. What was then a grassy quadrangle has since been covered by the most magnificent of reading-rooms, peopled from morn to dewy

12

eve by hundreds of students,[1] authors, compilers, journalists, of both sexes and of many ages, in quest of information of every kind, from that pertaining to the remotest antiquity down to an unknown or uncertain address discoverable in the Post Office London Directory, which is not the least sedulously consulted of the thousands of volumes accessible on the shelves of the Reading-room itself.[2]

Then, as now, the highest official functionary of the Museum was styled 'Principal Librarian.' The title of his office was and is somewhat a misnomer, since he had and has nothing to do specifically with the Library. He is the commander-in-chief, as it were, of the army of Museum *employés*, his generals and colonels being

---

[1] In the memoir, which Lord Beaconsfield prefixed to the 1858 edition of Isaac Disraeli's *Curiosities of Literature*, he wrote : ' When my father first frequented the Reading-room of the British Museum at the end of the last century, his companions never numbered half-a-dozen ; now those daily pilgrims of research may be counted by as many hundreds.' After Lord Beaconsfield, then Mr. Disraeli, became a trustee of the British Museum, and visited the interior recesses of the Library, he greeted very cordially one of the senior attendants who had been in the service of Isaac Disraeli, and who had often carried in his arms as a child the future Earl of Beaconsfield and Prime Minister of England. Probably it was to Isaac Disraeli that his old servant owed his subordinate employment in the Museum Library.

[2] A friend furnishes me with the following illustration of the strange uses which the privilege of admission to the Museum Reading-room is sometimes made to serve : 'Some weeks ago,' he says, 'I was searching in the catalogue for the *editio princeps* of an obscure work of Petrarch. Beside me was a lady engaged in a very different quest, as it proved. She was evidently perplexed while she turned over, with a look of weary disappointment, one of those catalogue-volumes devoted to Periodical Publications, which are certainly rather puzzling to the wholly uninitiated. With what you know to be my usual gallantry, I offered the lady my aid, and, on this being accepted, I asked her the precise object of her search. 'Oh,' was her reply, 'I want to find Bradshaw. I am going to Exeter this afternoon and I wish to know the hour at which my train starts !' I was able to save her further trouble with the catalogue by informing her that in the entrance-hall both a Bradshaw and another less complex Railway Guide are obligingly kept for general reference.

the Keepers and Assistant-Keepers of the various departments, under whom, as subordinate officers, are the Assistants, lowest in the scale being an array of attendants, the rank and file of the Museum force, with their sergeants and corporals. The real head of the Library proper was and is called the Keeper of the Printed Books as distinct from the Manuscripts, which have a Keeper of their own. Under the Keeper of the Printed Books, was one Assistant-Keeper—there are now three—with some eight or ten Assistants, of whom there are now nearly forty. Few as were the Assistants in the Library then, compared with their present number, they were probably twice as many as had been found sufficient not long before. When I became one of them, they had been gradually increased in order to assist in compiling, on quasi-scientific principles, a new catalogue of the contents of the vast Library, to be substituted for the old chaotic and imperfect chief catalogue which had become confusion worse confounded, and to include the contents of other subordinate but still important catalogues, all of which the unfortunate reader had sometimes to consult before he could be sure that the book required by him was or was not in the Library. Of the New Catalogue more hereafter.

The titular Principal Librarian fifty years ago was the late Sir Henry Ellis, an antiquary of some eminence in his day and generation, the editor of Dugdale's *Monasticon* among other monumental works. He himself had little of the Dryasdust in his composition. He was a short, dumpy, red-faced man, so fat that he waddled rather than walked. Being apparently of a social turn, he used often to stroll about the Library and chat familiarly with the assistants—practices wholly discontinued by his successors in the Principal Librarianship. Sir Henry was full of jest and anecdote, and some of his stories were not of a kind that ought to have been told to his juniors by a senior of his age and position in that Temple of the Muses. The real head of the Library, as Keeper of the Printed Books, was the well-known Panizzi. He was an Italian refugee, who, on finding shelter in England, had taught his native language in Liverpool, where Roscoe the historian introduced him to Brougham. Brougham took a fancy to him, and procured him a subordinate position in the Museum Library. In the course of time, when there was a vacancy in the Keepership of the Printed Books, Panizzi was pitchforked into it, over the head of that venerable and admirable scholar the late Rev. Henry Cary, translator of the greatest poet of Panizzi's own fatherland—Dante. The appointment of a foreigner to such a position gave great dissatisfaction to the English world of letters in general and to Cary in particular, who retired from the Museum in dudgeon.[1] Panizzi becoming a member of the Holland House circle, and intimate with Macaulay, Hallam, and other Whigs of 'light and leading,' was taken a good deal of notice of in London Society, which did not diminish his originally high opinion of himself. He was a big, boisterous, rather blustering man, with likes and still more with dislikes, a dangerous foe, and if he was also a helpful patron his patronage was generally bestowed on those in whom he found subserviency and sycophancy united to mediocrity. In

---

[1] A bust of Cary has been recently presented to the Museum by his daughter. Readers of Charles Lamb's correspondence may remember his penitential missive to his host after imbibing too freely as the guest of Cary in his rooms at the Museum.

striking contrast to Panizzi was the Assistant-Keeper of the Printed Books, the Rev. Richard Garnett, a philologist of great attainments and originality, and of the gentlest disposition, his shyness being only equalled by his amiability. He was the officer to apply to if a holiday was wanted and Panizzi absent, and it was granted as if the applicant were doing him a favour instead of asking one. He did not live long enough to succeed to the Keepership of Printed Books when Panizzi was promoted to be Principal Librarian. But the office, which by seniority would have been the father's, is now filled by the son, the eminent and amiable Dr. Richard Garnett, whose distinguished merits as a Librarian and an author are too well known and widely appreciated to need a tribute of recognition from me.

Panizzi was a man of considerable energy of a kind, and naturally he wished to show what could be done for the enlargement of the Library by a foreigner, whose appointment to its headship was so generally unpopular. His social connections aided him in this effort. He paid great court to public men,—especially if like Macaulay they belonged to the governing body of the Museum, its Trustees—whose influence could be effective in procuring an increase of Parliamentary Grants for the Library, and who were thus led to credit him with great zeal for its improvement. In this way it came to pass, that with his appointment to the Principal Librarianship, he became absolute monarch of all he surveyed, and so dominated the Trustees that, on and after resigning his high office, and retiring into private life, he was able just as much as before to influence them in the distribution of patronage. He had already persuaded them to appoint to the Keeper-

ship of the Printed Books an ex-attorney's-clerk, a man
of not the slightest mark or likelihood, whose only literary
achievement had been a very indifferent translation of the
Latin and other quotations in Blackstone's Commentaries.
He was next, on Panizzi's resignation and at his recommendation, placed at the head of the whole establishment as
Principal Librarian. In the attorney's office this fortunate
individual had had as a fellow-clerk a young man even more
mediocre than himself, and for him he procured a subordinate position in the Library. Through the favour of
Panizzi, ex-attorney's-clerk No. 2 was gradually raised to
be Keeper of the Printed Books, when his former fellow-
clerk was appointed Principal Librarian. Thus was presented one of the strangest spectacles. The highest office
in such a national establishment as the British Museum,
and the highest office in its Library, positions which men
of great literary and scientific eminence would have been
proud to fill, had, to the disgust of the world of literature
and science, fallen to the lot of these two ex-attorney's-
clerks.

In striking contrast to Panizzi's promotion of the two
ex-attorney's-clerks was his treatment of one of the most
competent of my colleagues of the New Catalogue, the late
Edward Edwards, a born librarian if ever there was one.
Edwards had earned his position in the Museum by pamphlets full of ingenious suggestions for the improvement of
the Library, and by the copious evidence on the same
subject, showing a thorough knowledge of it, which he
gave before a Select Committee of the House of Commons
appointed to inquire into the management of the Museum.
Panizzi took a violent dislike to him, I know not why,
unless it were that he had not that obsequiousness of

B

manner, which is perhaps nowhere learned better than in an
attorney's office.   Both the pettiest and the most effective
methods of harassing Edwards were employed by Panizzi.
Among the pettiest was that of compelling Edwards
to shave his moustache, the existence of which, Panizzi
declared, was incompatible with the status of an assistant in
the Library of the British Museum!   More effective was
his frequent reporting of Edwards to the Trustees, on what
were doubtless the most trivial grounds.   At last they
got tired of it.   'One or other of them,' Macaulay said,
'must go,' and of course it was not Panizzi who went.   After
having written vigorously in favour of the institution, at the
public expense, of Free Libraries, and aided the late
William Ewart, M.P., in his ultimately successful movement
for their statutory establishment, Edwards became the
first Librarian of the Free Public Library at Manchester,
which was one of the fruits of Ewart's Public Libraries
Act.   He was a most industrious as well as capable
man.   In the course of his subsequent career he did a
great deal of useful and praiseworthy literary work, such
as the production of an excellent biography of Sir Walter
Raleigh, based on original research, and of two valuable books (among several), which were labours of love,
Memoirs of Libraries and *Founders of the British
Museum.*   This last work he brought down to 1870, and
in it he heaped coals of fire on Panizzi's head, by doing
the amplest justice to his old persecutor's success in
greatly increasing the number of volumes in the Museum
Library.   Inside the Museum and out of it Panizzi
was always squabbling with somebody.   He was at
daggers drawing with Sir Henry Ellis, with the amiable
and courteous Keeper of the Manuscripts, the late Sir

Frederick Madden, and with the Secretary to the Trustees. Early in his career he was engaged to make a catalogue of the Library of the Royal Society. Over this task he had with his employers a quarrel which nearly ended in litigation. The history of his feud with Carlyle will be told hereafter. He had one with Sir Harris Nicolas too, and another with Sir Francis Palgrave. Panizzi took advantage of his control over the Library to avenge himself on the last mentioned of these two eminent antiquaries in a characteristically petty and spiteful way. Sir Francis was the son of a Jewish stockbroker named Cohen, and on becoming a Christian assumed the surname of Palgrave. In order to vex him Panizzi had all his books and so forth catalogued under his original name of Cohen, one which Sir Francis Palgrave wished to be forgotten or ignored !

Panizzi acquired a reputation for administrative ability, but certainly he did not show even common-sense in regulating the one task to which I had to contribute a quota of performance. The New Catalogue was compiled according to a code of ninety-one rules (I suppose there are now half as many again), for which, if they were not all of them actually drawn up by him, Panizzi was certainly responsible. Some system, of course, had to be adopted, but that which he elaborated was the very pedantry of cataloguing. Two illustrations of the absurdity which pervaded it must suffice. Suppose the work to be catalogued was the first edition of *Waverley*. Common-sense would suggest that it should be entered under Scott. But, no ! according to the ninety-one rules, it had, because anonymous, to be catalogued under *Waverley*, with a reference to *Waverley* from Scott ! Still more strikingly absurd was Panizzi's mode of dealing with the first edition of Milton's 'Comus,' the authorship of which is pretty well known to a good many persons much less instructed than Lord Macaulay's Schoolboy. Because it was anonymous, the ninety-one rules bade it be catalogued not even under 'Comus,' but under 'Ludlow Castle,' where, as the title-page testified, the noble 'masque' had been first 'presented!' Imagine this pedantry extended in every direction, and it will cease to be wonderful that it took more than thirty years to complete the New Catalogue, at a cost probably of a quarter of a million sterling.[1]

Another hindrance to the progress of the New Catalogue, and one which, in addition to the many absurdities of the ninety-one rules made the task of compiling it needlessly distasteful, was the want of a division of labour. Some there was but not nearly enough, and in a general way every assistant was expected to know everything. After fifty years I still remember well my dismay at the first cataloguing operation which I was called on to perform, and how I longed for the advent of one of those beneficent fairies of the story-books of childhood, who come to the rescue of distressed princes and princesses condemned to the discharge of seemingly impossible tasks. Before me was a long row of dumpy quartos, each of them containing some hundreds of detached printed pieces, street placards, fly-sheets, and pamphlets, of which the origin was this: From 1785 to 1787 the usually phlegmatic Dutch were in a state of great effervescence. There was

---

[1] In justice to the later administration of the Library, it should be added that in such special catalogues, as those of the books in the galleries of the Reading-room and in Mr. Fortescue's excellent classed catalogues of recent additions to the Library, common-sense has been allowed to triumph over the pedantry and absurdity of the ninety-one rules.

in Holland a republican party bent on reducing the Stadtholder to a cipher, and even in ejecting him altogether. There was a smaller party opposed to this movement, and hence much strife and turmoil, amounting to a petty civil war. At last the King of Prussia (Frederick the Great's successor), whose sister was wife of the Stadtholder, sent troops to Holland and restored the *status quo ante*. The reader can easily imagine how great in those years of tumult was the activity of the Dutch printing-presses in producing such ephemeral matter as I have described. Common-sense cataloguing would have disposed of the whole row of quartos as so many volumes of pamphlets and so forth relating to that period of Dutch political history, but no! the ninety-one rules ordained that every one of these pieces should be catalogued separately and intelligently,[1] so that where there was, as often happened, no tangible title, some rational account of the contents of the piece, fly-sheet, street placard, or what not, should be given, and that by a cataloguer who knew no Dutch. How I got through the task I know not, but got through it was, somehow. Luckily none of the revisers of the New Catalogue knew as much Dutch as I contrived to pick up for the nonce. Probably no mortal will ever ask for one of those quartos, or at least compare their contents with the entries in the catalogue, so that my sins of omission and commission run a very good chance of escaping discovery.

[1] The plan still dominant of separately cataloguing every detached publication, however trivial, added to the Library, fly-sheet, street placard, and so forth, has been and is productive of very great expense, and to this proceeding is largely due the enormous and growing bulk of the general catalogue in the Reading-room. It has been computed that the cost of registering, cataloguing, binding, and providing space on the shelves for a sheaf of street ballads would keep a poor family for a month.

Besides Edward Edwards there was noticeable among my colleagues of the New Catalogue John Humffries Parry, afterwards well known as Mr. Serjeant Parry. Besides cataloguing according to the ninety-one rules he was eating his dinners before being called to the Bar ; and occasionally in the evening he lectured at mechanics' and other institutions. His lectures were chiefly on the oratory of the French Revolution, a congenial subject, for although the son of a Bishop (of Barbadoes, if I remember rightly) he held, both in politics and religion, very advanced opinions. In his lectures, which were popular, he inter- spersed his biographical and historical sketches of the French Revolution with extracts from the speeches of Vergniaud and others, which he declaimed with great effect. He began his forensic career at the Old Bailey, but gradually worked his way upward to a higher plane, and had great success with juries, as I had agreeable reason to discover when many years afterwards his eloquence gained for me a cause in which I had more of justice than of law on my side. I often wondered that, with his strong political feeling and gift of popular oratory, he never found his way into the House of Commons. A very different man from Mr. Serjeant Parry was another assistant of my time who was not engaged on the New Catalogue of the Library proper, but who catalogued unaided, and with a code of rules of his own forming, the pretty large and daily increasing collection of music whether married or not to (rarely) immortal verse. This was the late Thomas, commonly called 'Tom,' Oliphant, except myself the only Scotchman among the assistants of fifty years ago. Tom was a cadet of the family of Oliphant of Condie, a younger brother of Sir

Anthony Oliphant, Chief Justice of Ceylon, and uncle of the far-famed Laurence Oliphant of varied and singular career. Tom had, I think, been in business in the city or elsewhere, and was unsuccessful ; but he retained some private means, and added to his income by song-writing. He became known as a musical expert (ultimately he was President of the Madrigal Society), and to his reputation in this way he owed his post in the Museum. Many a popular drawing-room song of those days bore on its title-page the intimation, 'Words by Thomas Oliphant, Esq.' Tom knew no German, and when he was told of a song in that noble tongue which was likely to suit him commercially, he asked me to give him a bare English prose translation of it, which he then turned into metre, better or worse. 'The Standard-Bearer' was one of the most successful of the many prose-skeleton songs of which I thus furnished him. Often in drawing-room and concert-room, when I have heard a vocalist musically announce that the Lady of his love he durst not name, my heart reverting fondly turned to Tom. He was full of dry humour, a Scottish gentleman of the old school and no sycophant. For this reason, I suppose,—I never could discover any other,—he was far from being a favourite of Panizzi's. Once when he made an application for an increase of salary, the only reply which he received was that his services were no longer required, and forthwith his place in the Museum Library knew him no more.[1]

[1] In what may be called Museum Circles there is still current a good story of the reply given by one of the previously mentioned ex-attorney's-clerks, as Keeper of the Printed Books, to a similar application made on behalf of the attendants in the Library. He was waited upon by a deputation of highly respectable seniors, most of whom had been many years in the service of the Museum, and who came to him to represent the financial grievances of the

But of the then Assistants in the Museum Library the late Thomas Watts was *facile princeps*. He had ceased, when I first knew him, to work on the New Catalogue, and his chief employment was the more appropriate as well as important one of preparing lists of books in many languages, which were not in the Library, but should, he thought, be acquired for it. The origin of his official connection with the Museum and his early career have been slurred over by his biographers, though they were very creditable to him. This is the story of both as it was told me long ago. His family, people of some substance, were the proprietors of a large public bath, known as Peerless Pool, in the City Road region (I think), and it was said that Watts often sat there at the receipt of custom, reading, as was his wont, many books and learning many languages. From Chinese to Icelandic, from Russian and Hungarian to Welsh, the range of his numerous linguistic conquests extended. He told me, in reply to a question of mine, that he generally began the study of a new language in one of the translations of the Scriptures executed under the auspices of the Bible Society; and there are very few languages a mastery of which cannot be thus facilitated. In the intervals of business and of home-study he visited

whole body. It was at a time of high prices for the necessaries of life, which pressed heavily on men who, like the attendants in the Museum Library, had small fixed incomes. The ex-attorney's-clerk to whom, occupying undeservedly a high position, they appealed for an increase of salaries, was noted for his taciturnity; having in a general way little or nothing to say, he had in a general way the prudence to say little or nothing. When the spokesman of the deputation had explained their claim there ensued a long pause, during which the person addressed, with his eyes fixed on the ground, seemed absorbed in meditative calculation, thus inspiring hopeful expectancy. At last he raised his head, opened his lips, and delivered himself of the extraordinary reply, in the form of a question: 'Don't you think that your wives could——take in washing?'

occasionally the old over-crowded, stuffy, and inconvenient Reading-room of the Museum. One of his favourite studies, for its own sake, was Russian literature, and he more often asked for than received Russian books, of which the Museum Library appears to have been nearly devoid. In consequence of Watts's repeated appeals, a batch of Russian books was at last purchased for the Library. But there was nobody in the Museum who knew Russian and could catalogue them. In this emergency Watts volunteered his services, and they were accepted. He came, he saw, he catalogued. The next step was to appoint to be an assistant a man so accomplished and promising. One of his first achievements in this position possessed and possesses considerable general interest. It had long been universally believed, and a statement of the belief had been undoubtingly made in numerous works of reference, British and Foreign, and in such a book as Isaac Disraeli's *Curiosities of Literature*, that the earliest English newspaper was the *English Mercurie*. It professed to have been issued by authority in those months of 1588 which witnessed the arrival in the Channel of the Spanish Armada with its subsequent discomfiture and dispersion. The only known copy of the *English Mercurie* was in the Library of the Museum. Watts on inspecting it saw at once that it was a forgery, and after due investigation proved it to be such, in a pamphlet which for ever dispelled the long-accepted journalistic myth. Great accessions of books in languages then little studied were procured for the Museum through Watts's exertions. Moreover, it is pretty certain that the erection of the new Reading-room on its present site—an achievement for which Panizzi received the credit—was first suggested by Watts in a communication to the *Mechanics' Magazine*, made years before he became officially connected with the Museum. When the new Reading-room was finished, he was appointed its superintendent, as many of its frequenters still remember gratefully. At his death he had risen to be one of Panizzi's successors in the Keepership of the Printed Books, but had not lived to enjoy his merited elevation long. His personal appearance was not prepossessing, and his manner was brusque. But, with a rough exterior, he had a kind heart and generous disposition.

Fifty years ago the superintendent of the Reading-room was a venerable and fine-looking old gentleman, who, in his customary suit of solemn black, and with his dignified benevolence of manner, might have passed for a bishop or an archdeacon at least. His antecedents, however, were not at all ecclesiastical. He had entered the service of the Museum, in the opening decade of this century, from the household of the fourth Duke of Grafton, to whom doubtless he owed his first appointment in the Library, whatever it may have been. In his Grace's household he was known as a pugilist of great skill, and in later years he was fond of reciting incidents of boxing-matches in which he had taken part. Years of service in the Library had made him familiar with the titles of books, but very little with their contents. For those readers whom his dignified appearance deterred from asking the superintendent of the Reading-room for information there was provided a subordinate, whose appearance certainly could not have a similarly deterrent effect. He was a little man with a face like a crab-apple, who eked out his doubtless scanty income from the Museum by copying manuscripts. Consequently any and every frac-

tion of time withdrawn from this employment to satisfy
the inquiries of readers involved a corresponding pecuniary loss. Therefore his answers to querists were brevity
itself, and, as soon as the shortest reply was given, his
upturned head was down again and his pen resumed its
scratch, scratch, scratch ! What a transition in the super-
intendence of the Reading-room from the venerable
ex-pugilist and his crab-apple-faced deputy to Thomas
Watts and to his accomplished as well as courteous
successors ! [1]

[1] Fifty years ago Mudie's Library, which is now an institution, existed only
in germ. Its founder, the late Charles Edward Mudie, was in some respects
a remarkable man. His father was for many years the head of a large and
successful stationery establishment in Coventry Street. The young Mudie
started one of the same kind as his father's, though on a much smaller scale,
in King Street, Holborn, now Southampton Row. He was of a studious and
thoughtful disposition and of somewhat 'advanced' theological views. He
collected for his own use a little library of books of a progressive kind, such
as the writings of Theodore Parker, Emerson's and Margaret Fuller's periodical
the *Dial*, etc. At that time they were not easily accessible in London, and he
converted his collection into a small circulating library, as an adjunct to his
ordinary business. I was one of the not very numerous circle of readers who
gladly availed themselves of what was then a unique collection, and who
were additionally attracted to King Street by the intelligence and amiability
of their owner. That collection was the nucleus of what has become, I suppose, the largest circulating library in the world. When the great hall in
New Oxford Street, now teeming daily with subscribers, was finished,
Mudie gave in it a reception, invitations to which were issued to, and largely
accepted by, literary people, among others. When I presented myself at it,
Mudie said, referring to my early connection with the modest establishment
in King Street, 'Nobody has a better right than you to be here to-night.'
Mudie was himself an author, besides circulating, on an enormous scale, the
writings of others. He gave me some years ago a pleasing little volume
of poems, all of them thoughtful and many of them devotional, the authorship of which was modestly denoted on the title-page by his initials
alone, 'C. E. M.,' and which was privately printed solely for distribution
among personal friends. He was generous to struggling worth, and at least
one meritorious literary acquaintance of mine was, at a difficult crisis, spontaneously as well as munificently aided by him.

III. CONCERNING THE ORGANISA-
TION OF LITERATURE

[ABOUT thirty years since I wrote an article to which probably I gave some such title as 'The French Academies and the British Museum.' The more ambitious title 'Concerning the Organisation of Literature,' with which it was published then, and is republished now, was given it by Professor Masson, at that time Editor of *Macmillan's Magazine*, in which it made its first appearance.

In now republishing the article just as it was when it appeared in the Magazine, I have added to the original notes a few which are distinguishable by being enclosed in brackets. During the last thirty years the functions of the French Academies of which an account is given, have remained, so far as I know, unaltered. Certainly there has been no change in the Constitution, so to speak, of the British Museum, although it will be seen that a complete reconstruction of its Governing Body was strongly recommended in the Report of the Royal Commission appointed in 1850, to investigate thoroughly the condition of that National Establishment. Until now their recommendation has been completely ignored by successive Ministries, Liberal and Conservative. Finally, there has for years been fitfully proceeding, in the periodical and newspaper press, a discussion (Matthew Arnold took part in it) on the desirability and feasibility of instituting an English Academy of Literature resembling the *Académie Française* at least in its composition and constitution. That is to say, its members would be distinguished men of letters, and they alone would elect new members to fill the vacancies caused by death. Whatever may be the value of the suggestions made in the following article with a view to the formation of an English Academy, the question itself though not one of the hour is, to a certain extent, one of the time :—]

THE chronicles of the year 1863 record two incidents little noticed by the public or its instructors of the press, but which possess a certain importance, from their relation to what is called the Organisation of Literature. In one of these incidents, the publication of the remodelled programme of the Guild of Literature and Art, lurks the admission of a failure, or at least of the inability of its promoters to perform the most important of the promises contained in their original plan. The other incident exhibits the germ of a new and fruitful project, which also aims at introducing an organic principle into the literary chaos. It is Lord Stanhope's[1] speech at the dinner of the Literary Fund, when he deplored the present isolation of men of letters from each other, the absence among them of class-combination and concert, and when he indicated the desirability of organising out of them an English body more or less resembling the French Academy.

The Guild of Literature and Art was founded in or about 1851, more than twelve years ago. Its founders were prominent authors and artists; Sir Edward Bulwer-Lytton[2] was and is its President, with Mr. Charles Dickens for Vice-President. Its members were to consist of persons following Literature or the Fine Arts as a profession, and mere membership was to be easily attainable. When the needful funds had been raised, the Guild was to be organised in quasi-collegiate fashion. There was to

[1] [Fourth Earl Stanhope, the historian, who died in 1876.]
[2] [The first Lord Lytton, the novelist, who died in 1873.]

be a Warden, with a house and a salary of £200 a year, presiding over two classes of recipients of the bounty of the Guild. One class was to consist of 'members for life,' elected by the Council from the ordinary members; they were to be persons who had achieved some distinction in Literature or Art, and each was to receive an annuity of £200 without a house, or of £170 with it. The other class, also elected by the Council, was to consist of 'Associates,'—men rather of literary or artistic promise than of distinction or note; each of these was to receive an annuity of £100 for life, or for a term of years, according to circumstances. As a condition attendant on the receipt of his annuity, each Life Member was to deliver annually three Lectures at Mechanics' Institutions in town and country; the Associates, again, were to employ a portion of their time 'in gratuitous assistance to any learned bodies, societies for the diffusion of useful knowledge, etc., or, as funds increase, and the utilities of the Institution develop themselves, *in co-operating towards works of national interest and importance*, but on subjects of a nature more popular, and at a price more accessible, than those which usually emanate from professed Academies.'[1] Such was the original scheme of the Guild of Literature and Art.

Now, let us suppose the needful funds had been collected for carrying out, on a scale of tolerable magnitude, this well-meant project. What, in that case, would have been the most important, fruitful principle in the scheme, distinguishing it from all others in operation, and claiming for it the sympathy and support of the public? Certainly not that involved in the granting of annuities

[1] Prospectus of the Guild of Literature and Art. 1851.

to authors and artists of some distinction; for, out of funds provided by Parliament, the State, through the Pension Fund, already grants such annuities to such persons. I am speaking of the principle merely, as one already recognised and acted on by the State. I do not mean to say that every author and artist of merit who both needs and deserves a pension receives one; but simply that, in granting pensions, the Government does so befriend such persons, and that there was, therefore, nothing novel in this part of the scheme of the Guild of Literature and Art, which simply proposed to do, with its own machinery and funds, what the State already attempted to do through the Government of the day, by the application of a Parliamentary Grant. The striking and original item in the project of the Guild of Literature and Art, was its proposal to pension the more promising of younger authors and artists, and to require from them in return, useful and honourable labour, with pen or pencil, on 'works of national interest and importance.' This, and this alone, removed the aid to be given by the Guild from the category to which belongs the eleemosynary bounty of the Pension Fund, and of the Royal Literary Fund. It thus became to them, in some measure, what a system of reproductive employment is to the operations of the New Poor Law. In return for slender, but acceptable pecuniary assistance, the juniors of Literature and Art were to perform profitable and worthy tasks, prescribed to them by their more experienced seniors; and here, at last, it might be fondly hoped, was a kind of Organisation of Literature.

Alas, it is precisely this and its kindred items which make no appearance in the remodelled programme of the

Guild of Literature and Art. The Guild received its charter of incorporation in 1854; and after nine years of a delay, caused, it is said, by some legal difficulty or obstruction, its matured scheme of operations, to be executed at its early convenience, was shaped and published a few months ago. The Warden has disappeared, and with him the old classification of members and associates. We see and hear nothing now of lectures to be delivered at mechanics' institutions, nothing of 'gratuitous aid to learned societies,' nothing of 'co-operation in the production of works of national interest or importance.' In the remodelled programme, under the rubric of 'Objects,' there are two paragraphs which thus define the present aims of the Association: 'The Guild shall, in the first instance, confine its operations to the foundation and endowment of an institution to be called the "Guild Institution."' And then: 'The Guild shall grant annuities to which professional members of either sex, and the widows of professional members, shall be eligible. It will also erect a limited number of free residences on land to be presented for this purpose by Sir Edward Bulwer-Lytton, and which will be occupied by members elected on this foundation. The several annuitants shall be elected by the Council,' etc., etc. This is all. The members of the Guild are now in number fifty. After twelve years or so its funds amount to £3694, of which £3334 were 'received for copyright and performance of Sir E. Bulwer-Lytton's play of *Not so Bad as we Seem.*' When the free residences have been built, and a few slender annuities awarded, what is there to make the public or men of letters zealously promote the further working of the scheme? Duly recognising the disinterestedness and kindly motives of its founders, one may predict, with something very like certainty, that the world is not destined to hear much more of the Guild of Literature and Art.[1]

I turn now to Lord Stanhope's proposal for the formation of an English Academy or Institute, somewhat resembling the famous *Académie Française*. Lord Stanhope is entitled to a hearing, were it only as a man of letters, who has done good service to his untitled order. Recently the Parliamentary originator of the National Portrait Gallery, it was he who conducted, years ago, through the House of Commons, the Literary Copyright Act, on which the relations between authors and publishers are still based. His career has been one of considerable official as well as of continuous literary labour. He is a man of business, and not merely a man of letters; no young enthusiast, but an experienced legislator, he is not likely to make a practical suggestion without having weighed all difficulties of execution and detail. There needs no demonstration of the truth of his assertion respecting the unorganised state of literature and its cultivators in England. The fact is patent to all the world. But what, it may be asked, could be gained by the foundation in England of an Academy, or Institute, resembling the *Académie Française?* It will be partly answering the question to give some account of the constitution and functions of the French Academy. First, however, a few words on the composition of the French Institute, of which the French Academy forms but a single section.

[1] [The Guild died long ago, and that it ever existed has been generally forgotten. What became of the funds raised for its establishment and support, I do not know.]

C

Five smaller bodies, with very different aims and occupations, make up the French Institute, to belong to which is considered a high honour by men of letters and science throughout Europe. These five bodies are (1) the *Académie Française*, (2) the *Académie des Inscriptions et Belles Lettres*, (3) the *Académie des Sciences*, (4) the *Académie des Beaux Arts*, (5) the *Académie des Sciences Morales et Politiques*. The oldest of them, the *Académie Française*, was founded by the great Cardinal Richelieu, with the special function of watching over the condition of the French language, in consonance with which trust the well-known Dictionary of the Academy has been produced by it. The *Académie des Inscriptions* deals with archæology and philology. Students of Gibbon may remember how frequently its *Mémoires*—'Transactions,' as we should say—are cited in the notes to the *Decline and Fall*. The *Académie des Beaux Arts* of course devotes itself to the fine arts; the *Académie des Sciences* to the physical sciences; the *Académie des Sciences Morales et Politiques* to ethics, philosophy, and politics, but, above all, to that wide department of things which in this country we call Social Science. Each of these five bodies has a special organisation of its own, governs itself, and is perfectly independent of its neighbours. Together, however, they compose the Institute, and a member of any one of them is a member of the Institute, which also in its collective capacity has a constitution and office-bearers. They have all of them analogues in England. If an attempt were made to realise what is understood to have been at one time a project of the late Prince Consort, namely, to collect the accredited 'Societies' of London under one roof, and, while leaving each its independence,

to organise them into one body,[1] for purposes of general
utility, the five bodies which compose the French Institute
would thus find analogues in England:—The Royal
Society would be the analogue of the *Académie des Sciences*;
the Royal Academy, of the *Académie des Beaux Arts*;
the Society of Antiquaries, of the *Académie des Inscriptions*; the modern Social Science Association, of the also
modern *Académie des Sciences Morales et Politiques*; and,
with a considerable stretch of imagination, the Royal
Society of Literature might pass for the analogue of the
Académie Française—the French Academy itself.

Analogy, however, is one thing; identity, another.
These five English Societies and those five French Academies may be analogous, but they lack anything like identity
of constitution. The English Societies are composed of
members paying subscriptions, and, virtually, not limited
as to number. I suppose that any person of respectable
position and attainments, with fair social connections, may
become a member of any of the learned societies of
London, if he is prepared to pay the needful entrance-fee
and subscription. It is not so with the French Academies.
The number of members in the case of each of them is
strictly limited, and no new member is elected but to fill
up a vacancy caused by death. The expenses of the
French Academies are not defrayed by the subscriptions
of the members, but by the State, which, while leaving
them complete self-government, adopts them as National
Institutions. Instead of making an annual payment,
every member of the Institute receives an annual salary
of 1500 francs, which marks his connection with the State,

---

[1] [Since then they have been domiciled under one roof, at Burlington
House, but their organisation 'into one body' has not been attempted.]

but is not large enough to make him feel himself dependent on its bounty. Generally, I believe, the French
budget contains an allocation of a sum of money to be
devoted to medals and other prizes placed at the disposal
of the Institute, or to defray the expenses of such of its
members as are sent on scientific and literary missions by
the Government. Possessing, from the incontestable
eminence and high character of their members, the
confidence of the nation, the Institute and the Academies
which compose it have acquired large corporate funds,
the result of the bequests and donations of private
individuals, and applied to the specific purposes named
by the testators and donors. Of these, more hereafter.
Suffice it for the present to say that the funds thus
acquired by the Academies which make up the Institute
yielded in 1848 an annual revenue, now doubtless much
increased, of upwards 130,000 francs, say £5200.[1] Even
in England this would be no inconsiderable sum to be
devoted yearly to prizes for literary merit and scientific
achievement.

To indicate more clearly the difference between the
London 'Societies' and the French Academies of the
Institute, let me compare the constitution and functions,
the *status* and condition of the *Académie Française* with
those of what I have called its English analogue, the
Royal Society of Literature. This Society was founded,
in the words of its own prospectus, 'to promote literature
in its most important branches, with a special attention to
the improvement of the English language,' and it was
incorporated by Royal Charter in 1825. His Majesty

---

[1] *Annuaire des Sociétés Savantes de la France*, etc. 1846. (Published by
authority.)

George IV. gave it annually, out of his private purse, the sum of eleven hundred guineas. A thousand of these were to be divided among Associates 'of approved learning;' the remaining hundred went to purchase two gold medals, presentable to the authors of new and distinguished works—Hallam and Washington Irving were, I think, the last, or about the last, recipients of them. The Royal Society of Literature, says a sympathetic chronicler of its career,[1] 'has the merit of rescuing the last years of Coleridge's life from complete dependence on a friend, and of placing the learned Dr. Jamieson above the wants and necessities of a man fast sinking to the grave.' But unfortunately the sympathetic chronicler is obliged to add: 'The annual grant of 1100 guineas was discontinued by William IV., and the Society has since sunk into a Transaction Society, with a small but increasing library.' Let *me* add, however, that even in its decadence, it contributed to a useful result. The liberality of some of its members enabled Mr. Thomas Wright to produce and to publish two volumes, comprehending the Anglo-Saxon and Anglo-Norman periods, of his learned and accurate *Biographia Britannica Literaria*. But that useful enterprise has gone no further. The Royal Society of Literature 'has sunk into a Transaction Society.' It publishes an occasional volume of Transactions, containing papers on all sorts of subjects, from Hellenic inscriptions to the breed of Merino sheep. That is all it does. The world knows little and hears nothing of it.

Contrast this state of things with that presented by the French Academy. It consists of forty members only.

---

[1] Mr. Peter Cunningham, *Handbook of London* (1850). 'Royal Society of Literature.'

Any vacancy which death causes in its ranks is filled up by a careful vote of the survivors. The honour of belonging to it is coveted by the highest in the land—if report speaks truly, by the present Emperor himself.[1] It contains a small proportion of men of rank and dignified ecclesiastics—a Duke de Broglie, a Duke de Noailles, a Bishop of Orleans; but even members of those classes must have done something in authorship. The list of its forty members in 1862 contained the following twenty names :—Villemain, Barante, Lamartine, Thiers, Guizot, Mignet, Victor Hugo, Saint Marc Girardin, Sainte-Beuve, Mérimée, Alfred de Vigny, Charles de Remusat, Ampère, D. Nisard, Montalembert, S. de Sacy, Legouvé, Ponsard, Emile Augier, Jules Sandeau—the flower of French literature, historical, æsthetic, critical, journalistic. Men like these are entitled to sit in judgment on the literary performances of their juniors and contemporaries, to praise here, and to reward there. This is exactly what the French Academy does. The English public knows it chiefly as a body, admission into which is keenly sought and is accompanied by great glorification of the dead and of the living; each new member on taking his seat bestowing a formal eulogium on his predecessor, and receiving in return an elaborate address of congratulation and praise from some one of his new colleagues. There are, however, other and much more important functions than this discharged by the French Academy. I do not attach so much importance to the two prizes of 2000 francs (or so) each, which, apparently from funds supplied by the State, are annually awarded by the Academy to the authors of two pieces of prose and verse on subjects

---

[1] [Napoleon III.]

named beforehand, the competition being open to all comers,—I attach more to the result of the Academy's vigilant inspection of the current literature of France, with the view of distinguishing those published works in which a high or pure ethical element is directly or indirectly prominent. Once a year, at the great annual meeting of the Academy in May, an elaborate report is read by its Perpetual Secretary. This document contains, among other things, the names and characteristics of some of the works recently published most remarkable for their ethical tone or moral usefulness. Money-prizes or medals, varying in amount and value (generally from 2000 to 3000 francs each) are awarded to the authors, and their works are said to be 'crowned' by the Academy—itself an honourable and welcome distinction in a country singularly jealous of social inequalities, but enthusiastically cognisant of the gradations of proved intellectual ability. The deficiencies, oversights, and caprices of newspaper and periodical criticism are to some extent compensated for and corrected by the elaborate examination to which the Academy subjects the literature of the day, and many a worthy book of an obscure and modest author has thus attention pointed to its merits. These prizes are defrayed out of the proceeds of a legacy left by the Baron de Monthyon to be devoted to rewarding the works of French authorship 'most useful to morals;' and, in the survey made by the Academy before awarding them, it includes all departments of literature. The famous 'prize of virtue' was also bequeathed by the Baron de Monthyon (1733—1820), a distinguished member of the *noblesse* of the gown in the pre-revolutionary period, and a munificent benefactor to more than one of the Academies which compose the Institute. The Monthyon prize of virtue, too, is awarded by the French Academy; but, as it is not connected with literature, it does not fall within the scope of the present article. Otherwise is it with the *prix* Gobert which the Academy likewise awards. This was founded by Baron Gobert (1807—1833), and amounts annually to upwards of 11,000 francs, say £440, nine-tenths to be given to the author of the best, one-tenth to the author of the second best, work in French History actually and recently published. In awarding this historical prize, the Academy exerts a certain discretion of its own, and prolongs the principal grant for a series of years to the author of one and the same work, if the non-appearance of any better or greater one seems to authorise such a continuance. It is evident of what assistance a grant like this may be to a historical writer of limited means, during the composition of some long and elaborate work. The *prix* Gobert was held for many years by Augustin Thierry, one of the founders of the Modern French Historical School. After his death it was awarded for two years to M. Poirson, the author of the well-known history of Henri Quatre. It has now been held for years, I believe, by Henri Martin, the author of the best recent history of France—at least the best produced by any French writer not of the Institute, whose members voluntarily debar themselves from competing for such prizes. These, then, are some of the functions discharged by the French Academy, and I may add that no murmur of complaint, or whispered charge of partiality, is ever heard to throw a doubt on the sense or justice of its verdicts and awards.

Had the French Academy been founded in modern

times, under a political system of even comparative freedom, in an age full of social problems calling for discussion
and solution, very probably it would have been so constituted as to include what now forms a separate section of
the Institute—the *Académie des Sciences Morales et
Politiques*. This body, for the discussion of political and
ethical questions, more especially those belonging to the
large domain of Social Economy, was founded in the time
of the First French Republic. It was suppressed by
Napoleon I. in his hatred of 'ideologists,' and of the public
discussion of matters bearing on the action of the State.
After the Revolution of 1830, it was resuscitated by
Guizot, when Minister of Public Instruction, and it has
since been one of the most quietly useful departments of
the Institute. It consists of forty French members, and
is divided into five sections. The section of *Philosophie*
included in 1862 Cousin, Damiron, Barthélemy St. Hil-
aire, and Charles de Remusat ;—that of *Morale*, Villeneuve,
Gustave de Beaumont, and Louis Reybaud ;—that of
Economie, Politique et Statistique, Charles Dupin, Passy,
Duchâtel, Michel Chevalier, Wolowski, and Léonce de La-
vergne ;—that of *Histoire Générale et Philosophique*, Guizot,
Mignet, Michelet, Thiers, and Amédée Thierry ;—Schelling was, Lord Brougham and Leopold Ranke are, among
its foreign members. It publishes copious Transactions ;
and, since its resuscitation, various of its members have
been commissioned by itself and by successive governments to investigate, at home and abroad, the conditions
of special sections of industrial populations. It was
through this Academy that, in earlier years, Blanqui prosecuted his remarkable inquiries into the state of the
manufacturing populations of the Continent, and that, in

recent years, M. Louis Reybaud (known to English readers chiefly as the author of the amusing *Jerome Paturot*) was stimulated to produce social monographs on the condition of the operatives employed in the silk and cotton manufactures of France. It is seemingly from the State chiefly that the *Académie des Sciences Morales et Politiques* derives the funds to provide for its rather numerous prizes. These are given not so much to the authors of works already published, as in the case of the *Académie Française*, but rather to the successful competitors in the composition of Essays on subjects proposed by the Academy. Dipping casually into the *Comptes Rendus* of the *Académie des Sciences Morales et Politiques*, I find that in one particular year the following were the subjects given out to the competing essayists :—in the section of 'Philosophy,' (1) a critical examination of the Scholastic Philosophy, (2) an investigation of the influence exercised on the morality of a nation by the progress and the love of material well-being ; in the section of 'Legislation, Public Law, and Jurisprudence,' the Theory and Principles of Life Assurance, its History, and the useful applications of which it is susceptible ; in the section of 'Political Economy,' the Laws that ought to regulate the proportionate relations of note-circulation to a metallic currency, so that the State may enjoy all the advantages of credit without suffering from its abuses ; in the section of 'General and Philosophical History,' to show how the progress of Criminal Justice in the prosecution and punishment of offences against the person and property follows and marks the progress of civilisation from the savage state to that of the best-governed nations. These are all subjects more or less interesting and important ; and the elucidation of them is at least as profitable to society as the production of 'sensation novels,' so abundantly encouraged, without prizes, on both sides of the Channel. The money-value of the prizes awarded to the successful competitors averages 1500 francs each. Small as is this amount, the adjudicating sections are very critical and not easily pleased. Sometimes, year after year, I observe, the same subject is declared still open to competition, the essays sent in having fallen short of the standard required by the adjudicators. This Academy publishes Transactions of considerable worth, consisting of disquisitions contributed by its eminent members. Its peculiar influence on the intellectual culture of France must be valuable. Should a British Academy ever be founded, certainly it would be well to combine in it the functions of both of these French Academies, the *Académie Française* and the *Académie des Sciences Morales et Politiques*. In a practical country like ours, an Academy which included men of eminence in social, legislative, economical, and political science would have more weight and greater prospects of usefulness than one composed exclusively of poets, novelists, critics, and historians.

But do these French Academies, then, embody in their constitution and functions principles generally applicable, true and valuable in England as in France? Surely yes. There is the principle that in the world of intellect differences of capacity and power of labour exist, and that, when these are proved by their results, the upper and the under should be formally recognised and duly ranked. There is the principle that the young and aspiring deserve reward and encouragement when, through talent and toil, they have achieved success, and that none are so well fitted as the more wise and more experienced of their own order to reward and to encourage. The literary and socio-economical criticism of the periodical and newspaper press does much ; but, from the very nature of the case, it must be hurried, or perfunctory, or limited. It would be something to have, in one Academy in England, as France has in these two Academies, the men of the highest proved and realised intellect collected, and formed into a conspicuous, honourable, and honoured body—after the heat of the battle and a victorious struggle, taking their seats in a House of Peers of their own. It would be something to have them, as in France, judging, rewarding, encouraging, guiding, their younger or less experienced brethren, when these did not disdain to be so subordinated. The proud and self-sufficing might hold aloof, while the modest yet aspiring would profit alike by encouragement and by discouragement. If it were thought desirable to copy the prize-systems of France, the small funds needful would not long be wanting, were the body once extant to which they could be safely intrusted. The wealthiest and most generous of nations has not less than France its Monthyons and Goberts, but it has no Institute to receive, to accumulate, and to apply their thoughtful bounty. Once let there exist a British Institute, comprising the most eminent men, as do the two French Academies which have been sketched—and with a guarantee in its constitution that only the distinguished can succeed the distinguished —all the rest will follow. There are even important national objects which such an Institute might subserve and which would make a wise Premier thankful for its existence and advice. It would be a body which he might consult in the disposal, for instance, of the Pension Fund ;

and its counsel would preserve him from becoming the official patron of a Poet Close.[1] The time must arrive, too, when our purely party-antagonisms will be dead, buried, and forgotten. Then Governments will be able, as well as willing, to prosecute, with concentrated energy the work of internal reform—social, legal, educational. Then will be undertaken extensive inquiries into the state of our population at home and throughout our vast empire, and into what can be learned from or suggested by foreign nations. For such a task, men of trained intelligence and the gift of clear and vivid expression will be needed ; and it may be that to a National Institute an English Government will turn to supply them, just as successive French Governments have so applied to the French Institute, and more particularly to the *Académie des Sciences Morales et Politiques.* Even as it is, compare a report by Mr. Tremenheere—brief, lucid, suggestive, conclusive—on a mining district or a baking trade with an average blue-book—*rudis indigestaque moles*—entombing the thousands upon thousands of questions and answers produced by a Select Committee of the House of Commons and the cloud of witnesses which it examines—the useful and the useless

---

[1] [This worthy was a Westmorland rhymer, of the semi-mendicant class, who produced a quantity of the most wretched doggerel. However, a memorial recommending him to the Royal bounty was good-naturedly signed by Lord Lonsdale and a number of Westmorland gentlemen. ‘Merit’ was once defined by Lord Palmerston to be ‘the opinion one man has of another,’ and as a number of men, in Westmorland at least, had, or professed to have, a high opinion of the local bard, Lord Palmerston, who was then Prime Minister, gave ‘ the Poet Close’ a Civil List Pension of £50 a year. This act excited a great ferment of protest in the press, and was sharply criticised in the House of Commons. Lord Palmerston, who never forsook a *protégé*, however undeserving, defended himself by making the following extraordinary statement : The Poet Close, he said, had ‘ raised himself from a humble station, with very little education, to a distinguished position ! His poetical merits were not equal to Burns, but they deserved to be placed in the same category ’ ! !]

jumbled together in inextricable confusion, and yielding frequently no result of any kind—for how often is the committee's report rendered colourless and neutral by the disagreement of its members? Tell me in what Parliamentary or official document or statement—and there have been very many tons of them printed—the relations between Europeans and natives in our Indian empire have received as much light and been made as clearly and generally intelligible as in the few letters which Mr. Wingrove Cook despatched from Bengal when returning home from his newspaper-mission to China,[1] or in the communications with which a 'Competition Wallah'[2] at once entertains and instructs the readers of *Macmillan's Magazine*.[3]

Such possible results, however, of the existence of a National Institute, recognised and honoured by the State, perhaps belong to a rather distant future. Perhaps, too, even although the suggestion of it comes from Lord Stanhope, a British Institute will not be founded until after many years. Yet even now, and without the creation of any new body, the claims of eminent men of letters could be partly recognised by intrusting them with useful, honourable, and dignified functions, which might in time develop into a government and direction of their dis-

---

[1] [They were republished in the volume, *China and Lower Bengal*, 5th edition, 1861.]

[2] [The present Sir George Trevelyan, Secretary of State for Scotland. Those *Macmillan*-papers of his were republished in volume-form in 1864, with the title 'The Competition Wallah.']

[3] [The late Lord Houghton strove, for many years, but always unsuccessfully, to become an Elected Trustee. Various reasons were given for his failure. Among them was not mentioned what perhaps was the strongest of all, his protest in the House of Commons (he was then Mr. Monckton Milnes and M.P. for Pontefract) against the elevation of a foreigner like Panizzi to the headship of the Museum Library.]

tinguished juniors. Some years ago an Edinburgh Reviewer, discussing the subject of an Order of Merit, for the reward and recognition of men eminent in literature and science, made the following remarks, which, from one point of view, have a certain truth and pertinence: 'An order created solely,' he said, 'for men of science and letters, as has been more than once suggested, would wholly fail in its object. There is no reason why they should be separated from others who deserve well of their country. On the contrary, it is to amalgamate them with their fellow-citizens in honours as in labours that we desire, and to suffer them to rank (when their reputation so entitles them) with whomsoever be the other claimants to social consideration. There is not a city knight who would not jest at an order consisting only of authors, to whose united rent-roll he would prefer even half-a-dozen railway debentures. If any practical honours ever be accorded to authors, philosophers, or artists, agreeably to the usual principles of our aristocratic monarchy, we fear, strange though it may appear to say, that they must be honours shared with dukes and earls, ambassadors and generals.'[1] Now, there is one body, fulfilling all the requirements of the Edinburgh Reviewer and to which eminent men of letters have belonged, do belong, and are entitled to belong in much more considerable numbers than at present. I mean the Board of so-called Trustees which governs our great national institution, the British Museum.

The British Museum is supported wholly by the British nation, and the British Parliament possesses the right, rarely exercised hitherto, of supreme control over its

---

[1] *Edinburgh Review*, lviii. 220 (July 1848, Art. 'Goldsmith.')

affairs. The grant of money annually voted by Parliament for the support of the Museum amounts to £100,000; £10,000 seems to be the amount of the ordinary annual grant for the department of printed books alone. The Parliamentary Grant and the whole affairs of the Museum are administered by the Board of Trustees, at present fifty in number, and in which there are four constituent elements. One section of them is hereditary, and consists of what are called 'Family Trustees,' representing the families of personages who have made magnificent bequests of collections of various kinds to the Museum. These are the Sloane, Cotton, Harley, Townley, Elgin, and Knight families. The Family Trustees are nine in number, and among them is the present Earl of Derby. One trustee, called the Royal Trustee, is appointed by the Sovereign, in recognition of George IV.'s gift of the Royal Library to the Museum and the nation. Then there are twenty-five Trustees who are members of the Board *ex officio*. These, called Official Trustees, include the chief dignitaries of the State and Church, from the Archbishop of Canterbury and the First Lord of the Treasury to the Solicitor-General, while with them are associated the Presidents of the Royal Society, the College of Physicians, the Society of Antiquaries, and the Royal Academy. We have now thirty-five out of the fifty Trustees. The remaining fifteen are called Elected Trustees, and are chosen by the thirty-five. The Elected Trustees are trustees for life, and, with one important exception, share all the rights and privileges of their colleagues. This important exception is that, when a vacancy occurs in their own number, they have no voice or vote in filling it up. The choice of a new Elected Trustee is made by the thirty-five without the intervention of the Trustees already elected.

In the existence of a body of Elected Trustees, we seem to have a provision for the recognition of some of the claims of men eminent in literature, archæology, and science. The honour of a seat at the Board is one which they would share, as the Edinburgh Reviewer expressed it, 'with dukes and earls, ambassadors and generals.' Eminent men of letters, moreover, are precisely the persons best fitted to superintend the management of a vast library of books and manuscripts, kept up and augmented chiefly for the sake of the very class to which they belong : as elected trustees they would be called on to perform with advantage to the public, functions pleasant to themselves. Accordingly, the elective trusteeship of the British Museum has been termed 'the Blue-Riband of Literature,' and as such it was bestowed on Hallam and on Macaulay.[1] Let us note, however, the collective results of a system which throws the choice of the fifteen Elected Trustees exclusively into the hands of the nine Family Trustees, of the Royal Trustee, and of the thirty-five Official Trustees.

[1] [The following is a list of the Elected Trustees in 1893. Italics mark the names of those who have achieved distinction in literature or science, in either or in both. The Prince of Wales, who is understood to be very diligent in his attendance at the meetings of the Trustees—*Duke of Argyll*, Marquis of Bath, Earl of Crawford (President of the Camden Society, past President of the Astronomical Society), *Earl of Rosebery* (biographer of the second William Pitt), Lord Walsingham, *Lord Acton*, *Mr. Justice Bowen*, translator of Virgil), Right Hon. Spencer Walpole, *Sir George Trevelyan*, *Sir Henry Rawlinson*, *Sir John Lubbock*, *Professor Huxley*, Sir John Evans (past President of the Camden Society, Treasurer of the Royal Society), and Mr. C. D. E. Fortnum. Two at least of these, the Duke of Argyll and Lord Rosebery, would doubtless have been elected Trustees even if they had written nothing, nor does a translation of portions of Virgil appear, in the case of Mr. Justice Bowen, to be a sufficiently valid claim to 'the Blue Riband of Literature.')

It has been seen that out of the forty members of the French Academy, in 1862, at least twenty—one-half of the whole—were among the most eminent men of letters in France. Here is the list of the Elected Trustees of the British Museum as it stood at the beginning of 1863 :— The Marquis of Lansdowne, Sir David Dundas, Sir Philip Egerton, the Duke of Somerset, *Sir Roderick Murchison, Dean Milman*, Earl Russell, Mr. Gladstone, Sir G. C. Lewis, Mr. Walpole, Lord Eversley, *Mr. Grote*, Lord Taunton, the Duke of Northumberland, and Sir Thomas Phillips. In this list the claims of literature and science are represented by one-fifth of the body—Sir Roderick Murchison, Dean Milman, and Mr. Grote. It may be said that Sir G. C. Lewis was an author, and that Earl Russell and Mr. Gladstone are authors of more or less note. But when it is observed that with them are associated as Elected Trustees, officials and ex-officials—the Duke of Northumberland, Lord Taunton, Lord Eversley, Mr. Walpole—who have no such pretensions, one is led to surmise that they would have been elected Trustees had Mr. Gladstone never written on Homer, Earl Russell on the History of Europe in the eighteenth century, or the late Sir G. C. Lewis on the Credibility of Early Roman History. The hardship is that official personages like the Duke of Somerset, Earl Russell, and Mr. Gladstone are at this moment trustees in virtue of their respective offices, and that by sitting as Elected Trustees they simply displace men intellectually eminent, but without high political position. To such an extent has this accumulation of the same honours on the same head been carried, that from the evidence given before the Royal Commission, appointed in 1850 to inquire into the management of the Museum, the late Lord

Aberdeen, it appears, was once a Trustee in a threefold capacity. He was a Trustee as Secretary of State, a Trustee as President of the Society of Antiquaries, and he was also an Elected Trustee! It is worth noting that Her Majesty has set the electing Trustees of the Museum an example which they might lay to heart. Until recently, the solitary Royal Trustee had always been one of the highest personages in the kingdom, generally a member of the Royal Family. The Royal Trusteeship was held by the late Duke of Cambridge at his death in 1850. Lately, however, it has been conferred by the Crown on Dr. Cureton, who is, at least, an eminent Syriac scholar, and who, having been formerly an officer of the Museum, has a practical acquaintance with the details of the establishment which he is called upon to co-operate in governing.[1]

The Royal Commission of 1850 saw the injustice and the evils of the present system, and recommended a sweeping change in the government of the Museum. According to the scheme of the Commission, the government of the Museum was to be intrusted to an Executive Council, consisting of a chairman and six members. The Trustees were to elect from their own body four members of the Board of Government; the Crown was to appoint the chairman, with the two remaining members of the Board—one of them to be distinguished for his literary attainments, the other for his attainments in natural history. No action has been taken upon this Report, and

[1] [As a Royal Trustee, the late Dr. Cureton was succeeded by Dr. Wellesley, the late Dean of Windsor. His successor was the late Duke of Albany, who manifested a great interest in the affairs of the Museum. The present Royal Trustee is the Bishop of Rochester (Dr. Randall Davidson) formerly Dean of Windsor.]

the constitution and government of the Museum remain
in 1863 much the same as they were in 1850. The leaders
of the two great political parties in the State have been
adroitly conciliated and gained over by being chosen
Elected Trustees, and no organic change will be proposed by them. It is to the House of Commons that
we must look for a reform : and, strange to say, in the
matter of the National Collections, literary, artistic, and
scientific, the House of Commons has more than once
of late years shown a singular independence, and refused to follow the advice of its accredited party leaders.
It has rejected by large majorities the proposal, supported by the leaders of parties on both sides of the
House, to break up the Museum and scatter its collections.[2] It remains for the House of Commons to make
amends for the inertia displayed by successive Governments, whether Liberal or Conservative, in carrying into
effect neither the spirit nor the letter of the recommenda-
tions of the Royal Commission of 1850. The House of
Commons could easily pass a resolution recommending
that all vacancies among the Elected Trustees should be
filled up from men eminent in literature, scholarship,
archæology, and science, and that the Elected Trustees
should themselves have a voice in the election of their
colleagues. As the whole constitution of the Museum
depends on the will of the House of Commons, which
votes the funds for its support, such a resolution, though
merely recommendatory, would doubtless have the force

---

[1] Mr. Disraeli has been lately elected a trustee. [The late Lord Beaconsfield continued to be an elected trustee, after he became an official trustee in
virtue of his Ministerial office.]

[2] [Since then, however, the contents of the Museum have been broken up,
by the formation of the National History Museum at South Kensington.]

of a command. Parliamentary and public opinion steadily operating, we should in course of time have in the Elected Trustees of the British Museum a British Institute, comprehending the intellectual notabilities of the country, possessing the confidence of the nation, appealing successfully for funds to Parliaments and Governments, and worthy to be appointed the executors of the British Monthyons and Goberts. They would find the objects of the Institution which they governed capable of being expanded and varied. Presiding over the State Paper and the Record Offices, the Master of the Rolls[1] has developed enterprises wider than the customary calendaring and cataloguing, useful and indispensable as they are. We owe to him, among other benefits conferred, the publication, at an expense insignificant to the country, of the series of *Chronicles and Memorials of Great Britain and Ireland during the Middle Ages ;* important contributions, which could or would never have been made by private publishing enterprise, to the political, ecclesiastical, social —nay, to the intellectual and scientific history of mediæval England, for the series includes a careful edition of the works of Roger Bacon. Men of originality and intelligence, of experience and energy, placed at the head, or in the headship, of the Museum, with that vast library of books and manuscripts under their care, might soon find the example of the Master of the Rolls worthy of imitation, and Government as ready in their case as in his to give the needful preliminary aid. What 'Materials for English History' of the post-mediæval ages lie buried in the

---

[1] [The late Lord Romilly. Since his death, in 1874, the execution of the useful enterprise, initiated under his auspices, has been continued by his successors in the office of Master of the Rolls.]

manuscript masses of the Museum that might be made to yield new gold to skilful 'prospectors' wisely directed and suitably equipped ! As regards the reproduction of books, take but a single instance. If the student wishes to consult a collection of the memoirs illustrating the history of the great civil war of the seventeenth century, and edited with even a glimmer of modern light, he must betake himself to the twenty-six volumes of the French translation of them, which Guizot published forty years ago! Such a collection edited by competent Englishmen, would not only be a boon to the student, but would enrich the historic literature of the country, and claim the aid of a Parliamentary Grant surely not less strongly than the chronicles of mediæval England. Many are the enterprises of this kind, from which the ordinary publisher naturally holds aloof, that would reward the encouragement of the State, and if well managed—wisdom above directing intelligent industry below—would entail but slight, if any, pecuniary loss in the long-run. Thus a reform in the government of the Museum might be the precursor of an important step towards the solution of the hard problem with which this article started—the organisation of literature.

IV. THE CARLYLES AND A SEGMENT OF THEIR CIRCLE: RECOLLECTIONS AND REFLECTIONS

CHAPTER I

FIRST ACQUAINTANCE WITH THE CARLYLES

IT was in the year of Queen Victoria's accession that the words, 'By Thomas Carlyle,' first appeared on a title-page. The work was his *French Revolution*, of which he once said to me, 'I put more of my life into that than into any of my books.' The times were not favourable to the success of the great prose epic. There was little seriousness in the literature of the day, and little demand for serious literature. The favourites of the reading public were Macaulay, with his brilliant common sense; Bulwer, with his glittering sentimentalism; and Dickens, with his genial drollery. 1837 was the year of the appearance of Macaulay's essay on Bacon and of Bulwer's *Ernest Maltravers*; it was the second year of the issue of *Pickwick*, which had suddenly leapt into boundless popularity. In politics the quasi-revolutionary excitement which carried the first Reform Bill seemed to have died out. Conservatism was rallying for its victory of a few years later over Lord Melbourne's dawdling Ministry. Whatever earnestness there was among cultivated Liberals was monopolised by those of the Radicals who called themselves 'philo-

sophical,' and intent on translating Benthamism into legislation, for the most part turned away from the glow and
gloom of Carlyle's vivid pictorialism. To the average
Conservative his treatment of the great uprising of the
French people seemed, of course, far too sympathetic.
Then, the startling originality of the style repelled at the
threshold many readers, and exasperated almost all the
critics. In the most popular literary periodical of the day
it was hinted that the author of *The French Revolution :
a History*, must have graduated in 'the University of
Bedlam.'[1]

There were readers, however, Conservative and Radical,
high and humble, old and young, who were spellbound by
the wonderful book, which, as Wordsworth has said of
genuine poetry, created the taste by which it was enjoyed.
Among them were two Edinburgh youths, friends from
childhood, school-fellows and college-mates, daily associated in their studies, readings, rambles, and amusements.
One of the effects produced on them by *The French Revolution* was an incitement to acquaint themselves, if possible,

[1] Of a very different kind was John Stuart Mill's article on *The French
Revolution* (*London and Westminster Review*, July 1837), and Thackeray's
in the *Times* (August 1837), both of which appeared soon after the publication of the book. Although Mill's article was the first noticeable
recognition of the greatness of the work, Carlyle nowhere makes any
reference to it in his letters or journals, at least as they have been
printed. The keynote of Mill's article is struck in the following, its opening
sentence : 'This is not so much a history as an epic poem, and notwithstanding, or even in consequence of this, the truest of histories. It is the
history of the French Revolution and the poetry of it both in one, and, on the
whole, no work of greater genius, either historical or poetical, has been produced in this country for many years.' Thackeray naturally was staggered
by what seemed to him the eccentric originality of the style of *The French
Revolution*, but he too recognised its transcendent merits. 'After perusing,'
he said, 'the whole of this extraordinary work, we can allow, almost to their
fullest extent, the high qualities with which Mr. Carlyle's idolaters endow
him.'

with whatever else the author of such a book might have
written.   There had then been issued no collection of
Carlyle's contributions to periodicals, and all of them were
anonymous.   Aided, however, by a few suggestions from
seniors more or less conversant with his scattered writings,
these young enthusiasts were fairly successful in tracking
Carlyle through volume upon volume of reviews and
magazines.   One of them has never forgotten the joy with
which, in a thumbed volume of *Fraser's Magazine*, he
lighted on *Sartor Resartus*, and with what intensity of
interest he followed the spiritual autobiography of Diogenes
Teufelsdröckh—the *Pilgrim's Progress*, it seemed to him,
of the nineteenth century, from doubt and despair to
'blessedness' and belief.   If Scotland was the country of
John Knox, it was also that of David Hume, and to the
teaching of the Westminster Assembly of Divines had
been superadded a knowledge of the scoffing of Voltaire,
whose works were in one's father's library, hidden away,
but not inaccessible.   Carlyle had in his own case recon-
ciled reason with faith ; this, above all things, it was that
attracted to him those two striplings.   And he had indicated that for others this consummation so devoutly to be
wished was attainable through a right study of German
literature.   What promise, what hope was there not in
such a passage as this of his essay, ' Characteristics ' ?
' A faith in religion has again become possible and
inevitable for the scientific mind, and the word Freethinker no longer means the Denier or Caviller, but the
Believer or the Ready to believe.   Nay, in the higher
literature of Germany there already lies for him that can
read it the beginning of a new revelation of the Godlike,
as yet unrecognised by the mass of the world, but waiting

there for recognition, and sure to find it when the fit hour comes.'

With limited resources, to say nothing of limited abilities, we had essayed to decipher this new revelation. But though the effort brought us much knowledge, its object still eluded us. Then, in an impatient mood, we indited a brief letter to Carlyle, in which something was said of what seemed to us his supreme position in contemporary English literature. We mentioned our slender studies in German philosophy, and, with the audacity of youth, an audacity which in the retrospect astonishes me, we asked him for a solution of the mystery of existence. To our surprise, as well as to our delight, there arrived before long an answer from Carlyle. Our foolish epistle had found him in a genial mood, and possibly he was a little pleased to receive, even from two unknown youths, that recognition of his intellectual supremacy which in all likelihood none of his coevals in the republic of letters would then have cheerfully conceded to him.

Here is Carlyle's epistle, one which speaks for itself:—

'SCOTSBRIG, ECCLEFECHAN,
'*August* 28*th*, 1841.

'MY GOOD YOUNG FRIENDS,—It is many years since I ceased reading German or any other metaphysics, and gradually came to discern that I had happily got done with that matter altogether. By what steps, series of books, and other influences, such result was brought about, it would now be extremely difficult to say. Few books stand prominently with me above the general dimness. My power to serve you in this matter is accordingly very small. I can only say that my curiosity was once as intense as yours; my obstructions and obscurations perhaps greater than yours; that by studying of great thinkers (wheresoever met with, howsoever named or rubricked), above all, by thinking and struggling earnestly myself, help and victory were certain for me, as they will be for you and for all that do the like.

'Those two little books of Fichte's and Schelling's [1] are bright in my memory beyond all others that I read on that subject. Perhaps there is not elsewhere, for a British student, as much of interest and novelty extant, in equal compression, in the whole literature of German philosophy. One other book I also favourably remember: *The Life of Fichte*, by his Son, two moderate German volumes, of recent date comparatively, in which, I think, you will find some glimpses of the general field of German metaphysics, and indications for you of roads, towards whatever quarter you may be bound. It is easily read, too, which is an advantage. I may say further that after all the Fichteisms, Schellingisms, Hegelisms, I still understand *Kant* to be the grand novelty, the prime author of the new spiritual world, of whom all the others are but superficial, transient modifications. If you do decide to penetrate into this matter, what better can you do than vigorously set to the *Kritik der reinen Vernunft*, a very attainable book, and resolutely study it and re-study it till you understand it? You will find it actually capable of being understood, rigorously sequent, like a book of mathematics; labour that pays itself; really one of the best metaphysical studies that I know of. Once master of Kant, you have attained what I reckon most precious, perhaps alone precious in that multifarious business of German philosophy: namely, deliverance from the fatal incubus of Scotch or French philosophy, with its mechanisms and its Atheisms, and be able perhaps to wend on your way leaving both of them behind you. In fine, if you prosecute the study, it will be well to consult Sir William Hamilton, your neighbour, probably your former teacher; he of all men, British or foreign, is the best acquainted with the bibliography of German and other metaphysics, the ablest, therefore, to direct you towards books in any specific case. A Mr. Ferrier of your city I believe to be likewise worth inquiring

---

[1] Fichte, *Ueber das Wesen des Gelehrten*; Schelling, *Ueber die Methode des Academischen Studium*, of which we had made mention in our letter as having been read by us.

of. On this business of metaphysics, I know not that I can safely counsel further. Go on, and prosper.

'For the rest, let it be no disappointment, if, after all study, you do not learn ' what we are ;' nay, if you discover that metaphysics cannot by possibility teach us *such* a result, or even that metaphysics is but a kind of disease, and the inquiry itself a kind of disease. We shall never know " what we are ;" on the other hand, we can always partly know, what beautiful or noble things we are fit to do, and that is the grand inquiry for us. The Hebrew Psalmist said, " I am fearfully and wonderfully made ;" *God* so made me. No Kant or Hegel, as I take it, can do much more than say the like, in the wider, complicated dialect we now have.

'On the whole, we learn better what man is by seeing extensively what good or great things have come out of man ; I mean practically here : that the literature of Germany is perhaps likely to be a far greater possession for you than its metaphysics. The anatomical skeleton,—nay, we will call it the impalpable, unembodied soul ; contrast that with the living man, visible and audible there ! Your rule in reading for self-culture is to get acquainted with great men, and great thinkers, on what subject soever they may write ; it will be a *humane* subject, or they will not deserve the name of great. Goethe, Schiller, Jean Paul ! I will name these three to you. It seems to me there lies more in these men, and in men like them, than in all bodies of philosophy. He who has discerned the world as these men discerned it,—is not he educated to the highest point of vision human kind has yet attained to, an authentic man of *this* generation, with all past generations lying obedient under his feet, not *dis*obedient round his legs, round his very throat ?

'Good young friends ! I have no time to write more. I bid you persist in the same noble temper. Through many difficulties and confusions, you need not doubt a good issue, if you have strength to endure honestly, manfully. Your help lies within yourself ; your hindrance too lies there. Courage. Forward, forward !

'Yours with true good wishes,

'T. CARLYLE.'

A year or two afterwards an opportunity occurred for us to show, as we thought, our grateful devotion to the man whom we regarded as chief teacher in Israel. The chair of 'Civil History' in the University of Edinburgh became vacant. Knowing little or nothing of Carlyle apart from his writings, we resolved on attempting to get up a requisition from students of the University asking him to become a candidate. The patrons of the chair were the Edinburgh Town Council; but, if I remember rightly, they had to select one of two names presented to them by the Faculty of Advocates. Mr. Froude's narrative of this little episode in Carlyle's career contains several inaccuracies and exaggerations. For instance, 'A History Chair,' he says, 'was about to be established.' On the contrary, it was established some hundred and twenty years before, and in Carlyle's own day and generation it had been filled (1821-37) by Sir William Hamilton. His class was always a very small one, because to attend it was not necessary for a degree or made compulsory on law or divinity students. Hamilton urged on the patrons the desirability of making attendance on his historical prelections necessary, at least for the M.A. degree, but he pleaded in vain. At last, when in 1833 the City of Edinburgh became bankrupt, the Town Council withdrew the modest stipend of £100 a year attached to the chair, and Hamilton gave up lecturing. The chief promoter of the students' requisition was the young friend who had joined me in inditing that letter, previously mentioned, of anxious inquiry to Carlyle, and whose name was Dunipace, not Duniface, as Mr. Froude prints it. My college days were over, and my share in the movement was that of a mere outsider, though a zealous one. There has been preserved (by others not by me) a contemporary transcript of the following communication, which was my handiwork, and in which the wish of his student-admirers to have him nominated as a candidate for the History Chair was first formally notified to Carlyle :—

'A Memorial has been drawn up, and in the course of a few days subscribed by upwards of a hundred students attending Edinburgh College, requesting the Faculty of Advocates to nominate Mr. Thomas Carlyle as candidate for the Chair of Universal History at present vacant in their University.

'From a letter of Mr. Carlyle to Goethe, published in the poet's posthumous works,[1] they concluded that he was not unwilling to accept an official literary situation of some kind, and they thought that this Professorship approximated very nearly in extensiveness of subject to Herr Teufelsdröckh's one of " Things in General," although unhappily sharing along with it the disadvantage of being wholly unendowed.   They trust that this peculiar mode of testifying their respect will not be displeasing to Mr. Carlyle : he will remember, they hope, that their feelings towards him are also peculiar.   .

'Should Mr. Carlyle have no objection, the Memorial

---

[1] No doubt, but it, or rather Goethe's German version of the letter from its original English, appeared during his lifetime, being printed in his introduction to the German translation of Carlyle's *Life of Schiller*.   It was first published in any English form in a translation of it, by me, from Goethe's German version.   Goethe made Carlyle say, speaking of his home at Craigenputtock : ' Hier wohnen wir in Ermangelung einer Lehr - oder - anderen öffentlichen Stelle.'   This I translated ' Professorial.'   By a printer's error, ' Professorial' became 'professional,' which, besides being inaccurate, is nonsense, or something very near it.   I was surprised to find the same error committed, in the printing of the original English letter, in the American Professor Norton's *Correspondence between Goethe and Carlyle* (1887), where Carlyle is represented as saying that he is ' settled down' at Craigenputtock, ' in defect of any professional or other official appointment.'

will be sent without delay for presentation to the Faculty ; and perhaps he will have the kindness to address a few lines on this subject to Henry Dunipace, student, care of Messrs. McLachlan and Stewart, Booksellers, Edinburgh.'

Carlyle naturally declined to become a candidate for a Chair as unendowed as his own Teufelsdröckh's in the University of Weissnichto. His cordial and touching reply to the requisitionists is given by Mr. Froude, according to whom he wrote to some one at the time : 'I must take care the dogs do not print it in their newspapers.' Whether or not Carlyle sent a monition of the kind I do not remember, but 'the dogs' did not print his reply in the newspapers. The Chair of History was accepted by James Ferrier (*ante*, p. 59), son-in-law of Professor Wilson ('Christopher North'), and afterwards a distinguished metaphysician, but then known only to a few by some contributions to *Blackwood's Magazine* ; among them the series of remarkable papers, 'An Introduction to the Philosophy of Consciousness.' He held it, actively or passively, in all likelihood passively, for several years, until he became Professor of Moral Philosophy at St. Andrews.

Settling in London a few years afterwards, I was taken one evening by a Scotch friend, an Edinburgh man, to the famous 'little house in Chelsea,' then No. 5 Cheyne Row. My friend occasionally visited there, and had answered some inquiry of Carlyle's respecting his two young Edinburgh disciples. Carlyle, the servant said, was out of town, but Mrs. Carlyle was at home. Our cards were taken to her, and we were told that she would be with us soon. We were then ushered into that little front parlour in which so

many distinguished (and undistinguished) visitors have held
colloquy and commune with Carlyle, or listened to his
vehement and often violent monologues.   It was modestly
furnished, the only object in it to attract the least attention
being a shelf pendent on one of the walls, containing several
books.   One of them was a copy of the original edition of
Carlyle's translation of *Wilhelm Meister's Apprenticeship*,
a gift from him to the lady before their marriage, with the
words, 'Von meinem liebsten Freunde,' in her handwriting
on the fly-leaf of the first of the three volumes.   Another
was one of those copies of *Sartor Resartus*, which, when
every London publisher of note refused to be at the cost
of reprinting it from *Fraser*, had been formed by detaching
from the magazine the sheets containing the successive
instalments of the now famous book, and stitching them
into volume-form.   At the beginning of it was an inscription
to ' my dear little Jane Carlyle,' describing it as ' another
milestone in our desolate' journey or other analogous sub-
stantive.   On a table in the back parlour, shut off from
the front one by folding doors, there lay in those years
a miniature portrait of Mrs. Carlyle in the bloom of youth
and with flower-decked head, a striking contrast to the
little lady, plain and rather sallow, but with beautiful dark
eyes, and the most expressive of countenances, who, entering the room, welcomed us to her tea-table.   Conversation
was soon in full flow, for she knew something of one's
Edinburgh belongings, and this was never, in her husband's
absence, a silent hostess.   The first of her peculiarities
which struck me was her Scotch accent.   It was as marked
as I afterwards found her husband's to be, and differed
from it not in degree but in kind, as Haddingtonshire
differs from Dumfriesshire.   She talked of Edinburgh, and

listened with apparent interest to my account of a spectacle which I had witnessed there. It was the impressive wending of a procession of some hundreds of ministers and elders of the Kirk through the streets of Edinburgh from their meeting-place at the old General Assembly to the Hall of a new one. Many of the ministers were old men, and all of them had given up their livings and homes for conscience' sake, to found a Free Kirk in which the accursed thing patronage should be unknown. Mrs. Carlyle declared that if she had been there she would have cried. *Apropos* of Edinburgh and of Scottish clericalism she gave us an amusing account of a recent visitor of hers, Bishop Terrot, a Scottish Episcopalian prelate who called himself Bishop of Edinburgh. Mrs. Carlyle laughingly described the complacency with which he had dwelt on some sermon or other recently preached by him in London, to show Londoners what a Scotch bishop could do.[1] If Carlyle had been there

---

[1] This passage as it was published in the *Bookman* having been shown to Miss Terrot, daughter of the late Bishop Terrot, by my friend the Rev. W. H. Langhorne, who was quoting it in his 'Reminiscences' (1893), he received from her a communication, from which I extract the following: 'As regards your quotation from the *Bookman*, I daresay you do not know how my father came to know the Carlyles. He was located first at Haddington; and one day Jennie Welsh, aged fourteen at that time, who was sliding on the Tyne, fell, and my father ran forward to help her up, and this was their first introduction. She kept up intercourse with him after her marriage, coming frequently to see him, and writing and being very friendly, but afterwards changed, probably through her husband's influence. Long years afterwards, in the early part of my father's illness, she wrote him a very beautiful letter expressive of much regard and sympathy, which was accidentally burnt soon after being received, though far better worth publishing than the smart letters edited by Froude.' Terrot is the 'Cuittikins,' of one of whose visits to her there is a contemptuous account in a letter of Mrs. Carlyle to her husband, and he is also the 'Bishop of ——' in Carlyle's equally contemptuous prefatory note to that letter. Referring to the territorial title, which Mr. Froude has left in blank, Carlyle speaks of it as one which 'we used to think analogous to Great Mogul of London.'

E

he would have been indignant, as he generally was, looking
in his wonted fashion at the present in the light of the past,
when that insignificant Scottish Episcopal Church was
referred to. Trodden under foot by 'the brutal hoof of
tyranny and oppression' was his summary description of
Scotland when Episcopacy was dominant. But Carlyle
was not there. He was visiting some simple-minded
admirer in Wales, whose conversation, the lady told us in
her frank way, he had spoken of in his last letter to her as
'verging on the inane.' My friend and I took our leave
early, Mrs. Carlyle having given me the impression of a
very clever and agreeable woman, with a vein in her both
of satire and of sentiment.

In course of time I received an invitation to revisit
Cheyne Row, on a specified evening, when Carlyle would
be at home. I remember that evening well. It was with
no small awe that I found myself at last in the presence
of the man whom, since boyhood, I had looked up to as
the greatest of seers and the deepest of thinkers, who had
solved, as far as they could be solved, the chief problems
of existence. I found husband and wife in the upper
chamber, which was Carlyle's workshop. His writing-table
was there, and there was his library, not a very large one,
prominent among its contents being the folios which he
was consulting for his *Cromwell*—Rushworth, Thurloe,
Whitelocke, and the rest. Mrs. Carlyle received me
amiably, and I was placed at comparative ease by the
not very appalling statement from the great man that he
had found the streets 'rather sloppy.' The conversation,
if conversation it can be called, since the youngest of the
party naturally said little, and Mrs. Carlyle nothing, ranged
over a great variety of topics. There were inquiries by

Carlyle respecting my occupations and studies. In the course of references to Scotland and the Scotch, Carlyle complained of the interest which his countrymen took in what to him were the merest trivialities of literature, and that, when he last visited his fatherland, he was pestered with questions as to who it was that wrote this, that, and the other thing in *Punch.* Emerson being mentioned, Carlyle said that it was wonderful how as a lecturer he 'insinuated' himself into his hearers. He told laughingly an incident reported to him by a friend who had been visiting Emerson at Concord. The philosopher's little boy being very fretful and tearful, the optimistic parent took the urchin in his arms, and said, caressing him, 'I will love the devil out of him.' Carlyle evidently thought that for such an extrusion a sterner mode of treatment would have been more effective or appropriate. The triumvirate of Lake Poets coming under review, Carlyle declared that he had never given in to the worship of Wordsworth, whom, however, he admitted to be a 'dignified preacher and teacher.' Southey's prose he called 'watery;' and spoke contemptuously of his 'coquettings with the Church.' He repeated with a certain glee Hazlitt's verdict on Coleridge as a reasoner, 'No premises, sir, and no conclusions.' In connection with Coleridge and his expositor, John A. Heraud, he told a story, amusing, though it may sound a little profane. Heraud, besides being the author of some grandiose epics—*The Descent into Hell* and *The Judgment of the Flood*, which had their admirers—was a German scholar at a time when German was little known, and he tried occasionally to popularise German metaphysics. Carlyle, before coming to London, had read some of Heraud's disquisitions, and after he came to London there

seems to have been a kind of intimacy between the two.
In any case, he was one of the audience to whom Heraud
delivered a very eulogistic and rather high-flown funeral
oration on Coleridge. Carlyle sat beside an obese, rubi-
cund city man, who, when Heraud had ended, turned to
Carlyle, and giving 'a great guff of port-wine' in his face,
said, with due solemnity: 'Sir, one drop of the blood of
Christ is worth it all!' Something that Brougham had
said or done (I think in a Corn-Law controversy with John
Bright) led Carlyle into a monologue on Brougham's
vagaries after he became Chancellor, which he made the
text for an emphatic deliverance on the dangers attending
gratified ambition, and the duty of a man to remain contented with the position marked out for him, and not to
strive for a higher one. It was not unusual for him to
wind up a denunciation by discovering some good in the
person or thing denounced. Brougham's promotion of
Thirlwall would, he said, be placed to the credit side of
his account, or words to that effect. Thirlwall had to
resign his tutorship at Cambridge as the result of his plain-
spoken pamphlet in support of the admission of Dissenters
to the Universities. Whereupon Brougham, then Chancellor, presented him to a living in Yorkshire, which
enabled him to finish his *History of Greece*. In the fulness
of time he was made by Lord Melbourne Bishop of St.
David's, to the great indignation of High and other orthodox Churchmen, to whom Broad-church Thirlwall, as
co-translator of Niebuhr, translator, too (though before he
took orders), of a quasi-heterodox essay of Schleiermacher's
on St. Luke, was a man suspect. Of the movement of
contemporary German literature, Carlyle said he knew
little or nothing, and asked me what Uhland was about,

to which I replied, if I remember rightly, that he was taking an active part in the debates of the Würtemberg Parliament. Carlyle spoke sympathetically of the then King of Prussia, Frederick William IV., as placed in a difficult position between the claims of his hereditary kingship and the demands of Prussian Liberalism. On the whole, he was doing the best that could be done under the circumstances, summoning to Berlin men of intellectual distinction ; by which, I suppose, Carlyle meant the King's patronage of Schelling, Tieck, and younger men of promise. In talk like this the evening passed very pleasantly for the junior of the party, who had lost the awe with which he entered that upper chamber. As I was leaving it, Mrs. Carlyle pointed out to me a portrait of Jean Paul Richter, which hung on one of its walls. 'His nose is put out of joint,' Carlyle remarked significantly. German literature, and a great deal else, was being effaced for him by the Letters and Speeches of Oliver Cromwell, 'the best fellow I have fallen in with,' I once heard him say.

CHAPTER II

THE CROMWELLIAD

DURING the earlier period of my personal acquaintance with Carlyle he was verging on his fiftieth
year, and his fame was approaching its zenith. The publication, in 1837, of his *French Revolution* had been followed,
in 1838, by that (in volume form, though still anonymously)
of *Sartor Resartus*, which he compared to a stone thrown
into a sheet of water: he saw the circle of its influence
constantly widening. In the succeeding year, 1839, appeared
the first collective edition of his scattered essays. With
1840, he promulgated, in his thoughtful and eloquent
Chartism, his first direct message to the governing classes
of England, pointing out to them their duty at a seemingly
perilous crisis. In the year after, 1841, he printed his
lectures on *Heroes and Hero-Worship*, which had crowned
his success as a lecturer, his audiences at them having
included persons of high social as well as intellectual distinction. Two years later, in 1843, during the revolt of the
middle classes against the aristocracy, which as a body
resisted the repeal of the corn-laws, appeared *Past and
Present*, in its modern section full of what had become
fierce and fiery protests against misgovernment and no-
government alike. Meanwhile he was receiving considerable social recognition from the great. Since his arrival in
London he had been intimate with the best and foremost
of his brother men of letters. But he had a thorn in

the flesh—weak health. Headaches and insomnia were the ailments of which he most complained orally ; and for the headaches I have known him make a characteristic attempt to console himself by remembering that they had afflicted some of the greatest of the early German Reformers. Scotland never sent forth a stronger man, his medical brother John said of him ; but if he gained much in many ways by his migration to London—'literature written out of London,' he once said to me, 'has always a provincial look,' not to speak of British Museum libraries and Public Record offices—he also suffered much by it. It was a trying exchange, that of the perfect stillness and pure air of his Dumfriesshire solitude, for our smoky and foggy Babylon, with its noises, to which he was morbidly sensitive, and its social excitements, which he could not altogether avoid, unless he was to remain in Chelsea, as at Craigen-puttock, a lonely hermit. 'Ill health has cast a funeral pall over my life,' he said to me soon after I made his personal acquaintance. With better health he might have been if not happy—one cannot well conceive Carlyle a happy man—at least not so irritable, with considerable benefit to himself and to others. Much in Carlyle and in what flowed from him was, as Goethe said of Schiller, 'pathological.'

At the period of which I am writing Carlyle was absorbed in the laborious task of editing and elucidating the letters and speeches of Cromwell. I had opportunities for observing the keenness and diligence of his research, seldom equalled by the most industrious of antiquaries engaged during a lifetime in the composition of a county history. An Edinburgh gentleman of some antiquarian eminence sent him a fragment of manuscript, intimating, with a flourish of trumpets, that it contained what might prove to be an important contribution to Cromwellian history. At the close of one of my occasional visits to the Chelsea household, Carlyle gave it me, saying that he could make nothing of it, and asking me, if so disposed, to endeavour to find out whether its contents could have any value for him. This was the first of a good many slight (and purely honorary) services which I was able to render him in connection with his *Cromwell* book. I was then so placed as to have somewhat peculiar facilities for such investigations. I found that the mysterious fragment was simply a transcript of a passage in one of the perfectly accessible newspapers of the Commonwealth time, and had, moreover, no value whatsoever. The discovery pleased Carlyle, and thenceforth there came to me, pretty frequently, notes from him, with little historical and other queries. To answer them gave me no trouble that was not a pleasure, and saved him what was worse than trouble, loss of patience and of temper. For ordinary copying work at the British Museum and elsewhere he then employed an amanuensis, a forlorn-looking young Scotchman, whom he called a 'much-enduring man,' and whom, I observed, he treated with considerable delicacy. For something more than mere copying, however, he had himself often to visit the old reading-room of the Museum, the overcrowding, bad ventilation, and general stuffiness of which had given rise to a malady which Carlyle called 'the Museum headache,' and had encouraged the propagation of a maleficent organism known to others as 'the Museum flea.' To these inconveniences was added a confused and almost chaotic catalogue (since superseded by one far superior to it), full of perplexing cross-references and of innumerable interlineations, made in an attempt to produce something like alphabetical sequence. It was painful to see Carlyle stooping as he groped, perplexed and irritated, in the confused and confusing catalogue trying to find out whether the book which he wanted was in it, and therefore in the library. If it was there, like every one else, he had next to write on a ticket the title of the work and the press-mark, given in the catalogue, indicating where it stood on the library shelves. The book was then, and not till then, procurable. With grim humour Carlyle called this indispensable ticket 'the talisman,' and bestowed anything but a benison on the framers of the regulation which made necessary this, to him, harassing preliminary quest, one, moreover, sometimes altogether unsuccessful. He maintained that all that ought to be incumbent on the reader was to give the name of the book which he wanted, and that it was the duty of the librarian, without more ado, to find it for him. If you go, he argued, into a shop to purchase something, you are not expected to indicate to the shopman the whereabouts of the article to be purchased. What was faulty in this analogy and somewhat unreasonable in his complaint need scarcely be indicated. Thus, however, it came about that by saving him visits to the Museum and irksome hunts in quest of the talisman, my slender assistance was valued by him. Thus, too, and perhaps a little in other ways—I being, moreover, domiciled not far from him in Chelsea—there was formed for me the sort of intimacy with him that might under favourable auspices arise between an obscure, insignificant youth and a man of great literary distinction, whose presence was welcomed in some of the highest circles of English society.

At last *Cromwell's Letters and Speeches*, edited and elucidated, were in the printer's hands, to be issued in two bulky and rather costly volumes ; and with their appearance Carlyle's literary fame reached its zenith. ' It was to his own surprise, and still more to that of his publishers, that the success of his *Cromwell* proved to be so great. According to Mrs. Carlyle, if I understood her rightly, they undertook its publication with considerable reluctance, and only on the understanding that he would give them afterwards a complete biography of Cromwell. She herself expressed satisfaction at having no longer to breathe what she called 'the Cromwell atmosphere,' and thought the English a singular people in having received with comparative indifference a book so interesting as *Past and Present* to bestow on the *Cromwell* such a cordial reception. By another member of Carlyle's family, who had not, like Mrs. Carlyle, been a daily and hourly witness of the toilsome effort which produced it, the book was welcomed more heartily than any of his previous writings. Carlyle spoke of the delight with which his pious Presbyterian mother read the large type of the Puritan hero's letters and speeches, neglecting her son's copious smaller type elucidations of them. She looked on Cromwell as on some good and great King of Judah, reappearing on earth in English guise. The financial result of the book to Carlyle was considerable. According to report, he received £1000 for this the first edition of it. One never heard him refer to the subject, though he spoke freely enough of the very different result, at one stage at least, of the first English edition of his *French Revolution*. In the first account rendered him by its publisher, the expenses of production so balanced the receipts from the sales as to leave the author for all his toil and trouble exactly *nil*! The *Cromwell* he himself predicted would be 'the most lasting of all his books.' It was the only work of his of which one heard him say, or rather hint, that its execution did not fall far short of his ideal.

Of course there were readers of the famous book who protested against Carlyle's presentation of Cromwell as from first to last the sincerest of men, inspired by the one desire that the Kingdom of his Father in heaven should come and His will be done on earth. On the other hand, there reached him numerous expressions of sympathetic approval of his estimate of Cromwell. Many of them were from 'Evangelicals' of all communions, and Carlyle might then be heard declaring that among Evangelicals were to be found some of the best people in England. From High Churchmen he neither expected nor received any but an unfavourable verdict on Cromwell's character and career. Their view was to some extent shared even by his own familiar friend, Richard Monckton Milnes, the first Lord Houghton of after years. Milnes was professedly a Tory, though of a subdued type. 'He takes mildly to his Conservatism,' Carlyle said of him about this time, 'and sees that it is a falling cause.' In his *One Tract More* (1841), written from the point of view of a philosophical Churchman (later on he called himself a 'Puseyite sceptic'), Milnes had delivered himself of an interesting *apologia* for the growing Tractarianism and germinating Ritualism of fifty years since. Nevertheless he was among the first to recognise and proclaim Carlyle's genius and that of Emerson also. The year before the appearance of the first English edition of Emerson's *Essays*, with a commendatory preface by Carlyle, Milnes contributed to the *London and*

Westminster Review an article on Emerson, which was the earliest recognition in any British periodical of the American philosopher's rare and peculiar merits. It appeared in the number of the *Review* for October 1839, immediately following that in which John Sterling gave a similar first and glowing recognition of Carlyle as a great and original teacher of men.[1] Milnes's was a finely appreciative estimate, yet he showed in it a certain intellectual conservatism by a friendly protest against Emerson's 'declaration of independence' in the spiritual region, and proclamation of the right and duty of every man to think for himself about everything. In spite of his general breadth of view, Milnes could not bring himself to sympathise with Puritanism. Very soon after the publication of his *Cromwell* Carlyle called on him, and found him, as regarded the great Protector, in substantial agreement with a really able as well

[1] In a very striking passage of his *Life of John Sterling* Carlyle has recorded the effect produced on him by this article. Speaking of Sterling at Clifton Carlyle says : ' He wrote there and sent forth in this autumn of 1839, his most important contribution to John Mill's Review, the article on Carlyle, which stands also in Mr. Hare's collection. What its effect on the public was I knew not, and know not ; but remember well, and may here be permitted to acknowledge, the deep, silent joy, not of a weak or ignoble nature, which it gave to myself in my then mood and situation, as it well might. This first generous human recognition, expressed with heroic emphasis, and clear conviction visible amid its fiery exaggeration, that one's poor battle in this world is not quite a mad and futile, that it is perhaps a worthy and manful one, which will come to something yet : this fact is a memorable one in every history ; and for me Sterling, often enough the stiff gainsayer in our private communings, was the doer of this. The thought burnt in me like a lamp for several days ; lighting up into a kind of heroic splendour the sad volcanic wrecks, abysses, and convulsions of said poor battle, and secretly I was very grateful to my daring friend, and am still and ought to be. What the public might be thinking about him and his audacities, and me in consequence, or whether it thought at all, I never learnt or much heeded to learn.' One, doubtless, of the effects of Sterling's article, aided by the appearance about the same time of the first collected edition of Carlyle's *Essays*, was to produce rather elaborate articles on Carlyle's writings and teaching in the *Edinburgh* and *Quarterly Reviews*. That in the

as elaborate article[1] contributed to the *Christian Remem-brancer* (April 1849), by J. B. Mozley, in which Carlyle's character and estimate of Cromwell were strenuously im-pugned. Mozley was a prominent High Churchman of the time, whom Mr. Gladstone made a Canon, and finally Regius Professor of Divinity at Oxford. Carlyle was too proud a man, and perhaps knew too much of the idiosyn-crasy of his friend and junior to display any chagrin, although he would have been better pleased if Milnes had appreciated *Cromwell* more and Mozley on Cromwell less. Among the distinguished young men of high cultivation who admired him and courted his society, Milnes was a chief favourite. Carlyle appreciated his 'sunny humani-ties' and cheerful contentment with a 'saloon celebrity' as a poet, while Mrs. Carlyle, touching gently on what she styled his 'ridicules,' praised his 'delightful little notes.' Carlyle, however, was sometimes nettled by what appears to have been Milnes's occasional fondness for contradicting him, or saying something unpalatable merely to produce an outburst of indignant protest. Carlyle took seriously whatever sounded like serious speech. I have heard him describe Milnes as 'going about talking the most palpable

Edinburgh (for July 1840) was by Herman Merivale, who became Permanent Under Secretary of State for India. It was patronising in tone, but did jus-tice to the vivid picturesqueness of *The French Revolution*, with which mainly it dealt. Carlyle, strange to say, at first fancied that it was by Macaulay, to whose strongly-marked style it bears not the slightest resem-blance. The article in the *Quarterly* (September 1840) was by William Sewell, an Oxford Tractarian cleric, whose *Christian Morals* and other books aroused some attention in their day. It was Sewell who, as sub-rector and tutor of Exeter College, Oxford, indignantly flung Mr. Froude's *Nemesis of Faith* into the blazing college fire, and, poker in hand, zealously stimulated its cremation. Mr. Froude was a fellow of that college. In Sewell's article there is an exhibition of some sympathy with Carlyle as a denouncer of the materialism of the age, but Carlyle's religion of hero-worship was of course repugnant to a champion of Tractarian orthodoxy.

[1] Reprinted in *Essays* by J. B. Mozley (1884).

sophistry,' which doubtless amounted to nothing more than some persistent attempts to draw out Carlyle.[1] He told me, quite good-humouredly, of a little practical joke which Milnes played on him. He received one day a visit from an American, who had been floating about rather extensively in London society. The visitor, who was homeward bound, stayed an unconscionable time. At last, when he was about to depart, he said that he could not return to the States without paying a farewell visit to Carlyle, who, Milnes had told him, 'was talking of him yesterday for two hours.' Carlyle had indeed been speaking of him for a considerable period on the previous day, but it was to denounce him as a bore of the first magnitude! Once, when Carlyle was in a less serene mood, and I happened to say something, I know not in what connection, of his early intimacy with Milnes, 'Yes,' was the reply, 'he looked at you out of the boxes.' After his tardy victory over circumstances, Carlyle had not forgotten the contrast between his former poverty and the splendour and wealth of the great people who, regarding him during his painful struggle as 'a curious thing'—his own expression in the *Reminiscences*—invited him to their banquets and receptions to be looked at and listened to—'out of the boxes.'

[1] In his *Life of Lord Houghton* Mr. T. W. Reid prints a letter written to a friend, in which W. E. Forster, afterwards the well-known statesman, thus describes Milnes teasing Carlyle when both were his guests at Rawdon, near Leeds: 'Monckton Milnes came yesterday, and left this morning—a pleasant, companionable little man, well-fed, and fattening, with some small remnant of poetry in his eyes, and nowhere else; delighting in paradoxes, but good-humoured ones; defending all manner of people and principles in order to provoke Carlyle to abuse them, in which laudable enterprise he must have succeeded to his heart's content, and for a time we had a most amusing evening; reminding me of a naughty boy rubbing a fierce cat's tail backwards, and, getting in between furious growls and fiery sparks, he managed to avoid the threatened scratches.'

CHAPTER III

AFTER THE CROMWELLIAD.

HIS book on Cromwell finished, Carlyle found himself for the first time during many years without occupation. The *dolce far niente* of ordinary workers was never a boon to him, and he longed to be in harness again. Mr. Froude hints that a life of Frederick the Great was already suggesting itself to him. My impression was a very different one. From Carlyle's conversation at this time, I inferred that he was looking for a theme to the England of the eleventh century rather than to the Germany of the eighteenth, and that William the Conqueror, not Frederick the Great, was to be his new hero. He came with his brother John to the Library of the British Museum, and carefully inspected there the engraved reproduction of the Bayeux Tapestry, chapters of Anglo-Norman history in needlework, once thought to have been the handiwork of Matilda, the Conqueror's spouse, and undoubtedly that of a contemporary of the Conquest. In the rude but genuine delineations of successive scenes and events, from Harold taking leave of the Confessor before starting for Normandy, onward to the fierce *mêlée* of Saxons and Normans at the battle of Hastings, there was exactly that visuality in which Carlyle delighted. The quaint antique panorama would have furnished him with many a picturesque touch had he undertaken the task towards which his thoughts seemed to be tending, and which has since been performed by other and very different hands. He had long been impressed by the gigantic figure of the Conqueror looming through the mist of ages, and, as he thought, greatly distorted by the prepossessions and prejudices of modern historians. To begin with, under Harold, Carlyle thought, England would have lapsed into hopeless anarchy. The rebellion of Harold's own brother Tostig, supported by a Danish invasion, prefigured in all likelihood a series of rebellions and invasions by which England would have been harassed and harried but for the Norman Conquest. In the rule of the Conqueror Carlyle saw a great deal more than the ruthlessness with which it was established, and he looked on William and his Normans as the true makers of the greatness of England. His keen interest in the Conqueror and the Conquest had apparently been first aroused by Thierry's well-known History. Carlyle could not believe that the England fashioned by William was the result of nothing better than the Norman cruelty and rapacity with pictures of which Thierry's pages teemed. Such a notion was entirely false, and had produced, he thought, practically mischievous conceptions of the course of human affairs. I heard him maintain in all seriousness that the acceptance of Thierry's theory of the Norman Conquest had contributed to produce the cruelties then recently perpetrated by the French in Algeria! In the very year of the issue of Carlyle's *Cromwell* there was a general outburst of indignation in England at the tidings of a terrible Algerian atrocity. A body of Arab fugitives had taken refuge in a cavern, and refused to surrender to their French pursuers. A fire of fagots was lighted at the entrance of the cavern, and when at last the French troops entered it, they found the corpses of some five hundred suffocated Arabs. The

French officer in command was the Colonel Pelissier, who became twenty years later Commander-in-Chief of the French army before Sebastopol. Afterwards, as Marshal Duke of Malakhoff, and created a British G.C.B., he figured as French ambassador in London.

Whatever Carlyle's intentions in regard to William the Conqueror—the study of whose history he resumed subsequently—he was suddenly summoned to complete a familiar task. Only a few months after the issue of *Cromwell's Letters and Speeches,* a second edition was demanded. During the interval, so great had been the interest generally taken in the contents of the book, that many unpublished letters of Cromwell's and documents relating to him were disinterred from private repositories throughout the country, and forwarded to his zealous biographer. Among the contributors was the then Duke of Manchester, whose ancestor, an Earl of Manchester, was one of the Parliament's Generals early in the Civil War, having at one time for his Lieutenant-General Cromwell himself, who, however, got rid of him, through the famous self-denying ordinance, as suspected of lukewarmness in the cause. The Duke found among the Kimbolton papers unpublished letters of Cromwell; and not caring to intrust them to the post, brought them on foot to Chelsea, and delivered them to the servant as if he were any ordinary messenger. I know not whether it was the disclosure of his Grace's rank that led, or helped to lead, the handmaiden of the Chelsea household to an inference tentatively communicated by her to her mistress, whom it amused, and who reported it with a certain satisfaction. One day, in an interval of business, she looked at Mrs. Carlyle, and said, in a tone of interrogation, 'Master, ma'am, is the

F

cleverest man as is?' the reply of her mistress being, 'We fondly hope so.' However this may have been, all letters undoubtedly Cromwell's were welcomed by Carlyle, and with elucidations wherever needful, were duly inserted in the new edition; while, with a conscientious thoughtfulness too rare among successful editors, he printed the new letters and elucidations in a detached supplement for the benefit of possessors of the first edition.

The labour required for an artistic fusion of the new matter with the old was considerable, but to Carlyle it was a labour of love. The demand for a second edition of one of his more elaborate works so soon after the appearance of the first, was unique in his experience. He prized his success no doubt for its own sake, but also because he attached great importance to his countrymen's adoption of his estimate of Cromwell. Once more his conversation, or his monologues, turned much on Cromwell, who for a long time coloured his thoughts and waking dreams. I can see him now, in an old brown dressing-gown, seated on a footstool on the hearthrug, close to the fireplace in the little parlour, sending most deftly up the chimney whiffs from a long clay pipe, so that the room might not be odorous of tobacco-smoke. I can hear him between the whiffs, which served as commas and colons (there was never a full stop), pouring forth in the strongest possible of Scotch accents, an oral Latter-Day Pamphlet, contrasting Cromwell and his Puritans with contemporary English politicians and the multitudes whom they were leading by the nose to the abyss. I see Mrs. Carlyle, with head bent and one hand covering her face, listening in silence. She had heard it all so often before, poor lady, and knew how little would come of it. I can hear her, when Carlyle's denunciations of the present became terribly fierce, make the considerate appeal, 'Don't be angry with Mr. Espinasse; he is not to blame,' or, before the pipe had been substituted for the tea-cup, 'My dear, your tea is getting quite cold; that is the way with reformers.' Then perhaps the wild tempest of words would cease, and the Latter-Day Prophet break out into a hearty laugh at his own vehemence.

Carlyle's theory of government was, as all the world knows, that in an age and country like ours the wisest man should rule. If you asked how the wisest was 'to be discovered, he replied that first of all we had to recognise the necessity for the supremacy of wisdom, together with the utter futility of our present method of choosing our governors by counting votes at the polling-booth. Once, when I ventured to hint that even were the wisest man discovered and chosen to rule over us he would not be immortal, and there might be 'a difficulty about the succession,' Carlyle replied in rather an irate tone, 'That is the sort of twaddle that used to be poured into me when I was young,' and proceeded to speak of the good government enjoyed by the world under those five great Roman Emperors of whom Nerva was the first and Marcus Aurelius the last, and who succeeded each other by adoption. Yet Marcus Aurelius, to say nothing of his persecution of the Christians, appointed as his successor his vile son Commodus; and Carlyle had no great opinion of the 'wisdom' embodied in the Meditations of the contemplative Emperor, though they furnished him with one of the epigraphs of his history of the French Revolution. On quite another occasion, when I spoke of the stoical grandeur of the Meditations, he cut me short with the contemptuous remark, 'The unreading Germans came in and put an end to all that sentimentality.' In truth, it was this very matter of the succession which proved to be the weakness of the Protectorate instituted by Cromwell and his officers. In the latest form of the Protectoral constitution, Cromwell was authorised to nominate his successor. It is not certain, but it is probable, that he nominated the incapable Richard, who did succeed him, and wrecked the Protectorate. In his book, following a tradition, Carlyle suggested that Fleetwood, Cromwell's son-in-law, was nominated his successor in 'the sealed piece of paper' in which Cromwell is supposed to have named one, and which could not be found when searched for at Hampton Court when Cromwell was dying. In conversation, Carlyle said that if Cromwell had nominated as his successor his capable younger son, Henry, who was governing Ireland for him when he died, the Protectorate might have been firmly established, and thus the pernicious restoration of the Stuarts been averted.[1] Carlyle's opinion, of some ten years afterwards, on the interesting point, is given in his unpublished pencil jottings on the proof-sheets of an article on the Civil War and Cromwell, contributed to the *Edinburgh Review* for January 1856, by his friend the late well-known John Forster. Forster sent

---

[1] The late Mr. Venables gave (*Fortnightly Review* for May 1893) the following interesting account of a discussion, of which he was an ear-witness, between Carlyle and Macaulay on the character of Henry Cromwell : 'Almost the only occasion on which I remember to have heard Carlyle engaged in an elaborate defence of his opinions or assertions was at a breakfast party in London, against an opponent no less formidable than Lord Macaulay. The subject of dispute was the character of Henry Cromwell, whom Lord Macaulay described, in words quoted from Mrs. Hutchinson's *Memoirs*, as a "deboshed cavalier." Carlyle maintained not only that the charge was unjust, but that Henry Cromwell was an able and upright statesman. Both disputants were equally vigorous and voluble; but, not pretending to have any independent opinions on the subject, I observed that Carlyle referred to many contem-

the proof to Carlyle for corrections or suggestions, and Carlyle's comments pencilled on its margin, though few, are for the most part strikingly characteristic. The ground-work of Forster's article was Guizot's *Histoire de la Répub-lique d'Angleterre, et de Cromwell* (1854), a continuation of his former work, which closed with the execution of Charles I., and which Carlyle had praised in his *Cromwell.* The continuation came down to the death of Cromwell, and contained some really curious matter taken from the unpublished despatches of French ambassadors in England during the Commonwealth. But in the interval Louis Philippe had fallen, and his Prime Minister had become, for Carlyle, 'Sophist Guizot.' More than once in these jottings Carlyle calls Guizot a 'galvanised dead dog,' pronouncing him incapable of understanding such a man as Cromwell, and calling his later book—in which Crom-well's religious fervour was represented as tempered by statecraft—'a dirty French pamphlet.' Forster having quoted a passage in which Guizot spoke of the Protector as desirous of founding a dynasty, Carlyle thus retorts on the fallen French statesman : ' It is false that he ever wanted to found a dynasty. His notion was (and that very loose) a dynasty like the Hebrew Judges.' In his

porary authorities, while Lord Macaulay, at the end of every rhetorical period, invariably reverted to Mrs. Hutchinson and her "deboshed cavalier." " I have read," Carlyle once answered, not without impatience, "all that shrill female ever wrote, and I can assert that she knew nothing of Henry Cromwell. I have read every existing letter which she" (*sic*, a misprint surely for "he ") ever wrote, "and all that is written about him, and know that he was not a deboshed cavalier." The only other speaker who intervened was Sir George Lewis, whose sceptical instinct never failed him. In answer to Carlyle's argument from the letters, he suggested that Henry Cromwell, when he was Lord Deputy in Ireland, probably saved himself the trouble of writing, by merely signing letters written by his secretary. I forget whether Lord Macaulay accepted the aid of his unexpected ally.'

Edinburgh article, Forster not only adopted this theory, but broached it as his own. If Cromwell, in however 'loose' a fashion, did entertain such a notion, what a comment on it was the 'Happy Restoration'!

For the time being Carlyle was satisfied that he had done enough in the way of rehabilitating Cromwell, and was disposed to leave it to others to fill up his outline of the great English revolution of the seventeenth century. To aid those who might come after him, he bethought him of a little project suggested by his own experience. While editing and elucidating *Cromwell's Letters and Speeches*, he had consulted, and guided others to consult for him, the vast mass of so-called King's Pamphlets, in number between thirty and forty thousand, in the library of the British Museum. They cover the period between the meeting of the Long Parliament and the Restoration. The collector of them had purchased day by day and week by week whatever issued from the printing-press—newspapers, political pamphlets, sermons, plays, poems, and pasquinades. He had also formed a rough manuscript catalogue of them in several volumes (they still repose on one of the shelves of the Museum Reading Room), the titles being arranged in the chronological order of the issue of the publications themselves, of all arrangements the most useful for the serious historian. Carlyle thought that much of the unknown history of the eventful period lay buried in this mass of so-called pamphlets, and if extricated from it would be an invaluable aid towards the composition of a true Cromwelliad. The first step to be taken was to have the old manuscript catalogue printed, so that whoever wished to explore the collection would have before him a guide to and synopsis of its contents. I heard him say, with his usual emphasis, that the mere titles, often very quaint, of those old pamphlets would be more amusing than most of the books issued in our day and generation. Accordingly he drew up a Memorial, addressed to the Trustees, the governing body, of the British Museum, strongly urging them to have that catalogue printed. He showed me the Memorial, which has never been published, and which perhaps is still preserved somewhere in the Museum archives. I recollect little of it beyond its general purport. He indicated that a Cromwelliad worthy of its subject would in time be worked out by 'the genius of the English people.' He affirmed that the England of the Civil War and Commonwealth times might be restored to life by a proper exploration of the King's Pamphlets, and he added, I remember, 'even the age of Elizabeth is irrecoverable.' He said something at the close about 'the Michelets and Mignets' being intrusted with the care of the French national archives; by way, I suppose, of hinting that they managed these things better in France than in England. He told me at the time that to procure support for his Memorial he called on 'old Hallam,' the historian, who was one of the Trustees of the Museum. Neither from him nor from any one else did Carlyle receive the slightest encouragement, and his proposal fell to the ground. Some time afterwards, when he was again at leisure, I heard him talk, though rather vaguely, of forming a company of 'a few faithful men,' to conduct under his guidance an exploration of those pamphlets and of other neglected materials for the history of the Civil War and the Commonwealth, above all, of Cromwell's Protectorate. He lamented often the talent, undirected and misdirected, which was wasted on current literature, too frequently little better, he thought, than 'intellectual prostitution,' men 'blazing themselves out in newspapers,' as he phrased it, who, under proper guidance, might produce something noble; or at least contribute to its production. To that 'organisation of literature' which he sometimes dreamt of, and which he desiderated above all things, the execution of this project of his might have been a contribution, small in itself, but important as a beginning. It never came to anything; perhaps the 'few faithful men' were not forthcoming. This is one of the most original and interesting of all Carlyle's schemes of reconstruction in an age of revolution. The organisation of literature remains a dream which can be realised only in a very distant future.

CHAPTER IV

THE ASHBURTONS

WHILE Carlyle was working at the second edition of his *Cromwell* the Corn Laws were being repealed. Though generally indifferent to the details of contemporary politics, he watched that operation with considerable interest. In *Past and Present* he had thundered against the Corn Laws, and denounced Sir Robert Peel as Sir Jabesh Windbag, emptying on him and his 'sliding scale' a vial of contemptuous indignation. What was now happening, however, greatly altered for the better his opinion of the statesman who was carrying Corn Law repeal through Parliament, and Peel was to become for Carlyle an 'approximate hero.' As usual, he assigned to the 'hero' all the merit of the great achievement, ignoring the other persons and events who and which co-operated to bring it about. With Sir Robert's conversion to Corn Law repeal his Cabinet was broken up, and he resigned the Premiership. He resumed it when Lord John Russell found himself, not very unwillingly, unable to form an Administration. 'He has the courage of a lion,' Carlyle then said to me; and declared his belief that Peel 'would set up a permanent establishment in this country.' So little did he understand the working of our beautiful system of party government, or foresee that Peel's share in repealing the Corn Laws was in a few weeks to extrude him from Downing Street, and exclude him from it for the few remaining years of his life! But Carlyle did foresee that Corn Law repeal was the precursor of great political changes, nearer or more remote, in the direction of democracy; and the feeling with which he anticipated them was by no means one of unalloyed complacency. In his pessimistic forecast it was as if he had to live on and work in a decayed and tottering house, the fall of which was inevitable. The prospect of such a consummation did not seem altogether delightful to this one of the occupiers of the rickety tenement, as he considered it to be. In view of the ultimate downfall of 'great masses of humbug,' he said to me then: 'You may live to see it; I hope that I shall not.'

One subordinate cause of the welcome which Carlyle gave to Corn Law repeal was his hope that it would preserve the aristocracy from a violent death, and allow its members breathing-time for reflection on their position and duties. No man ever spoke more plainly of the worthlessness of the merely idle, pleasure-seeking, game-preserving aristocrat, but he cherished a high estimate of the possibilities for good which had fallen to the lot of the English aristocracy as a whole. His own personal experience of some of its members had indeed inspired him with a kindly feeling towards the order to which they belonged. For several years before the repeal of the Corn Laws he had enjoyed a close intimacy with Mr. Bingham Baring and his wife, Lady Harriet, afterwards the second Lord and Lady Ashburton, who appreciated his genius and conversation, and of whom he was often the welcome guest. This intimacy ripened into cordial friendship, and brought him into contact with many of their compeers, his fellow-guests in town and country, by whom he was treated with the utmost courtesy and respect. Carlyle's lot had been very different from that of Macaulay, for instance, who was his junior, and made his appearance in literature about the same time as himself. Early in life Macaulay attained literary and political distinction, speedily finding favour in the eyes of the Whig leaders, and obtaining a seat in Parliament, with substantial official benefits, from his party, as soon as it was raised to power. Slowly and painfully, for more than twenty years after his adoption of a literary career, Carlyle had to 'cut his way,' as he phrased it, 'through the jungle of poverty and obscurity.' He would have been more than human if the Radical sternness of his youth had not relaxed a little when, having acquired a modest independence, he found his society welcomed by those whom he calls in his *Reminiscences* 'the selectest specimens of the English aristocracy.' Once, with the severe rigour of inexperienced youth, I expressed to him surprise at the great complacency with which a prominent democratic leader of those days, on platforms a vehement denouncer of all placed in authority over him, had been talking to me of some civil speech or other made to him by a Cabinet Minister. When I had finished, Carlyle ejaculated, in a tone expressive of no very strong condemnation of the delinquent; 'Poor human nature! Poor human nature!'

A fraction of the winter holiday taken by Carlyle after finishing his *Cromwell* he passed with his wife in Hampshire, where they were the guests of Mr. and Lady Harriet Baring. After his return to London in the spring, to work at the second edition of the successful book, Mrs. Carlyle went again on a visit to the Barings, this time at Addiscombe, where they had another country-house, Carlyle generally joining her there for a day or two at the end of the week. As the guest, then, of these particular Barings, he was in the society of staunch adherents of Sir Robert Peel. From the formation of Peel's second Ministry in 1841, Carlyle's host, Mr. Bingham Baring, had been the Parliamentary Secretary of the Board of Control, until in 1845 he was appointed Paymaster-General of the Forces. This office had been held by Lord John Russell when charged with the conduct of the first Reform Bill, and Mr. Baring was succeeded in it by Macaulay. The work probably was not very heavy, but, whatever its nature, the Carlyles reported, as something singular, that so long as Mr. Baring was in town 'he went to his office every day.' When Sir Robert, on declaring his conversion to Corn Law repeal, was deserted by many of the magnates of his Ministry and party, Mr. Bingham Baring adhered to him, and resumed his former office on his chief's restoration to the Premiership. If Peel had set up that 'permanent establishment in this country' which Carlyle fondly hoped for, or even if he had remained in office for a year or two more, it is possible that with such influential friends as the Barings, especially when they became Lord and Lady Ashburton, Carlyle might have been enabled to serve his country as a 'doer,' and not merely as a 'speaker.' 'Goethe,' he once said to me, 'was the most successful speaker of the century, but I would have been better pleased if he had done something ;' and to 'do something, to do almost anything that was useful and honourable rather than spend his days in painfully writing books, which he felt too keenly to be an inadequate expression of himself, was so strong a desire of Carlyle's that, in the middle of his literary career, he actually thought of abandon-

ing literature and becoming—a civil engineer! Now that
he was famous and successful he might well aspire to some
higher practical work, and, without parading, he did not
conceal his aspiration. There was no need for him to
conceal it. His was not the vulgar ambition to be dubbed
the 'Right Honourable Thomas,' with a salary of some
thousands a year, paid quarterly, as had been the lot of
Macaulay. Carlyle was ready to work, for the work's sake,
with Herculean energy, at any of several highly useful
public tasks. *Dis aliter visum.*

Of Carlyle's two friendly Barings, Lady Harriet alone
belonged to the hereditary aristocracy. She was the eldest
daughter of the sixth Earl of Sandwich, and was doubtless
none the less interesting to Carlyle because her ancestor,
Edward Montagu, the first Earl, 'enlisted,' he told me,
'with Oliver when he was sixteen.' As an Admiral of the
Fleet under the Protectorate, he fought with Blake against
the Spaniard, but when the Commonwealth fell to pieces
after Cromwell's death, he played a prominent part in
bringing about the Restoration, and was rewarded with
an earldom. The Barings were, in comparison with the
Montagus, people of yesterday. German in origin, they
traced their descent to the pastor, in the last century, of
a Lutheran Church at Bremen, who migrated to London.
His son John settled in England, and was a cloth manufacturer near Exeter. The cloth manufacturer's son
Francis, who in time was created a baronet, laid the
foundations of the financial house of Baring, once so pre-
eminently great, but somewhat eclipsed in these later
days. Alexander, the second son of Sir Francis, ultimately
became the head of his father's house of business, and
amassed a colossal fortune, so much of which he sank in

the purchase of land that Carlyle, who knew him and liked him, told me that 'he might be pricked for a sheriff in any county in England.' He was President of the Board of Trade in Peel's first Ministry of 1834-35, at the close of which he became the first Lord Ashburton of the modern creation, and during Sir Robert's second Administration of 1841-45, he negotiated the well-known Ashburton Treaty, which settled various boundary and other thorny differences between the British and American Governments. The affairs of the financial house, known later as Baring Brothers, seem to have finally fallen into the hands of descendants of this first Lord Ashburton's elder brother. His eldest son, who, as second Lord Ashburton, succeeded him some two years later than the time of which I am writing, was Carlyle's kind and steadfast friend.

Carlyle, Thackeray, Emerson when in England, for a time John Stuart Mill, Tennyson,[1] Monckton Milnes (Lord Houghton), Charles Kingsley, Jowett, Goldwin Smith, Spedding, Sir Henry Taylor, Tom Taylor, and Venables,[2] who at his death was *doyen* of the *Saturday Review*, and from whom his friend Thackeray borrowed the nobler traits in the character of George Warrington in *Pendennis*, figured as members, some intermittently, others

[1] In an unpublished letter of Carlyle's from the Hampshire seat of the Ashburtons, 'The Grange,' dated January 2nd, 1856, he writes thus of Tennyson as a fellow-guest: 'We are a fluctuating company, come like shadows, so depart. The agreeable phenomenon at present is Alfred Tennyson. He has a big moustache, carefully cultivated, and with his new wide-awake looks flourishing. Good company to smoke with in the conservatory of the place, though he often loses his pipe,—more power to it!'

[2] As he was not only an intimate friend of Carlyle, but saw much of him in the Ashburton circle to which both belonged, the admirable article of Venables, 'Carlyle in Society and at Home,' previously quoted (*ante*, p. 84), is, so far as it goes, a contribution of the greatest value to Carlyle's biography.

permanently, of the literary circle which Mr. and Lady
Harriet Baring gathered round them before and after
they became Lord and Lady Ashburton. Yet, but for
Lord Houghton's interesting sketch of both of them in
the chapter, 'Lady Ashburton,' in his little-read volume,
Monographs, not much would be known of the second
Lord and Lady Ashburton, otherwise than through Mr.
Froude's needlessly elaborate narrative of the mental disturbance occasioned to Mrs. Carlyle by the homage which
her husband paid to the lady, and his desire that it should
be also paid to her by his wife. Lord Houghton's Monograph is the main authority for what follows. Mr. Bingham
Baring formed in early life a warm friendship with Charles
Buller, who remained until his premature death a constant
and favourite guest of Lord and Lady Ashburton, as they
shall henceforth be called. Carlyle, as is well known, had
been Charles Buller's tutor, and as long as both were alive,
their intimacy survived this connection. It was through
Buller apparently that Carlyle and Lord Ashburton became acquainted. Lord Ashburton was a man of superior
intelligence, and felt strongly the responsibilities of his
position. He was very shy and retiring, and, with all her
efforts, his brilliant wife could not succeed in exciting in
him a political ambition, which, if he had possessed it,
could have been easily gratified. He was content to fulfil
the duties of his station, to admire his gifted wife, and to
enjoy the homage which every one rendered to her. It
had been partly with the hope, Lord Houghton intimates,
of advancing him in political life that she first gathered
round her such a circle as had scarcely ever before been
seen in London *salon* or English country-house—statesmen, high officials, prominent politicians and ecclesiastics,

not a few men of purely intellectual and literary distinction, of all schools and opinions, with a large and doubtless judicious admixture of people of mere rank and fashion. The Châtelaine herself was one of the cleverest and wittiest of women. The Princess Lieven said of her, *qu'il vaudrait bien s'abonner pour entendre causer cette femme*; but even the amiable Lord Houghton speaks of her 'natural rudeness of temperament and despotism of disposition.' She was satirical, and could be sarcastic. The *parcere subjectis* was much less congenial to her than the *debellare superbos*. 'Many who would not have cared for a quiet defeat shrank from the merriment of her victory.' 'I do not mind being knocked down,' moaned one of the victims of her wit, 'but I can't stand being danced upon afterwards.' The impression made by all that one has read and heard of this famous lady is that she had a great deal more head than heart. She treated even her husband's family with a certain disdain. 'The Barings are everywhere,' she said, 'and get everything.' 'The only check upon them,' she added, 'is that they are all members of the Church of England;' by which observation she meant presumably to hint that, had it been otherwise, a Baring might have sat in the chair of St. Peter! Himself not always sparing of others with his tongue, Thackeray took such umbrage at some of her personal sallies, that for a time he declined her invitations, and said harsh things of her. He gave in, however, when, resentment on either side having cooled down with the lapse of months, he received from her a card of invitation to dinner. He returned it with a drawing on the back, 'representing himself kneeling at her feet with his hair all aflame from the hot coals she was energetically pouring on his head out of an ornamental brazier.' The reconciliation was complete, and the after-friendship of the peeress and the novelist was thenceforth uninterrupted. This deference to intellect was the redeeming point in the great lady's character. 'Ask me to meet your printers!' a lady of fashion once said to her, the 'printers' being a scornful appellation for such distinguished men of letters as have been already named. '"My printers," as they call them, have become a sort of Order of the Garter,' Lord Houghton reports Lady Ashburton as saying. 'I dare not talk to the Knights as I could do to fine ladies and gentlemen.' She could, however, be capricious to her 'Knights'; and in a letter written home by Sir Henry Taylor when visiting her, with Tennyson as a fellow-guest, there are proofs that her caprices did not fail to provoke envyings and jealousies among the notable men who composed her little court. But it is admitted that her, like her husband's, regard for Carlyle never wavered, however imperious her manner to him might sometimes be. 'Coming back to the society of Carlyle,' she said once, 'after the dons at Oxford, is like returning from some conventional world to the human race.' According to Lord Houghton, 'the frequent presence of the great moralist of itself gave to the life of Bath House and the Grange a reality that made the most ordinary worldly component parts of it more human and worthy than elsewhere.'

Lord Ashburton is described by Lord Houghton as a nobleman with an 'unquenchable thirst for information,' who loved to bring about him 'every special capacity.' Lady Ashburton delighted chiefly in the society of her 'printers.' To her husband it was due that among their guests were men of science like Lyon Playfair and Dr.

G

William Carpenter, or such industrialists as the eminent mechanical engineer, the praises of whom being sung after his departure, Carlyle was content to say 'he seems to be a clean veracious smith.' But while others among her 'printers' shared with Carlyle more or less, and fitfully or otherwise, the favour which Lady Ashburton always showed him, he appears to have been the only one of them whom her lord not only cherished as a friend but as a companion, taking the sage with him in journeyings often to Scotland and to France. Mr. Froude even says that he found among Carlyle's papers notes in which Lord Ashburton expressed sympathetic approval of those schemes of social reconstruction which were rejected by almost all of Carlyle's contemporaries. After Lord Ashburton's death, Lord Houghton spoke of him as 'the noblest and purest-minded man I have ever known'—Lord Houghton had known nearly everybody who was worth knowing—and he adds, 'If he' (Lord Ashburton) 'had had powers and facility of expression he would have been a great one.' Of such a nobleman more ought to have been than is recorded. Since these Carlyle papers were first printed, I have been able to collect a little information about Lord Ashburton which has not been published in any contribution to the enormous mass of Carlyle literature. One creditable anecdote of his earlier manhood I lighted on in a very unexpected quarter.[1] It relates to the frightful agrarian outrages which marked the year 1830: Carlyle's Lord Ashburton, then Mr. Bingham Baring, was born in 1799. Bands of agricultural labourers went about destroying threshing machines as diminishing employment and

[1] Charles Roach Smith, *Retrospections: Social and Archæological* (1883), ii. 44-8 and 244-6.

lowering wages, and threatening letters, demanding their disuse, were addressed to the farmers who had adopted them. Night after night incendiary fires destroyed corn-stacks, farm buildings, and live stock. Hampshire, where Mr. Baring's father, the first Lord Ashburton of that creation, had estates, was one of the areas visited by these outrages. The rioters were at their destructive work on a farm near the Grange, which afterwards became so famous as the scene of the second Lord and Lady Ashburton's splendid and comprehensive hospitality. Mr. Bingham Baring, with a few servants and dependants, sallied forth to resist the rioters. In the *mêlée* which ensued, a young fellow of the name of Cooke struck Mr. Baring with one of the sledge-hammers which the rioters used in destroying the obnoxious threshing machines. Mr. Baring was seriously injured, and the blow might have been fatal had it not been partly warded off by one of those who had accompanied him to the fray. Cooke was arrested, and, with a number of others, was tried before a special commission of judges at Winchester, early in 1831. He was found guilty, and, under a statute since repealed, condemned to death. At the trial, Mr. Baring, on oath, distinctly declared his belief that Cooke did not strike him with malicious, far less with murderous, intent. After the sentence Mr. Baring and his family used all their considerable influence to procure a commutation of the death penalty. The judges appear to have refused to intervene, and Lord Melbourne, then Home Secretary, thought that an example had to be made. Through no fault of his Mr. Baring's amiable intention was defeated, and Cooke was executed.

After Mr. Bingham Baring became Lord Ashburton he

was twice President of the Royal Geographical Society, but specialists supplied the bulk of his one presidential address. I have, however, found in print a full report of what was probably the longest speech which Lord Ashburton ever made, an interesting speech, and delivered on an interesting occasion. It was an address to the elementary teachers of the diocese of Winchester (1855), in explanation of his establishment of a set of 'Ashburton prizes'—money prizes, 'for the teaching of common things' —rudimentary physics, physiology, domestic economy, and so much of political economy as related to work and wages ; for the speaker did not share the steady aversion from the 'dismal science,' felt and expressed by his guide, philosopher, and friend, Carlyle. In the course of the address Lord Ashburton let fall this little bit of autobiography :—

'Between Eton and Oxford I studied six months in the University of Geneva. I did not indeed learn much, but my eyes were opened to mark and understand what had before passed unheeded. Faculties were called into play which lay till then undeveloped, and I found my mind ripen more rapidly during those few months than in years previous ; and now, advancing in age, I still continue to add more and more to my knowledge by the application of the general principles of common things which I then learnt.'

The following remarks on the teaching of science and its absence from the education of the higher as well as of the humbler classes were more striking then than they will appear to be now, though they still deserve to be laid to heart :—

'Remember that it is by the daily use of the powers of nature that man feeds and clothes and houses himself. He employs fire in a hundred ways for a hundred purposes;

why should he not be taught the doctrine of heat? For some purposes he may learn to use it better ; he may learn to use it for more.

'Again, he passes the livelong day in the application of the mechanical powers ; why should he not be instructed in their principles also? It is true that princes in this land are ignorant of them as well as peasants. In this progressive country we neglect the knowledge in which there is progress, to devote ourselves to those branches in which we are scarcely, if at all, superior to our ancestors. In this practical country the knowledge which gives power over nature is left to be picked up by chance on a man's way through life. In this religious country the knowledge of God's works forms no part of the education of the people, no part even of the accomplishments of a gentleman ; but this judicial blindness cannot much longer exist. If we wish to hold our rank among nations, if we intend to maintain that manufacturing ascendency which is the chief source of our national strength, we must carry this study of common things not only into the schools of the poor, but into our colleges and universities.'

Then came some remarks, more original than these, but too long for quotation, in which Lord Ashburton developed the thesis that the labourer and the artisan would take a much greater interest in their work, if, instead of making it a matter of monotonous routine, they understood the principles on which their procedure was based. The whole address reads like the product of a thoughtful and even penetrating man, animated by a generous desire to increase the well-being and happiness of those socially beneath him.

Lord Ashburton's attachment to Carlyle led him to

welcome Carlyle's friends and to encourage and aid Carlyle's struggling *protégés*.   Instances of his munificence to these will be given hereafter.   Meanwhile, here is an amusing anecdote illustrating Lord Ashburton's generosity, when Carlyle was even indirectly concerned.   An artist, who frequented the Carlyles, painted a picture of them as they looked in their little parlour where guests were generally received,—Carlyle in his dressing-gown smoking a pipe by the fireside, the lady in an arm-chair sitting opposite him.   The picture was hung at one of the Royal Academy's Exhibitions, but was by no means a striking work of art.   So great, however, was Lord Ashburton's interest in the subject that he bought it for £500.   The delighted artist hurried off to Chelsea, expecting congratulations on his own account, and some manifestation of pleasure on the part of the Carlyles at having such a value set on a delineation of themselves and their domestic interior.   When he had delivered himself of what he fancied to be the glad tidings, all the response received by him from Carlyle was the by no means complimentary or complacent remark : 'Well, in my opinion, £500 was just £495 too much !'

CHAPTER V

MAZZINI AND THE CARLYLE BROTHERHOOD

CARLYLE was still at work on the second edition of his *Cromwell* when there occurred the painful episode in his married life to which reference has been previously made. Mrs. Carlyle was dissatisfied with Lady Harriet Baring's demeanour to her as a guest, and was disinclined to reappear in that character. Though Carlyle thought her repugnance unreasonable, and allowed it to irritate him extremely, he deferred to it so far as even to think of discontinuing his own visits to the Barings. He hinted as much to Lady Harriet, who received the intimation, he wrote to his wife, 'with fully more indifference than I expected,' a response characteristic of 'the high lady,' as Carlyle was wont to call her. Before very long matters were made up for a time at least, and Mrs. Carlyle resumed her visits to the Barings.

From the dates given by Mr. Froude, I see that I was an occasional visitor to the Chelsea household when this unhappy disagreement arose. I observed at the time that Carlyle was more than usually irritable. 'Women are very silly creatures,' was one of the hasty generalisations in which he indulged, and he protested against his wife's then admiration of George Sand—ebullitions which she bore in silence. I knew nothing of what was doubtless the cause of Carlyle's irritation, and like the rest of the world, would have known nothing of it but for Mr. Froude's revelations.

Indeed, it is very noticeable that when editing his wife's letters for possible publication, Carlyle omitted all those of them written when she left London for the North, a little later, in a very angry mood, and that when expressing penitence, in the *Reminiscences*, for his marital shortcomings, he forbore any mention of this Baring episode. But, if the episode is one which yields little or nothing in the way of 'Recollections,' it may well be suggestive of 'Reflections.' Strange irony of fate! Mrs. Carlyle had worked unweariedly, and suffered uncomplainingly, for some twenty years, to forward her husband on his toilsome path to eminence, and now it was the very altitude, which in this intimacy with the Barings he had reached, that led to the first great breach between the two. Mr. Froude blames both of them impartially, Carlyle for not sufficiently considering the feelings of his wife, and Mrs. Carlyle for exaggerating her grievance. But surely there is a third person involved in this unhappy business who has escaped well-deserved censure—Lady Ashburton herself. Mr. Froude tells the very edifying story of an invitation from Lady Ashburton to Mrs. Carlyle, asking her to spend December at the Grange, the chief country-seat of the Ashburtons, while Carlyle was to remain at home busy with one of his books, the motive of the invitation being that Mrs. Carlyle should help in amusing some of her hostess's guests. 'She did not wish to go,' Mr. Froude says, 'and yet she hardly dared say no. She consulted John Carlyle,' her husband's medical brother, and this is an extract from her letter to him: 'Heaven knows what is to be said from me individually. If I refuse this time she,' Lady Ashburton, 'will quarrel with me outright. That is her way, and to quarrel with her involves also quarrelling with Mr. Carlyle. It is not a thing to be done lightly.' Why should Lady Ashburton 'quarrel outright' with Mrs. Carlyle for refusing to be dragged from home to spend December in amusing the great lady's guests? It was wrong of Carlyle to be ready to quarrel with his wife because Lady Ashburton quarrelled with her on that paltry ground. But the prime offender was the great lady, who showed so much selfishness and so little delicacy of feeling in trying to coerce the wife into becoming an unwilling guest, knowing doubtless very well that the husband's wrath would be the penalty of refusal.

Mr. Froude has printed two replies of Mazzini to appeals made to him by Mrs. Carlyle for sympathy in the dire distress of mind which the Baring episode was causing her. Among her complaints was that of a profound feeling of loneliness ; another was that her life was an 'empty' one. Mazzini's consolations on the first of these laments point to previous conversations between the two on life and death, and on the commune of the living with the beloved dead— references to which may have surprised those who knew Mrs. Carlyle only as a brilliant and satirical hostess. To her complaint of leading an 'empty' life, Mazzini's admonitory response was naturally 'do good,' 'get up and work'—advice more easily given than followed. Mrs. Carlyle had a kindly disposition, and often in an impulsive way 'did good' to a greater extent than she received credit for. But the objects of her kindness were those in whom she took a personal interest, and the comprehensive feminine philanthropy now so rife was not at all in her way. I asked her once why she did not write a book. She replied that her 'ideal was too high.' Otherwise, to judge from little pieces of hers in prose and verse printed since her death, composed with more deliberation than the letters which she dashed off in hot haste, and exhibiting keen insight and a peculiar delicacy of thought and feeling, she might have made some very interesting and striking contributions to modern literature.

When Mrs. Carlyle made these appeals to Mazzini her intimacy with him and admiration for him were at their highest. He had been then nearly ten years an exile in England. While carrying on, under constant espionage, with ceaseless activity and marvellous dexterity and fertility of resource, his ' Young Italy' propagandism, he supported himself partly by writing high-toned articles for magazines and reviews. Among these was the *Monthly Chronicle*, which was edited by Bulwer (afterwards the first Lord Lytton), then a Liberal and something more, and which came to grief, with the also long-defunct *British and Foreign Review*. This periodical was founded and munificently supported by a wealthy northern M.P., Mr. Wentworth Beaumont, an advanced Liberal and ardent anti-Russian, its editor being John Mitchell Kemble (a son of Charles), the ' J. M. K.' to whom Tennyson, his early friend, addressed a fine sonnet, but who, instead of becoming, as predicted by the poet, a ' latter Luther and a soldier-priest,' achieved distinction as an Anglo-Saxon scholar. To each of these periodicals Mazzini contributed an article on Carlyle, eloquent and highly appreciative, but containing a friendly and sorrowful protest against Carlyle's view of ' heroes' as the all-important factors in the history of man, Mazzini opposing to it what he described as ' the great religious idea, the continuous development of humanity, according to an educational plan designed by Providence.' But in spite of all differences of opinion, theoretical and practical, Carlyle greatly admired the noble-minded Italian patriot. There is still remembered Carlyle's indignant protest against the opening, for the benefit of the Austrian Government, at the General Post Office, of Mazzini's letters by Sir James Graham, then Peel's Home Secretary, whom Carlyle defined to me as a 'border-reiver' disguised as a Minister of State. In his protest, addressed to and published by the *Times*, Carlyle spoke of Mazzini as 'a man of genius and virtue, . . . one of those rare men numerable unfortunately but as units in this world, who are worthy to be called martyr-souls.' Years afterwards I heard Carlyle say, 'When I first met Mazzini I thought him the most beautiful creature I had ever seen—but entirely unpractical,' Mrs. Carlyle, by this time a little disenchanted, quietly adding, 'he twaddled.' This was just after the arrival of the news of the crushing defeat inflicted at Novara on Charles Albert and his Piedmontese army by Radetzky and his Austrians —another illustration, Carlyle said, of what 'Dutch bottom' could do. Whatever material progress there had been in Italy, such as road-making, was due, he opined, to the Austrians. However, he wound up with the avowal, made, I thought, rather reluctantly, 'But I hope they' (the Austrians) 'will be driven out.'

Next to his wife in devotion to Carlyle, but at a considerable distance, was his brother John, 'Jack,' or 'The Doctor,' his junior by some six years. Of his three brothers, John was the only one who was enabled to adopt a profession, and that mainly through Carlyle's generosity to him, and at a time when he himself had a hard struggle to maintain. Carlyle's favourite brother, however, was, he told me, Alexander, 'Alec,' two years his junior, whose 'little white nieves' (*Anglicè*, fists) he could still see gleaming in the summer evening dusk, raised in defence of his elder brother in boyish school or village-fights. Farming was Alec's vocation, but after several failures he migrated to Canada, and was the first of the brothers to die. Carlyle said he 'wanted patience,' and spoke self-reproachingly of having done him no good by putting the Abbé Raynal's and other fiery books into his hands. The remaining and youngest brother James was, like Alec, a farmer, but 'he adapted himself,' Carlyle told me, 'to the new modes of farming,' and throve in his native district. James must have been the brother whom I once saw casually in his native village. During a walking tour, wending my way Edinburgh-wards from the English Lakes, I had to visit a friend who was temporarily sojourning in the neighbourhood of Ecclefechan. I turned aside to see the hamlet in which my favourite sage was born and partly bred. One of his brothers, whom I took to have been James, kept there a little general shop. I entered and bought from the brother an ounce of snuff. He was a shock-headed common-looking Scotchman, the father apparently of some bare-footed children who were running in and out of the shop. James appears to have been far the least cultivated of the three—Carlyle called him a 'very inarticulate man.' He survived all his brothers.

Dr. John Carlyle, at the time of which I write, had almost but not quite given up practising as a physician, and, being an accomplished Italian scholar, was employing his ample leisure in executing his well-known and excellent English prose translation of Dante's 'Inferno.' As travelling physician to the then Countess of Clare, and afterwards to the late Duke of Buccleuch, he had seen a great deal of the Continent, besides having in

earlier years studied medicine in Germany. While attending on Lady Clare he saw much of Italy and the Italians,
and he spoke to me in praise of the dignified manners
of the Italian aristocracy, intimacy with whom, he said,
was seldom conceded to English tourists. In Italy, he
acquired that thorough mastery of its language and knowledge of its older literature which is conspicuous in his
prose translation, with copious annotations, of Dante's
'Inferno.' He had that love of arguing which Benjamin
Franklin discovered in 'all attorneys and men educated at
Edinburgh,' where he took his M.D. degree. Carlyle has not
too amiably described him as 'a logic-chopper from his
infancy,' and, while recognising his excellent qualities, is
found, in one of his notes to Mrs. Carlyle's letters, speaking
of him as an element of disturbance in the Chelsea household, though to me he appeared one of the quietest of men.
While the poor Doctor was labouring hard at his translation
of Dante, Carlyle rather pooh-poohed his zeal as expended
on an 'obsolete' theme. Mrs. Carlyle's liking for him was
fitful. The good Doctor was indeed rather prosaic, and,
according to his sister-in-law, 'looked on love as a disease
of the nerves.' When he left London to settle for a time
in Edinburgh she said, not too good-naturedly, 'John is
somebody there, he is nobody here.' The Countess of
Clare left him a pension sufficient for his modest wants.
In later years he married an opulent widow, one of his very
few remaining patients. When I first knew him he lived
in lodgings not far from the Carlyles, of whom he was a
constant visitor. He gave them medical advice when it
was needed, was his brother's companion on many a London
expedition, and was always ready to do for him anything
in reason. 'I preach cheerfulness to him,' the Doctor told

me ; he did not say with what result. He was very intelligent and well-informed, a harder, drier, more reticent
Carlyle, I thought, with as little of his brother's irritability
as of his genius. He admired that brother greatly, and
had adopted some of his opinions, but he was much the
more democratic of the two, and would sometimes meekly
champion the elective principle in politics in opposition to
his brother's scornful denunciations of franchise, ballot,
and all the rest of it. He spoke to me with admiration of
the mode in which official medical posts were filled in
Paris by the suffrages of members of the profession who
generally elected the most suitable men, whereas everything of that kind was settled in London by outside
influence, canvassing, and so forth. Like his brother he
loved thoroughness of knowledge and despised super-
ficiality. One of his favourite amusements when he had
an unfamiliar visitor who said that he knew such and such
a language, was to test the pretender's knowledge by
setting him to translate a passage in a book in that language. It was whispered that even the great Emerson's
knowledge of German was thus tested by the Doctor,
and that the Sage of Concord himself had been found
wanting !

Dr. Carlyle contributed, though indirectly, to the production of *Sartor Resartus.* It is evident that his brother's
fragment of a novel, *Wotton Reinfried*, published for the
first time in a contemporary periodical (and afterwards, 1892,
in the volume with the surely inappropriate title, *Last
Words of Thomas Carlyle*), was laid aside to make way
and to furnish at least some material for the *Life and
Opinions of Diogenes Teufelsdröckh.* Whole passages of
the novel are transferred to *Sartor*, notably a very fine

one descriptive of mountain scenery, which in the later redaction the forlorn and footsore Teufelsdröckh is contemplating when the faithless Blumine and her husband are driven past him on their wedding tour in a barouche and four. In the novel, the first evening passed by the hero in the society of Jane Montagu, with whom he falls in love (Jane was Mrs. Carlyle's Christian name, and the Basil Montagus were among Carlyle's earliest friends in London), and their final parting are described in almost the same words as those of the analogous scenes in *Sartor*. When the conception of a Clothes philosophy flashed on Carlyle, as recorded by him in the *Reminiscences*, he needed a setting for it more appropriate and adequate than a Scottish fiction afforded.[1] Dr. Carlyle supplied what was wanted. His early residence in Munich enabled him to furnish his brother with descriptions of the life, habits, and surroundings of German Professors, from their philosophic beer-drinking in the *Grüne Gans* to their transcendental musings in such a watch-tower as that of the Wahngasse. During a later visit of Dr. Carlyle's to Munich (in 1835) Carlyle writes to him (with a complimentary message to ' Herr Schelling,' then a Professor at Munich): ' It seems to me always that you ought to meet Teufelsdröckh in some of the coffee-houses of Munich. Do they meet at that one yet '—the *Grüne Gans*—'and drink beer ?' Three years before he wrote thus, the British scenery and characters of *Wotton Reinfried* having been discarded,

---

[1] These indications of the development of *Wotton Reinfried* into *Sartor Resartus* appeared in the *Bookman* months before a Mr. Strachey, in the *Nineteenth Century* for September 1892, indulged in the following baseless taunt : ' It says little for the depth of Grub Street acquaintance with Carlyle's writings that criticism has not remarked that this story, *Wotton Reinfried*, is the protoplasm from which *Sartor Resartus* was afterwards evolved.'

Sartor Resartus had begun to dawn on a reading public which knew not what to make of it, and it was dismissed by one Sir Oracle of literary opinion as 'clotted nonsense.' 'These London men,' Dr. Carlyle once said to me, with more feeling than he was wont to show, 'tried to keep my brother down, but they couldn't.' The book, which was to London publishers a stumbling-block and to London critics foolishness, has now its millions of readers, and is enrolled among the classics of the world.

CHAPTER VI

JOHN FORSTER

GOETHE has said somewhere that the most trying situation for a man is to find himself in completely altered circumstances without being mentally and otherwise in the least prepared for the change. One fine day this was my painful predicament. With goodwill towards me Carlyle harboured a strong dislike for the person to whom the perplexities of my position were mainly due, so that sympathy and antipathy combined to induce him to interest himself in my behalf. 'You may lead,' he said to me, 'a wild Ishmaelitish life as a man of letters,' a vocation for which I felt little fitted. For a man of letters, he was of opinion in his then mood, 'historical research or to guide the people onward from day to day'—through the press, of course—was the worthiest employment. Historical research was in my circumstances out of the question. When in regard to his other alternative I pleaded my ignorance of politics, he replied, 'Politics are the grandest of all things,' though it might be well for me to wait a little before meddling with them. These opinions of his on politics and the press he modified profoundly in the course of not many years. He offered, as what he could do best for me, to introduce me—and introduce me he did—to two friends of his, both of them connected with the newspaper press, John Forster and John Robertson.

Forster was then one of the busiest of London journalists, and Carlyle's influence was needed to procure for an obscure aspirant easy access to him. To begin with, he had only recently entered on the editorship of the *Daily News*, at that time a very troublesome post. Charles Dickens, having had some differences with his old allies of the *Morning Chronicle*, projected a new daily paper, which was to be more thoroughgoing than the Whig *Chronicle*, and to combine a strenuous support of Corn-Law Repeal, with philanthropy of the familiar Dickens kind. The result was the issue of the *Daily News*, with Dickens for its editor-in-chief. He was soon disgusted with the uncongenial and embarrassing task, for the performance of which few men of his miscellaneous literary experience were more unfitted. In a very few weeks he threw up the editorship, rather abruptly, but not before he had induced his faithful and loyal friend Forster to become his reluctant successor. Forster did not retain the post many months, but, while fulfilling its duties with his usual energy, he continued his work on the *Examiner*, of which he had been for many years the literary and dramatic critic, and which, partly through him, but still more through the pungent political articles of its proprietor and editor-in-chief, Albany Fonblanque, had, after a period of decadence, regained the old position won for it by Leigh Hunt and his coadjutors. In his own department Forster had brought things so far that praise of a new book or a new play in the *Examiner* was a feather in the cap of an ordinary author or dramatist. At this time he had not become the biographer of Goldsmith, and his only noticeable book was his *Statesmen of the Commonwealth* (produced, I was told at Chelsea, 'in eight months'), contributed to Lardner's *Cabinet Cyclopædia*, and followed in the same series by his *Life of Oliver Cromwell*, of which more hereafter. It was as a critic that he had become the friend of some of the most prominent men of letters of his time, especially of Bulwer and Dickens. His intimacy with and somewhat exuberant loyalty to Bulwer drew down on him the ire of Lady Bulwer after her separation from her husband. When reviling Bulwer in her once-famous novel, *Cheveley ; or, the Man of Honour* (which Carlyle owned to having read through at a sitting), she introduced his two journalistic intimates, Fonblanque and Forster, as Fonnoir and Fuzboz, hence the nickname of 'Fuz' by which Forster is designated by Carlyle in many of his letters to his wife. Of Lady Bulwer's two portraits, Forster's is far the most unflattering. 'Mr. Fonnoir, editor of *The Investigator*,' is admitted to be, with all his faults, 'about the most agreeable man in England ;' but not a single good word is vouchsafed to poor Fuzboz. He is represented as 'a very ugly and noseless likeness of a great tragedian whom he tried to imitate . . . even to his handwriting, . . . a sort of lick-dust to Mr. Fonnoir and to Mr. Anybody and everybody else to whom he could gain access.' There just was a grain of truth in this decidedly spiteful caricature. Forster was a little of a tuft-hunter, and in view of the exuberant praise which he showered on any and every of Bulwer's performances, Carlyle, even when he came at last to have a very friendly feeling towards him, admitted that there was in Forster 'a certain laxity of mind.' It is also true that he imitated in everyday life the stage-mannerism of Macready, Lady Bulwer's 'great tragedian,' of whom he was the intimate friend. I remember being in this way rather overpowered at one of my first interviews with him. I called on him by appointment, and he kept me a few minutes waiting. Then he strode into the room, and striking an attitude, exclaimed in a tragic tone: 'It is with infinite regret that I have caused you this delay. Believe me,' and here he placed his hand upon his heart, 'I feel it sensibly.' He had as famulus and factotum a youth well known to all of Forster's friends as Henry, who amused them sometimes by a trick of identifying himself with his master. On another occasion Forster had made an appointment with me at one of the residences of his bachelor days, those chambers in 58 Lincoln's Inn Fields, where he gave many a pleasant little dinner party, and where Dickens was wont to read to select audiences, which occasionally included Carlyle, his Christmas stories before their publication. Something came in the way, and he wrote, to put me off, a note which I did not receive in time. Punctually, therefore, at the appointed hour I knocked at his door. Henry opened it, and having surveyed me with an air of dignified surprise, said in a tone slightly reproachful: ' *We* wrote to you this morning!' Forster's foibles were a source of occasional merriment to his friends. His resolute and rather despotic disposition procured for him, however, a good deal of outward respect, especially as he could be, in and out of the *Examiner*, very useful and helpful to all whom he liked. It was credibly reported of Dickens that Forster was the only man of whom he stood a little in awe.[1] On the whole, Forster's good qualities far outshone his faults. He was an honourable as well as an able man, diligent and painstaking in

---

[1] There is a lifelike miniature sketch of Forster in his own biography of Dickens, and done by the latter. Mrs. Gamp is supposed to have resolved on accompanying Dickens and his troupe of amateur actors, bound for Manchester and Liverpool, to perform ' Every Man in his Humour,' for the benefit of Leigh Hunt's exchequer. Forster was to play Master Kitely. Mrs. Gamp is standing on the platform, and an *attaché* of Dickens's company points out to her its various members as they make their appearance to enter the train— Douglas Jerrold, Leech, etc. In her own inimitable style she is reporting, in a

business, and his friendship, when once won, was remarkably steadfast.

At first Carlyle did not like Forster, who, however, gained on him, he told me, by the exhibition of a resolute desire to 'improve himself.' Anything like intimacy began, I think, with Carlyle's efforts to establish the London Library, when he found Forster's energetic aid most valuable. It was by Forster that he was introduced to the firm which for half a century until his death published all his books, and the head of which at one time was the 'hard-fisted bibliopole' of the *Reminiscences*, converted by an amusing blunder of Mr. Froude's into a 'hard-fisted bibliophile,' a distinction with a difference. Up to the time of which I am writing, Carlyle had contributed only one article to the *Examiner*; of his subsequent contributions to it more in a future chapter. He did not include that one article in any edition of his works, and it has escaped the notice not only of his biographers, but what is more remarkable, of his bibliographers. It was a pleasant little review [1] of Heintze's German translation of selected poems of Burns, from which, not then such a Prussophile as he became, Carlyle noted the absence of any version of 'A man's a man for a' that,' as a lay the sentiment of which would not be acceptable to certain persons in the Berlin of those days. He contributed to the revived *Foreign Quarterly*, which was edited for a year or two by Forster—very ably, Carlyle thought—his strik-

---

letter to Mrs. Harris, what she saw and heard. When Forster arrives, ' this resolute gent,' she is told, 'a-coming along here as is aperrantly going to take the railways by storm—him with the tight legs, and his weskit very much buttoned, and his mouth very much shut, and his coat a-flying open, and his heels a-giving it to the platform, is a crikit and beeogruffer and our principal tragegian.' [1] Printed in the *Examiner* of Sept. 27, 1840.

ing article on Dr. Francia, the Dictator of Paraguay, a country the history of which, after Francia's death, proved that a despotism possibly beneficent may become one positively maleficent. But the strongest of the literary ties that united them was their common interest in the great Civil War of the seventeenth century, and the events that immediately preceded and succeeded it. Forster had finished his *Life of Cromwell* when Carlyle was beginning his seventeenth century studies, and their unpublished correspondence is full of applications made at one time by Carlyle for the loan of books on the period, and of queries to be answered by Forster. In regard to Cromwell's later career there was then a vital difference between them; Forster, as a decided Liberal, denouncing Cromwell's *coup d'état*, the expulsion of the Long Parliament, and the subsequent establishment of the Protectorate, as a reprehensible destruction of a free Commonwealth and a pernicious usurpation of supreme authority; while, as all the world knows, Carlyle bestowed the heartiest approval on Cromwell's conduct throughout. In time, Forster avowed his conversion to Carlyle's view, who was not a little pleased by it. But long before there had grown up the friendliest social intimacy between Forster and the Carlyles, from whose correspondence the somewhat contemptuous designation 'Fuz' disappears after a time. Forster was a frequent visitor of the Carlyles, and they were frequent guests of his at Lincoln's Inn Fields, always the more willingly on Carlyle's part when he was to meet Dickens, for whom in his notes to Forster he professed a genuine affection, though in conversation he was given to talk contemptuously of 'Dickens and his squad.' One short break in their friendship will be mentioned hereafter, but it may be said, I think, that Carlyle grew to like Forster most of all his London literary contemporaries, after beginning by liking him not at all.

A very interesting memorial of their friendship lies all but unknown, and, so far as I am aware, thoroughly inspected by no one save myself, in the manuscript and other matter relating to Carlyle bequeathed, with a great many other valuable things, a fine library among them, by John Forster to the South Kensington Museum. The Carlyliana of the collection include a long series of letters written to Forster by Carlyle, covering a period of some forty years, from the beginning of their acquaintance to the end, only with Forster's death, of what became their friendship. With the exception of his letters to members of his own family there are none so interesting and instructive as these of Carlyle to Forster, and a well-edited selection from them would be an extremely valuable contribution to Carlyle's biography. This being the case, it is singular that Mr. Froude should have made no use of them in his four volumes on Carlyle. Such neglect is the more singular inasmuch as Carlyle's letters to Forster abound with interesting matter respecting some of those later years of Carlyle's life, Mr. Froude's account of which is extremely meagre, partly, but not wholly, because when compelled to cease writing with his own hand Carlyle no longer, of course, confided as previously his thoughts and feelings to his Journal. When age and infirmity prevented Carlyle from wielding a pen he employed an amanuensis, and, as it happens, such letters to Forster are ampler and more interesting than those which were written by his own hand. This is easily accounted for. As relatives and old friends sank one after another into the grave Carlyle clung more and more to Forster, his ally of forty years, who remained indefatigable in his attentions, and who, in his frequent, kindly, and thoughtful hospitality to the veteran, was aided by his 'dear little wife,' as Carlyle, in his letters, fondly calls Mrs. Forster. (She had been the wealthy widow of Henry Colburn, the once well-known publisher who made a fortune by vending loads of novels and compilation, much of them unmitigated trash.) Moreover, Forster continued to the last, as he had done for many years, to help Carlyle in his bargaining with his publishers, who, it appears from one of Carlyle's notes to Forster, originally offered £800 for the first two volumes of *Frederick the Great*, each of them to consist of 400 pages. It is no wonder if Carlyle had for Forster a grateful and very friendly regard, and gave it profuse and sincere expression. I doubt whether, at the end of any but letters to his own relatives, Carlyle ever subscribed himself as, in one to Forster, 'Yours very affectionately.' Those later letters of his to Forster abound in records of his varying moods, some of them mournful enough, but they are seldom marked by the bitterness which disfigures his Journal and still more his *Reminiscences*, and there is often a beautiful pathos in his wail not merely over himself, but over friends departing and departed, especially Dickens. There are sketches of Ruskin at home, of Browning's possible poetic future, of Mr. Justice Stephen as a companion of his walks, of a visit in old age to Kirkcaldy, where in youth he had been a schoolmaster, and they vie in interest with anything in the *Reminiscences*. One would not have thought Owen Meredith likely to prove attractive to Carlyle, but he tells Forster that not only has Mr. Froude fallen in love with the second Lord Lytton, but that he himself has some thoughts of doing so also: the first Lord Lytton Carlyle never liked. Among other references to Mr. Froude is a censure on him for his wild-goose chase to the United States in search of an American verdict on the controversy between England and Ireland. Carlyle opined that Mr. Froude had better not have taken 'our extremely dirty Irish linen' to wash there, and 'call America to see.' Sometimes light is thrown on what Mr. Froude has left enigmatic and obscure. For instance, he prints a letter written to the then Countess of Derby in which Carlyle ascribes to her influence (perhaps wrongly) Lord Beaconsfield's offer to him of a pension and the dignity of G.C.B. There is no hint elsewhere in Mr. Froude's volumes of any intimacy between that lady and Carlyle. But, from Carlyle's letters to Forster, it appears that Lady Derby had a regard for him so great that she once insisted on himself and his niece taking up their abode at Lord Derby's Kentish seat, Keston Lodge. One of the most idyllic of his letters to Forster, breathing a spirit of serene and thankful repose, is an account of his sojourn there, and of his enjoyment of the beautiful adjacent region, which, by the way, teems with memories of the great Chatham and his famous son. In exploring Carlyle's many letters to Forster few things struck me more than Carlyle's mode of recommending to him the execution of a literary enterprise which Forster was well fitted to undertake. In 1855, Forster was appointed Secretary to the Lunacy Commissioners, of whom Barry Cornwall (he first introduced Carlyle to Jeffrey and the *Edinburgh Review*) was one, and to him, I rather think, Forster owed the welcome appointment which made him independent of journalism and literature. Six years afterwards Forster was promoted to a Commissionership in Lunacy, with a salary raised from £800 to £1500 a year. On his appointment to the former of these posts, he resigned the editorship of the *Examiner* (in which he was succeeded by Professor Henry Morley), and never afterwards contributed a line to the newspaper or periodical press. But though the offices which he held were very far from being sinecures, he wrote, in the intervals of business, the best of his historical and biographical works. When at one time he was looking about him for a new subject, Carlyle advised him to undertake a life of Strafford. Forster had years before, in his *Lives of British Statesmen*, written a biography of Strafford, the amount of Browning's recently discovered participation in which has probably been greatly exaggerated. But since then, masses of new material for the history of the period had accumulated, and Forster's knowledge of it had greatly increased. There was, and there is, room for a new biography of Strafford. What is curious in the remarks with which Carlyle accompanied his recommendation was that he expressed himself as if he thought that, after two centuries of obloquy, Puritanism had had full justice done it, and it was now time to see what could be said for the Royalist side of the great controversy, and for by far the greatest man who had taken that side. For Strafford, even in his *Cromwell*—as in his *French Revolution* for Mirabeau, who, if he had lived a little longer, might have saved the French Monarchy—Carlyle had shown a certain admiration, and his recommendation of such a subject to be so treated is another proof of that love of his for absolutism, and dislike of democracy, both of which became more intense with his advancing years ; scornful references to 'the People's

William' are frequent in his later letters to Forster. Forster acted on Carlyle's advice and began a life of Strafford. Some of the proof-sheets of it are among his papers at the South Kensington Museum, but, as in the case of his biography of Swift, death did not allow him to finish it. He died five years before Carlyle, who had appointed him one of his executors. After Forster's death Carlyle substituted Mr. Froude for him as an executor, the other being Sir James Fitzjames Stephen, afterwards Mr. Justice Stephen, who had become a most intimate friend of Carlyle in his later years.

CHAPTER VII

JOHN ROBERTSON

AS the biographer of Goldsmith, Dickens, Walter
Savage Landor, and as the author of what promised
to be, when his death rendered it a fragment, our best life
of Swift, to say nothing of his life of Sir John Eliot and
other solid contributions, some of them already glanced at,
to the history of England in the seventeenth century, or of
his agreeable essays on Steele and Defoe, Foote and
Churchill, John Forster may be long read and remembered.
But probably very few of my readers know even the name
of John Robertson, the other journalistic friend of Carlyle,
to whom he gave me an introduction simultaneously with
that to Forster, and who, though then in far from flourishing circumstances, showed me some active kindness.
Mostly forgotten if he now be, Robertson was at one time
a stirring man in the periodical and newspaper press of
London. A Scotchman, and like Carlyle bred for the
Scottish Church, he also like Carlyle broke loose from it,
and found a fitful literary career in London. He was a
vigorous and vivid writer and talker, and in time became
a prominent political contributor to the great Whig organ
of those days, the *Morning Chronicle*. From his antecedents he had a knowledge, rare among London
journalists, of Scottish ecclesiastical affairs, and it proved
useful to him at a time when the controversy which led to
the disruption of the Kirk (and in which he strenuously

124

supported the anti-patronage cause) was growing very lively. On this account he was personally introduced to Lord Melbourne, then Prime Minister, who declared that his peace of mind was much less disturbed by the Chartist movement than by 'that d—d Scotch Kirk,' as he called it in his usual imprecatory fashion. Robertson's talents and political ardour procured him an intimacy with several distinguished literary Liberals, among them Bulwer (afterwards the first Lord Lytton) and John Stuart Mill, whose biographer intimates that Robertson's 'impetus and suggestiveness in conversation drew out Mill, who never talked better than he did with him.' Robertson had much to tell me of Bulwer, in whom he had discovered a goodness of heart for which few of the famous novelist's literary contemporaries gave him credit. Among other and less commendable traits, which Robertson reported to me, was Bulwer's fondness for personal metamorphoses, so to speak. One day he would appear in black from top to toe, with a dark-complexioned visage to match. Another day he would be all brown, and on a third he would be all in white, with blonde hair and a fair complexion lighted up by rouge!

Robertson's intimacy with John Stuart Mill gained him a position which made him for a time a man of some importance in London literature, but of which circumstances had deprived him several years before my acquaintance with him. That munificent Radical and free-thinking baronet, Sir William Molesworth, having founded the *London Review*—of which Carlyle faintly and fruitlessly hoped to be made the editor—after a time bought the *Westminster* (for £1000 from General Perronet Thompson, once well known as the author of the Anti-Corn Law

Catechism) and from his fusion of the two sprang the
London and Westminster Review. In a few years Molesworth grew weary of the steady drain upon his purse
for the support of the unprofitable periodical. It was then
that, as recorded in his Autobiography, Mill, to his cost,
was induced to purchase the *London and Westminster,*
'mainly,' he says, 'in reliance on the representations of a
young Scotchman of the name of Robertson, who had
some ability and information, much industry, and an active,
scheming head full of devices for making the *Review* more
saleable.' Among the proofs of ability which Robertson
had given were articles on Shakespeare and Bacon, contributed to Sir William Molesworth's *London Review.*
Robertson was appointed acting editor, Mill's official
connection with the India Office making him reluctant to
be known as the actual editor. He retained, however,
complete control over the *Review,* and had often to use the
bridle-rein with the fiery young Scotchman, whom he is
even found, more than once, reproving for writing slip-shod
English. But Robertson continued to edit the *London and
Westminster,* with vigour and ability, during the whole
of Mill's proprietorship (1837-40), and boasted that he had
reduced to £33 the loss from the *London* of £100 on each
number. Whatever his editorial merits, he appears to have
become inflated by such authority as he was allowed to
wield, and to have given a good deal of offence to contributors in *esse* and in *posse.* Carlyle, one of whose
contributions to the *London and Westminster* was the well-
known article on Sir Walter Scott (1838), writes at this
time of the wane of his intimacy with Mill, whose 'editor,'
he adds, 'one Robertson, a burly Aberdeen Scotchman of
seven-and-twenty, full of laughter, vanity, pepticity, and

hope, amuses me considerably more' than Mill himself.
Robertson was very soon to yield Carlyle anything but
amusement. According to Mr. Froude, in the December
of 1838, Carlyle had agreed with Mill to write for the
Review an article on Cromwell. Mill went abroad, and
Robertson, who was left in undisputed command, informed
Carlyle that he need not trouble himself to write about
Cromwell, as he himself intended to 'do' Cromwell.
Carlyle's indignation was great. He broke off at once his
connection with the *London and Westminster*, and began
to study Cromwell's life and times as the subject of a
possible book. Robertson's article appeared in the *London
and Westminster* for October 1839, in which was also
published, perhaps to soothe Carlyle, John Sterling's
glowing eulogium on him (*ante*, p. 76). What is very
noticeable in Robertson's article, though neither Mr.
Froude nor any one else has noticed it, is, that it was the
first distinct and emphatic attempt made in the literature
of that generation to vindicate Cromwell in all his doings,
especially in his expulsion of the Long Parliament, which
even Forster had strenuously protested against—and
Robertson's Liberalism was quite as 'advanced' as
Forster's. Some seven years elapsed after the publication
of Robertson's really able and eloquent article before the
appearance of Carlyle's great work on Cromwell. To
Robertson, therefore, belongs the merit, and he was not
at all backward in claiming it, of being an earlier and
thoroughgoing vindicator of Cromwell.[1]

[1] The following vigorous sketch of Cromwell's character in *Wotton Reinfried*, supposed to be suggested by a portrait of him, seems to show that at
Craigenputtock, Carlyle had not got beyond the hero-hypocrite theory of the
great Protector. 'This is the man whose words no one could interpret, but
whose thoughts were clearest wisdom, who spoke in laborious folly, in volun-

Ignorant of the genesis of Robertson's article, the story
of which was first told by Mr. Froude, I unwittingly spoke
in praise of it to Carlyle. ' I never read his trash,' Carlyle
replied. ' I thought it very beautiful,' Mrs. Carlyle
remarked—a verdict on Robertson's article much juster
than her husband's, if his could be called a verdict on an
article which he had not read. ' Robertson,' Carlyle
rejoined, ' could not form a coherent image of anything.'
The subject of Robertson being thus broached, Carlyle
spoke of a letter which had appeared in some London
newspaper, addressed to the then Duke of Buccleuch, and
signed ' John Robertson, Reform Club.' In all likelihood
it was an indignant effusion provoked by the Duke's refusal
of a site for a projected Free Kirk on one of his Scottish
estates. Carlyle gave a long, loud, and scornful laugh at
the juxtaposition of the Duke of Buccleuch and ' John
Robertson, Reform Club.' To my unsophisticated mind
there seemed nothing to laugh at. The matter was one
either of fact or of argument, and in neither case could its
rights or its wrongs be in any way affected by the relative
social positions of the many-acred Duke of Buccleuch and
' John Robertson,' who could only hail from the ' Reform
Club.' During the first week of April 1848—one of great
excitement in London—I saw Robertson for the last time,
as he was just stepping out of that Reform Club a
particular parade of his membership of which had excited

tary or involuntary enigmas, but saw and acted unerringly his fate. Confusion,
ineptitude, dishonesty, are pictured on his countenance, but through these
there shines a fiery strength, nay, a grandeur as of a true hero. You see there
he was fearless, resolute as a Scanderbeg, yet cunning and double withal,
like some paltry pettifogger. He is your true, enthusiastic hypocrite, at once
crack-brained and inspired; a knave and a demigod, in brief, old Noll as he
looked and lived.'

Carlyle's contemptuous merriment. He was on his way to attend a meeting of the Chartist Convention then in session, organising the 'demonstration' of the famous 10th of April, the prospect of which, following as it did on the French Revolution of the preceding February, was viewed by the higher and middle classes with great and, as it proved, with needless apprehension. When I told Carlyle of my meeting with Robertson, he said, 'Robertson ought to go into the Chartist movement and make it respectable,' for Carlyle was then, though only for the time being, in a rather revolutionary mood, as will be told more amply in a future chapter. Robertson did *not* go into the movement with that or any other result, and, without his aid, most of what was essential in the 'People's Charter' has since been conceded, or is now being accepted, by Respectability in high places. Of Robertson subsequently little or nothing was seen or heard in public. Later in life he made, I believe, a good marriage, and 'lived happy ever after.' An interesting correspondence between him and Mill relating to the conduct of the *London and Westminster* was published, with elucidations, by Robertson's daughter in the number of the *Atlantic Monthly* for the January of 1892.[1]

---

[1] Robertson's admiration for the fair sex was considerable, but not always disinterested. I knew one clever literary lady who was wooed, and might have been won, by him, had his behaviour not created a suspicion that he wished her for a wife chiefly to make her of use to him in his literary labours. His gallantry, with an eye to business, is amusingly brought out in the following vivacious letter of Mrs. Carlyle to her friend Miss Bölte (*Last Words of Thomas Carlyle*, p. 293) :—

December 23, 1843.

'Your little friend, Miss Swanwick, called here the other day, looking ineffably sweet! almost too sweet for practical purposes! That minds me (as my Helen says) I received by post a little while since a letter in a handwriting not new to me, but I could not tell, in the first minute, whose it was. I read the first words : " Oh those bright sweet eyes !" I stop amazed " as in presence

While Carlyle, as has been told, practically aided me to start on my enforced journey into the wilderness, he bestowed on me several monitions. One of his most emphatic warnings was against literary vanity. 'In literature a man can do nothing worth doing until he has killed his vanity.' As an illustration of literary magnanimity and superiority to personal feeling he told me at full length an anecdote of Diderot which is only very briefly referred to in his fine essay on that famous *philosophe*. Visited by one of the tribe of out-at-elbows authors whom his well-known good-nature brought about him, Diderot asked him if he had anything to show of his composition in print or manuscript. After a good deal of very natural hesitation the visitor produced from his pocket a manuscript which turned out to be a lampoon on Diderot himself. Instead of being offended, the generous Diderot looked it over, corrected it, and wrote for it a dedication to the then Duke of Orleans (father of *Égalité* Orleans) who, as it happened, was *dévot*, and therefore anything but friendly to *philosophes*

of the Infinite !" *What* man has gone out of his wits? In what year of grace was I? What was it at all? I looked for a signature, there was none! I turned to the beginning again and read a few words more : "There is no escaping their bewitching influence!" "Idiot," said I, "whoever you be," having now got up a due matronly rage! I read on, however. "It is impossible those sweet eyes should be unaccompanied with a benevolent heart ; could you not then intercede with the possessor of them to do me a kindness? The time of *young ladies* is in general so uselessly employed that I should think you would really be benefiting (!) Miss Swanwick in persuading her to—translate for me those *French Laws on Pawnbroking*." Now the riddle was satisfactorily solved. The "bright sweet eyes" were none of *mine*, but Miss Swanwick's; and the writer of the letter was Robertson, who, you may remember, I told you raved about those same eyes to a weariness. My virtuous married-woman indignation blushes had been entirely thrown away! It was too ridiculous! But could you have conceived of such stupidity—even among authors—as this of beginning a letter to one woman with an apostrophe to the eyes of another?"' What a combination, bright sweet eyes, and the French Laws on Pawnbroking!

of Diderot's way of thinking. The result was the purchase of the manuscript by a bookseller, and 24 gold Louis in the pocket of the starveling scribbler thus unexpectedly befriended. More appropriate than warnings against indulgence in a vanity which, from the nature of the case could not then exist, was an admonition which doubtless he thought to be needed: 'Avoid hypochondria, pride, and gloom: they are a waste of faculty.' On anything like over-fastidiousness, in regard to the literary employment offered to a beginner, he expressed himself forcibly: 'A man is an indestructible fragment of the universe, but, if he wishes to live, he must not be nice.' Of deeper import and more lasting value was the wise advice not to mistake 'the shriek of self-love' for the voice of conscience. And so I sallied forth into the wide world, fortified by Carlyle's oral monitions, who added, among others, these written words of encouragement: 'The heart that remained true to itself never yet found this big universe finally faithless to it.'

CHAPTER VIII

GERALDINE JEWSBURY

THE scene now changes from London to Manchester, 'perhaps one of the best soils in this era,' so Carlyle wrote to me when I informed him that I found myself domiciled in the metropolis of the cotton manufacture. Among its then denizens was a very intimate lady-friend of Mrs. Carlyle, whose introduction of me to her procured me a cordial welcome. This was Miss Jewsbury, the 'Geraldine' who figures so often and so prominently in Mrs. Carlyle's correspondence. Losing her mother at an early age, she was brought up by her elder sister, Maria Jane Jewsbury, a gifted and remarkable woman, whose prose and verse won for her the admiration and friendship of Wordsworth. He has left it on record that within the whole range of his acquaintance she had 'no equal' as regards 'quickness in the motions of her mind.', In this respect Geraldine resembled her, but her mental development was very different from that of her sister. The elder Miss Jewsbury became deeply religious, and married a chaplain in the East India Company's service, with whom she proceeded to India, where she died, when her sister was in her twenty-first year. Geraldine fell under the influence, not of Wordsworth, but of Shelley, and with the result that was to be expected. She lost the faith of her childhood without gaining a new one, and for this she yearned. While harassed by what she afterwards half playfully, half sadly called 'bother in her soul,' she lighted on some of Carlyle's earlier writings. She found in them indications that there was still possible a faith in the Supernal which harmonised with Reason. Like many others in her predicament in those days, she wrote to Carlyle and confided to him her spiritual perplexities. Both he and his wife were impressed by the tone and tenor of Miss Jewsbury's ingenuous and anxious inquiries, and she was asked to visit them. Personal knowledge heightened their previous favourable impression of her. She was verging on thirty when Carlyle wrote of her as 'one of the most interesting young women I have seen for years, clear delicate sense and courage looking out of her small sylph-like figure.' He objected strongly to what he soon discovered to be her enthusiasm for George Sand, but this was not thought an objection by his wife, who greatly admired the genius, while disapproving of the ethics, of the famous Frenchwoman. She and Miss Jewsbury soon contracted a warm friendship, which, with occasional intermissions, lasted for nearly half a century, and ended only with Mrs. Carlyle's death.

At the time when, during the first of my sojourns in Manchester, I made Miss Jewsbury's acquaintance, she kept house for her brother Frank, who was in business there. He was a young man of quick observation and much intelligence, well read in some departments of literature, highly social, and, like the model bishop of the great apostle, 'given to hospitality.' They lived in Greenheyes, the suburb of Manchester in which Thomas De Quincey was born. Their house looked pleasantly on the green fields in which is laid the scene of the opening chapter of Mrs. Gaskell's *Mary Barton*, but which with the growth of Manchester since then have suffered an invasion of bricks and mortar. Here Mrs. Carlyle sometimes visited her Geraldine, on her way to or from Liverpool, where she had both friends and relatives. Her visits to both places were paid without her husband, the Carlyles having adopted the sensible practice of separating for at least a month in each year. Mrs. Carlyle was never happier than during these visits to the North. She could say and do what she liked, and was courted and caressed for her own sake, and not for her husband's. This pleased her not a little, proud though she was of him, and whether with him or away from him, always occupied with his interests and his comfort. Now and then, as will happen with clever and sensitive women, she and Miss Jewsbury had their differences. Mrs. Carlyle was nearly twelve years Miss Jewsbury's senior. She had seen much more of the world than her less experienced and more impulsive junior, whom at this and the other little crisis she sometimes lectured when sympathy rather than rebuke was expected. 'Mrs. Carlyle pours oil into your wounds, but it is oil of vitriol,' Miss Jewsbury once remarked to me when she was smarting under some infliction from her London friend's reproving pen. But these were mere brief episodes of a friendship during which Mrs. Carlyle did much to help Miss Jewsbury, both socially and in her literary career, and was repaid by her junior's affectionate sympathy and attentions of every kind.

A year or two before my arrival in Manchester Miss Jewsbury had produced her first of several novels, one which Mrs. Carlyle, or through her, the ever-helpful John Forster, induced her husband's publishers to issue. This was *Zoe, or the Two Lives*, which, though mostly forgotten now, was the precursor not only of Mr. Froude's *Nemesis of Faith*, published three years after it, but of *Robert Elsmere*, and the progeny to which it has given birth. The 'two lives' were those of a hero and a heroine. The hero, belonging to a good English and Roman Catholic family, resolves, being full of enthusiastic piety, to enter the Romish priesthood, and goes to an ecclesiastical college at Rome to fit himself for it. He becomes a priest and a professor, and his abilities and fervid religious zeal being recognised by his superiors, he seems destined to rise to a very high position in the hierarchy of his Church. But reading and reflection lead him to doubt the truth not only of Romish but of all Christian theology, and doubt leads him gradually to denial. After a not unnatural struggle, he determines to sacrifice his position and prospects in the Church rather than hypocritically continue to profess a faith which his reason has forced him to reject. The long and painful conflict in his mind between old associations and the course which conscience dictates to him, the desolate aspect of the universe and human life to a man so educated and trained, when the sun of faith has ceased to illumine them, are depicted with great power and vividness.

The wish to serve his fellow-men which had led him into the ancient Church and had been strengthened and developed in it survives his departure from it. He resolves to attempt to civilise and humanise, without the aid of dogmatic theology, in one of the wildest iron districts of South Wales, its half-savage population which has no 'idea of a God, except to swear by.' He takes up his abode among them, and finding that he can do nothing with the parents, however much he does for them by relieving the sick and the suffering, he founds schools for the children. At last his unwearied kindness is beginning to tell and to earn him a little gratitude.   But just then, the time of the novel is the period preceding the first French Revolution, and Mirabeau in England is introduced making very fierce love to the heroine—the Methodist movement reaches the village in which the hero is settled.   Very striking is the way in which the nullity of the cultivated philanthropic gentleman's teaching is contrasted with the fierce religious excitement produced by the preaching of a rude and ignorant Methodist orator.   The hero begins to be distrusted for attaching more efficacy to good works than to faith, and at last he is driven, bitterly disappointed, from the village, amid a storm of obloquy, as an emissary of Satan.

Thus the career of Miss Jewsbury's hero, after his abandonment of the orthodox faith is far less commonplace than the sequel of Robert Elsmere's similar proceeding, though, like that, it ends in premature death. So far as my acquaintance with modern English fiction extends, *Zoe* was the first novel in which the hero's career is made dependent on the victory of modern scepticism over ancient belief.

At home, or in society, Miss Jewsbury did not give one the impression of having grappled with the problems which *Zoe* showed to have been familiar to her.   She was not in the least a blue-stocking, never speaking of her own books, and not very much of other people's.   'A cheerful, transparent little creature,' was Carlyle's later verdict on her, when she had got rid of 'bother in her soul,' and he had condoned her devotion to George Sand.   Her conversation was full of wit and point.   She was a most agreeable hostess, and never seemed happier than when witnessing the enjoyment of her brother's friends at his frequent symposia. To me one of the greatest charms of the Jewsbury circle was that politics, general and local, were eschewed by its members, so that its sociality was never disturbed by the party-spirit which then ran so high in Manchester. Of literary and artistic society there was not much during my first sojourn there, but Londoners of more or less intellectual note who visited Manchester generally found their way to the Jewsburys, and were welcomed by brother as well as by sister. One of them was Westland Marston, the dramatist, a polished, gentleman-like young man, author of *The Patrician's Daughter* (and afterwards father of the late Philip Bourke Marston), which had considerable success on the London stage ; he died only a few years ago, having been long before left stranded by the indifference of the public to the poetic drama, which he had fondly hoped to revive. Marston came to lecture at the Manchester Athenæum. Another London visitor was Gallenga, then known by his *nom de plume* of Mariotti. He had written a book about Italy, his fatherland, from which he was a political exile, and in after-years was to become, under Delane, a travelling correspondent of the *Times* in several widely-separated regions of the globe. A clever, rather cynical Italian, he came to Manchester to lecture on Dante before a more select audience than that of the Athenæum, thanks to the recommendation of his countryman, Gambardella, who had been painting portraits in Manchester, among them those of the family of one of its wealthiest German merchants. Mariotti, or Gallenga, found more than an audience for his lectures on Dante. He wooed and won a daughter of that wealthy German family, and the struggling Italian exile was a made man for life. During my second and somewhat later sojourn in Manchester, Mr. Froude was for a time settled there under circumstances which seemed to preclude the possibility that he would ever become, as he not long ago became, a Professor at Oxford, of all places in the world. George Henry Lewes was also in Manchester about the same time, though he, compared with Mr. Froude, was a bird of passage. Both Mr. Froude and Lewes were frequent guests of the Jewsburys. Mr. Froude, who was then a little over thirty, had a year or so before come before the world as the author of the *Nemesis of Faith*. The book had the misfortune to be not only banned by the orthodox and burned by the sub-rector of Exeter College, Oxford (*ante*, p. 77), of which its author was a fellow, but was denounced by his friend that was to be, Carlyle himself, for its somewhat prurient sentimentality and parade of doubts which the doubter had better have kept to himself.[1] Under the influence of his brother, Hurrell Froude, and John Henry Newman and Co., Mr. Froude had in his youth been a Tractarian, contributing to the Lives of the Saints, and taking Deacon's orders with a view to the Anglican priesthood. His theological opinions, of course, had been completely transformed when he wrote the *Nemesis of Faith*. In the storm of academic indignation which the book excited he resigned his fellowship and quitted Oxford, little thinking that more than forty years afterwards he was to return to it as its Regius Professor of History and thus successor of his persistent assailant the late Edward Freeman. On leaving Oxford he became Principal (I think) of some

---

[1] In an unpublished letter to John Forster, written just after the publication of the *Nemesis of Faith*, the book is denounced by Carlyle in language almost savage in its plain speaking.

university or college in an Australian colony, but the *Nemesis of Faith* followed him there and his appointment was cancelled. On this part of his history it may be permissible to quote a passage from so well known a book as the Life of Lord Houghton, who wrote thus to one of his correspondents: 'A bomb has fallen into the midst of the religious world in the shape of a book called *The Nemesis of Faith* by the brother of Froude the dead Puseyite. It is a sort of religious anti-religious Wilhelm Meister, and balances itself between fact and fiction in an uncomfortable manner, though with great ability, and has caused the poor man to lose his fellowship and a college in Van Diemen's Land'—the Tasmania of to-day—'and to fall into utter poverty.' After Mr. Froude's return from Australia he found a temporary home at Manchester as tutor to the sons of a wealthy and much respected Unitarian solicitor. There is an amusing record in a letter to Mrs. Carlyle of Miss Jewsbury's first acquaintance with Mr. Froude, of whose opinions when he came to Manchester, and of the drift of his *Nemesis of Faith*, she appeared to have been completely ignorant.

'I am going out to-night,' she writes, 'to meet the author of *Nemesis of Faith*, a very nice natural young man, though rather like "a lost sheep" at present. He has only been used to the Oxford part of the world, so that sectarianism and unbelievers (!) are strange to him.' Miss Jewsbury soon knew Mr. Froude's opinions very much better than when she penned those lines. They became fast friends. He was of some practical use to her after her brother's marriage and her own migration to London, and he was her frequent visitor during the lingering illness which, in her 69th year, proved fatal to her.

Another of Miss Jewsbury's notable friends and occasional visitors, whose acquaintance she owed to the Carlyles, was William Edward Forster, the young, vigorous, and cultivated woollen manufacturer of Rawdon, near Leeds. He was then little known out of Yorkshire, but afterwards very well known as a statesman.

In the company of Forster, early in 1848, Miss Jewsbury paid a visit to Paris, where Emerson and Arthur Clough were also sojourning. Some of her experiences there she utilised in what appears to me the most interesting of all her fugitive compositions, one written from the heart as well as the head. This is the article on 'Religious Faith and Scepticism' which she contributed to the *Westminster Review* for January 1850. The books which served as basis for the article were, besides an anonymous work attributed to John Henry Newman, Mr. Froude's *Nemesis of Faith*, and a volume of politico-religious letters by Père Enfantin who was the head of the St. Simonian Society at the time of its dissolution. Miss Jewsbury had seen him in Paris during her visit of 1848, and gave in her article some interesting particulars respecting him and his former St. Simonian followers. From being the chief of an organisation which was to reform society the Père had become the engineer and manager of a French railway, but he still enlightened the world through the press. Miss Jewsbury had a special reason for being interested in St. Simonians. One of her dearest friends, whom she regarded with great affection and respect, was a St. Simonian Frenchman who, on the dissolution of the Society, entered the service of the Pacha of Egypt, turned Mahometan (if I remember rightly) and was made a Bey. She looked up to him as a spiritual father (any Mahometanism of his could be only nominal), and she corresponded with him while he was in Egypt. His were the letters ' from Cairo,' the arrival of which made her happy and their absence unhappy, as appears from sundry references to them and him in her recently published letters to Mrs. Carlyle, references, like so much else in them, left unintelligible by the editress of the volume. The Bey, in full Oriental costume, paid a visit to her in Manchester while I was there, and I heard him on various occasions hold forth on politics, ethics, and religion. I remember Miss Jewsbury sitting literally at his feet, and, looking up to him reverently from her footstool say, interrogatively in her English-French : *Mais moi, je veux connaître qu'est-ce que c'est que la morale !* I took no note of what his answer was, if answer he gave. After a few weeks ' Geraldine's Bey,' as her friends used to call him, disappeared, and one never heard of him again.

The most salient passages, however, in Miss Jewsbury's *Westminster* article, were those in which she dealt with Mr. Froude's *Nemesis of Faith*, and it is very much to her credit, her intimacy with its author being remembered, that she expressed herself thus freely and frankly in regard to it :

'The *Nemesis of Faith* is a very powerful picture of the struggle of a religiously disposed sceptic ; the language is eloquent and powerful, and goes to the heart of the matter : it is "a voice of crying heard and loud lament," but nothing more ; there is no attempt to discover by what right this state of things exists. Doubt is treated as a painful phenomenon, and not as a legitimate phasis in the transition of humanity from one condition to another : therefore the work is oppressive and painful ; it suggests nothing ; there is no outlet from it—not even into the wilderness, where one might at least breathe—for the author insists on setting his face towards the Past ; and yet his book is constructed like a town in which every street should be a *cul de sac.*'

Such a passage, too, as the following is worth quoting, for it is applicable to a class of books which have been distressingly numerous since Miss Jewsbury wrote these thoughtful and suggestive words :—

' While we desire that men should examine courageously, and " try all things " which they feel moved to try and examine, still, the more modesty and reserve men observe, during their periods of transition, the better. The fashion of writing sceptical books, full of sentimental regret and interesting struggle is highly to be deprecated. . . . It is very difficult to lay down sympathy which has been over excited, and the danger is that the man who began his utterance in sincerity, may end by enjoying his sorrows and draping himself becomingly in his "doubts," "sorrows," ' positions," or whatever may chance to be the point in which the interest of society has been enlisted. . . . The more rigid the discipline of silence to which sceptics condemn themselves during their transition to sòme sort of solution, the better for themselves and the world : afterwards, as full a history of their spiritual progress as they feel (what Carlyle calls) " a healthy desire " to impart.'

Lewes was in Manchester when the article was written, and he sent it for Miss Jewsbury to the editor of the *Westminster Review*, naming ten pounds as the remuneration expected for it. The article was declined for one reason and another. Miss Jewsbury divined the real cause, and waived the remuneration. The article was then inserted.

During my first sojourn in Manchester I saw something of Miss Jewsbury's very intimate friends the two Cushmans, American actresses, the elder of whom had astonished the Londoners by playing Romeo to her sister's Juliet. In due time she was introduced to Mrs. Carlyle, of whom in one at least of her social phases—and Mrs. Carlyle had several —Miss Cushman has given a brief but lifelike word-portrait in a letter printed by one of her American biographers. [1] It was probably through the keen interest in the stage created in Miss Jewsbury by this intimacy with the Cushmans that she was led to make a gifted and enthusiastic actress one of the heroines of her second novel, *The Half Sisters*. Like her subsequent fictions, it sustained without increasing the reputation as a novelist which *Zoe* had gained her. The proofs of *The Half Sisters* were sent to Mrs. Carlyle to be corrected. But Carlyle, who had a contempt for novel-writing, and perhaps thought that Miss Jewsbury's new fiction was George Sandish, objected, rather crustily declaring, Mrs. Carlyle wrote to John Forster, 'I do not know bad grammar when I see it any better than she does,' and 'if I had any faculty I might find better employment for it, etc., etc.' Accordingly Mrs. Carlyle 'resigned.' Without telling me of the withdrawal of so distinguished a predecessor, Miss Jewsbury asked me to undertake the task of proof-correcting. I performed it with so much of youthful zeal that she

---

[1] ' On Sunday who should come self-invited to meet me but Mrs. Carlyle ? She came at one o'clock and stayed until eight. And such a day I have not known. Clever, witty, calm, cool, unsmiling, unsparing, a *raconteur* unparalleled, a manner inimitable, a behaviour scrupulous, and a power invincible —a combination rare and strange exists in that plain, keen, unattractive, yet unescapable woman ! Oh, I must tell you of that day for I cannot write it ! After she left, of course we talked *her* until the small hours of the morning.'

thought me, I fancied, to have overshot the mark. However, she thanked me for having, as she phrased it, 'set her sentences on their legs,' and indeed whatever she wrote, books or letters, had an irrepressible tendency to sprawl, her punctuation consisting mainly of dashes. Carlyle's interference to prevent his wife from becoming in this instance a correctress of the press was singular, since only a month before he had visited Manchester, where he was hospitably entertained by Miss Jewsbury and her brother, and had shown himself most amiably disposed towards her. But some account of his sayings and doings during that visit to Manchester must be reserved for another chapter.

CHAPTER IX

CARLYLE IN MANCHESTER

CARLYLE'S Manchester visit, foreshadowed at the close of the preceding chapter, was paid mainly to a little group of friendly admirers which had recently formed itself there. He came to them from the neighbourhood of Leeds, where he had been the guest of William Edward Forster (*ante*, p. 78), an ardent Liberal, but not at all of the Manchester and *laissez-faire* school, a diligent and appreciative student of Carlyle's writings and a great friend of Mrs. Carlyle. I found Carlyle newly arrived in the afternoon at a Manchester railway-station, grumbling at a decrepit porter who was not adjusting on his back with adequate symmetry the philosopher's luggage. In the evening I piloted him to Greenheyes and the Jewsburys, whose home was his, I think, during most of his stay in Manchester. On the way he talked much of France and the French, starting from the Praslin tragedy,[1] which had been recently enacted in Paris and had moved him greatly. France was, moreover, in a state of unrest, longing for Parliamentary reform, indignant at Louis

---

[1] This domestic tragedy, mostly forgotten now, excited the utmost horror throughout Europe. In August 1847, under circumstances of peculiar atrocity, the Duke de Praslin, a French peer of ancient descent, murdered his wife, who was the daughter of Marshal Sebastiani, formerly French ambassador in London. The cause of the crime was supposed to be the discovery by the Duchess, of an undue intimacy between her husband and the family-governess. Before he could be tried, the Duke committed suicide.

K

Philippe's and Guizot's repressive policy at home and scandalous intrigues abroad in the matter of the Spanish marriages, and stirred to its depths by disclosures of infamous corruption in high places, military and civil, a Minister of Public Works having in consequence attempted to commit suicide. Before long there was good reason for me to remember what fell from Carlyle's lips while I convoyed him that autumn evening through the streets of Manchester and its suburban byways. France, he said, was on the verge of another insurrectionary convulsion, and, with the French Revolution of the ensuing February, his prophecy came true indeed.

Lancashire and its Industrialism had for years interested Carlyle. The reader of 'Chartism' will (if he has a good memory) remember that vivid apostrophe in it : 'Hast thou heard with sound ears the awakening of a Manchester, on Monday morning, at half-past five by the clock, the rushing off of its thousand mills, like the boom of an Atlantic tide, ten thousand times ten thousand spools and spindles all set humming there—it is perhaps, if thou knew it well, sublime as a Niagara or more so.' Carlyle urged his friend John Chorley, a Lancashire man (of whom more hereafter), to write a history of Lancashire, than which, he said, 'there is not a bigger baby born of Time in these late centuries.' On the margins of the copy, in the London library, of Edward Baines's *History of the Cotton Manufacture*, I found pencil-jottings of Carlyle's which testified to the care and interest with which he had conned it. With Dr. Aikin's useful History of the Country 40 miles round Manchester, Carlyle showed considerable acquaintance. He bracketed Brindley with Arkwright as the two heroes of English industrialism in the eighteenth century, and declared the

Duke of Bridgewater, the founder of British canal-navigation, to be worth almost all the English Dukes put together whom recent centuries had produced. What surprised us more than this was the familiarity which he displayed with such a piece of rude humour, written in the homeliest Lancashire dialect, as 'Tim Bobbin' (which he called a 'Schwank'), and with the biography of its author, John Collier. Carlyle dilated genially on Collier's speedy return to his little cottage and cheerful semi-idyllic poverty at Milnrow, after having been tempted away to Yorkshire to enter the well-paid service of some magnate of the woollen trade.

Before visiting W. E. Forster in Yorkshire, Carlyle had spent a fortnight at Matlock, and inspected the neighbouring village of Cromford, as almost from the first, and thenceforward to the last, the headquarters of Richard Arkwright, and chief scene of those cotton-spinning operations of his with which Lancashire Industrialism took the earliest of its gigantic strides. As many passages in Carlyle's writings testify, Arkwright was one of his heroes, and, notwithstanding occasional gibes at 'Plugson of Undershot,' he had pronounced the future of England to lie with such 'Captains of Industry' as Arkwright's Lancashire had produced : they, moreover, since he uttered that prediction, had conquered the English aristocracy and repealed the Corn Laws. Almost fresh from an exploration of Cromford, Carlyle in Manchester was full of Arkwright. In fact, he hinted to us that, having then no literary enterprise on hand, he thought of settling for a longer or shorter time in our neighbourhood, and writing a life of Arkwright with appropriate comments. It was an evanescent project and came to nothing. The first biography which Carlyle wrote after his Cromwell was one not of Arkwright, but of John Sterling, a very different person from the founder of the modern cotton manufacture.

The late Mr. (afterwards Sir) Joseph Whitworth was a friend of Miss Jewsbury's, and, accompanied by her and by me, Carlyle visited and carefully inspected the great tool-making works of that eminent mechanician. Carlyle said of Whitworth personally that he put him in mind of (now the late) Thomas Watts of the British Museum, 'he had a face like a watch.' Of the many marvels of mechanical ingenuity disclosed to us during our visit, two specially interested Carlyle. One of them was a model of a knitting machine, newly invented by Whitworth (I know not whether it ever came into practical use), which imitated so exactly the movements of the feminine fingers, with their final jerk, when knitting stockings, that Carlyle, contemplating it at work, burst into a hearty laugh. The other machine was one which could measure the millionth part of an inch, and a hair from each of the heads of the three visitors was subjected to its delicate admeasurement. That belonging to the junior male of the party was adjudged the finest, Miss Jewsbury's came next, while the Sage's was found to be the coarsest of the three. During an interval for refreshment, Carlyle thought fit to improve the occasion by giving Whitworth an account of Dr. Francia's Workman's Gallows, on which the terrible Dictator hung negligent artificers, and with the sight of which he so frightened an unhappy shoemaker, who had brought him a pair of badly-made grenadier's belts that, within twelve hours, the culprit had turned out two of the best belts to be found in all Paraguay. This, with one exception, to be noted presently, was the only industrial establishment in visiting which

Carlyle was accompanied by the writer of these pages. But Carlyle inspected several others. Before he left us he expressed a doubt whether 'spinning clothes' was a desirable employment for great masses of human beings, 'without,' he was careful to add, 'strong counteracting influences.' Years afterwards, looking back to what he had seen in Manchester and Lancashire, he came to the conclusion thus expressed: 'They would do very well down there if the factory-inspectors did their duty,' as no doubt they have done, are doing, and will continue to do.

Among the more noticeable episodes of Carlyle's Manchester visit was his excursion to 'Brightdom,' as he called it, the Rochdale domain of the Brights. Before the excursion was talked of, Carlyle said to me, *à propos* of I know not what, 'there is good in Bright,' the famous John, of course. Carlyle's Rochdale visit was, however, not to him, but to his younger brother, Mr. Jacob Bright, now a well-known M.P. Among Carlyle's Manchester companions in the excursion there were friends of Mr. Jacob Bright, who, though not a Carlylian, was ready to welcome the distinguished author and denouncer of the Corn Laws. Carlyle's host for the day was then a bachelor, domiciled with brothers and sisters, while higher up the Rochdale acclivity on which he abode was the residence of his brother John, newly elected, for the first time, Member for Manchester, and he, as it happened, was then at home. A part of the afternoon was spent by Carlyle and his Manchester companions in an inspection of a new, or newish, mill belonging to the Brights, and of the most modern and improved construction and equipment. The rest of the afternoon was passed at Mr. Jacob Bright's in general conversation, accompanied by a considerable consumption of tobacco in various forms, Carlyle, of course, taking an active part in both of these occupations. I was rather amused by the deference which, consciously or unconsciously, Carlyle paid to the *genius loci*. He launched into a fiscal disquisition full of facts and figures, the object of which was to show how unjustly the demands of the Imperial Exchequer mulcted the poor, onwards from the old woman smoking her pipe of enormously taxed tobacco. The composition of the newly-elected Parliament coming under review, Carlyle expressed a grim satisfaction with the rejection of 'flowery rhetoricians,' by which he meant the defeat, at Edinburgh, of Macaulay, whose procedure in the Corn-Law controversy had brought him into great disfavour with the Anti-Corn-Law Leaguers. He laughed heartily, and it seemed sympathetically, at the statement of one of the party that the extension of manufacturing industry in and round Rochdale had driven from it all but a solitary survivor of the once numerous squirearchy of the district, substituting the mill for the manor-house. A report of some sayings and doings of a local High Church cleric, I think, led Carlyle to say with considerable emphasis that if the Church of England went on quietly in the old ways it might last for a long time, but that it would soon be sent about its business if it asserted sacerdotal pretensions.

Before and during the evening repast all went harmoniously. After it there was an adjournment to the drawing-room, where were Mr. and Mrs. John Bright. It was the first, and proved to be the last, meeting of the famous orator and the famous author. By some mischance the subject of negro-slavery was broached, and almost forthwith the two celebrities plunged into unpleasant controversy. Carlyle passionately defended the peculiar institution in the strain with which his denunciations of Quashee made his readers afterwards familiar, asserting that negro emancipation had ruined the West Indies. John Bright as strenuously, but not as violently, denounced slavery, and averred that statistics showed the exports of produce from Jamaica to have increased, not diminished, since emancipation. The railway system was another bone of contention, John Bright, of course, expatiating on the benefits which it had conferred on trade and manufactures, while Carlyle contended vehemently that it had dislocated and disorganised much of the quiet industry of the country, clinching his argument by describing the fate of some once prosperous Dumfriesshire watchmaker of his acquaintance, whom he had found adrift in the world, and who ascribed his ruin to a new railway by which his customers were allured to traffic with watchmakers at a distance! An illustration this, by the way, of the *Kleinstädterei* which Emerson said that he occasionally detected in Carlyle's conversation. Even in regard to the benefits of education the two disputants fell out, Carlyle opposing to his adversary's high estimate of them one of the sagacity and applicable knowledge of his own uneducated father, although the said father 'could not tell you of the bitter ale consumed in the City of Prophets.' This was a hit at Thackeray, who, in his entertaining record of Eastern travel (Mr. Michael Angelo Titmarsh's Journey from Cornhill to Cairo), had chronicled the joy which he felt when a camel-load of Hodson's pale ale arrived from Beyrout at Jerusalem during his visit to that 'City of Prophets!' When we had taken our leave, and were wending on our way towards Manchester, Carlyle spoke regretfully of his vehemence, and ascribed the painful scene to the introduction, with *malice prepense* of controversial topics, seeming to blame for it a certain junior of the party,—which, however, was not among that junior's many sins.

Mr. Froude, in his brief (and inaccurate) account of this visit of Carlyle's to Manchester, makes him 'talk with some of the leaders of the working men who were studying his works with passionate earnestness,' etc. As it happens there were no working men's leaders in the Manchester of that time. Mr. Froude was probably led into error by seeing, in Carlyle's Journal of his Manchester visit, references, which he can scarcely have failed to make, to Samuel Bamford, the author of *Passages in the Life of a Radical.* He was a great admirer of Carlyle, and Carlyle had a great regard for Bamford, whom, in his unpublished correspondence with John Forster he calls 'the brave Bamford.' The two met more than once at the Jewsburys' during Carlyle's stay in Manchester, and had much friendly talk. Bamford, who was at one time a hand-loom weaver, had been at Peterloo, and, though there with the most peaceable intentions, was arrested, tried, and imprisoned. But, while a genuine Radical and a zealous champion of the claims of labour, he was so far from being a leader of the working men that they looked askance at him, because all along, before, during, and after the Chartist agitation, he had steadily raised his voice against the use of physical force or recourse to violence of any kind. The geniality and good sense, combined with manliness and honesty, displayed in the *Passages*, at once commended him to Carlyle. Soon after the appearance of the modest little book it was noticed very favourably in the Tory *Quarterly Review* itself, I have little doubt through Carlyle's recommendation of it to Lockhart. I have still less doubt that to a similar recommendation was due the kind present of £100 which Carlyle's Lord Ashburton spontaneously made to Bamford, who himself told me of it.

At the little parties, which the hospitable Jewsburys gave in his honour to his friends and the friends of his friends, Carlyle was always genial, pleasantly conversible, never vehement. Miss Jewsbury, who was one of the acutest of observers, declared that during his Manchester visit there was a sort, to use her own phrase, of 'devil-may-care' air about him which she had never seen him wear before. Among his new Manchester acquaintances, he seemed to be struck by an interesting member of the Greek colony established there. This was Stavros Dilberoglue, the Manchester representative of a Greek House in London, a very handsome and cultivated young man, of singular refinement of mind and manners. He was a friend of Miss Jewsbury's, and became through her one of Mrs. Carlyle's. He was the donor to Mrs. Carlyle of the pet dog Nero, so often and so fondly mentioned in her correspondence, her fondness for whom procured her from Lady Ashburton the appellation of Agrippina, one not redeeming by its wit a conspicuous absence of good taste and good feeling in the giver. It was to Dilberoglue that Carlyle, enjoining on him a 'due depth of silence,' intrusted the commission to procure, as a birthday present for his wife, a little machine for making those cigarettes in which at one time she liked to indulge. Among Dilberoglue's personal characteristics was a certain longitude of neck, and, seizing on this with his usual quickness of eye for physical peculiarities, Carlyle compared him to a crane that had alighted on our shores and would one day wing his way to his distant home. Dilberoglue, however, when he had

made a fortune, settled in London, where, from his knowledge of Lancashire, he proved a very useful member of the
Mansion House Committee during the cotton-famine. A
little more of him hereafter. Of Carlyle's table-talk during
this Manchester visit there is not much to add to what has
already been reported of it. A discussion in a company
where he was, on the relative claims, then slightly agitating
the literary world, of Sheridan Knowles and Leigh Hunt,
to a pension, he cut short by saying 'Pension them both!'
On another occasion one of the Jewsburys' Scottish guests
sang very expressively to a plaintive air, a song by an
ill-fated Clydesdale poet, 'There's nae Covenant noo,' a
lament over the passing away of the creed of the Scottish
Covenanters. Doubtless he thought it a lyric that would
please the champion of seventeenth-century British Puritanism. But when it was finished Carlyle shook his head,
and hinted that the emotion expressed in the song had
ceased to be genuine, and was in truth factitious. Of the
advent of Emerson, which was expected in Manchester, he
spoke without enthusiasm, calling him 'a flowing poetic
man,' whose teaching he did not regard as of much importance. He expressed himself very pleased with his Manchester visit, and, when urged to remain a little longer, settled
the matter in a way usual with him in such cases, tossing up
a penny so as to leave the question of stay or departure to
the arbitrament of heads or tails, and the result of the toss
decided him to depart. Missing the first train by which
he intended to travel northward, he was bitterly self-
reproachful, and one could not help laughing inwardly to
hear his plaintive exclamation, 'If my wife had been here,
this would not have happened!' Mrs. Carlyle was at
home, doubtless busily superintending the operations of

carpenters, house-painters, etc. Soon after arriving at his destination in his beloved Dumfriesshire, he wrote Miss Jewsbury one of those beautiful letters in the inditing of which none could equal him, encouraging her in her attempt to make the home over which she presided the socially intellectual centre so much needed in such a place as Manchester then was. A few weeks after Carlyle's departure from Manchester Emerson arrived there to begin a lecturing tour in England. Of Emerson in Manchester and in London much will be said in the next chapter.

CHAPTER X

EMERSON IN ENGLAND

A LETTER, warmly inviting Emerson to proceed to Chelsea immediately on arriving in England, had been sent by Carlyle to Manchester. I went with it to Liverpool to place it in Emerson's hands as soon as he should touch the soil of England. But the packet-ship which had borne him across the Atlantic did not arrive until two days after it was due, so I returned with the letter to Manchester. It was posted to Emerson at Liverpool, and reached him when he landed. On receiving it he came to Manchester only for an hour or two, and then went straight to the Carlyles at Chelsea. It was just after that visit, and on his return to Manchester, that I saw him in private for the first time. His commune with Carlyle at this their second meeting had not been quite so satisfactory as at their first one some 'fourteen years before, when Emerson made that well-remembered pilgrimage to Craigenputtock. To say nothing of other differences, Carlyle, still full of Cromwell, resented with needless heat Emerson's refusal to fall down and worship the Puritan hero. There was just a trace of irritation, the only one which I ever perceived in Emerson, in his first references to his Chelsea visit ; but it soon disappeared, never to reappear. Sorrowing admiration was expressed in the remark made to one of us early during his stay in Manchester : ' Carlyle's heart is as large as the world, but he is growing morbid.' Emerson was lost in wonder at the vividness of Carlyle's conversation, which he compared to 'sculpture,' and pronounced to be even more marvellous than his books.

Emerson made Manchester his headquarters for several months, not only lecturing there, but returning to it every now and then from his lecturing tours in the manufacturing districts, and as far north as Edinburgh. He delivered two courses of lectures in Manchester, one of them at the Athenæum, the other, intended to be of a homelier kind, at the Mechanics' Institution. Those at the Athenæum belonged mainly to the series so well known afterwards under the title of 'Representative Men.' Emerson's manner in the lecture-room, like that which distinguished him in private, was one of perfect serenity. For any emotion that he displayed, there might have been no audience before him. He always read his lectures, and in a grave monotone for the most part, with rarely any emphasis. Much in them must have been 'caviare to the general,' but ever and anon some striking thought, strikingly expressed, produced a ripple of response from the audience, and the close of his finely discriminating lecture on Napoleon was followed by several rounds of applause, all this confirming what he once said to me, that such lecturing triumphs as fell to him were achieved by 'hits.' To the public success or failure of his lectures he appeared to be profoundly indifferent, a mood to which his experiences in American lecture-rooms had habituated him. He told me, with perfect equanimity, that at home he was accustomed to see hearers, after listening to him a little, walk out of the room, as much as to say that they had had enough of him. At his Manchester lectures the audiences were numerous and attentive. Whatever they might fail to understand, they evidently felt that this was a man of genius and of high and pure mind.

Out of the lecture-room Emerson's only public appearance in Manchester was at the annual soirée of the Manchester Athenæum, the late Sir Archibald (then plain Mr.) Alison in the chair. Emerson delivered on the occasion an effective little speech, unusually complimentary for him, since he made in it laudatory references to the Tory chairman's History of Europe, to Dickens, who had sent a letter of apology for non-attendance, and even to *Punch.* Better than this, it contained a noble passage on the greatness of the English character, afterwards expanded and minutely illustrated in the *English Traits*, of all Emerson's books the most interesting to English readers. As a silent auditor Emerson was present at a great 'demonstration' in the Free Trade Hall to celebrate the victory of the Anti‑Corn‑Law League. Among the speakers was Cobden, who had not long before returned to England, flushed with the success of his triumphal progress through the Continent after the repeal of the Corn Laws. Cobden was then beginning what proved to be a rather futile crusade against our military and naval expenditure. But in his speech he announced his new programme in such guarded language that, as Emerson told me, Cobden impressed him as 'the embodiment of English discretion.' However, I see that Emerson spoke more exuberantly and enthusiastically of Cobden in a letter which he wrote at the time to his friend Thoreau at Concord, and which is printed in the *Atlantic Monthly* for June 1892.

Emerson's associates in Manchester were chiefly members of the little circle which had welcomed Carlyle to the cotton city some weeks before. He honoured my domicile with several visits. Coming on one occasion to breakfast, he brought with him photographs of his wife and children, saying *à propos* of that of Mrs. Emerson, 'If any of our family are saved, it will be through her merits.' On the same occasion he took up *The Christian Year*, which was lying about, and I was a little surprised to find so ethnic a philosopher point admiringly to the opening stanza, ' Hues of the rich unfolding morn,' etc. As an evening guest, among a circle of his juniors not given to silence, Emerson was very reticent but very amiable, listening patiently, with a benignant smile, to the argumentation and other talk going on. If he did broach a comment or an opinion it was generally, I observed, to cite something said by a thoughtful friend at home. In private conversation he told me that Carlyle had advised him to try some historical subject, his reply being that he had no genius for history. Referring to Carlyle's vehement denunciations of authorship, he said, ' If Mr. Carlyle can show me any better employment than literature, I shall be happy to betake myself to it.' Before finally quitting Manchester, Emerson gave a dinner-party to his Manchester friends and others from the northern and midland counties, with some of whom he had corresponded from Concord on high or deep spiritual matters. The guests were a strange collection of mystics, poets, prose-rhapsodists, editors, schoolmasters, ex-Unitarian ministers, and cultivated manufacturers, the only bond of union among them being a common regard and respect for Emerson. One of the guests (he still survives) was a vegetarian, for whom a dinner of herbs had been considerately prepared. He was then a young man and had written a mystical book, which Emerson admired and which made him hopeful of its writer's future. It is a little characteristic of the difference between the Sage of Concord and the Sage of Chelsea,—that Carlyle's only comment on this and another mystical book by the same writer, was a contemptuous expression of wonder that 'a lad in a provincial town' should have presumed to handle such themes as he had dealt with. After the prandial and post-prandial babblement, to which our host as usual contributed nothing, he gave a serene close to the evening by reading to us his lecture on Plato. He had omitted it, probably as above the heads of an ordinary audience, from his series of lectures at the Manchester Athenæum on Representative Men, of which it now forms part.

Soon afterwards I pitched my tent in London again, and saw something of Emerson there, at the Carlyles' and elsewhere. 'The seraphic man,' as Carlyle called him, was, like most other visitors at Chelsea, silent when Carlyle held forth. However, it was at the Carlyles' that I listened to the most copious utterance which in private I ever heard come from Emerson's lips—and it was not very copious. I can give only a very imperfect report of it. It may have been a deliverance of Emerson's own, but, as was not uncommon with him, he professed to be only repeating what had been said to him by a friend who complained of the far too general and exclusive domination of 'the alphabet.' In the course of his European travels this friend had been struck with the much that had been said and was known about men who had had to do with 'the alphabet,' that is, who had written anything, compared with the obscurity which had been left to enshroud great workers and doers from the first architect of Cologne Cathedral, Erwin of Steinbach onwards. A catalogue of illustrative contrasts followed. This apparent depreciation of literature from one who prized it so highly as Emerson did seem to me singular, but was, of course, echoed sympathetically by Carlyle. On another evening the conversation turning on lectures and lecturing, Carlyle good-humouredly bantered Emerson on the easiness of his platform-tasks, reading 'from a paper before him,' and its contrast with his own difficulties, those of 'a poor fellow, set up to hold forth without any paper' to help him. Emerson said nothing. In such very little private conversation as I had with him in London he laid great stress on the scholarship of England, especially its Oriental scholarship. Really the Englishman in whom Emerson seemed to me as much interested as in any other was that strange being Thomas Taylor, the Platonist and Neo-pagan whom some visitor once found in an attitude of worship before a silver shrine of Mercury! Taylor lived in Walworth, whither Emerson told me that he made a pilgrimage—the only literary pilgrimage which I knew him make in London—in search of memorials of this reviver of the worship of the gods of antiquity.

Between Carlyle and Bancroft, the historian of the United States and then American minister in London, Emerson was introduced everywhere, his reputation as a thinker of course powerfully aiding, and both in the aristocratic and intellectual circles of London society he saw everybody whom he could have cared to see, Carlyle reporting (what ought to have pleased that great apostle of silence) the complaint of 'the high people' that (unlike himself) Emerson had little to say to them. One of the effects on Emerson of the brilliancy of the society in which he found himself lionised for the first time was to make him very reluctant to lecture in London. To overcome this reluctance, resort was had to a device of which I heard no whisper at the time, and which, either through modesty or pride, Emerson seems never to have mentioned even in his letters to relatives and friends at home. It came to my knowledge only recently, when exploring the paper-masses left behind him by the late John Forster. Among them is the original, with the signatories' autographs attached, of a memorial addressed to Emerson, respectfully requesting him to deliver a course of lectures in London, signed by Bulwer Lytton, Carlyle, Procter (Barry Cornwall), Charles Dickens, and the inevitable Forster himself. Two courses of lectures by Emerson in London did come off, the earlier of them (on the 'Mind and Manners of the Nineteenth Century') being delivered to a guinea-paying audience in a hall in Edward Street, Portman Square. On the first day the audience was numerous, aristocratic as well as in-tellectual, two daughters of the then Duchess of Suther-land (who had been Emerson's hostess at Stafford House) being seated on the platform by the Lecturer's side. I had a long talk with Carlyle about one of these Edward Street lectures. When I spoke of the high ethical ideal which Emerson held up to us, Carlyle replied that Emerson's ethics consisted chiefly of 'prohibitions.' In a striking passage of the lecture, Emerson, whom again I report very imperfectly, had compared man's life on earth to a bird alighting on a rock, resting for a while, and then flying away into infinite space. I made some reference to this similitude, and Carlyle rejoined 'Merchant! you figure well.' On asking for some explanation of this enigmatic deliverance, Carlyle told me the story of an impecunious Dumfriesshire man, to whom, on entering a shop, a tradesman (in old days every Scotch shopkeeper was called a merchant) had tendered an account. The debtor had no money with which to settle the bill, but after carefully inspecting its caligraphy and arithmetic he said to his creditor in a mournfully complimentary tone : 'Merchant! you figure well.' The bearing of this anecdote on Emerson's similitude, I leave it to the reader to discover. Mrs. Carlyle was more dissatisfied than her husband with Emerson's ethics. Dilating in his high-flown optimistic way on the ultimate triumph of good over evil, the lecturer went the length of saying that even when in a certain haunt of sensual vice, unmentionable to ears polite (though Emerson called it by its plain English name), man is still tending upwards, or words to that effect. Mrs. Carlyle's moral indignation at this statement knew no bounds, and for some time she could scarcely speak of Emerson with patience. I now and then fancied that after Emerson had been banqueted and welcomed by so many great and distinguished people in London, she viewed him, with a certain wife-like jealousy, as a sort of rival of her husband. Emerson's admiration for her abated visibly, till at last he was heard to say that the society of 'the lady' (Mrs. Carlyle made no pretension to profundity) was worth cultivating, mainly because she was the person who could tell you most about the husband. Very soon after the delivery of the first lecture I accompanied Carlyle to Emerson's domicile, a visit apparently intended to be one of congratulation on his lecturing success. Emerson was at home, and Carlyle seemed to find the process of congratulation rather embarrassing. He could get out little more than that the lecture was 'very Emersonian,' which, considering that Emerson had been the lecturer, was not striking or enthusiastic praise. Then the subject was swiftly dismissed and succeeded by a conversation on a common friend, *à propos* of whom Carlyle, who was one of the keenest-sighted of physiognomists, laid it down as an ascertained physiognomico-spiritual fact that a long upper lip denoted in its possessor 'a certain resonance to the noble,' and the brief visit ended. Elsewhere than in Emerson's presence, 'Moonshine' pithily expressed Carlyle's opinion on his London lectures. But, before Emerson left England for home a few weeks afterwards, Carlyle spoke more kindly of his friend's lectures as 'intellectual sonatas,' and of the friend himself as 'a beautiful figure among those talking Yankees,' and the ideal of an American gentleman.

In his *English Traits* Emerson has given an agreeable description of an excursion which he made with Carlyle to see Stonehenge, and of their subsequent visit to the Hampshire county house of 'A. H.' 'A. H.' was no other a person than the late amiable Arthur (afterwards Sir Arthur) Helps, who was an old friend of Carlyle's, and whom Emerson had met in London. Speaking some time subsequently to a friend of mine about this welcome visit of the two Sages, Helps said that, when taking his walks abroad with them, he was surprised by their display of a very minute knowledge of—grasses! It would have been well if their conversation had never turned on more dangerous and controversial themes. It was during this visit that Emerson startled his host and fellow-guest by propounding the doctrine of non-resistance in its extremest form. As far as I was able at the time to make out, Emerson's theory was that the wise man should have such perfect confidence in the ongoings of the universe, the development of the human race included, as to refrain from fighting with pen or tongue, not less than with sword, for the good and against the bad, and should regard even the best government and legislation as superfluous interferences with the ordained economy of things. I saw Carlyle immediately after his return from the Stonehenge expedition, and he was full of indignant protest against Emerson's doctrine of limitless *laissez-faire*, which if acted on would, he said, prevent a man from so much as 'rooting out a thistle.' At any time, even during that memorable and pleasant early visit of Emerson's to Craigenputtock where Carlyle was quietly thinking and studying, his vigorous, not to say vehement, nature would have led him to reject Emerson's spiritual Quakerism. Much more must it have been repugnant to Carlyle during that tumultuous revolutionary year 1848, when he was boiling over with an almost insurrectionary indignation against things in general. It was most unfortunate for the renewed intercourse between the two Sages that it should have taken place at such a time. Considering the deep material obligations under which Carlyle was to Emerson he might, however, I think, have treated Emerson more tenderly than he did, but his then stormy mood of mind is a sort of palliation of his conduct to his brother-Sage, and some compensation was made for it in his correspondence with Concord after Emerson's return home. When the war between North and South broke out, Emerson, it may be noted, flung to the winds his cherished doctrine of non-resistance.

Not one (so far as I know) of Carlyle's biographers and bibliographers has noticed a slight but interesting literary memorial of his intimacy with Emerson, and of their friendly correspondence after Emerson's return to Concord. This is an article on 'Indian Meal' in *Fraser's Magazine* for May 1849, signed ' C.,' Carlyle's authorship of which is undoubted, though he did not include it in any collective edition of his writings. Cobbett had endeavoured unsuccessfully to persuade the English farmer to raise Indian corn, and Carlyle wished, in those days of potato-disease, to see Indian meal an article of general consumption. He found that the Indian meal then in use among us, whether ground in the exporting country, or at home from imported Indian corn, was tainted by a bitterness which made even the starving Irish pauper turn against it. Moreover, English millstones being generally too soft for that kind of grain there was found a considerable admixture of sand in the meal which they turned out, and this did not at all improve matters. He corresponded on the subject with Emerson at Concord, who sent him from his own barn a barrel of Indian corn in its natural state, which had not been subjected to the process of kiln-drying, and to this process, Emerson reported, was said to be due the *amari aliquid* in the meal as then consumed in England and Ireland. At Carlyle's instance, his friend Lord Ashburton had Emerson's sample ground by a miller of his own, and prepared for the table by his own French cook. The result, according to Carlyle in *Fraser*, was ' meal which was sweet among the sweetest; with an excellent rich taste something like that of nuts, indeed it seemed to me, perhaps from novelty in part, decidedly sweeter than wheat or any other grain I have ever tasted. So that, it would appear, all our experiments hitherto in Indian meal have been vitiated to the heart by a deadly original sin or fundamental falsity to start with—as if in experimenting on Westphalian ham, all the ham presented to us hitherto for trial had been in a rancid state. . . Ground by a reason-

able miller, who grinds only it and not his millstones
along with it, this grain, I can already promise, will make
excellent, cleanly, wholesome, and palatable eating ; and
be fit for the cook's art under all manner of conditions,
ready to combine with whatever judicious condiment, and
reward well whatever wise treatment he applies to it : and
indeed, on the whole, I should say, a more promising
article could not well be submitted to him, if his art is
really a useful one.' On it, Carlyle continued, 'a grown man
could be supported wholesomely, and even agreeably, at the
rate of little more than a penny a day, which surely is cheap
enough. Neither, as the article is not grown at home, and
can be procured only by commerce, need political econo-
mists dread new "Irish difficulties" from the cheapness of
it. Nor is there danger, for unlimited periods yet, of it
becoming dearer : it grows, in the warm latitudes of the
earth, profusely with the whole impulse of the sun ; can
grow over huge tracts and continents lying vacant hitherto,
festering hitherto as pestiferous jungles, yielding only
rattle-snakes and yellow-fever : it is probable, if we were
driven to it, the planet Earth, sown where fit with Indian
corn, might produce a million times as much food as it now
does or has ever done. To the disconsolate Malthusian
this grain ought to be a sovereign comfort.' In the single
valley of the Mississippi alone, ' were the rest of the earth
all lying fallow, there could Indian corn enough be given
to support the whole posterity of Adam now alive.'
Announcing these good tidings, Carlyle bade 'the disconsolate Malthusian fling his "geometrical series" into the
córner, assist wisely in the Free Trade movement, and dry
up his tears.' Carlyle told me that he sent his article, in
the first instance, to the editor of the *Times*, who rejected

and returned it.[1] In the collective editions of his writings, from which Carlyle excluded it, there are surely things more trivial and less interesting than the striking piece in which the Sage of Chelsea, aided by the Sage of Concord, sought to indicate how every son of Adam could live on little more than a penny a day !

[1] In a letter to Emerson (19th April 1849), after describing what had been done with the Indian Corn sent from Concord, Carlyle goes on to say : ' I, on my side, have already drawn up a fit proclamation of the excellencies of this invaluable corn, and admonitions as to the benighted state of English eaters in regard to it, to appear in *Fraser's Magazine*, or I know not where, very soon.' The article being on a subject of general importance, Carlyle sent it, in the first instance, to the *Times*, if published in which it would have a far greater number of readers than the magazine could ensure it.

CHAPTER XI

CARLYLE IN 1848

AN insurrectionary movement in France had, as pre-viously reported, been predicted by Carlyle in the autumn of 1847. The Revolution of February 1848 gave him therefore more satisfaction than surprise, though even he had scarcely looked for the 'beautiful radiancy,' as he called it to me, which the French displayed in flinging out Louis Philippe. ' It will be a long time,' Carlyle said to me, ' before another man has such a chance as Louis Philippe had,' for, like the rest of the world, he little foresaw the sudden rise of Louis Napoleon. Since the publication of his *Cromwell*, Carlyle's pen had been lying idle, though his mind was seething with literary projects. Suddenly the French Revolution blazed forth amid what he had described to me as 'this vile murk of things,' and seemed to offer a stirring and pregnant theme, a text for much prophetic utterance. While its results were undeveloped, his new and very un-Burke-like ' Reflections on the French Revolu-tion' were less suited for a book than for 'articles,' and the startling phenomenon in Paris led to Carlyle's first appearance in political journalism. He was encouraged to make the attempt all the more because his intimate friend and warm admirer, John Forster, had become editor of the *Examiner*, in succession to Albany Fonblanque, whom the Whigs, on their return to power after the repeal of the Corn Laws, appointed chief of the Statistical Department of the Board of Trade. Carlyle's first essay in political journalism was an anonymous contribution to the leading columns of the *Examiner*, a most vivid and vigorous article on 'Louis Philippe,' whose downfall he greeted with 'a stern, almost sacred joy.' This and his few other newspaper articles he himself never cared to reprint, so that they are unknown to the great mass of the readers of his works. Moreover, there has remained until now quite unnoticed a second article on French affairs, which was written by him for the *Examiner*, which was set up in type, and of which he corrected the proof, yet which was never published in that or any other journal, and lies buried in the multifarious paper-masses left by the late John Forster. The piece is curious as testifying, rather unexpectedly, to Carlyle's impetuous enthusiasm for the Second French Republic, to celebrate the birth of which it was written. He went the length of declaring that if the Czar with his 'Scythians' attempted to crush the nascent republic, it would be the duty of England to fight by the side of France in resistance to Russia ! It is little to be wondered at that the prudent Forster withdrew from publication in what had become a Whig organ an article written in this spirit. In the course of years there was formed an Anglo-French alliance against Russia, but it was one which, in the altered circumstances, was fiercely denounced by Carlyle.

Carlyle's enthusiasm for the Second French Republic died out as this lapsed into anarchy and bloodshed, and he thoroughly detested the 'Saviour of Society,' Louis Napoleon, whom he had known in England and whom the French, still dazzled by the Napoleonic legend, preferred as President of the Republic to the upright General Cavaignac, father of the Cavaignac now a prominent French politician and brother of Godefroi Cavaignac, a great friend of Carlyle's, as will be more fully noted hereafter. In the earlier history of the Second French Republic there occurred an episode which was trifling in itself, but which struck me at the time as illustrating Carlyle's far too great liability to have his judgments affected by his personal prepossessions, or, as in this case, prejudices. When a new National Assembly was convoked, there appeared an address to the electors which caused a considerable sensation. It advised them to give their suffrages to none but plain honest men who would make all the better deputies if they were uneducated, or had very little to do with 'the alphabet,' as Emerson's friend, previously cited, might have phrased it. Carlyle warmly approved of the tone and tenor of this address, but some time afterwards, when it turned out that it was the handiwork of George Sand, by which time, it is true, the prospects of the French Republic were growing decidedly dubious, he just as warmly condemned it. On hearing of the Revolution of February 1848, George Sand had rushed off to Paris to fling herself into the political *mêlée*, and Mazzini, in his Italian-English, complained to Mrs. Carlyle, as she herself told me, that Madame Dudevant was then 'living on credits!' With the collapse of Carlyle's hopes from France, he made Ireland the subject of his few remaining contributions to the newspaper press. Two were published by Forster, one of them a very powerful protest against 'The Repeal of the Union,' and then Carlyle's connection with the *Examiner* ceased. Like his other articles, they were written in the purest Carlylese, little to the taste of readers of the *Examiner*, whom Fonblanque had fed on nothing stronger than illustrations of contemporary politics drawn from Molière's plays and

Fielding's novels. Forster himself told me that, 'splendid'
as he admitted Carlyle's papers to be, he had received protests against them from subscribers, and doubtless Carlyle's
indignant criticisms on Ministerial legislation and no-
legislation for Ireland had given offence in quarters where
Forster was anxious that offence should not be taken.
But these were considerations to which Carlyle in his then
mood paid no heed. He was nettled at the stop put to his
earnest disquisitions by his own familiar friend. He was
chagrined to see his passionate denunciations of a futile
policy in famine-stricken Ireland and his daringly original
suggestions of a new one superseded by the common-
places of Whiggism. Forster, I heard him say, 'will write the
Examiner down.' The result was that he cooled considerably towards Forster. But the coolness did not last long.
Forster was too devoted and useful, and Carlyle had too
much sense for that—their friendship was soon as cordial
as ever. From Forster and the *Examiner* Carlyle turned
to the hard-headed Rintoul and the *Spectator*, busy on the
editorial staff of which was Thornton Hunt, the eldest son
of his old friend Leigh Hunt, and himself a great admirer
of Carlyle. Rintoul failed to tolerate more than two articles
of Carlyle's, those in which he propounded his scheme of
'Irish regiments of the New Era.' The famine-stricken
peasantry of Ireland, instead of being fed in eleemosynary
fashion out of rates and Parliamentary Grants, were to earn
their own living through spade husbandry, organised by the
Government, which was to support them until they could be
supported by the fruits of their industry. The Irishman,
according to Carlyle, had a special talent for that kind of
husbandry, and was known to be when drilled one of the
bravest of soldiers. 'Digging,' said Carlyle, 'can be regi-

mented as well as fighting,' and so forth. This was enough
—too much—for Rintoul. Carlyle was now convinced that
he could not find in British journalism as then constituted
a pulpit from which to preach to the governing classes. He
began to talk of starting an organ of his own, which
(following Cobbett) he spoke of as 'Twopenny Trash.'
The project, like so many others of his, went no further
than talk, and a year and a half passed away before the
world was startled by the thunder and lightning of the
Latter-Day Pamphlets.

Meanwhile, Carlyle's friends and admirers of the Young
Ireland party had been arrested, and were being tried for
the violence of their inflammatory language. Carlyle, who
had all along sorrowfully reprobated their insurrectionary
schemes, showed himself full of pitying sympathy with them
in the time of their adversity. Of his friendship with the
'Irish Rebel' of 1848, now 'Sir Charles Gavan Duffy,
K.C.M.G.,' that much-experienced veteran has given the
world an interesting memorial in his 'Conversations with
Carlyle.' For the most violent of the Young Ireland party,
John Mitchell, who adopted some of Carlyle's heretical
notions, those on slavery for instance, Carlyle had a very
strong liking. Indeed, his knowledge of, and personal commune with, these young Irishmen and their friends appears
to have opened his eyes to something good in the national
character of a people of whose faults alone he had been
formerly cognisant. 'The English,' he was heard to say,
'are torpid, and the Scotch are harsh, but the Irish are
affectionate.' He told me that once, when taking a walk
with Mitchell in London, he asked whether the Young
Irelander, who was denouncing and threatening the Saxon,
thought that he had much chance in a conflict with a

nation to whose strength and resources such a capital as London bore testimony. Mitchell's answer was that he would 'try.' When Mitchell was suffering a felon's doom, in the 'still-vexed Bermoothes,' he wrote to Carlyle, who in his reply, he informed me, endeavoured to console Mitchell by telling him that 'this was still the country of Shakespeare and Milton,'—a consolation, it seemed to me, which would have been more suitably addressed to a depressed poet than to a banished, imprisoned, and exasperated 'rebel.'

A mild literary phenomenon, presenting a striking contrast to the tumultuous revolutionism of that *annus mirabilis*, claims mention through its connection with Carlyle. In the spring of 1848 Eckermann sent him from Weimar the final instalment of the *Conversations with Goethe*. A letter accompanied it, Carlyle told me, in which the then recent French Revolution was treated by Eckermann as 'ein anderer Beweis der menschlichen Schwacheit' ('another proof of the weakness of man'), Carlyle laughing heartily at the calmly contemptuous way in which Goethe's Boswell spoke of an event of such importance to Europe. Eckermann, he said, was 'a beautiful mirror-soul; he doesn't know how clever he is.' He was, Carlyle added, 'miserably poor,' and had once sent him the autograph manuscript of one of Goethe's dramas to be offered for sale to the authorities of the British Museum. Carlyle went with it to the late Sir Frederick Madden, then at the head of the Manuscript Department of the Museum, and met with a courteous refusal. A similar refusal would not be given now. In Eckermann's new volume there was a genial letter from Sir Walter Scott to Goethe, giving some account of himself and his family. Lockhart and his devotion to Goethe were mentioned in it, and Goethe expressed to Eckermann his surprise that Sir Walter said nothing of Carlyle, who had done so much to diffuse in Great Britain a knowledge of German literature. It was on this occasion that Goethe spoke to Eckermann of Carlyle as 'a moral force of great significance,' as 'having in him much for the future,' and as a man concerning whom 'it was difficult to conceive all that he might produce and effect.' Carlyle made no remark on this, but laughed a little at Sir Walter's truly Scott-like mention in the letter to Goethe of 'my friend Sir John Hope of Pinkie,' and spoke in his usual depreciatory tone of 'Wattie' as having 'turned the history of his country into an opera.'

Towards the close of the book, Eckermann reported a remarkable discourse by Goethe on sacred things. It was a discourse, full of serene wisdom, on religion, natural and revealed, on the Protestant Church's relation to it, on the inestimable value, for ethical culture, of the Gospels, on the debt which we owe to Luther and the Reformation, and on the life beyond the grave. At any time the thoughts of a Goethe on such themes as these would have been impressive, but their impressiveness was greatly enhanced by the fact that they were uttered only some ten days before the death of the venerable poet-sage. Speaking of the Founder of Christianity, Goethe said, 'Ich beuge mich vor Ihm'— 'I bow down before him.'[1] Carlyle gave me the volume

[1] I give the whole of the passage, in the late John Oxenford's translation. After some judicial remarks on the controversy respecting the authenticity of the Gospels, Goethe went on to say : 'Nevertheless, I look upon all the four Gospels as thoroughly genuine ; for there is in them the reflection of a greatness which emanates from the person of Jesus and which is of as divine a kind as ever was seen upon earth. If I am asked whether it is in my nature to pay Him devout reverence I say "certainly." I bow before Him as the divine manifestation of the highest principle of morality.' Let there be

to review, and I observed that he had underlined the *Ich* of the foregoing sentence, and pencilled opposite to it an emphatic note of exclamation, one among the slightest but not the least expressive and significant of his innumerable Marginalia.

quoted, too, the same translator's version of the closing passage of Goethe's discourse : 'God did not retire to rest after the well-known six days of creation, but, on the contrary, is constantly active as on the first.   It would have been for Him a poor occupation to compose this heavy world out of simple elements, and to keep it rolling in the sunbeams from year to year, if He had not had the plan of founding a nursery for a world of spirits.'   A theory of Evolution without an Evolver would have been banned by Goethe.

CHAPTER XII

THE ORGANISATION OF LABOUR

CARLYLE'S pupil in earlier and friend in later years, Charles Buller, died towards the close of 1848, and Carlyle wrote a kindly obituary notice of him, which appeared in the *Examiner*. Buller had been President of the Poor-Law Board since the return of the Whigs to office, after the Repeal of the Corn Laws. With all his affection for the man, Carlyle spoke to me rather slightingly of him as an administrator, approaching, 'with kid gloves on, that grimy phenomenon,' pauperism. This meant nothing more than that Buller managed his department as his predecessors in office had done, and as his successors were to do. The connection with Poor-Law Administration of so old and intimate a friend had led Carlyle to look a little into the unsatisfactory statistics of English pauperism—the magnitude of Irish pauperism was glaring—and, as was seen in the last chapter, Carlyle had promulgated a scheme for its reproductive employment. By degrees he formed a gigantic and far-reaching scheme of the same kind, embracing English as well as Irish pauperism. A statement of it, made with immense emphasis, was to be thrown here and there into those *Latter-Day Pamphlets* which, with their tumultuous vehemence of protest against everything under heaven, have become, in spite of the enormous literary power displayed in them, wearisome in their monotony. They are now probably the least read of all Carlyle's

M

writings, and possess mainly a biographical and psychological interest. It was unfortunate that Carlyle's project of social reconstruction should have been communicated through that turbid, that tempestuous medium. The *Latter-Day Pamphlets* provoked a howling storm of wrathful criticism. Furious at Carlyle's assaults on the popular idols and dominant ideas of their time, the great majority of his critics were in no mood to examine his one solitary proposal of a practical, I am far from saying of a practicable, kind, for the gradual abolition of the social anarchy which he denounced with a terrible earnestness almost unknown in the world's literature since the record of Hebrew prophecy was closed.

No. I. of the *Latter-Day Pamphlets* (1st February 1850) contained Carlyle's scheme, in its rudimentary form, of ' Industrial Regiments,' British as well as Irish. Poor-Law Relief of any kind was to be sternly refused to all paupers capable of working. Work was to be offered them by the State. If they shirked it, they were to be flogged ; and if, after this operation, they remained disobedient, they were to be shot, an unnecessary exhibition of the harshness which, rightly or wrongly, Carlyle, the reader has seen, considered a characteristic of his countrymen north of the Tweed. Great numbers of convicted criminals were in Carlyle's day—as they are in ours—kept at work—sometimes very hard work—without either flogging or shooting. No. V. of the *Pamphlets* expanded the original scheme. The Industrial Regiments were no longer to consist of paupers solely. Enlistment in them was to be open to any worker who was dissatisfied with the conditions of his actual employment. The sweated might thus escape from the sweater, the underpaid and overtasked in any department of labour would find work under rigorous but just and wholesome conditions in Carlyle's Industrial Regiments. Thus, Carlyle thought, the ordinary employer of labour would have to concede to his workers equally just and wholesome conditions, or he would find them deserting him and enlisting in the State's Industrial Army. This was Carlyle's solution of the 'Labour Question,' which is always with us. That in those days of triumphant *laissez-faire* Carlyle's scheme should have received no approval, and only a slight contemptuous attention from statesmen and politicians, is not to be wondered at. It is more wonderful that it should have been utterly neglected by the most prominent and vociferous of Carlyle's enthusiastic disciples. Mr. Froude, the Elisha of that Elijah, is never weary of proclaiming his belief that Carlyle was the wisest as well as the noblest man of his generation, and that only in following Carlyle's precepts is political and social salvation to be found. Yet nowhere in Mr. Froude's writings is there to be found any reference to the Industrial Regiments. When, in the course of his elaborate biography of Carlyle, he comes to the *Latter-Day Pamphlets*, he has a good deal to say about almost everything in them except the one thing which can chiefly preserve them from neglect. He ignores altogether the scheme on which Carlyle based his hopes of national regeneration, his one noticeable reply to the reproach with which he was frequently assailed, that he could only denounce social evils and had no remedy to propose for them, that he was wholly aggressive and not in the least constructive.

Having been absent a second time from London, I returned to it soon after the appearance of No. 1. of the *Latter-Day Pamphlets*. I found Carlyle in one of his sternest moods. So unwelcome to him were visitors that 'nobody comes to the house now,' Mrs. Carlyle said, not at all complacently, 'but a few followers of mine.' A single gleam of humour did for a moment lighten the gloom of his denunciations of idle pauperism, Poor-Law Relief, charitable dole-giving, and all the rest of it. He illustrated his attitude towards them by citing what he spoke of as 'one of the drollest things that ever came from Dickens.' When on the occasion of Mr. Dombey's second marriage he enters the church in which it is to be solemnised, attired in a new blue coat, fawn-coloured pantaloons and lilac waistcoat, Mr. Toots, surveying the scene from the gallery, informs in an undertone his neighbour and friend The Chicken that this gorgeous personage is the bridegroom. The confident pugilist hoarsely whispers in reply that Mr. Dombey is 'as stiff a cove as ever he see, but that it is within the resources of science to double him up, with one blow in the waistcoat.' Carlyle, with grim glee, boasted (rashly, it has turned out) that fashionable and complacent as was the Philanthropy of the day, it was within the resources of *his* science to 'double it up'! In this anti-philanthropic temper of mind, he spoke with some impatience even of Factory Legislation,—an improvement in which was then being mooted,—and of Lord Ashley, the Earl of Shaftesbury that was to be, whom he had praised in *Past and Present.* 'Why,' he said, 'can't the operatives make their own bargains with the mill-owners?' though he admitted that Factory Legislation was indispensable for the protection of women and children. When I asked him whether he did not think that Lord Ashley was sincere, he would only reply, 'He is not consciously insincere;' and added, 'what he is doing will come out in a way which he little expects.' One small episode in Carlyle's biography at this time is worth noting. Some of the Aberdeen students started him, not successfully, as a candidate for their Lord Rectorship against, I think, the Duke of Argyll. 'I suppose,' he said to me, 'the young fellows look on me as an embodiment of German neology.' Of the Rectorship, he said : 'It is nothing in itself, but it is thought to be something here.' There were reasons, quite unconnected with personal vanity (of which few distinguished men had less than Carlyle), why he should wish just then to receive what would be regarded as 'something' in London.

There was, indeed, no doubt in my mind that in those days Carlyle would have cheerfully accepted an office under Government which might have enabled him to carry out, to some extent, his scheme for the reproductive employment of pauperism. But the Whigs of 1847-50 (with the exception, perhaps, of Earl Grey, and his distrust of Lord Palmerston's policy had prevented him from joining the Ministry) did not love Carlyle, nor was there love lost between him and them. The Presidency of the Poor-Law Board, vacant through the death of Charles Buller, was given to a 'safe' Whig lawyer, who and whose newspaper connections were useful to the party. The Permanent (as distinct from the Parliamentary) Secretaryship of the same Board became vacant not long afterwards. From some faint indications at the time, I half-surmised that Carlyle had an eye on it, but it was given to the son of a considerable Whig earl. Carlyle did not spare the Whigs in the *Latter-Day Pamphlets*, and some sarcasms in them on Lord John Russell drew from his lordship, speaking in the House of Commons, an unmistakable reference to Carlyle as 'a clever but whimsical writer.' A great Whig brother-man-of-letters—Macaulay—was an ardent adherent of *laissez-faire*, and he, it was said, made merry over a slight linguistic error committed by Carlyle (but corrected afterwards), who in the first of the *Pamphlets* had written ἔθνοι instead of ἔθνη! Carlyle turned his face towards Peel, whom he had met occasionally at Lord Ashburton's, and for whom, since the Repeal of the Corn Laws, he had a considerable regard. The Peelites having bought the *Morning Chronicle*, there began to appear in it, towards the close of 1849, a striking series of articles on Labour and the Poor, in London and elsewhere. At the beginning of 1850 there were even faint rumours that some of the leading Peelites were in favour of a determined attempt to grapple with the Labour question. However this may have been, in the *Latter-Day Pamphlet* on 'The New Downing Street,' which was to set the pauper to work and to do a great deal else, Carlyle called on Peel to undertake the Premiership, as if in such a case the will were equivalent to the way. That pamphlet appeared on the 15th of April (1850), and within a month Carlyle was invited by Peel to the dinner-party, Carlyle's graphic account of which and of his host has been printed by Mr. Froude. Some six weeks afterwards Sir Robert Peel was in his grave. With his death there vanished Carlyle's never confident hope of being given an opportunity to realise his dream of social reform. I still remember the tone of sadness, blended with resignation, in which at that time he said to me: 'The world is a poor slave, and will always be governed in a low way.'

The fundamental idea of Carlyle's scheme for the reconstruction of society, as originally conceived by him, was that paupers having been defeated, as it were, in the battle of life they should be made slaves of, just as the Greeks and Romans made slaves of those whom they conquered and took captive in warfare. This notion he derived from Andrew Fletcher of Saltoun, whose works he was studying in those years, Fletcher having proposed that the beggars and sturdy vagabonds by whom the Scotland of his day was infested should be seized and reduced to servitude. Carlyle's original conception was a little mitigated when, instead of enslaving them, he proposed the compulsory enlistment of all paupers in an industrial army, the voluntary enlistment in which of all workers, outside pauperism, discontented with the condition of their employment, was not merely permitted but invited. An organisation like that of a modern army became Carlyle's social ideal. Speaking of what could be, and was done by military drill, he said to me, 'it is beautiful to see that men have such a faculty left' as that of being drilled. In his industrial army there were to be the same implicit obedience to authority, and the same punishments for disobedience, as in the army which conquered at Waterloo. No democratic element was to be admitted into its constitution; it was to be controlled despotically from above. Herein lay a great difference between Carlyle's scheme and such continental state-socialism as that, for instance, of Louis Blanc, in whom, however, he recognised 'something chivalrous.' In his *Organisation du Travail*, Louis Blanc proposed that the soldiers of any one of his Industrial Regiments should elect their own officers, a project to which Carlyle would not listen for a moment.

Carlyle did not appear to me to know much about the working of the Poor-Law legislation which he wished to revolutionise, or to have more than glanced at the statistics of pauperism. Henry Fielding's well-meant and even practical, but rather out of date, proposals for the repression of mendicancy and crime in London lay on Carlyle's table, but not a single Blue Book or Parliamentary Return was visible there. He said vaguely that the amount of the poor-rate levied annually in England and Wales was approaching that levied in the days of the old and wasteful poor-law. But he did not take into account the increase of population during the interval, or the fact that considerable portions of the poor-rate under the new law, were expended on purposes only indirectly connected with pauper-relief. He seemed to have a notion that if a man was once a pauper, he was always a pauper, infecting his neighbourhood with pauperism. He never deigned to look into the fluctuations of pauperism, and its decrease or increase varying with the state of trade. He did not even gauge the amount of that adult able-bodied pauperism with which he proposed to deal so stringently. If you spoke to him of any of these things, he made some impatient reply about not wishing to be pestered with 'details,' as if it was not the adjustment of these very details that made the difference between a Utopian and a practicable scheme. When all was over, or at least when no statesman or prominent politician was found taking any notice of his scheme, and the death of Sir Robert Peel extinguished some hopes that have been hinted at, Carlyle surveyed the situation more calmly than when he was in the volcanic state which produced the *Latter-Day Pamphlets.* 'It'—the execution of his scheme—'would,' he avowed, 'have been very difficult.' 'I would have called together,' he said, 'the Boards of Guardians throughout the country.' In fact he would have instituted, on a large scale, inquiries which surely he ought to have instituted, on however small a scale, before he broached his grandiose project. What seemed to me another omission on his part was his neglect to inquire into the history of the various attempts, by no means insignificant in number, during the eighteenth century, to employ paupers reproductively, or at least to make the English work-house really a house of work. Some of these attempts, notably one in the Isle of Wight, were persevered in to a comparatively recent period. They all failed or were abandoned, and the causes which produced that disappointing consummation might have been profitably studied by Carlyle when he was advocating a scheme involving the renewal of undoubtedly unsuccessful experiments. Carlyle spent ungrudgingly any quantity of time in fixing a date, or discovering all that could be discovered respecting the places and persons, often unimportant, which and who happened to be mentioned in a letter of Oliver Cromwell's. But it surprised me much to see that he would not take the slightest pains to master the details necessary for the execution of a scheme which involved nothing less than a reconstruction of the social system of his country. He had perhaps become a little conscious of the importance of this neglect when he said the last word that I heard from him on the subject : 'I don't wish to do anything, I only wish to say my say !'

One result, though it was evanescent, of Carlyle's promulgation of his pauper-scheme claims a passing notice. It was in obedience to the impulse given by him in the *Latter-Day Pamphlets* that there was formed at Manchester a Society the object of which was to promote the reproductive employment of paupers. The originator of the movement was Archibald Stark, a clever young man who during the famine-time had visited the south of Ireland, as a newspaper correspondent, I fancy, and found in the Cork Union Workhouse, strange to say, Carlyle's notions partly realised. Stark associated to himself in his difficult enterprise another clever young man, Thomas Worthington Barlow, who had a good reputation as a diligent Cheshire and Lancashire antiquary. After great exertion Stark formed his Poor-Law Association, and succeeded in obtaining for it as Vice-Presidents a number of persons chiefly of 'position:' Carlyle was one of them. With him were conjoined the then Bishop of Ripon, and the good Dr. Hook of Leeds, afterwards Dean of Chichester. The list of vice-Presidents contained also a sprinkling of baronets and M.P.'s. None of the M.P.'s were politically important, but among them was the late Henry Thomas Hope, to whom Disraeli dedicated *Coningsby*, it having been written in the 'shades' of Deepdene, the beautiful Surrey seat which Hope inherited from his father, the author of *Anastasius*. Through Stark's energy the Association was got under weigh, and public meetings in support of it were held. When it seemed coming to something Carlyle encouraged it in a long letter, never reprinted from the newspapers in which it appeared, and much more temperate than his deliverances on pauperism in the *Latter-Day Pamphlets*. But the leading men of Manchester held aloof from the movement. It threatened to empty that reservoir of unemployed labour on which employers can draw when it suits their purpose, and in fact it tended to make labour, to a certain extent, independent of capital. In the course of time the movement died out for want of adequately active support. There had been some talk of forming a

London committee, but Carlyle, who was beginning to
occupy himself with *Frederick the Great*, did not care to
put his shoulder to the wheel. Stark migrated to London,
to become for a short time editor of the *Daily Telegraph* in
its prehistoric days (it was then owned, I think, by a Colonel
Sleigh), and at a salary less, I suppose, than a thirtieth of
that received by the present editor. Afterwards he went
to Calcutta to engage in Anglo-Indian Journalism, and,
since then, I have heard nothing of him. Barlow obtained
a legal appointment on the West Coast of Africa, and,
before long, died in due course at Sierra Leone. Thus it
is that 'Society' rewards those who aspire to benefit it,
without appealing to the passions and prejudices of parties,
sects, and classes. The seed, however, sown by Carlyle
has not been altogether unproductive. Here and there in
England there are now more human and profitable methods
of employing paupers than the stone-breaking and oakum-
picking of the days of yore. General Booth's *In Darkest
England* contains, in support of its thesis, several quotations
from Carlyle on the organisation of labour, and the results
of the General's scheme appear to have proved that private
enterprise is inadequate for the success of what he undertook. It remains to be seen whether Carlyle's idea will
be partly realised in those Municipal Workshops—the
establishment of which is now being fitfully demanded.

When the *Latter-Day Pamphlets* were finished Carlyle
spoke of them as a kind of 'drain' carrying off the peccant
humours which had accumulated in him. But this was
only a temporary deliverance from them. Disheartened
by the death of Sir Robert Peel, and by the reception of
his scheme for the organisation of labour, above all with
nothing to do, he soon relapsed into a mournful mood.

One day at that time I was chatting with Mrs. Carlyle while he sat by himself, grumbling occasionally and looking very gloomy. Mrs. Carlyle, seeing how the land lay, suddenly turned round and said to him, 'You ought to write a book.' 'I can't write as I used to do' was Carlyle's sorrowful reply. How strangely he had under-estimated the opulence of literary power that remained in him was proved by what followed,—whether as the result of Mrs. Carlyle's suggestion, I cannot say. Before many months were over there was written and published his *Life of John Sterling*, which both in matter and manner is perhaps the most agreeable, though, of course, far from being the greatest, of all his books. It was the first of them, moreover, in which there was anything about himself as he lived, moved, and had his being in the London of the middle of the nineteenth century. Previously he had been to the majority of his readers and admirers a mysterious voice vaguely understood to be issuing from somewhere in Chelsea. His *Life of Sterling* showed him a living, breathing, flesh-and-blood man, consorting freely and socially with his fellows, among them the distinguished members of the Sterling Club, and himself endeared by friendly guidance and advice to its gifted founder and sponsor, whose early recognition of him (*ante*, p. 76) he never forgot.

The delightful biography of Sterling is one of Carlyle's minor works, and several more important literary projects flitted before him during the years which elapsed between the issue of the last of the *Latter-Day Pamphlets* and his decision to grapple with the history of Frederick the Great. Some account of those projects—none of them came to anything—has been given by Mr. Froude, presumably deriving his knowledge of them from Carlyle's journals.

One passage in Mr. Froude's record claims attention and explanation. After reciting various non-historical themes which Carlyle thought transiently of handling, Mr. Froude says : There were, too, the Conqueror, 'Simon de Montfort,' 'the battle of Towton.' 'But what' (Mr. Froude continues), he asked himself, 'could be done with a British Museum under fat pedants?' etc., etc. It was one 'fat pedant' whose want of helpfulness and whose obstructiveness Carlyle had in his eye. This was Panizzi, then Keeper of the Printed Books in the British Museum, that is, head of its vast library, whose story has been already partly told in the chapter on the British Museum Library, as it was fifty years ago. In the same chapter the administrative organisation of that library was explained, and it was pointed out that the officer styled Principal Librarian was at the head of the whole establishment, and had nothing specifically to do with the library. As was also stated, Sir Henry Ellis, a well-known antiquary, was at the time the Principal Librarian of the Museum. With Sir Henry Ellis, Carlyle (as he told me) had once a passage of arms which did not tend to make him regard with a favourable eye the officialism of the British Museum. Carlyle, according to the usual practice, had recommended to Sir Henry Ellis some friend or acquaintance as a proper person to receive the ticket required for admission to the reading-room of the Museum Library. Sir Henry replied, somewhat superciliously, that he did not know who 'Mr. Thomas Carlyle' was. 'Mr. Thomas Carlyle' rejoined, in a tone easily imaginable, that Sir Henry Ellis had better acquire forthwith the knowledge in which he avowed himself deficient. The suggestion appears to have been acted on, and the ticket to have been procured. This was a passage-at-arms pretty quickly over, but the antagonism between Carlyle and Panizzi lasted during their joint lives. As has been seen, Carlyle allowed it, according to Mr. Froude, to prevent him from writing a book of English history which might have been more interesting to his countrymen than his biography of the Prussian Frederick, perhaps the most marvellous, but certainly not the most attractive, of his works. The long-continued antagonism between Carlyle and Panizzi, which had a negative result so important, was a mystery to those of their contemporaries who took any interest in it. An explanation of its origin may not be out of place.

Years after Carlyle dubbed Panizzi a fat pedant, the highest office in the Museum, the so-called Principal Librarianship, fell vacant. Two names were submitted to the Queen from which to select one for the post, those of Panizzi and the accomplished Anglo-Saxon scholar, John Mitchell Kemble (*ante*, p. 106). Lord Palmerston was Prime Minister, and, through his correspondence with Cavour and other Italian statesmen, Panizzi had been serviceable to him and Lord Clarendon. Doubtless, it was at the instance of Lord Palmerston that the Queen appointed Panizzi to the most important literary office in the gift of the Crown, far more important than the Laureateship. The origin and progress of the controversy between Panizzi and Carlyle were the following :—

While Carlyle was writing his history of the French Revolution, he contributed to the *Westminster Review* an article ('Histories of the French Revolution') on the materials accessible for the composition of a book on that great theme, with some trenchant criticisms on such of his predecessors in the attempt as Thiers and Mignet. In the course of the article he mentioned the existence in Paris of a vast collection of the pamphlets, newspapers, broad-sheets, and even street placards which were issued in the French capital day by day, as the Revolution evolved itself. Then he subjoined the following note: 'It is generally known that a similar collection, perhaps still larger and more curious, lies buried in the British Museum here, inaccessible for want of a proper catalogue. Some fifteen months ago the respectable Sub-librarian seemed to be working on such a thing. By respectful application to him you could gain access to his room, and have the satisfaction of mounting on ladders and reading the outside titles of his books, which,' the satirical Carlyle added, 'was a great help.' After 'weary months of waiting' for greater help than this, Carlyle gave up dancing attendance on Panizzi as, he wrote, 'a game not worth the candle.'

Panizzi never forgave Carlyle this caustic comment on his procedure. It was offensive enough to find himself represented as in his official capacity at the head of the National Library, obstructing the progress of a great historical work. But still more offensive, in his eyes, was in all probability the designation of 'respectable Sub-librarian,' applied to the high and mighty Keeper of the Printed Books in the British Museum, a man who dined at Holland House, who was intimate with Macaulay and Brougham, with the leading Whig statesmen of the day, 'and Mr. Panizzi, etc.,' closing the lists, in the *Morning Post*, of guests at numbers of aristocratic receptions in London. Panizzi resented ever afterwards that sarcastic note in the *Westminster Review*, as Carlyle found to his cost. When he came to write his *Cromwell* he would fain have consulted somewhere, in the quiet interior recesses of the Museum Library, the unique collection which it contains of pamphlets and so forth issued in London from day to day during the great English Civil War of the seventeenth century and the Protectorate which followed it (*ante*, p. 86). The 'respectable Sub-librarian' would not hear of such a concession, and Carlyle was left, with what assistance he could command, to do his best in the crowded and incommodious reading-room of those days, his sufferings in which have been already described (*ante*, p. 73). Carlyle detailed his grievance when giving evidence—very interesting and instructive, sometimes even entertaining—before the Royal Commission subsequently appointed to inquire into the affairs of the British Museum, and he mentioned as one of his reasons for wishing to escape from the reading-room into the interior of the library that he was 'thin-skinned.' Panizzi retorted in his evidence that he 'did not feel readers' skins.' Years afterwards, and deep in the composition of Frederick, Carlyle renewed his application, in a letter to Panizzi, which was for him not only calm but conciliatory. All the return which he received was a reply from the vindictive Italian so insolent that Panizzi's biographer and panegyrist refrained from printing it. The great Lady Ashburton herself was applied to exert, on behalf of Carlyle's application, her influence with Panizzi whom she knew, but the appearance on the scene of even this *Dea ex machinâ* was fruitless. Carlyle in his journal might call Panizzi a fat pedant, and in conversation 'an Italian language-master' as contemptuously as Dr. Johnson may have spoken of Mrs. Thrale's Mr. Piozzi. Clothed in a little brief authority, and having completely gained the ear of the working members of the Museum's Board of Trustees, the fat pedant and Italian language-master proved more than a match for the Scottish man of genius.

CHAPTER XIII

POLITICS, RELIGION, EDUCATION

CARLYLE'S political opinions and theories, up to a late period of his life, are pretty well known to the students of his writings. He confronted with a tyranno-mania, so to speak, what he scoffed at as the eleuthero-mania of his age, and his ideal Government was a beneficent despotism. England, he said to me, was governed by a 'miserable bureaucracy.' Parliament he regarded for some years, after the appearance of his *Cromwell*, with a detestation that was fanatical, and his favourite episode in English history was Cromwell's forcible ejection of the Long Parliament. Once, but at least in my hearing once only, when speaking of the futility of Parliament, he exclaimed 'the Protectionists might do it,' that is, send the Free Trade House of Commons about its business. This was at a time (I think) when an audacious agriculturist, a Mr. Chowler, enraged at the repeal of the Corn Laws, talked of the horses of the country being in the hands of the farmers, and threatened a march of amateur mounted yeomanry upon London, or rather upon Westminster! Once, but again only once, he spoke of going into Parliament to tell it his mind, but his wife immediately raised the formidable objection that he would have in that case to keep late hours, and he never recurred to the subject. On one occasion, when he was declaiming, in his usual style, on the wretched kind of men whom, in his opinion, we had

N

for governors, the late Professor Craik—he was making a call at Chelsea—asked who were the men that he would put in their place. 'I am one,' Carlyle replied, 'you are one, and he,' pointing to another of the persons present, 'he is one,' adding something in a tone of unforgetable bitterness about being 'crushed down here.' When he found Governments and Parliaments, in spite of his passionate appeals, going on in the old routine jog-trot, he sometimes expressed a desire for universal suffrage, and the anarchy which he thought would be its inevitable result, as in that event possibly despotism would follow. Carlyle, however, had from the first no love for that 'Saviour of Society,' Napoleon III., although he did deal summarily with a Parliament. When I spoke to Carlyle of the *coup d'état*, as a feat likely to commend itself to Cromwell's biographer, he replied that Louis Napoleon had 'done some very ugly things,' but also that amongst things not ugly which he had done was 'the putting down of newspapers.' This last sally reminded me, though I did not venture to tell him so, of his sarcastic reference to the German Tory nobleman, the Count von Zähdarm, of Professor Teufelsdröckh's famous epitaph, whose one cherished wish was 'die auszurottende Journalistik!' Not long after the *coup d'état*, Carlyle talked much of Louis Napoleon's aggressive designs, and, being myself of French extraction, I was rather indignant when he declared that France, if she did not take care, would be partitioned one of these days. Events have unhappily led to at least a partial fulfilment of his prediction.

For leading English statesmen, after the death of Sir Robert Peel, Carlyle expressed great contempt. Lord John Russell 'thought of nothing but his quarter's salary.' Lord Palmerston was 'the ugliest man he had ever seen.'

Disraeli's *Coningsby* Carlyle had saluted with the cry:
'Ou' Clo,' and the last chapters of Tancred convinced him,
he said, that its author was a thorough quack. But Carlyle's
judgments on public men, and indeed on other men, were
liable to revision when he became personally acquainted
with them. After he had seen Lord John Russell at Lord
Ashburton's, I myself heard Carlyle speak of him in quite
an altered tone, as 'having something of the old English
gentleman about him,' and the late Mr. Venables, who
moved in the Ashburton circle, saw Carlyle, at Bath
House, chatting gaily with Lord Palmerston himself, and
judged from their laughter that the two were on the best
of terms. Soon after the repeal of the Corn Laws, Carlyle
said to me of Mr. Gladstone, 'he has no convictions, but
he is a long-headed fellow.' When there was a vacancy
through death, in the Librarianship of the London Library,
Mr. Gladstone called on Carlyle (so I understood him to
say) in order to urge the claims, real or supposed, which
some one of his Italian or Hellenic protégés had, he opined,
to the post. Carlyle told me that he spoke to him very
plainly on the inadmissibility of the proposal. The post,
Carlyle said, ought to be given to an Englishman, and
given to an Englishman it was. Mr. Venables has also
recorded that when, with great difficulty, Carlyle was
induced to meet Disraeli at dinner, and the two had some
conversation, the man of letters at parting said, that, if he
had met the statesman earlier, his opinion of his fellow-
guest would have been different. But such personal intercourse as he had with Mr. Gladstone never induced Carlyle
to abate his dislike for Disraeli's rival, and for that rival's
general policy.

A man at once so meditative, and so ready to unbosom

himself as Carlyle was, could not fail to speak of religion and of the great problems involved in it, though these were not topics to which he cared often to advert, or long to dwell on. His rejection of the popular theology is well known, and he used to say that he never felt spiritually at ease until he left the Church and the Churches behind him, and went out into the 'bare desert' where was a temple not made with hands. At the same time, and in spite of all the harsh things that he wrote concerning the creed of orthodoxy, he recognised its hold on human nature, and said to me once, 'it will be a long time before they give it up.' He was fond of repeating the alleged reply of Confucius to some anxious Chinese inquirer, 'You ask me what death is, I know not what life is; you ask me what heaven is, I know not what earth is,' and so on. I was foolish enough, early in my acquaintance with Carlyle, to inflict on him a vague notion of mine that a man's fate in the other world might depend on the state in which he was when he arrived in it from this world. It is a rude and crude form of a notion of this kind, I have been told, which leads a modern Chinaman to die for another at the hands of the executioner in return for a few dollars to be paid to his widow or other heirs. Just before execution, having been dressed in fine garments and fed sumptuously, he goes cheerfully to death believing that he will find himself in the other world as comfortable as when he left this. Carlyle gave me and my theory of a future life no encouragement, silencing me at once with the concise and emphatic rejoinder, 'We know nothing about it!' Keen as was his moral sense and rigorous, I do believe, his practice of self-examination, 'I never troubled myself,' he told me, 'about my faults, it was only not struggling enough.'. As to Hell, 'every man,' he said to me, 'must feel that he is a damned scoundrel,' and therefore deserves it. Quoting a gibe of Leigh Hunt's at the Glasgow people, as 'so stingy that they would not subscribe to put down hell,' Carlyle opined that it would scarcely be desirable to have that operation completely performed. A young relative of mine, belonging to the softer sex, was sitting by us when Carlyle delivered this opinion, but, being a little deaf, she did not catch what he said. I turned to her and said, 'F., do you think we could get on without hell?' 'Hell?' she repeated with a shudder. 'Ah!' said Carlyle encouragingly, 'she hasn't turned that over in her mind yet!' Carlyle desired the retention of hell, of course, because it might be a terror to evil-doers. But I fancied I caught an echo from the faith of his young years when I heard him once repeat, with seeming awe, one of Oliver Cromwell's exclamations on his death-bed, the verse of Scripture: 'It is a fearful thing to fall into the hands of the living God.' In a serener mood Carlyle asked, 'What are we?' and replied to his own question, 'A thought shot down from yon blue sky,' which is, I opine, a saying of Emerson's. Then again, speaking of the darkness in which the destiny of man is shrouded, he said, 'It would never do for us to know the plan of the campaign.' 'Walking itself,' he has written somewhere, 'is a series of falls,' and I heard him say, in the same spirit and jubilantly trustful, 'Defeat is victory.' In a strain, rather unusual for him, he talked to me, but only once, of the ultimate supremacy of the beautiful which, he has also written somewhere, 'is higher than the good.' He illustrated his meaning by saying that, in describing their celestial visions, the mediæval saints dwelt chiefly on the beauty and splendour of the heaven thus revealed to them. .

In time, he prophesied, beauty would be all-in-all. (I can give the thought, but not the words, in which he clothed it. 'For the few?' I said interrogatively. 'No!' he replied, 'for the many.' Popery and the Papacy Carlyle held in an abhorrence, already recorded and familiar to all readers of his writings. He thought that the misfortunes of the Irish were in great part clearly traceable to their rejection of the Reformation. The Irish peasant, he said, if left to commune with his own soul, would feel that murder was a damnable crime, but he knows that the priest will give him absolution for it, and so he thinks little of it. Yet Carlyle felt compelled to add the qualifying admission (Young Ireland was in prison at the time) that the Irish priests alone stood up persistently for the Irish people. When I referred to a revival of the old scheme for a State endowment of the Irish Roman Catholic clergy he replied, that if it were to be done at all, 'it would have to be done by statesmen of a much higher morality than any we have at present,' a deliverance somewhat enigmatic, but in which reflection may discover considerable meaning.

For the Church of England as an institution, and apart from its theology, Carlyle had a certain toleration, but, when Lord John Russell created a see of Manchester, Carlyle thought the phenomenon so incongruous that he applied to the first Bishop of the new diocese, officially not personally, epithets which will not bear reproduction. For English dissent he expressed contempt, and great as was his appreciation of the old Puritan faith, he spoke of the 'rubbishing Puritanism' of the present as a thing to be attacked and destroyed wherever found. Unitarianism he regarded as a hollow compromise, though he admitted that many clever and worthy people were Unitarians. 'There,' he said to me once, 'are two young men,' naming the late William Maccall and another common friend, still living, 'who took up with it,' Unitarianism, 'and are now completely stranded.' With the Broad Church movement, among the promoters of which were such personal friends as Frederick Denison Maurice and Charles Kingsley, he had only a moderate sympathy. The utmost he would predict of their efforts—and that in a half-contemptuous tone—was: 'They will get up something' as a substitute for the Thirty-Nine Articles and all the rest of it. The Founder of Christianity he called 'a beautiful moral phenomenon,' and the Jewish history, as told in the Old and New Testaments, 'a grand symbol, if one could take up with it.' But Carlyle, as his wife once said to me, was 'not one man, but many men;' and many accordingly were his moods, his expressed opinions often varying with them. There came a time when he thought of writing a book or pamphlet proclaiming the necessity for an 'Exodus from Houndsditch,' and wrote to Emerson that he was almost disposed to echo the exclamation attributed, perhaps wrongly, to the dying Voltaire, '*Ne me parlez plus de cet homme-là!*' This was his frame of mind when I was the sole listener to a dialogue between him and Professor Blackie who was paying him a visit at Chelsea. The conversation turned at one time on Goethe, in whom the Professor, otherwise a profound admirer of the great German, said that he discovered a lack of sympathy with earnest men, Luther for instance. To this Carlyle gave the rather striking reply that it could not well have been otherwise, since Luther was 'a savage'! and Goethe anything but that. The conversation, having taken this turn, continued on our adjournment—it was a fine summer or autumn evening—to the little flagged space between the house and the back garden, where, when the temperature and the elements favoured the occupation, Carlyle was wont to smoke a pipe, or several pipes. Professor Blackie happening to say something eulogistic of John Wesley, Carlyle burst forth with a 'd——n Wesley for bringing in a——;' but, no! the conclusion of the sentence is unprintable. Seeing something like astonishment painted on the Professor's face—the youngest of the party was too much accustomed to Carlyle's strong sayings to be surprised at anything that fell from him—Carlyle graciously added, 'Well, I withdraw the d——n!' Of Professor Blackie he said afterwards that there was 'something of the old scholar about him.'

'Universal Education and general emigration' were, when Carlyle wrote 'Chartism,' two remedies which he proposed to apply as at least partial cures for what was diseased in the body-politic. While he was enthusiastic about emigration he told Earl Grey, then Secretary of State for the Colonies (who 'blushed,' he said, on being introduced to him) that he would do in a single year all that needed to be done for emigration, though officialism pronounced it impossible of performance in any number of years. But he cooled very considerably on emigration when and after he framed his scheme for the reproductive employment of pauperism. He was far more faithful to the cause of education than to that of emigration, though I heard him once at least speak doubtfully of the value of an extension of education if it enabled the multitude to indulge more freely than before in the products of what he wittily called 'Eliza Cookery.' Eliza Cook was a popular poetess and editress of the day who conducted a cheap periodical in which 'social progress' was advocated in the most sentimental, sugary, and flowery style. But this depreciation of education was only a transient ebullition. When the Lancashire Public School Association was formed, with the object of establishing throughout that county undenominational schools which were to be supported by local rates, and locally administered,—an anticipation, in fact, of the Board Schools created by William Edward Forster's Act of 1870,—Carlyle wrote a letter of earnest encouragement to the promoters of the scheme. 'No man,' he said in it, 'no generation of men, has a right to pass through this world, and leave his children in a state of ignorance which could have been avoided ; and if many generations among us English have already too much done so, it is a sadder case for England now, and the more pressing is the call for this generation of Englishmen. In all times and places it is man's solemn duty whether done or not, and, if in any time or place, I should say it was in Lancashire, in England, in these years that are now passing over us.' Soon after this letter was despatched I became Secretary of the Association, and was domiciled for a second time in Manchester, its head-quarters. More of my Secretaryship hereafter,—now be said only enough, in connection with it, to explain what follows. After a struggle against great opposition the Association promised to come to something. Accordingly there was to be held in the Free Trade Hall, which once resounded with the oratory of the Anti-Corn-Law League, a 'great' public meeting, or 'demonstration' to further the Association's object. Invitations to attend the meeting and to address it were issued to men of eminence and note, supposed to approve generally of the programme of the Association. Among those so invited was Carlyle.

He was evidently not disinclined to come, when he wrote to me asking what I thought of the matter. Probably, from over-fastidiousness on his account, I did not think that his appearance on such a stage with such a company of performers as had been secured would be desirable for him. On the other hand, it would have been a clear dereliction of duty on my part to advise him not to come. So I carried out his favourite doctrine of silence : never did man less practise what he preached than Carlyle in this matter of speech and silence. I left his letter unanswered. Whether *propter hoc* he never hinted, nor is it for me to surmise, but certainly *post hoc*, he wrote to decline attendance at our meeting, saying that his speculations as to the visit had been 'cut short by a cold.' I refer to the matter because, so far as I know, this was the only occasion on which Carlyle ever hinted at an intention of addressing a 'great' public meeting on an important public question. The programme and proceedings of the Association revived his interest in the education of the people. When my Secretaryship terminated, and I returned to London, I heard him descant on the scheme of education finely and symbolically unfolded in *Wilhelm Meister's Wanderjahre.* He went the length of announcing his intention, but he never carried it out, of having reprinted, in a separate form, the pages devoted by Goethe to that scheme in his otherwise disappointing book, and of scattering them broadcast. People, Carlyle complained, neglected Goethe on education, and 'ran after Jamie Simpson.' It appeared to me singular that Carlyle, and in such a connection, too, could remember what everybody else had forgotten. 'Jamie Simpson' was an Edinburgh advocate of very ordinary intelligence, but he had somehow been

seized by an enthusiasm for the cause of National Education. Many years before Carlyle made this reference to
him, 'Jamie' had appeared in London and delivered on
his favourite theme some lectures or addresses, which,
probably owing to influence exerted on his behalf by
Brougham and other leading friends of popular education,
appear to have been well attended. He and his lectures
had been forgotten by everybody except Carlyle, whose
indignation was doubtless aroused at the time by the
hearing vouchsafed to Simpson, and he still spoke of it
with that old indignation. If 'Jamie' be not consigned to
utter oblivion, he will owe his escape to an Edinburgh
incident in his biography, not to his London lectures on
National Education. He was one of the vainest of men.
In my younger days, it was still remembered in Edinburgh
that Sir Walter Scott and he entering the boxes of the
theatre there simultaneously, and the audience cheering
heartily, 'Jamie' advanced to the front of his box, and,
fancying that the applause was meant for him, duly and
gratefully bowed his acknowledgments!

CHAPTER XIV

AUTOBIOGRAPHICAL

THE opulent originality, vigour, and picturesqueness of Carlyle's talk astonished all who heard it. What he said might be wise, or only half-wise, or, as sometimes happened, wholly unwise, but it was always striking, never commonplace. It is true that both as a host and as a guest he was too fond of engrossing the conversation, that with him dialogue too often became monologue, that his prophet-like denunciations of the present, in season and out of season, were occasionally wearisome in their monotonous vehemence and iteration and reiteration long-drawn-out. But it was not always thus with him. In the society of two or three friends, if he could not help being emphatic, he could be calm and reasonable, take as well as give, and listen patiently to the expression of opinions opposite to his own. It was in such a gathering that he was most satisfactory, if not most astonishing. There was, moreover, one gift, that of oral narration, which he possessed in a more remarkable degree than any man of his generation, and his exhibition of it was always acceptable, combining as it did epic detail with lyrical emotion. I have heard of a distinguished company at a dinner-party suspending, at an early stage of the meal, the process of deglutition, to listen with rapt attention while Carlyle, starting from some chance remark by a fellow-guest, gave a vivid account of John Sobieski's defence of

Vienna against the Turk. Never surely was there an eminent man of letters—not Macaulay himself, for even he had his brilliant flashes of silence—to whom, as to this Apostle of Silence, it seemed in so great a degree a necessity of his nature to be always either speaking or writing. If Carlyle read, it was pencil in hand, to indite comments, grave or gay, and often pregnant, on the margin of the book. The volumes which he borrowed from the London Library might alone furnish a diligent and admiring student and collector with a mass of interesting marginalia. After a day spent in writing or in talking, in either or in both, he would often, before going to bed, seize his pen and soliloquize in his Journal. If you came upon him, when he was taking his walks abroad, you saw his lips moving, and knew that he was muttering to himself. Sometimes at home, when he thought the company dull or unsympathetic, he would, rather than be silent, recite, in impressive monotone, a favourite passage of an English poet, notably Milton's touching and noble lines on his blindness in the third book of ' Paradise Lost.' Once at the beginning of his acquaintance with me, when he had exhausted the monitions which he thought suited to my youthful mind, he entertained and instructed me with an account of the evolution of the Arabic numerals 2, 3, etc., up to 9, by the addition of strokes and curves to the perpendicular straight line which denotes the primitive numeral 1. Mrs. Carlyle did not, like her husband, write books, but in her own way she was, to use a favourite expression of his, as ' articulate' as her husband. She was too bright and clever a talker not to enjoy practising her gift. Naturally she shone more in conversation when her husband was absent than when he was present. Sometimes, when the company in the little house at Chelsea was miscellaneous, the claims of the hostess to be heard conflicted with those of the host, and there was between her and one or other of their guests a cross-fire of conversation which sadly irritated Carlyle. It was better, at least if they were at home, when they talked successively rather than simultaneously, but her husband did not always allow her that alternative. She once repeated to me, with quiet glee, a remark dropped by Samuel Rogers at one of his breakfast-parties at which Carlyle and she were among the guests. When Carlyle's thunder had been followed by his wife's sparkle, their sardonic host said in a half-soliloquy which was intended to be audible : ' As soon as that man's tongue stops, that woman's begins ! ' Finally, be it noted, that though Carlyle's accent was the broadest Dumfriesshire, he always, like David Hume, whose accent was the broadest Berwickshire, spoke perfectly pure, if often colloquial English, never Scotch, unless he was quoting what had been said by others in that expressive dialect. The ' I dinna's,' ' I canna's,' and so forth, sometimes put into his mouth, are due to the forgetfulness or the inventiveness of the reporters, real or pretended.

Carlyle showed no reluctance to talk about himself. Indeed his conversation abounded with little autobiographical episodes and reminiscences. He was specially fond of reverting to odd persons whom he had known, and to phrases current, in his native Dumfriesshire which had been more or less his home until he was in his fortieth year, for it was at that comparatively late age that he quitted Scotland to settle in London. Of his father he often cited traits, some of them absent from the fine monograph on ' James Carlyle ' in the *Reminiscences*.

Speaking of his own boyhood, 'when my father frowned the universe was darkened for me,' I have heard him say ; but also that the same stern father 'behaved to me with princely generosity when I decided on giving up the Church.' His mother he pronounced, in his own exaggerative way, 'the last of the Christians.' Of his brothers something has been already said. He spoke contemptuously of the teaching of his *alma mater*, Edinburgh University. Leslie was the only one of his professors for whom he retained a regard. He was a favourite pupil of Leslie's, and while Carlyle was an Edinburgh student, dependent on the small allowance which was all that his father could afford, Leslie aided him outside the college-walls by recommending him successfully as a private teacher of mathematics to 'an old gentleman in Prince's Street,' among others. Science, to which he was devoted in his youth, in later years he called 'cold.' He was given to quizzing the worthy Professor of Natural History of his student time, who, 'after quoting Dante and other odd fellows,' would say, by an abrupt transition, 'And now, gentlemen, we will proceed with the order *Glires*.' But he spoke with something faintly resembling enthusiasm of the effect produced on him by certain extra-mural lectures on chemistry which he attended, and of chemistry itself—though he does not appear to have prosecuted a study of it—as the most brilliant and fascinating of the physical sciences. The happiest time of his earlier years was, he told me, when, the labours of the day being over, evening after evening, in his solitary lodging, he worked his way through the *Principia* as edited by some Jesuits. This was, doubtless, the redaction of Newton's great book, the Jesuit editors of which, I have read somewhere, were

induced, by a fear of their superiors, to contradict in
hypocritical notes, otherwise valuable, those scientific truths
embodied in the text which were banned as heretical by
the heads of their Church and their order. If so, thus
early did Carlyle, by personal experience, come to know
something of both the good and the bad done in the world
by the followers of Loyola. At one time when Carlyle
thought, though not for long, of going to the Scottish bar,
he attended the Scots-law class of Baron Hume (as he
afterwards became), the great David's nephew. Much in
this Professor's prelections repelled Carlyle from the study
of law, and his disgust was completed, he said, when one of
them included an elaborate disquisition on the number of
taps which the Scottish analogue of the English bailiff had
to administer to the door before he could legally enter a
debtor's domicile as the representative of the Scottish
Themis ! 'On the whole,' to use one of Carlyle's very
favourite phrases, the chief result, according to his own
account, of the years which he spent at the University of
Edinburgh, was to throw him into an attitude of defiant
protest against its teachers and their teaching. Yet in old
age, after the Edinburgh students had elected him their
Lord Rector, Carlyle's heart softened towards his *alma
mater*, and he bequeathed to it the rents of the little
Dumfriesshire estate, which on his wife's death came to him
through her, and while residing on which he had written
Sartor Resartus.

On his literary career, earlier and later, Carlyle was far
from uncommunicative. When he thought of embracing
it, after resolving to become neither a minister of the Kirk
nor an Edinburgh advocate, he read, he told me, some
fifty volumes of the *Edinburgh Review*, little fancying, I

daresay, that he was to become one of its most illustrious contributors. Of anonymous reviewing, when he had ceased to be in any way dependent on it, he spoke disparagingly, the most that he would admit of it being that 'You get a sort of reputation at last.' He complained of Jeffrey's interpolations of his *Edinburgh Review* articles, such as 'It is but fair to say,' and other qualifying phrases, thrust in by the adroit editor, when, I suppose, Carlyle had been saying something too severe or trenchant about somebody. The dealings with him of editors in general he compared, in my hearing, to a practice prevalent among the poor people in certain parts of his beloved Dumfriesshire. In the hope of bestowing a little flavour on the miserably thin and insipid pottage, which was all that their poverty allowed them, they were glad to insert in it, each family in turn, a ham-bone—I forget the quaint Scotch name given it in this connection—which was sent round from cottage to cottage from I know what duly-appointed custodian. Carlyle said, with a touch of vanity rare in him, that a contribution from him was to British editors and their dull periodicals what that ham-bone was to the Dumfriesshire cottagers and their tasteless pottage!

His performance of one of his earliest literary tasks, the *Specimens of German Romance*, he described to me as a very pleasant occupation for him, an unusual admission, though, it is true, his work was one of translation mainly, not except in fractions, that of original composition, which was always painful to him. 'Those were among my happiest hours,' he said, 'spent in the company of poetic, genial men.' Of *Sartor Resartus* he said that it had been like a stone thrown into a sheet of water; he saw the circle produced by it widening every day. Of his *French*

Revolution he said, besides what I have already recorded, and conscious, doubtless, of the startling originality of the style, that it was a case of 'hit or miss.' Of his lectures generally, he said that the attention of his hearers was keenest when he touched on the career and personal character of the man of whom he happened to be speaking, and flagged when he went off into disquisition or literary criticism. His modest description of what he thought to be the impression produced by him on his audiences was, that he was 'a wild man, but with a certain Scotch coherency in him.' The Lectures on Heroes were the only series published during his lifetime. He delivered them, as usual, extempore, or with the aid only of a few notes ; but, when they were to be published, he wrote them off with the utmost rapidity. Mrs. Carlyle told me that his lecturing was first suggested by Miss Martineau, who, having as a frequent visitor listened to his marvellous talk, thought that it deserved a wider circle of hearers, and 'you know,' Mrs. Carlyle added with pathetic simplicity, 'something had to be done if we were to keep body and soul together.' The pain of gestation, when he was delivering a course of lectures, and his denunciations of lecturing as a trade, he has recorded vividly in his letters and journals. Yet when I told him that Leigh Hunt, according to report, had been invited by some persons of distinction to set up a sort of pulpit, and preach from it on Sundays his gospel of cheerful optimism, Carlyle replied, I fancied almost in a regretful tone, 'Ah! I could have cultivated myself into *that* very well.' To what has been said of his *Cromwell* I have nothing to add, and of the *Latter-Day Pamphlets* very little. Mr. Froude's remarks concerning them have produced an erroneous impression, that not only did their tone and tenor provoke the hostility of the critics, but that a falling off in their circulation led Carlyle to issue only eight of them instead of the twelve which he had planned at the outset. On the contrary, when soon after the appearance of the last of them I dined with Carlyle, having Mr. David (now Professor) Masson for my fellow-guest, our host told us that the sale of the *Latter-Day Pamphlets* had been very brisk, and that his publisher wished him to issue more of them. It was, I fancy, the death of Sir Robert Peel (*ante*, p. 182), that led him to discontinue them.

From his remark previously reported, on the view which, he thought, editors of periodicals took of his contributions, it will have been seen that Carlyle did not affect to be ignorant of at least the relative value of what he wrote. I have also heard him say that he had endeavoured to make his literature somewhat different from 'the ordinary school-boy scrawl.' But he spoke modestly of the absolute value of his writings. At a time when it was often complained that the high price at which his works were published prevented book-buyers of moderate means from purchasing them, I asked him if he did not attach importance to the issue of cheap popular editions of them. His only reply was that he regarded his books as 'contemptible performances compared with the idea which inspired them.'

CHAPTER XV

CARLYLE'S LITERARY TABLE-TALK

CARLYLE'S estimates of the British men of letters who were his contemporaries did not, it is well known, err on the side of over-appreciation. Some of the most famous or popular of them were poets and novelists, and against metre and fiction he waged perpetual war, although Goethe had been a poet, dramatist, and novelist, Schiller a poet and dramatist much more than a historian, and Jean Paul, from first to last a writer of fiction chiefly. Mainly, perhaps, this aversion from poetry and fiction was due not merely to Carlyle's love of reality, but to his own comparative failure in both. However this may have been, he was ever admonishing poets to write in prose, and novelists to write history or biography, as if there were not an infinite charm in the music of true verse as in the song of birds and the voices of the ocean, as if innumerable things worth saying could not be said better in verse than in prose, as if one of the greatest intellectual pleasures of life would not be lost if there were to be no novels, but only histories and biographies. So far did Carlyle carry his preference of prose to metre that I found him one day grumbling terribly because the pleasure which he had expected to derive from an English translation of some Indian drama, by 'a man of strong Hindoo genius,' had been spoilt through the rendering being in verse and not in prose.

Wordsworth as a poet, whatever may have been his opinion of him otherwise, Carlyle did not estimate very highly. 'Put Æschylus among those hills,' he exclaimed, 'and he will say something worth listening to!' I thought, though it was merely a surmise of mine, and not founded on anything ever said or hinted at by Carlyle, that, in his general depreciation of Wordsworth, he was a little influenced by one of the poet's sonnets [1] evidently directed against himself and his *French Revolution*,—for, great as was Carlyle's intellectual integrity, his estimates of his contemporaries, literary and unliterary, were often in a perceptible degree coloured by personal feeling. But certainly no adverse feeling of that kind influenced him if he did not form an adequate estimate of the value of Tennyson's exquisite verse. For Tennyson, the man, Carlyle had a considerable affection, though he liked him as a companion chiefly because, he told me, he found 'Alfred'—thus he always spoke of him—'an intelligent listener.' Of course he recognised Tennyson's poetic genius, but he thought it largely wasted on that which profiteth not. Of the lovely 'Princess,'

---

[1] 'In Allusion to various Recent Histories and Notices of the French Revolution.'

> 'Portentous change ! when History can appear
> As the cool Advocate of foul device ;
> Reckless audacity extol, and jeer
> At consciences perplexed with scruples nice.
> They who bewail not, must abhor, the sneer
> Born of Conceit, Power's blind Idolater ;
> Or haply sprung from vaunting Cowardice,
> Betrayed by mockery of holy fear.
> Hath it not long been said the wrath of Man
> Works not the righteousness of God ?   Oh bend,
> Bend, ye Perverse ! to judgments from on High,
> Laws that lay under Heaven's perpetual ban
> All principles of action that transcend
> The sacred limits of humanity.'

Carlyle said curtly, at its first appearance, that it 'had everything but common-sense.' I found him one forenoon deep in the *Acta Sanctorum*, and full of the story of the dealings of an early Christian missionary with some Scandinavian and heathen potentate. 'Alfred,' he declared, 'would be much better employed in making such an episode interesting and beautiful than in cobbling his odes,' the occupation in which, when visiting him some time before, Carlyle had found him engaged, and with the futility of which he had then and there reproached him. I asked Carlyle if the late Laureate did not 'stand up' for his literary procedure. 'No! he lay down for it,' Carlyle replied, doubtless with a reference to 'Alfred's' careless, indolent ways. At that time Tennyson was not so averse, as he became in later years, from being looked at, and positively enjoyed, Carlyle averred, the abundant lionising bestowed on him during his occasional visits to London. Mrs. Barrett Browning, the poetess, did not take as quietly as Tennyson the protest against verse-making and the advice to betake herself to prose, received by her in a letter from Carlyle, to whom she had sent some of her poems. She wrote him so touching a rejoinder that 'I had,' Carlyle confessed, 'to draw in my horns.'

Of the novel, as a kind of attempt to delineate the real, or the possible, and at least written in prose, Carlyle, though the translator of the two *Meisters* and of the *Specimens of German Romance*, was but slightly more tolerant than of the poem. 'On the whole,' to write a novel was, with him, 'to screw one's-self up one's big toe;' but he owned that there were some very clever men among the novelists, and that if he 'were to be hanged' he could not imitate their successes. Always since,

in *Sartor Resartus*, he had derided the dandiacal Pelham,
he spoke with contempt of its author, who was one of
his friend John Forster's most be-worshipped idols.   For
Carlyle the first Lord Lytton was 'a poor fribble,' and
Mrs. Carlyle, who had espoused the cause of the novelist's
wife, and championed her grievances, was still more plain-
spoken, calling him 'a lanthorn-jawed quack!'   She told
me that Carlyle had refused I know not how many invitations to dine with him.   For Charles Dickens Carlyle had
a personal liking, and thought it worth while to report to
me that he had seen him give a 'little bob,' when introduced to Lord Holland, of a kind intended to mean that he
did not much plume himself on making his Lordship's acquaintance.   Of Dickens he often said that he was the only
man of his time in whose writings genuine cheerfulness
was to be found.   Of Thackeray's earlier performances
Carlyle said that they showed 'something Hogarthian'
to be in him, but that his books were 'wretched.'   Of
course this was before the appearance of *Vanity Fair*,
the immense talent displayed in which Carlyle fully recognised, pronouncing Thackeray 'a man of much more judgment than Dickens.'   Yet, when *Vanity Fair* in its yellow
cover was being issued contemporaneously with *Dombey and
Son* in its green ditto, Carlyle spoke of the relief which he
found on turning from Thackeray's terrible cynicism to
the cheerful geniality of Dickens.   The highest praise
bestowed by him on Thackeray's lectures was that they
were 'ingenious.'   Personally Carlyle preferred Dickens,
who always treated him with deference, to Thackeray, who
often opposed to his inopportune denunciations of men
and things at miscellaneous dinner-parties some of that
persiflage which was more disconcerting to Carlyle than

direct contradiction. It was a startling parallel between two surely most dissimilar men which was drawn by Carlyle, when he once said to me, 'Thackeray is like Wilson of Edinburgh' (Christopher North), 'he has no convictions.' Possibly this was said after Carlyle had been more than usually irritated by Thackeray's persiflage. *Alton Locke* Carlyle had read, and evidently appreciated, but he spoke of it with reserve, probably from the references in it to himself and his teaching. He bestowed some slight praise on Mrs. Gaskell for having in her first novel, *Mary Barton*, discovered romance in the prosaic life of cotton-spinning Manchester. Anthony Trollope's novels he compared to 'alum,' and Jane Austen's, so bepraised by Macaulay, he summarily dismissed as mere 'dish-washings!'

For his brother historians Carlyle had scant reverence. With him Hallam was only a 'Dryasdust,' and he laughed heartily, I remember, at some critic—Philarète Chasles, I think—who, in the *Revue des Deux Mondes*, reproached him with having spoken of '*le respectable* Hallam' as '*sec comme poussière*!' With Macaulay, as a Whig of the Whigs and zealous champion of *laissez-faire*, he had prandial and post-prandial battles, and Carlyle harboured a dislike for him which seemed to me to have something personal in it. Once, when I ventured to praise Macaulay's history, Carlyle turned on me rather fiercely, averring that Macaulay had never said anything that was 'not entirely commonplace;' but, he had the grace to add 'he is a very brilliant fellow. Flow on, thou shining river!' Carlyle might have remembered that while he was, according to his own confession (as will appear presently), increasing the general intellectual confusion by translating *Wilhelm Meister* and proclaiming the transcendent importance of German literature, Macaulay, in his fine essay on Milton, was rehabilitating those Puritans, to have cleared the memory of the greatest of whom, Oliver Cromwell, did not become, until twenty years or so later, the chief glory of Carlyle's career of authorship.   Further, it is very probable that Carlyle was first attracted to Frederick the Great, as the subject for a book, by Macaulay's brilliant essay in the *Edinburgh Review*, in which he 'left half told the story' of that singular hero, promising to finish it some time or other.   He did not keep the promise, for to keep it was conditional on the completion of the compilation on Frederick the Great and his times, which was ushered into the world by the poet Campbell as its editor,—he died two years afterwards,—and the book, which came down only to the commencement of the Seven Years' War, was left a fragment.   The impetus thus given to Carlyle in his choice of Frederick as a subject was doubtless increased by the appearance of Ranke's elaborate, but inadequate, *Neun Bücher Preussischer Geschichte* (1847-48). Carlyle pronounced it to me a 'complete failure,' and made respecting its author a curiously characteristic remark. He had seen and conversed with Ranke, who was in London at the time, working among the manuscripts of the British Museum and the Record Office.   As is well known Carlyle was one of the most vigilant and keen-sighted of physiognomists, delighting to discover a connection between a man's intellect and character, on the one hand, and his facial or even his bodily aspects and peculiarities on the other.   It happened, at least this was Carlyle's statement to me, that something either congenital, or the result of external injury, was so much the matter with an upper section of Ranke's dorsal region that he had to link

the peccant parts together with an iron hook.   Carlyle
accordingly called him a 'broken-backed man,' and discovered analogies between Ranke's book and that physical
calamity !   Carlyle's oral criticism on the earliest volumes
of Mr. Froude's History was brief and abrupt : 'Meritorious, but too much raw material.'   On the publication of
John Stuart Mill's *Elements of Political Economy*, he sent
a presentation-copy of it to Carlyle, his intimacy with
whom, though there was no actual breach between them,
had ceased for some years.   Contemptuous though he was
of the 'dismal science,' Carlyle called Mill's a 'very clever
book,' while comparing its complex treatment of his subject to the operation of 'extracting the cube root in Roman
numerals.'   'It could be done, but was not worth doing,' a
rather striking Carlylian comment; whether it was a just
one is another matter.   Carlyle, in those days at least, always
spoke of Mill with a certain regard, his expression of which
seemed to indicate a regret that their active friendship had
come to an end.   His chief criticism on Mill as a companion was that he insisted on 'having everything demon-
strated.'   Mill might have replied that demonstration was
sometimes more trustworthy and practically useful than
Carlyle's favourite intuition, which experience proved to
be by no means an infallible guide either to himself or
to others.   Mill, he said, used at one time to come to him
every Sunday for a walk.   On one point, he added, they
were agreed.   It was that if the Bible could be buried for
a generation and then dug up again, it would in that case
be rightly enjoyed.   Of another friend, also a John, whose
intimacy with the Carlyles ceased only at his death, John
Sterling, Carlyle said that he was 'a beautiful figure in
our literature,' but that 'he has never done anything,'

meaning that he had never in fact written a substantial book. This reminds me of the story of the prolific, popular, and prosperous Scotch novelist, whose sketches of Scottish life and scenery having attracted Carlyle's notice he was invited to Chelsea. There, instead of being praised, as might under the circumstances be expected, for what he had done, the only encouragement he received from Carlyle was to have the question rather gruffly put to him, 'But when are you going to do something?' novels counting for nothing in the Sage's estimation at that late period of life. I asked Carlyle if Sterling was not ambitious, and received the frank reply, 'he had his ambition as we all have,' Carlyle adding, 'Sterling liked to be in the van, like Forster of Rawdon,' the William Edward in later years well known to fame. This was another of Carlyle's odd parallels, since John Sterling's 'van' was altogether different from Forster's. On the same occasion Mrs. Carlyle said of John Sterling, in her incisive way, that he 'wanted back-bone.'

'I saw that the French Revolution and German Literature were the cardinal phenomena of the century,' Carlyle once said in my presence, when speaking of his earlier literary aspirations and endeavours. Again, 'if it had not been for the French Revolution, I should never have had any hope,' he said to me during the first years of my acquaintance with him. His hopes of great results to mankind from the First French Revolution survived, though somewhat abated, those which he had founded on the extension of a knowledge and appreciation of German literature. When, about the middle of the century, the Grand Duke of Weimar of the time visited him at Chelsea (driving down in a kind of state which startled the inhabitants of modest Cheyne Row), his Serene Highness asked him why German literature was not more studied in England. 'I told him,' Carlyle informed me, 'that this was due to our sulky Radical temper.' Carlyle's own indignant broodings over the 'condition of England question,' his later Cromwell-worship, his conception of a project for the reorganisation of our industrial system through the reproductive employment of pauperism, led him by degrees far away from the ethereal region in which the literature of Goethe and Schiller had been evolved. Yet I was greatly surprised, not to say disappointed, by something that fell from him at the time when he was busy with the *Latter-Day Pamphlets.* Happening to refer to his efforts to make German literature known in England, I received for rejoinder the abrupt and chilling reply: 'It only increased the confusion.' This, then, was the end of that 'beginning of a new revelation of the Godlike,' which once he had told the world (*ante,* p. 57) was to be discerned in 'the higher literature of Germany!' Of Fichte he had at that time written in language of transcendent admiration as 'a colossal and adamantine spirit standing erect and clear like a Cato Major among degenerate men, fit to have been the teacher of the Stoa, and to have discovered beauty and virtue in the groves of Academe.' Yet when some twenty years later he had been reading a new volume in the series of translations from Fichte's works, executed by an Edinburgh man, he pronounced, to my great astonishment, the lauded Fichte of earlier years to be 'a thick-skinned fellow!'— a verdict, the grounds for which he did not explain, but which was too obviously contemptuous. Still, however, his appreciation of, and gratitude to, Kant remained comparatively unimpaired. 'Kant,' he said, 'taught me that I had a soul as well as a body.' To much of Humboldt's *Kosmos* he applied the expressive Scotch epithet 'dreigh ;' but, on the whole, he thought Humboldt had done very fairly in 'his own sentimental-atheistic way,' which, Carlyle thought, would astonish future generations. Speaking of his sojourn at Berlin, during his first visit to Germany in quest of material for his Frederick, he said that the man of letters whose society he most enjoyed was 'old Tieck,' whom he had helped to introduce to the reading public of England in the *Specimens of German Romance*.

Even in his once idolised Goethe—formerly called by him in conversation 'a colossal man who oversees everything' —Carlyle found latterly something to criticise pretty severely. He complained, in my hearing, that Goethe was too much given to what Carlyle rather scornfully called 'peering into nature.' He was referring to those optical and biological studies to which Goethe devoted much time and thought, and which he considered, especially the optical, so important that he said to Eckermann : 'As Napoleon fell heir to the French Revolution, so have I fallen heir to the Newtonian theory of colours,' one denounced by him with what was for him quite unusual vehemence. And although the main theory propounded in the *Farbenlehre* has been rejected by British men of science, both here and on the Continent Goethe is recognised by the highest authorities as the author of 'epoch-making' discoveries in the domain of morphology and comparative anatomy. But Carlyle, who admitted that he never could read a line of Charles Darwin, cared for none of these things. In later life, with an eye directed to the possible-practical, he spoke of Goethe chiefly in connection with the poetic and

symbolic scheme of education which was unfolded in
Wilhelm Meister's Wanderjahre (*ante*, p. 202). Some
other references to Goethe made by Carlyle in conversation
may as well be given now. In earlier years Carlyle had
been [attracted towards the St. Simonians. A more or
less sympathetic mention of them, in his letters to Goethe,
drew from the wise old German the emphatic monition :
' Von der St. Simonischen Gesellschaft, bitte Sie, halten
Sich fern '! ('From the St. Simonian Society, I beg of
you, keep yourself far apart.') When translating and
interpreting Goethe's mysterious piece Das Mährchen
(which belongs to what De Quincey called Goethe's ' conun-
drums '), Carlyle thought that he discovered in it a
number of allusions to the political and intellectual history
of modern Europe, and he asked Goethe whether his
surmises were correct. In Goethe's ambiguous, not to say
unsatisfactory reply, he neither denied nor admitted the
correctness of Carlyle's ingenious glosses, but contented
himself with saying, Carlyle told me that different people
interpreted these things in different ways. Of Goethe's
marriage Carlyle said that Schiller, speaking of him as *ein
alte Hagestolz* (an old bachelor), predicted that he would
be entrapped by some artful woman, and when allusion
was made to the aged Goethe's attachment to a very
young lady, an attachment so passionate that he wished to
marry her, Carlyle a little irreverently ejaculated ' poor
fellow ! ' In the course of his correspondence with Carlyle
Goethe addressed some very pretty complimentary verses
to Mrs. Carlyle, who, however, did not speak of him with
enthusiasm, and declared that it would have been much better for him if he had been capable of giving a good hearty
laugh. She had been told, she said, by Mrs. Jameson

that, when visiting Goethe at Weimar, she heard his daughter-in-law Ottilie screaming in another room, while her husband August, Goethe's only son, and indeed his only child, was beating her.   This was probably the little lady's exaggeration of something milder that Mrs. Jameson may have hinted at.   It was Ottilie von Goethe who said of Balzac's novels that each of them 'seemed dug out of the heart of a suffering woman.'   If only a little was true of what Mrs. Carlyle reported of the Weimar household, on Mrs. Jameson's authority, Ottilie must have indeed known what it was to be a 'suffering woman.'   But she did not suffer long.   Her husband, who died before his father, had a sad ending for the son whom Goethe loved, and some traits of whose young years he introduced in his delineation of Wilhelm Meister's Felix.

Carlyle read few modern French books, and spoke contemptuously of modern French literature.   But he recognised in Chateaubriand 'a man of real sensibility.'   One of the impressions given him by Thiers's *French Revolution* was that its author was 'a man without a conscience.' George Sand (with whom he conjoined Balzac in one and the same condemnation), it is well known to all readers of Carlyle, he could not away with, looking at, or at least generally speaking of, her books as distinguished by nothing better than a lax treatment of the sexual relation.   The only civil thing that I ever heard him say of the Pope and his obsolete creed was, that they might be a sort of barrier against something worse than themselves, George Sandism to wit.   Yet when brought face to face, as it were, with her genius, and placing himself on the judgment-seat to deliver a deliberate verdict on her, he could not help recognising the gifts of that extraordinary woman.   George

Henry Lewes told me that he once found Carlyle with some of George Sand's books spread out before him, and confessing that he had broken down in an attempt to indite a scathing invective against her and them. 'There is something Goethian about the woman,' he said to Lewes as an excuse for his failure. I was rather surprised when Carlyle spoke to me of her as 'a shrewd woman.' Shrewd she was undoubtedly, but *that* was hardly the characteristic of her to which one expected prominence to be given by Carlyle. And then, as if to neutralise even this faint praise, he repeated the scornful line from the Venetian epigrams—

'Ach! die zärtlichen Herzen! Ein Pfuscher vermag sie zu rühren.'

An exclamation of Goethe's, be it noted, introduced by him in a poetic apology for that devotion of his to science, which Carlyle, as formerly mentioned (*ante*, p. 221), spoke of contemptuously as 'peering into nature.'[1]

Apart from the enormous mass of books through which Carlyle had to plod his way, or which he had to consult, when writing his historical works, he was a considerable reader. He eschewed indeed the daily newspaper, being content with his weekly *Examiner*, which at one time he exchanged for the *Leader*. The *Times* he took in only for a brief period after the French Revolution of 1848 broke out. He expected from it, he told me, cleverer writing than he found in it, speaking, moreover, of the style of its article as Johnsonian (which seemed to me an inaccurate statement), and pronouncing the sentences to be all

---

[1] 'Mit Botanik giebst du dich ab? Mit Optik? Was thu'st du?
　　Ist es nicht schöner Gewinn rühren ein zärtliches Herz?
　　Ach! die zärtlichen Herzen! Ein Pfuscher vermag sie zu rühren;
　　Sei es mein einziges Glück, dich zu berühren, Natur!'

'properly balanced,' as if that were something astonishing in a 'leading journal.' His former conception of the journalist as one who guided the people forward from day to day had vanished by this time, and a harsh one was substituted for it. Referring to the clever gentlemen who enlighten the world through the daily press he asked me, 'What are these fellows doing? They only serve to cancel one another.' I replied that they were like barristers who put the cases of their clients more neatly and concisely than their clients themselves could, the clients of the journalist being the political party which his newspaper supported, and which supported his newspaper. In a general way, the little that Carlyle cared to know about public affairs, beyond what he chanced to read of them in his weekly newspaper, he gathered from conversation, while in such circles as that of the Ashburtons, he met, heard, and talked with men who were 'making history.' Current literature he professed to contemn, maintaining that a man was much better employed smoking his pipe, even he was pleased to concede (he himself being, for his stomach's sake and his often infirmities, mainly a water-drinker) with the addition of 'a moderate glass of beer,' than in reading 'such books as come out now.' Nevertheless, he read in, if not through, many of the books of the day which were recommended to him as possessing merit, and he dipped into most of the books and pamphlets which in considerable numbers were presented to him by their authors. Mrs. Carlyle occasionally read a novel aloud to him. I found her once thus occupied with a wild weird story of Emily Brontë's, which naturally was not much to her husband's taste. It was in old books that Carlyle chiefly delighted, and indeed altogether he lived very much in the past. Of

P

the London publishers as a class he spoke with a harshness
scarcely mitigated by the doubtful compliment that, 'considering what was behind, it was well to have in them such
a dead wall of dulness.' One bibliopolic phenomenon of
his own time, however, he greeted with rare cordiality—
the late Mr. Bohn's issue of the Standard Library,
especially the Antiquarian and Classical Sections thereof.
I had heard Carlyle protest retrospectively against the
mode of proceeding adopted by Lord Brougham's preten-
tious and once famous but now almost forgotten, as
well as long-extinct, Society for the Diffusion of Useful
Knowledge, which had books of various kinds written to
order for publication under its auspices. 'They treated
literature,' Carlyle said, 'as if it were a *tabula rasa*,' whereas
good books already existed in abundance, but needing to
be brought serially or systematically within the reach of
readers of moderate means. This was done by Bohn, and
Carlyle declared that, if he were Chancellor of the Exchequer, he would propose a Parliamentary Grant to him
in aid of his useful enterprise. One of the earliest volumes
of Bohn's Classical Library was Cary's English translation
of Herodotus. Carlyle read it with delight, pronouncing,
in his familiar fashion, the Father of History 'a beautiful
old fellow.' In a general way Carlyle cared little about
the classics, and never read them in the originals, his knowledge of Homer himself being derived chiefly, I fancied,
from Voss's admirable German version. As might be
expected, he protested strenuously against the time devoted
in our modern systems of education to Latin and Greek,
and did not estimate very highly the importance of classical
scholarship. It was not, he would say, by studying
Egyptian that the Greeks themselves came to produce

their literature. There was Goethe, he added, who was not a profound classical scholar, but 'he knew better than all your pedants what a Roman or Greek man thought and felt.'

I never heard Carlyle speak of Pope, Swift, and the other Queen Anne men, nor of Fielding, nor even of Sterne, for whom he had an early love. But he called the day on which he first read *Roderick Random* one of the sunniest of his life (!), and a good biography of Smollett, he thought, was among the few things of the kind which then remained to be done. Of the harshest saying that I ever heard fall from his lips about a man of genius, Goldsmith was the subject. When the biography of Goldsmith, by Carlyle's friend John Forster, appeared, he told me that he had written Forster a letter commending the book, but objecting to Goldsmith being made the central figure of a group composed of some of the most distinguished men of his time. Goldsmith, Carlyle continued, was 'an Irish black-guard' (how different from Dr. Johnson's verdict, 'great moralist' though he was !); but he had the grace to add, 'he wrote some of the most elegant things in the English language.' It was Johnson, Carlyle always insisted in conversation,—as he had asserted in his famous essay on Boswell's Life,—who kept England so loyal to the old that the French Revolution of 1789 was not followed by a similar phenomenon on this side the Channel. To me it appeared that Burke's *Reflections* had been far more effective in that way than anything or all that Johnson wrote. Carlyle's admiration of Burke, indeed, was of the scantiest. He admitted that there were 'gleams of insight' in Burke's speeches and writings, but thought that, instead of denouncing the French Revolution and all its works, Burke

had better have promoted reform at home. To reform alike
in Church and State (except, perhaps, in the case of administrative economy), Burke was generally opposed. As regards
post-Johnsonian literature, Carlyle's opinions, expressed
in private, on Wordsworth, Coleridge, Southey, Scott, have
already been referred to. I heard him say, what he said
to many others, that the life of Keats by his friend Richard
Monckton Milnes (the first Lord Houghton) was ' fricassee
of dead dog.' To me he added that the account, in the
book of Keats's last days and death in Rome, was as painful
as anything he had ever read. Byron, he predicted, would
be 'forgotten in fifty years.' Some decades have elapsed
since Carlyle emitted the prophecy, and, according to
present appearances, it will remain unfulfilled. The harsh
and hasty judgment on Charles Lamb, in the *Reminiscences*,
has been much and naturally censured, but I heard Carlyle
say of Lamb, that he did very well with 'that little mouse-
trap of his.' Concerning De Quincey Carlyle made the
really pregnant remark, 'he sees into the fibres of a thing.'
    When I first knew Carlyle, he took a melancholy view
of literature as of most things. Writing, which was not
commonplace, would not find an audience. 'There are no
people of any culture in England.' 'No man in England
can get himself developed.' Literature was 'dying out,' or
being 'ground down into penny journals,'—by which
he did not mean penny newspapers; they were a growth
of after-years. Of ordinary London *littérateurs*, journalists,
or what not, many of them, in those days, haunters of
taverns, while few of them had any aspiration beyond
satisfying the needs of the passing hour, he said: 'They
have no homes,' and still worse, 'they have no faith.'
Young men of talent, possessing any earnestness, were

being driven into Radicalism. ' I hope that they will go on rebelling until they get something to do,' from the State he meant, of course. After the success of *Cromwell*, he took a more hopeful view of the prospects of serious literature like his own. 'You get,' he said, 'an audience at last.'

CHAPTER XVI

VISITORS OF THE CARLYLES

IN spite of his dyspepsia, and though dining out, he declared, deranged him, Carlyle was generally ready, when in average health, to be a dinner-guest if he liked the host. One host, among Amphitryons far higher in the social scale, was John Gibson Lockhart, who became a great friend of his, although Carlyle always maintained (I cannot help thinking him mistaken) that it was Lockhart's verdict on *Sartor Resartus* which had led John Murray of Albemarle Street to decline it. I mention Lockhart among those of whose hospitality Carlyle partook, because Mrs. Carlyle said that, when her husband dined with Lockhart, he always came home full of too piquant anecdotes (a thing rare with him), chiefly of Edinburgh, a city with the men and manners of which host and guest had been from of old familiar. Carlyle might have dined out perpetually had he so chosen, but he did not choose. He told me of a curious computation, after a survey of London hospitality, which had been made by himself and Erasmus Darwin, a brother of the *Origin of Species*. It was that there were in town on any day during the London season, three thousand families at whose dinner-tables a man of any note would be welcome! Erasmus Darwin was a tall and very courteous gentleman of the old school, the kind of friend much affected by the Carlyles, with whom he was a great favourite. One peculiarity of his which, besides his

personal qualities, commended him to intimate visitors of
the Carlyles was that he had at all hours a cab in attendance, in which he was ready and willing to have any such
visitor of theirs driven to his destination in town, a mode
of conveyance more certain, definite, expeditious, than the
omnibus, and, of course, more economical than a cab hired
by one's-self.

Carlyle liked the company of distinguished people, in
whatever department of activity their distinction had been
won, and if any one, whether distinguished or undistinguished, had special knowledge of a subject, even of an
out-of-the-way subject, he could be silent, becoming the
most attentive of listeners, and interpolating an occasional
question, only to listen the more attentively. I remember
to have seen him at one of the *soirées* given by John
Chapman, then a publisher in the Strand (and in a house
which was for a time George Eliot's domicile), listening
during the best part of an hour, to what the late Dr. Elliot-
son had to say on Animal Magnetism, for his devotion
to the propagation of which he sacrificed a fine medical
practice. But Carlyle's most intimate friends were men
like Erasmus Darwin, who was not at all what the world
calls distinguished, but whom he prized for quiet intelligence, refinement of manners, and purity of life. One of
these, whom it seemed to me Carlyle liked as much as he
then liked anybody, was John Chorley, a brother of the
once well-known *Athenæum*-Chorley. Chorley had been
secretary, with a considerable salary, to some large
railway company, but gave up the post, it was said, from
a fastidious sense of honour, which was offended by I
know not what in the proceedings of the board whose
official organ he was. This endeared him additionally to

Carlyle, who much preferred an over-sensitive conscience to none at all. Chorley was a quiet, shy, proud, studious man, whose chief recreation, according to. Carlyle, was solitary performance on the bassoon. The Chorleys were Lancashire men, and, as has been previously recorded (*ante*, p. 146), Carlyle recommended John Chorley to write a history of Lancashire. The suggestion was fruitless. Chorley's studies lay in a very different direction, Spanish literature, and especially the Spanish drama, of which he had an unrivalled knowledge, and of the products of which he had formed a unique collection. A book about the Spanish drama, Carlyle, too, advised him to write. But Chorley was too fastidious even for that, and, as in the case of so many men that one has come across, much accumulated and unique knowledge, which ought to have borne fruit, perished with him. Another speciality of John Chorley, far away from Spanish or any other literature, was a singular conversancy with the navy in all its branches. This was a topic on which Carlyle, whose admiration of the British navy was considerable, delighted to hear him dilate. I remember passing a pleasant hour listening to ·Chorley while he described to Carlyle the hardships and privations endured in the Polar regions by the officers and men of a Government Arctic Expedition, and the devices by which the officers endeavoured to keep up the spirits of the men. Carlyle long survived Chorley, who left him a legacy of some thousands of pounds. Carlyle did not need it, and thought of sending to the Literary Fund, as a donation, the whole of the money thus bequeathed him. Whether he carried out this intention I know not. It is another illustration of the magnetism which Carlyle exercised on his friends that Chorley, a man very well to do, not only left him this legacy, but transcribed for him into clear manuscript the fragments of that history of James I. which Carlyle began as an introduction to his projected Cromwelliad—fragments which, perhaps, might still be worth publishing.

John Chorley's vast collection of Spanish plays, with his own MS. annotations, he gave to the Library of the British Museum. His only published book contained a weird drama to which was appended some stray poems of no great value. He contributed to the *Athenæum* at a time when his brother Henry was a prominent member of its staff, but that employment of his leisure hours, was, I take it, unknown, or little known to Carlyle. Among the books which fell to Chorley to be reviewed was a German one, by a clever German lady (Jewess, I think), a Miss Bölte, whose death abroad I saw chronicled not long ago in the newspapers, and who came a good deal about the Carlyles. Her correspondence with Mrs. Carlyle has been already noted, and a letter of Mrs. Carlyle's to her been quoted (*ante*, p. 129). In Berlin she had been a friend of Rahel, and remained a friend of Rahel's husband, Varnhagen von Ense ('a solid man' Carlyle called him), letters from whom, some of them containing, I remember, protests against 'John-Bullismus,' she used to bring with her and read aloud at Chelsea. Governessing was her main occupation, but she wrote among other things novels, chiefly sentimental, which appear to have had some vogue in Germany. Carlyle tolerated her as a correspondent of Varnhagen, and Mrs. Carlyle befriended her as a clever lone woman in a foreign land, and was successful in getting her situations. Several of them were in families of

some social distinction,—she was for a time with a section
of the Buller family,—and, seeing thus a little of the ways
of the fashionable world, she took it into her head to write,
from slender experience, sketches of high life in London,
and these contained noticeable exaggerations and blunders.
The volume was handled rather severely in the *Athenæum*.
One evening I heard her complain to the Carlyles of this
criticism of her book. 'Oh,' said Carlyle consolingly, 'the
man who wrote the article is probably in debt to his
landlady, and with very forlorn outlooks.' The reviewer,
as was soon known to Mrs. Carlyle at least, was no other
than the opulent Chorley! I, too, reviewed the same book
somewhere or other, and my review was, I daresay, more
favourable than Chorley's. Not long afterwards Miss
Bölte, John Chorley, and I, found ourselves together at the
Carlyles', and Mrs. Carlyle, in a laughing aside to me,
remarked how odd it was that the lady should be in the
company of two of her reviewers.

Among the visitors of more or less note whom I saw
cursorily at the Carlyles' was Mr. Venables (*ante*, p. 94), a
very pleasant man, then rising at the Parliamentary bar.
His chief literary distinction at that time was his contribution of an article on Miss Martineau's *Deerbrook* to
the *Edinburgh Review*. Mrs. Carlyle called him 'rather
dandiacal,' but he was a favourite both with husband and
wife. Another of their welcome visitors was that clever,
agreeable, amiable man, the late Arthur Helps. Carlyle
liked him, even speaking favourably of his books, though,
as regarded his dealings with the Spanish conquests in
America, Carlyle told him that he had lent too favourable
an ear to the glowing accounts given by some of the
Spanish chroniclers of the material splendours which

the conquerors were described as having found among their conquered victims. A Life and Correspondence of Arthur Helps is among our biographical desiderata, since few men of his generation had communed with as many distinguished persons, from the Sovereign downwards. Let me record one instance, which came under my own notice, of the thoughtful and wide beneficence of this kindly gentleman. A cultivated young Scottish friend of mine, well connected, came to London to study for the bar. After being called, no clients made their appearance, and, by degrees, his little patrimony melted away. He had a scholarly equipment, but not of the peculiar kind needed for the literary struggle. He was in great straits when he bethought him of offering, without an introduction, his services to Helps, who was then busy chronicling the early doings of the Spaniards in America. Helps saw at once from my friend's letter that his correspondent was a scholar and a gentleman. He invited him to his country-house, and employed him for a considerable time in making transcripts and researches. Still more generously, when he could not honestly find work for my friend, who returned to London, he arranged with him to call every week on his factotum in town, and receive a weekly stipend sufficient to keep the wolf from the door, until at last he found employment which enabled him to dispense with Helps's delicately-rendered assistance.

Among their visitors of minor note, the late Mr. Robert Farie was a favourite of the Carlyles, and specially intimate with 'Brother John.' Farie was a young amiable, thoughtful, and gentlemanlike Scotchman of good family, well-off, and without visible occupation. He was a great admirer of Mrs. Carlyle, to whom, when she said that she did not take horse-exercise because she had no riding-habit, he offered to present one—an offer, the acceptance of which was peremptorily vetoed by her husband, if indeed it would have been accepted by the wife. Early in my acquaintance with Carlyle I told him that I thought of translating an interesting, but very little known, work of Goethe's, the *Campaign in France*. He replied, looking at the project from a purely business point of view, 'Translations seldom answer.' It mattered little to Farie whether a translation answered or not, and he undertook, by way of intellectual amusement, the task which I had abandoned. His translation was duly published, but did not excite the attention which it deserved. The book is mainly a narrative of what Goethe, who accompanied the Weimar contingent, saw during that campaign of the allies in their invasion of France in 1792, which was undertaken to extinguish the French Revolution, but which ended in their own ignominious repulse. ' *Guai a chi la tocca*,' it is dangerous to meddle with France, I have heard Carlyle say, when otherwise depreciating, as not infrequently happened, France and the French. In his *French Revolution* he thought it worth while to quote from the *Campaign in France*, Goethe's account, from personal experience, of the 'cannon-fever,' an attack of which he voluntarily courted, from sheer curiosity, during a brush between the French and the allies. Goethe's little book is rememberable, were it only because it records the striking prophecy which he delivered on the evening of the battle of Valmy, at which Dumouriez drove back with great loss the Prussians and their allies, a defeat from which, in that campaign, they never recovered. After nightfall when some of Goethe's Prussian military friends, seated with him round a camp-fire, were talking over the incidents of the disastrous day, the keen-sighted and reflective poet uttered the memorable prediction: 'With this day begins a new epoch in the world's history, and you can say that you were present at its opening.' There are noticeable things in the book besides details of the epoch-making campaign. Carlyle's knowledge of it had been refreshed by Farie's translation, and he laughed heartily and characteristically at the passage in it, which describes Goethe when crossing a stream, fascinated by the sight of a piece of crockery in the water, and glittering in the sunbeams with effects of light and colour, which confirmed for him some optical theory of his afterwards expounded in the *Farbenlehre*. Far more important than this illustration of Goethe's fondness for 'peering into nature' (*ante*, p. 221) is the very interesting account of the visit paid by the kindly poet to a young German correspondent who had laid bare to him the sorrows and sufferings of a mind afflicted with grave spiritual hypochondriasis. The remedies for it, which Goethe suggested to the patient, are as applicable now as they were then to victims of that distressing psychical malady. I may note here that German having been, for obvious reasons, introduced into the curriculum of state-education in France since the Franco-German War of 1870, the favourite German school-book is this of Goethe's, no doubt because in it a great German tells the story of a crowning triumph of French patriotism and valour over the hated Prussians.

Of those friends of Carlyle during his early life in London who had departed to the other world before I knew him, John Sterling was the chief: to the oral verdict of the

Carlyles on him reference has been made already (*ante*, p. 219). Respecting a still earlier friend, Edward Irving, the only remark not in the *Reminiscences*, which I heard fall from Carlyle, was that Irving had given him the best piece of advice in the matter of reading which he ever received : it was 'always to read history with the map' beside you. Of the late George Darley, in some of whose poems there appears to have been of late a revival of interest, Carlyle spoke with great friendliness ; occasionally imitating—Carlyle was more given to mimicry than successful in it—the stutter with which Darley, like Charles Lamb, a stammerer, said his pointed things. He described Darley as wasting his talents on attempts to produce a Shakespearian drama, and as condemned to earn a living in the to him distasteful occupation of art critic. Besides Mazzini and his Italian friends there came about the Carlyles, during the earlier years of their residence in London, sundry French exiles, driven from their country for their republican zeal by the Governments of Louis Philippe. Carlyle had a great regard for one of them, Godefroi Cavaignac ; he sometimes brought with him to Chelsea Armand Marrast, afterwards a member of the Provisional Government of February 1848, whom Carlyle remembered as having sung to him rustic songs in vogue among the French peasantry, but a man otherwise not much to his taste. Godefroi Cavaignac was a son of the Cavaignac, one of the members of the French Convention who voted for the execution of Louis XVI., and a conspicuous man in the stormy days of the First French Republic. Godefroi's brother was the zealously republican General Cavaignac (*ante*, p. 170), one of the few contemporary Frenchmen admired by Carlyle. Godefroi himself had been very active and prominent in the movement which produced the French Revolution of 1830. From a report of it given by him Carlyle described to me an interview, just when that revolution was being consummated, between Cavaignac and Louis Philippe, then Duke of Orleans, in some 'big, gloomy room of the Palais Royal.' Cavaignac pleaded for the establishment of a republic. Louis Philippe, while raising objections, made some reference to his father Égalité Orleans. '*Altesse!*' was Cavaignac's reply, '*vous finirez comme lui,*' a prophecy which was far from being completely fulfilled. While I write, a son of General Cavaignac, and nephew of Godefroi, after having been Minister of Marine in one of the Governments of the Third French Republic, is spoken of as its probable future President.

CHAPTER XVII

SOME OF CARLYLE'S FRIENDS

ONE New Year's Eve, Carlyle jotted in his Journal :
' On Christmas-day Ballantyne, Maccall, and John
Welsh were with us at dinner.' John Welsh, a stranger to
me, was doubtless a relative of Mrs. Carlyle, but with his
fellow-guests I was intimate, and as they were at that time
esteemed by Carlyle, something may be said of both.
Ballantyne's had been rather an interesting career. Originally he was a weaver in Paisley, a town which has been,
and for aught I know is still, prolific of poets of humble
life. He was of a reading, and even a studious turn, conn-
ing many a volume, as well as crooning many a Scottish
song, while he plied the shuttle. Exchanging the shuttle
for the pen, and the loom for the press, he worked his way
up, I forget exactly how and by what steps, to be the editor
of a Bolton newspaper. He became early, and remained
to the end, an enthusiastic admirer of Carlyle's writings.
The admiration which he felt for them he wished others to
feel, and this he attempted to effect by giving in his paper
frequent extracts from them. In this way he really did a
great deal to make Carlyle's genius and name known in the
manufacturing districts, where at that time literary novelties were in very slight demand. He opened up a correspondence with Carlyle, who was doubtless both surprised
and pleased to find an effective journalistic admirer in a
hotbed of manufacturing Radicalism, and that, too, when he

himself was either slighted or ignored by the London press. More important to Ballantyne than his Carlylolatry, he edited the Bolton paper at a time when the Anti-Corn-Law League was beginning its Seven Years' War against Protection. Ballantyne had a turn for statistics, and, though never wielding a vigorous pen, wrote lucidly and logically on what he understood. He mastered thoroughly the details of the Corn-Law controversy, and his articles against the Corn Laws attracted the attention of Cobden, who prized lucidity and logic more than rhetoric, and who, according to Ballantyne's own account, often consulted him during the struggle of the League. In the success of that struggle Carlyle took a considerable interest, whatever his opinions in later years on Free Trade, when it was proclaimed to be the be-all and end-all of social progress. Ballantyne sent Carlyle regularly newspapers and private letters containing reports of anything specially interesting in the proceedings and progress of the League, and Carlyle responded sympathetically. From his editorship of the Bolton paper Ballantyne migrated to the staff of the *Manchester Guardian*, which was then Whig. Next he became the editor of the *Manchester Examiner*, when it was founded by John Bright and others to be the organ of a Liberalism more advanced than the *Guardian's*. At the time when he ate with William Maccall his Christmas dinner at the Carlyles' he was on the editorial staff of the *Leader*. Carlyle liked him for the sake of Auld Lang Syne, and for his own. He was then one of the cheeriest, hopefullest, and what is more, kindliest of men,—when a Scotchman is kindly he is very kindly,—and, however depressed his circumstances became, he was always eager to help any one as unfortunate as himself. He was argumentative and positive to a degree,

Q

and had withal an inexhaustible store of plausible projects, and singular powers of persuasiveness, which with persons of a higher rank, profoundly ignorant of the element in which he lived, moved, and had his being, sometimes stood him in wonderfully good stead.

When he left the *Leader* Ballantyne became sub-editor of the *Illustrated London News*, with the late Dr. Charles Mackay for his chief. The duties of the post were, if he had only known it, precisely those which suited him best, since he had a lynx-like eye for the salient and the interesting in any mass of matter that came before him. Indications of his great talent in this way, apart from its exercise on transitory journalism, survive in his *Essays in Mosaic* and his selection of *Passages from Carlyle's Writings*. But Ballantyne was ambitious. Like so many Scotchmen of literary proclivities, he thought journalism the greatest of human occupations, and pined for the editorial chair which he had not filled since leaving Lancashire. Some changes in the financial arrangements of the *Illustrated London News* being proposed, Ballantyne kicked against the traces, imprudently resigned his sub-editorship, and late in life entered on a new career of painful vicissitude. He resolved on starting a weekly newspaper of his own, with the ambitious title of the *Statesman*, as an organ of Palmerstonian Liberalism. The chief political contributor was Thornton Hunt, who had become a perfect leading-article machine, turning out daily and weekly I know not how many yards or miles of disquisition, of very fair quality, moreover, considering its quantity. The sub-editor was Frederic Martin, Carlyle's amanuensis or literary factotum : of him more hereafter. William Maccall, an old ally of Ballantyne's, was among the general contributors, as was

the writer of these pages, to whom also the literary department was intrusted. Ballantyne had not a farthing of capital
of his own, and the *Statesman* was started and carried on,
during its hand-to-mouth life of not many months, with
money borrowed, or rather given. In the extremity to
which he was now reduced, Ballantyne had come to look
on the moneyed classes, especially the moneyed aristocracy,
as bound to support a journalist and a journal in difficulties, and that was the predicament in which the *Statesman*
and its proprietor-editor soon found themselves. I remember him telling me, with exultation, of his discovery, that
Leigh Hunt had received from Shelley donations amounting
to £17,000. What Macaulay's famous cheque of £20,000
had been to many a literary aspirant, that £17,000 (if it was
really ever given) became to Ballantyne, who forgot that he
was not a Leigh Hunt, and that, if he had been one, men
of Shelley's peculiar beneficence and generosity are rare.
Into the financial secrets of the *Statesman* I never cared
to inquire, but several disclosures which Ballantyne volunteered to me threw some light on them, and one of them is
interesting in connection with Carlyle, who befriended him
from first to last. Carefully watching his opportunity, when
Mrs. Carlyle was out of town, Ballantyne asked Carlyle
for the loan of £50. Carlyle good-naturedly assented,
but stipulated for a little delay, as his surplus moneys were
in the Annan branch of the old-established Scottish bank,
the British Linen Company, so faithfully, even in finance,
did he cling to his native region. On a day appointed by
the lender, the borrower appeared in Cheyne Row and
found spread out on the table an elaborate deed recording
the transaction, and reciting Ballantyne's liability for the
sum to be lent. This document having been duly signed

and sealed, he received the money. On returning to town, and learning, of course, what had happened in her absence, Mrs. Carlyle reproached Ballantyne bitterly for his stratagem (I tell the story as he told it to me), and dilated on the losses which her husband had suffered by lending to impecunious friends. Loss, as it turned out, however, there was none to Carlyle, but a still greater gain to Ballantyne. By a further stretch of good-nature, Carlyle gave Ballantyne one of his visiting-cards as an introduction to his staunch and very wealthy friend Lord Ashburton. Carlyle's name operated as an 'open sesame' at the portals of Bath House, and procured the transmitter a courteous and even cordial reception from Lord Ashburton. What was thus begun by Ballantyne, was completed by his persuasiveness and declarations of his adhesion to the faith as it was in Carlyle, in whom Lord Ashburton was a firm believer. Before long Ballantyne was telling Lord Ashburton of Carlyle's loan, and lamenting that a man of such genius should be a loser by his beneficence. I don't remember whether he also told Lord Ashburton the amount of the sum which he had borrowed. In any case, the generous and trustful peer forthwith presented Ballantyne with a cheque for £500. From this Ballantyne repaid Carlyle the borrowed £50, and remained by the transaction a gainer of £450, much of which went, I do not doubt, to help to keep the *Statesman* in paper, print, and contributions.

Lord Ashburton did more for Ballantyne than give him the £500, if, indeed, this sum was the only pecuniary benefaction which he received from the munificent peer. Lord Ashburton introduced him to several of the great Whig leaders. I rather think that there was even a

dinner-party given at Bath House to allow Ballantyne to
expound his political programme to Lord Palmerston,
Lord Clarendon, and Lord John Russell among others.
In return he expected money to keep himself and the
Statesman afloat. Perhaps he got some, but certainly not
from Lord John Russell. He himself described to me an
unsatisfactory interview which he had with that statesman.
During it Lord John stood with his back to the fireplace,
looking exceedingly supercilious. When Ballantyne had
ended his flowing appeal for financial aid to the *Statesman*,
his Lordship replied curtly and frigidly that he never had
anything to do with subsidising the press, or words to that
effect. Ballantyne did find some favour in the eyes of
Lord Clarendon, but it was with Lord Palmerston that he
was most successful, personally at least; whether financially
or not I neither knew nor cared to inquire. Lord Palmerston
was given to patronising strange journalistic adventurers,
such, for instance, as Michele, an editor of the *Morning
Post*, whom, in gratitude for his newspaper support, and
perhaps for other reasons, he appointed Consul-General at
St. Petersburg, but to whom, for the very reasons which procured him the appointment, the Czar Nicholas refused the
exequatur needed for the discharge of his Consular functions.
Lord Palmerston invited Ballantyne to Broadlands, and
there, as at the time he told me with glee, he took Lady
Palmerston in to dinner, afterwards enlightening her on
the merits of Burns. In spite of patronage of this kind, the
funds of the *Statesman* dwindled away. Ballantyne's last
effort to replenish his exchequer was, I believe, to work on
the fears of coming democracy, which harassed the mind
of the once well-known Frances, Countess Waldegrave (a
daughter of Braham, the Hebrew vocalist), who aspired to

a feminine political leadership, and, probably supported by her bounty, the *Statesman* dragged out a little longer an existence which ended in death by starvation. After its decease, Ballantyne went to Manchester, where he persuaded a wealthy local notable to supply him with money to start a short-lived weekly journal in which he waged war against John Bright and the Manchester party, who, he thought, had behaved badly to him as editor of the *Manchester Examiner*. On the speedy failure of this new venture, Ballantyne tried Edinburgh, where he made the acquaintance of the shrewd and not unkindly John Blackwood, then at the head of the well-known publishing firm which issued and issues *Blackwood's Magazine*. John Blackwood told me that, during their first conversation, Ballantyne broached to him in half-an-hour some thirty or forty literary projects, 'all of them,' he added, 'clever,' though he did not adopt any of them, while admitting into his magazine, at least one article of Ballantyne's. What was more important, he gave Ballantyne an introduction to the late C. N. Newdegate, so long, in and out of the House of Commons, the zealous champion of Protestantism and vehement denouncer of all British statesmanship and legislation which seemed in his ever-wakeful eyes to favour in the least the Scarlet Lady. Newdegate had bought, or was buying, a journal of eighteenth century fame, but then in the last stage of senile decrepitude, the *St. James's Chronicle*, in order to convert it into an ultra-Protestant organ. He had a great respect for the opinion of John Blackwood as the editor of a magazine which then supported an old-fashioned Toryism in Church and State. Ballantyne's conversation aided the effect of Blackwood's introduction, and he was appointed editor of the *St. James's Chronicle*. He

compiled its news columns admirably, but former failures
and vicissitudes had told on his intellect, and indeed, for
political and general writing on the topics of the day, he
had never any great aptitude. In course of time, Newdegate wearied of him, and announced that there must be
a change in the editorship. In his extremity Ballantyne
invoked the intervention of Carlyle, and he good-naturedly
said that he would be happy to receive a visit from
Newdegate, whom, as a champion of Protestantism in a
degenerate age of universal toleration, he was perhaps a
little anxious to know. The tall, rigid-looking Newdegate,
nothing loth to become acquainted with the prose laureate
of seventeenth century Puritanism, duly made his appearance in Cheyne Row. At every pause in the conversation Carlyle, according to Ballantyne, put in a good
word for his old and most loyal ally, but it was evident that
Newdegate had 'come to certain conclusions,' as Carlyle
phrased it, which made intervention useless. Ballantyne
did not long survive his supercession in the editorship
of the *St. James's Chronicle* by Samuel Kydd, in his earlier
years a strenuous Chartist—such are the changes which
fleeting time procureth. One of Carlyle's last benefactions
to Ballantyne was the gift of the manuscript and copyright
of *Reminiscences of my Irish Journey in* 1847. The
recipient sold it for what it would fetch, and it was
published in 1882 with a preface by Mr. Froude.

A striking contrast in every way to the brisk, cheery,
light-hearted little Ballantyne of Carlyle's Christmas
dinner-party was presented by his fellow-guest, William
Maccall. This was a tall, erect man, with a military
bearing, who must have looked the very ideal of a cavalry
soldier when he mounted his charger, after enlisting in a

regiment of dragoons—as he told me he once did—at Jock's Lodge, near Edinburgh, only, however, to be soon bought off. He was an Ayrshire man, and was sent to the University of Glasgow to qualify himself for the Secession Ministry, the communion to which his parents belonged. Doubts as to the truth of Calvinism invaded his mind and were not to be ejected from it. A persuasive Glasgow Unitarian minister induced him to take up his abode in that half-way house between Belief and Denial—Unitarianism. As a Unitarian he ministered for a year to a small congregation at Greenock. How it came about I never heard him explain, but he then went for two years to the Theological Seminary at Geneva, the city which, though once dominated by the founder and sponsor of Calvinism had lapsed into Socinianism. There he learned and studied much and became a fervent admirer of another 'citizen of Geneva,' a very different man from Calvin, Jean Jacques Rousseau. On leaving Geneva he was for several years a Unitarian minister at Bolton (where he made the acquaintance of Thomas Ballantyne) and afterwards at Crediton in Devonshire. By this time he was a man of thirty, and had sketched out the system which he expounded in lectures to his little congregation of rustic Crediton folk, and which was afterwards embodied in his earliest and best-known book, the *Elements of Individualism*. His doctrine was propounded in it with a comparative modesty and reasonableness too often wanting in his later teachings and preachings. Maccall, a profoundly devout man, though not of the orthodox type, maintained that whereas all other religions insisted on the necessity of adding the Divine to the Human, in his system the Human was held to include the Divine, and

the more Human you became, the more Divine you were.
' I believe,' thus ran one of the many articles of his elaborate
credo, ' I believe that the revelations of God are perpetual,
and that every Individual, while a fresh revelation of God
and of the Universe, is the highest of all revelations to
himself.' Maccall was a man of passionate, glowing,
sensitive, and, unfortunately, of exceedingly aggressive
nature, simple-minded and unworldly to a degree. Whatever his circumstances might have been, some of these
qualities, especially his aggressiveness, directed as it was
too often against persons, and not, as in Carlyle's case,
against principles and society in general, would have made
success in literature and in life very difficult. But Maccall
found himself in extremely depressed circumstances when,
after he published the *Elements of Individualism*, he threw
himself on the world and on literature. No one of heart
and insight who knew him or read his book could doubt
his spirituality and noble-mindedness, but these are characteristics prized only by the few, and it is on the many, or
on publishers and editors who court the suffrages of the
many, that a British man of letters, without fortune, has
to depend for his subsistence. How he impressed personally a stranger to his writings, but one of gifts and
sympathies, he told me himself. He travelled once a
longish journey in a stage-coach with John Sterling, accidentally. They were quite unknown to each other when,
thus finding themselves together, they entered into conversation. Sterling afterwards declared that Maccall was
the most interesting man whom he had ever met with, and
introduced him to Carlyle, who, having read or looked into
his books, and on personal acquaintance with him, saw that
this was a man far above the common. ' I have a great

regard for poor Maccall,' Carlyle said to me; 'there never was a man who went about with any dignity on so little money,' adding that, though every one needed something of that individuality which Maccall preached, it was not to be 'perked up' into a doctrine for the guidance of a man's conduct through life. It was Carlyle who introduced me to Maccall at one of the *soirées* then given frequently by John Chapman the publisher (*ante*, p. 231), and thus began our long intimacy. On the same evening, Maccall afterwards told me, Carlyle bade him 'come out like an athlete,' in what arena the philosopher did not suggest. It was a monition very well suited to Maccall's character and temperament, but not at all to his then circumstances. Later on, however, Carlyle did a good deal more for Maccall than give him this inopportune advice.

When I first became acquainted with him, Maccall had contributed a little to the *Spectator*, but he was not adapted for that sailing close to the wind which is required from the political journalist, and his connection with it soon ceased. He depended chiefly on a meagre pittance derived from the *Critic*, then struggling painfully for existence, its contents being 'supported by voluntary contributions,' unpaid, and of great dulness, among which Maccall's shone with a certain radiancy. Of his connection with the *Critic* more hereafter. He was married and a father. His poverty was great, and so was his frugality. By and by, Carlyle introduced him to John Parker, the publisher in the Strand, who, for a time, both issued and edited *Fraser's Magazine* before it passed on his death, with the rest of his literary property, into the hands of the Messrs. Longman. Maccall contributed to it a striking article on Joseph de Maistre, that singular prophet of the reaction against the

First French Revolution.[1] This he followed up by sending an article on some book by the late Dr. Vaughan the Nonconformist. The article was in type, but was so virulent that it was withdrawn before publication, and his connection with that series of *Fraser's Magazine* also ceased. He was more successful with the *Gentleman's Magazine* when edited by the late John Bruce, the eminent antiquary, a very pleasant as well as accomplished man, and with *Fraser's Magazine* after it came to be edited by Mr. Froude,—to both of them he was introduced by Carlyle. As his contributions to these two magazines were chiefly in the sphere of foreign literature and biography, his aggressiveness was not so objectionable as when he was attacking living English men of letters and their writings, an occupation in which he took a savage delight. For a contemporary English author to have a literary reputation, was, except in a few cases, Carlyle and John Wilson among them, to expose himself to be tomahawked by Maccall, if he was allowed an opportunity; indeed he seemed to regard as a criminal offence the mere writing of an English book. These and similar manifestations of the 'Individuality of the Individual' did not contribute to make Maccall popular with editors. His connection, too, with those of them who had a friendly feeling towards him, came, in the course of nature, to an end. The *Gentleman's Magazine* passed into other hands and changed its character. The *Critic* died. In *Fraser's Magazine*, before its extinction, Mr. Froude was succeeded by an

---

[1] Carlyle wrote of Maccall to Parker: 'He is clearly a man of much worth, of many energies and talents, which ought to bear good fruit in the world one day.' And again, 'Maccall's *De Maistre* was very well; sincere and penetrating, though harsh. You might do something useful with Maccall, by a little faith, hope, charity, and prudence, four excellent virtues.'

editor, the late William Allingham, who knew not or cared not for Maccall. He threw himself into lecturing, in which for years he had been fitfully engaged. One of his earliest courses of lectures in London, delivered in a hall near Oxford Street, was, I remember, attended, at least once, by Monckton Milnes (Lord Houghton) and other friends of the Carlyles, but the lectures were both abstruse and virulent, and had no sequel. Maccall sank to far more plebeian audiences, but violent though he was, his violence was not plebeian, and with his new associates, Bradlaugh and others of that genus, he was soon at feud. He never forgot himself in his subject, and his self-assertion was not always attractive. I remember attending one of his later lectures. His theme was Genius under some aspect, which I forget, and the hall in which he delivered it was well filled with an audience somewhat above the working-class. It was the most painful lecture to which I ever listened. The biography of genius affords material for any number of lectures or of volumes. But this discourse was, though he never named himself or directly referred to himself, a dismal version of the autobiography of William Maccall. It was little more than a catalogue of his own struggles, disappointments, failures, baffled aspirations, physical miseries, and spiritual agonies, all generalised so as to represent the sufferings of genius in the abstract. For one solitary listener to it, who understood the meaning of it all, it had a melancholy interest, but to the mass of his hearers it was so uninteresting and so unintelligible that a most (to me) pathetic passage was interrupted by a voice from one of the audience who shouted ' Tell us about Chatterton, Mr. Maccall,' and the lecture was soon brought to an abrupt conclusion. His last years were spent in a perpetual and painful struggle with the direst poverty. But he never lost his manly bearing. In truth, William Maccall was one of the most honest and honourable of men, with noble qualities of head and heart. Even the intellectual arrogance and self-will, which barred his way to success, sprang from what was but an exaggeration, though a noxious one, of a profound spiritual truth. One saying of his survives and occasionally crops up in current literature. Maccall is 'the satirical friend of mine' whom Carlyle, in the first chapter of his *Frederick*, quotes as saying (it was of George Gilfillan that he said it): 'You may paint with a very big brush and yet not be a great painter!'

I cannot refrain from giving one or two specimens of the style and way of thinking of a man whom Carlyle esteemed very highly, but who is all but unknown to the present generation. The extracts which follow are from one of Maccall's later Tractates, *The Newest Materialism*: sundry papers on the books of Mill, Comte, Bain, Spencer, Atkinson, and Feuerbach. This is how Maccall regarded John Stuart Mill and his teaching, *à propos* of his once famous treatise on *Liberty*:

'Mr. Mill is a student: a student not of rich mind, but of fine intellect over-cultivated, not of warm and generous nature, but of a Rousseau sentimentality, which seldom aims to be pathetic without growing silly. Mr. Mill is a student, and he has the student's worst prejudices. He views Society as a kind of debating club for the reception or rejection of new ideas after boundless babblement. The two primordial facts in the past are for him, the Platonic Dialectics and the Dialectics of the School-men; for the Almighty created the universe not as a theatre of life, but for the sake of fair discussion, and you are fulfilling your mission as a Divine soul, not by achieving Divine victories, but by studying your neighbour's side of the question as well as your own.

'Verily, my brothers and sisters, crushed by tragic sin, crucified by tragic sorrow, yearning for regeneration, for consolation, and for effulgent, valiant martyr deeds, after the sharp hour of tribulation,—this is rather a shabby outlook. If ye cannot take your turn at dialectical fencing, ye had better bundle out of existence with convenient promptitude, seeing that earth has no existence, except as a dialectical fencing academy. We now know well what we were made for, and that is something—if, indeed, Mr. Mill, as a fanatical Malthusian, will allow that we ought to have been made at all. That little babies are a nuisance, and that big babies should spend all their time in what the Scotch call arglebargling, seems to be Mr. Mill's compendious creed. To be choked in your infancy, if some one has committed the crime of being your father, or if Rhadamanthine Malthusianism permits you to live, to chatter evermore about progress and liberty—such is the pleasant alternative offered you.'

This is one-sided but clever, and there is a grain of truth in it.

Ludwig Feuerbach's *Essence of Christianity* was translated into English by George Eliot, and her version of it is noted as the only literary performance of hers which appeared with her real name, 'Marion Evans,' on the title-page. By the way, there is in one of her letters (printed in Mr. Cross's biography) the following reference to Maccall in the early days of her editorship of the *Westminster Review*: 'You will be surprised at the notice of the *Westminster*, in *The People*, when you know that Maccall himself wrote it. I have not seen it, but have been told of its ill-nature. However, he is too good a man to write otherwise than sincerely, and our opinion of a book often depends on the state of the liver.' What now follows is Maccall's verdict on Feuerbach's philosophy, in a sketch of it suggested by George Eliot's translation of the *Essence of Christianity*.

'The cardinal principle of the book, which is iterated and reiterated without one touch of feeling or glow of imagination, and is mere arid dogmatic statement, is that there is no theology except what is based on anthropology, and that there is no god except each man's notion of a god. But if God is phantasmal, still more must everything else be so, and all things being phantasmal, we have no career before us saving that of imposture, if we have a single grain of common-sense left. Phantasms ourselves in the midst of phantasms, we must clutch what we can with the insatiate greed of a ferocious egoism. If born with an impulse to whatever is noble, our most loving and chivalrous deeds will be but wealth wasted, power insanely directed. We know that the instincts of mankind are more potent than these gigantic cobwebs spun by the brazen impudence of crazy metaphysicians. We know that there cannot cease to be virtue and faith among men; those affections opulent as ocean; those martyr heroisms that gird and garland our globe with sacredness; those grand organic agencies which blend families into tribes, and blend tribes into nations; that adoring gladness, the gladder for the awe wherewith it bows down to the everlasting immutabilities, which are pinnacled high as the firmaments and the archangels, and pillared in the deepest depths; and the clinging in life, and in death to God, to prayer, and to immortality. Still, is any of us enough of a philosopher to behold these impious extravagances of a pestilential philosophy without abhorrence and indignation?'

Vigorous writing certainly.

James Dodds was another Scotchman who for years found considerable favour in Carlyle's eyes. Dodds had a singularly varied career. He was a Roxburghshire man, and his people appear to have belonged to the peasant-class. But the Scottish peasant was, perhaps still is, distinguished among all others by his intelligence and love of knowledge, and Dodds owed something to the humble associates of his early years. Long afterwards, when he had attained, at least in Scotland, a certain distinction, he told a Scottish audience that the first copy of Milton which fell into his hands came from the book-shelf of a common blacksmith ; that he was introduced to *Don Quixote* by a ploughman in a lonely valley at the foot of the Cheviots ; and that he heard of Goethe for the first time when a forester's wife asked him to read to her the Sorrows of Werther ! The factor of the Duke of Roxburgh, on whose estate Dodds's grandfather lived, took an interest in the promising boy, and sent him to Edinburgh University. When in after-years I became acquainted with Dodds, he seemed to me a striking, but very rough embodiment of the national *perfervidum ingenium,* and in his earlier career it led him into tumultuous courses. He rebelled against his Professors, and for this he was reprimanded by his benefactor. Dodds would no longer accept his bounty, and flying in dudgeon from Edinburgh, started with three shillings in his pocket to walk to Newcastle, which he reached half-starved. Here. he joined a company of strolling players, and the future historian of the Covenant and laureate of the Covenanters enlisted with these vagrant Bohemians as their low comedian. From the wretched life of penury and semi-famine which he thus led for some time, he was rescued by old friends, and he is next heard of as teacher of a small adventure-school in his native region. He quitted this employment to be apprenticed for five years to a country 'writer' (a species of Scotch attorney) near Melrose, with some dim hope of working his way to the Scottish bar. Meanwhile he cultivated public speaking, for which he had a considerable natural gift, at political meetings of local Liberals, and composed an essay on Shakespeare. A kind clerical cousin wrote about him to

Carlyle, and in such a way as to interest him. A glowing essay in MS. on his *French Revolution* increased Carlyle's interest in his young countryman. A correspondence between the two ensued, much more copious on the part of the junior than of the senior. His country apprenticeship over, Dodds migrated to Edinburgh, where he became clerk to a solicitor, and, still with an eye to the Bar, attended the University law-classes, and joined a College debating-society, of which I too was a member. Thus my acquaintance with Dodds began. He seemed to me a man with a bursting heart, loud, exaggeratively emphatic, but of indisputable talent and sincerity. Socially, as well as intellectually, he was thoroughly fearless and independent, caring not a jot for the contemptuous wonderment with which many of his fellow-students contemplated the eccentric oddity of his careless rustic costume. Precisely how I know not, but he came to be looked on very favourably by the late John Hunter, who belonged to the highest class of Edinburgh solicitors. Hunter was a very amiable and cultivated man, a friend both of Carlyle and Leigh Hunt. His home was Craigcrook, famous as the beautifully situated residence of Lord Jeffrey, whom Hunter succeeded in its occupancy. Here he entertained literary visitors to Edinburgh, and Dodds was a frequent guest. Hunter's liking for him proved of great value. While working hard in Edinburgh to perfect himself in the theory and practice of Scottish law, Dodds contributed to Scottish periodicals his stirring and often touching *Lays of the Scottish Cove-nanters.* They were suggested, no doubt, by W. E. Aytoun's *Lays of the Scottish Cavaliers,* to which, of course, in tone as in theme, they were in striking contrast. To many Scotchmen the memory of the martyr heroes and

R   .

heroines of the Covenant was far dearer than that of their ruthless persecutors, some of whom were glorified by Aytoun. But Dodds, unlike Aytoun, was an unknown young man, and, indeed, his *Lays of the Covenanters* were not collected until after his death, when they were republished by the kind clerical cousin, with the same name and surname as his own, who had first brought him under the notice of Carlyle, several interesting letters from whom are printed in the memoir of Dodds, prefixed to the volume by its editor. Carlyle's original interest in Dodds was deepened when he saw that his young admirer's soaring spiritual and literary aspirations did not interfere with diligent industry in his vocation ; his letters to Dodds are kindly encouraging, as well as wisely monitory. So thoroughly did Dodds master a knowledge of his profession that, with Hunter's aid, he was enabled to settle in London as a Parliamentary solicitor. He was soon in considerable practice, chiefly in the promotion of Scotch railway bills and in the conduct of Scotch appeals. In London he was an occasional visitor of Carlyle's, and generally a silent one. Since we were at college together our roads had lain far apart, and I had seen and heard nothing of him until one evening I found myself seated with him, and his amiable Edinburgh friend John Hunter, at Mrs. Carlyle's tea-table. Her husband was away, and perhaps on that account Dodds, suddenly breaking into the quiet conversation that was going on, startled his hostess and his fellow-visitors by a tirade in favour of the insurgent Hungarians, which was violent in language, and delivered in a tone of voice far louder than was generally heard in that establishment, unless when Carlyle himself was the speaker. Dodds's vehement championship of 'civil and religious liberty all over the world' gradually withdrew him from cultivating the society of Carlyle, of whom, however, he always spoke with respect. He found in himself a greater affinity with Leigh Hunt than with Carlyle, and he became not only a close personal friend of Hunt's, but his confidant and honorary adviser in Hunt's continual pecuniary embarrassments, making arrangements with creditors, and so forth. Dodds had considerable literary ability, but his high-flown enthusiasm and glowing style were not suited to the newspaper and periodical press of London, with which he never endeavoured to form a connection. But he contributed to sundry Scotch newspapers very vigorous and telling sketches of notable contemporaries, which, in his indifference to literary fame, he never collected. Lecturing he much preferred to writing, and occasionally lectured very successfully in London. But Scotland was his favourite hunting-ground as a lecturer, and not long before his death he entertained me with a programme of a lecturing expedition which he had arranged, and which embraced an astonishing number of Scottish towns. The only book by which he was known in his lifetime, *The Fifty Years' Struggle of the Scottish Covenanters*, 1638-88, was originally a course of lectures, which he enlarged considerably before they appeared in volume-form. Dodds had studied for years the history of that struggle, and had visited the localities made memorable by its most striking incidents and episodes of heroism and martyrdom. His book, in its combination of compactness, accuracy, and enthusiasm, remains one of the best on the subject. It contains a series of word-portraits of heroes and martyrs of the Covenant unrivalled in their way, and the volume was successful, as it deserved to be, going through several editions with very little pecuniary profit to its author. No Scotchman as successful as Dodds was in London ever remained more faithful to the interests and memories of his fatherland. He was, of course, aided in his exhibition of this fidelity by the character of his professional occupations, which kept him continually in contact, as it were, with Scotland. Many are the useful branch-railways in Scotland which would not have existed but for Dodds, and several of the monuments erected at spots consecrated by the Covenanting heroism of which they are enduring memorials, owed much to his enthusiasm. When the Duke of Athole drove a party of naturalists from Glen Tilt, and the Scotch Court of Session sustained his claim thus to do what he liked with his own, it was Dodds who urged the appeal, which proved successful, to the House of Lords, and he threw himself into its conduct with a zeal which was far more patriotic than professional. His death, during a visit to his beloved Scotland, was startling in its suddenness.

Any sketch of the Carlyle *entourage*, however slight, must include the curious figure of a man, who for a considerable period drudged as the *famulus* and factotum of Carlyle, when toiling at his history of Frederick. Frederic Martin was a Sclavonic Jew of I forget what nationality, with a peculiarly servile demeanour, who played Wagner to Carlyle's Faust. He represented himself as having been secretary to Heine—possibly he had been the amanuensis of 'Blackguard Heine,' so Carlyle harshly called him, and as having seen a great deal of the Parisian Bohemia. Coming to England, he became an usher in some provincial Dotheboys Hall. In the hope of escaping from a miserable existence of this kind, he wrote offering his services to Carlyle as literary assistant. Carlyle tried him,

and found him useful. He was an excellent German
scholar, intelligent, even clever, and very industrious. He
transcribed, translated, fetched and carried, for Carlyle, on
what he described as an extremely small weekly stipend,
out of which, he complained, he had to pay for writing-
paper, omnibus-fares on journeys made for Carlyle, and for
I know not what beside. Carlyle was not a hero to this
famulus of his, nor was the *famulus*, however useful,
entirely admirable in the eyes of Carlyle. If the master
was always bewailing his lot, so also was the servant, and
Carlyle, who had little pity for any grievances but his own,
compared Martin, with his perpetual lamentations over
himself, to the 'peaseweep' of Scotland, a bird with a
peculiarly wailing note. On leaving Carlyle, his connection with whom was in itself a sort of recommendation, he
was seldom without literary employment, as newspaper
sub-editor, compiler, and so forth. He had rather a turn for
statistics, and it was in this department that he made a
considerable 'hit,' by the production of the well-known
Statesman's Year Book, which proved successful, and an
annual issue of which he edited until the end of his days.
In his later years Martin came into painful collision with
the earliest and most distinguished of his English literary
employers. He started a periodical, *The Biographical
Magazine*, which was to contain sketches of living celebrities. The first article in No. I. was headed, 'Thomas
Carlyle: a biography, with autobiographical notes. Chapter
I.' There were illustrations, too, among them drawings of
the houses successively occupied by Carlyle's father, with
one of the very small bedroom in which Carlyle himself
was born at Ecclefechan. His parading 'autobiographical
notes' was decidedly deceptive, and might well irritate

Carlyle, as seeming to promise not only his sanction but his co-operation. They consisted wholly of a translation by Martin of the German places and persons in Teufels-dröckh's early autobiography into the supposed Scottish originals—James Carlyle for Father Andreas ; Ecclefechan for Entepfuhl ; Annan Academy for Hinterschlag Gymnasium, and so on. Martin, moreover, had gone to Ecclefechan and picked up from oldest inhabitants sundry anecdotes and traits of the boy Carlyle and his progenitors, some of which Carlyle could not have relished. For instance, Carlyle's father, James, and his four uncles on the father's side, all of them stone-masons, were said by Martin to have been known as 'the fighting masons of Ecclefechan,' and as 'among the best drinkers and best head-splitters at the annual fairs of the village.' Nor were matters improved when Martin thus reported in half-Anglicised Scotch, what had been told him by an Ecclefechan nona-genarian, who as a boy had been apprenticed to Carlyle's father : ' You want to know about the Carlyles ? Weel, they were a curious sample of folks. There was not the like o' them. Pithy, bitter-speaking bodies, and awfu' fighters. Thomas and Frank '—two of Carlyle's uncles —' were plagues to fight ; they were always fighting and trying to get up disturbances. Old James, that is, you must know, the father of the great Thomas Carlyle, the book-author, liked a fight too, but not quite so much. He enjoyed a fight, but mostly kept out of it himself. But all the others went at it terribly ; they hurt the fairs with their fighting.' To this simple and unadorned recital Martin added in his own person : ' The look of old William Easton,' the nonagenarian narrator, his radiant countenance, while going back in memory to these glorious (!) scenes of his early life, was something to be remembered.' ' Something to be remembered' may also have been the aspect of Carlyle's countenance when he read this account of the ' glorious scenes ' in which his kinsmen were made to figure. The scathing protest which he wrote to Martin, Martin kept to himself. Suffice it to say that No. II. of the *Biographical Magazine* never appeared, and that Martin's biography of Carlyle never went beyond Chapter I. This disappointment was followed by the reception of an unexpected boon. Disraeli, struck by the conception and execution of *The Statesman's Year-Book*, conferred on its compiler a pension, if I remember rightly, of £100 a year. Martin did not, however, live to enjoy it long.

CHAPTER XVIII

CARLYLE AT HOME: CONCLUSION

CARLYLE'S daily life, especially if he were writing a book, was, when I first knew him, simplicity, not to say monotony, itself. He worked till three in the afternoon, with intermissions, occasional in the case of visitors, either familiar friends, or strangers who came properly introduced—frequent when he felt, which was often, the want of a pipe. At three, weather permitting, he sallied forth to walk (if he did not ride) till five, well pleased if he had a more or less intelligent companion of his pedestrianism to talk to, after what had generally been for him a long spell of silence. Then, Mrs. Carlyle presiding, he took his seat at the tea-table, where there seldom failed to be a guest or two. In summer there was usually, after tea, an adjournment of Carlyle and any smokers to the fireless kitchen, where was an abundant supply of churchwarden pipes and York River tobacco, with tumblers and a jug of fair water, though for dinner-guests (who were not very frequent) there was provided a bottle of excellent port (from Leith), with a post-prandial glass of brandy and water. The feast of reason and the flow of soul finished at ten, when Carlyle started for another walk, to 'purchase a sleep,' as he phrased it. He stepped out swiftly in those years, following the King's Road, and then turning up that 'long, unlovely' Sloane Street, at the top of which any companion he may have had was bidden Good-night, Carlyle retracing his steps to home, and, I believe, a supper of porridge, made of the best oat-meal, sent specially for him from Scotland. It was when accompanying him occasionally on these nocturnal walks that I found him readiest to afford glimpses of his innermost being. During one of them he spoke of his feeling towards his fellow-men as 'abhorrence mingled with pity.' Such a declaration from one's guide, philosopher, and friend was not of a kind to induce a disciple to take genial views of mankind. Emerson noted as 'depressing' any spiritual influence that Carlyle exerted on those who sat at his feet.

Carlyle talked sometimes of leaving Chelsea for a home in the country, not too far from town, but this intention, like many others, he never carried out. In spite of its fogs and noises, London, he said, possessed in his eyes 'an epic grandeur' all its own, and for comfort he knew no place like it. Nevertheless he admired Paris, compared with which the vaunted beauty of Edinburgh he deemed insignificant, and he lapsed into something like enthusiasm when speaking of the view of the French capital to be had from the heights of Montmartre. Of his own Chelsea domicile he said that he 'hated it less' than others. He made some attempts to buy it, which, had they proved effectual, might have prevented it from becoming, as after his death it did become, the abode of mediums, resonant with the raps and taps of Sludge's spirits, and noisome with animal realities almost as objectionable. It was well for Carlyle, and still better for his wife, that he did not leave London. Her sociality was undisguised, and in the country she would have been dreadfully dull. Carlyle professed a love of solitude, and grumbled at the want of genuine conversation in

London ; but he would have languished if he had had no-body to talk to, though he was more fastidious in the choice of his auditors than Coleridge. Of him Mrs. Carlyle told me, in her satirical way, that when he was staying with the Basil Montagus, and was alone in his room, they would send to him any stray child who happened to be at hand, and then the philosopher would harangue the little urchin or the little damsel quite contentedly ! Bores indeed, in an unusual proportion, Carlyle was troubled with, partly owing to his prophetic character. 'One great thing about London is that here no man is to bore another,' he said. But this maxim was ignored in Carlyle's own case by inquirers after truth, and to such a degree by Americans as to lead him to write in a splenetic mood that famous sentence, afterwards regretted, about the millions of trans-atlantic bores who had been brought into the world with unexampled rapidity. One American cleric, I remember, half-forced his way into the house to insist on Carlyle explaining to him difficulties which had occurred to him in studying 'the moral character of Goorty,'—such, according to Carlyle, was his pronunciation of Goethe's name. All he got out of Carlyle was a recommendation to restudy, in 'Goorty's' own writings, the 'moral character' the anomalies of which had perplexed him.

Carlyle had no amusements. Smoking and riding were his only relaxations : otherwise he was reading or writing or talking. Mrs. Grote, I think it is, who tells of a whist-party in which the players were Macaulay, the late Earl Stanhope, Grote, and Hallam, four grave historians joining in an innocent rubber. One cannot fancy Carlyle asking 'what are trumps ?' and defending himself from the charge of not returning his partner's lead ! Mrs. Carlyle, but never her husband, played at chess. I found her a very fair player, and I have seen her pitted at that game and holding her own against William Edward Forster.   In the London season, when Carlyle was 'hipped,' his wife would sometimes drive about with him to concerts, but except, in the rare case of a Chopin, he cared little for them, or for any music that was not Scotch and wedded to Scotch ballads. Mrs. Carlyle played and sang them very expressively, but I remember early in our acquaintance, the emphasis, it seemed afterwards a little significant, with which she refused a request from me to sing 'Auld Robin Gray.' As long as Macready, a great friend of the Carlyles, remained on the London stage, Carlyle went occasionally to the theatre, and I remember him telling me of his presence at the first performance of *Richelieu*, which Bulwer-Lytton wrote for Macready.   The Queen and everybody else was there, and Carlyle declared that he felt quite sorry for her, condemned to sit and see a King made as wicked, weak, and contemptible as Louis XIII. in Bulwer-Lytton's play.   With Macready's withdrawal from the stage, Carlyle seldom or never visited the theatre, though his wife was rather fond of it.   I remember him only once there.   It was when Dickens and his friends played *The Merry Wives of Windsor* for the benefit of the veteran Leigh Hunt. I was in the boxes, and seeing the Carlyles in a private box went to it, and found them there accompanied by Captain Sterling, John Sterling's military brother.   When the curtain fell, Carlyle said 'a poor play,' but cried '*plaudite, plaudite!*' Mrs. Carlyle took a good deal of interest in Mrs. Mary Cowden Clarke (she played Mrs. Quickly), whom she saw for the first time, and about whom, being questioned by her, I told the little that I knew.

On the relations between Carlyle and his wife, so abundantly discussed by others, I have very little, either in the way of recollections or reflections, to add to what has been said in previous pages. One thing is certain, if their married life was not throughout as happy as it might have been, this did not arise from any exaggerated estimate of what husbands and wives should expect from each other. How often have I heard each of them speak of the absurdity of supposing that a husband was to find in a wife, or a wife in a husband, 'another self!' I have heard Mrs. Carlyle say more than once that a wife could not expect from a husband the same attention after marriage as before it, and this was a theme on which she was rather fond of dilating. Another and more pregnant remark which she once let drop was, 'I can't bear to be thought of as only Mr. Carlyle's wife.' Of course too much is not to be made of a casual remark like this, but its evident sincerity explained several things in her procedure : her self-assertion, her constant intervention in conversation while Carlyle was leading it, and her readiness to tell, 'before company,' anecdotes of Carlyle which made him appear ever so slightly ridiculous. Nothing can exceed the quickness with which clever women pounce upon inconsistency in their husbands, especially when their husbands give themselves airs of superiority. Carlyle was full of inconsistencies, especially in the contrast between his doctrine of the sacredness of silence and his own incessant talk. This gave Mrs. Carlyle a handle of which, when irritated, she was not slow to avail herself for comment on the difference between her husband's preachment and practice. Once when he was declaiming against the love of perpetual locomotion, and insisting on the duty of staying where you are, the

little lady bowled him out very neatly by citing two lines
from his own translation of a distich in *Wilhelm Meister's
Wanderjahre*—

> 'To give room for wandering is it
> That the world was made so wide.'

Carlyle was silenced at once.   Another cause of dissidence
was a difference of temperament.   With gipsy blood in her
veins, Mrs. Carlyle was, in no offensive sense, somewhat
Bohemian, Carlyle not in the least, and her little vivacities
of speech and conduct, which would have amused many
another husband, made him sometimes turn rather roughly
on her.   Much that was faulty in Carlyle's behaviour has
been so amply told, and remorsefully repented of by himself,
that there is no need to enlarge on it.   But he was quite
conscious of all that he owed to her, and has been heard to
say : ' Had it not been for my dear little wife, I should never
have had any hope.'

Two faded-looking letters, out of several written to me
by Mrs. Carlyle, lie before me, having survived by some
accident the lapse of decades.   As they are characteristic of
her in her best and most amiable mood, I shall print them
here, and thus finish off these multifarious and discursive
jottings on the Carlyles and some of those who were
known to them.   Both of her letters refer more or less
directly to a little periodical paper, *The Inspector*, which
in younger and foolish years I started at Manchester, and
which, in spite of the kind efforts of Mrs. Carlyle and others
to keep it alive, came, as it deserved, to an untimely end.
Here is No. 1 of her amiable epistles—

'*New Year's Eve.*

' My dear Mr. Espinasse,—I shall not be able to sleep in
my grave, never to lay (*sic*) in my bed, if I let the year go off with-

out discharging my conscience of its business with you. I have to communicate the names, and also the 1s. 6d.'s, of two more sub-scribers to your dear little paper. The names are Mr. Neuberg, 25 Church Row, Hampstead, and Miss Williams Wynn, 20 Grafton Street. The 1s. and 6d.'s are, along with Captain Sterling's and Mr. Donne's in my pocket, waiting till the sum becomes worth getting a Post Office Order for. But here you have it, under my own hand, that I owe you six shillings.

'Good luck to you, our excellent "young friend," or whatever you like to call yourself, it is deuced hard if a man mayn't call himself what he pleases—and

'Good luck to *The Inspector*—make Geraldine write more in it. The people here said they would "give twopence a paper more for her articles."

'I will write you a letter some day, but just now I am a little *mad* with the tear and wear of *details* from which I cannot escape —I cannot even write to Geraldine, although she and I are "all right" now.

'New year's wishes to you if you care for them. All these horrid "I wish you etc's." make me quite mad and even suicidal.—Yours ever affectionately,

'JANE CARLYLE.'

'My angel of a dog sends his kind regards.'

The first mentioned of the four subscribers procured by Mrs. Carlyle for the ill-fated *Inspector*, 'Mr. Neuberg,' is well known to the readers of Mr. Froude's Biography of Carlyle, and of Carlyle's own *Reminiscences*. For this reason, and also because there is a monograph on him and his connection with Carlyle in *Macmillan's Magazine* (vol. 50, 1884), I have left him unnoticed in these Recollections. To Miss Williams Wynn, of the family of 'the King of Wales,' a very amiable and refined lady, there are also many references in the biographical and epistolary literature of the Carlyles. The late Mr. Donne, then Chief Librarian

of the London Library, afterwards Deputy Examiner of
Plays, is known by several contributions to literature,
among them Monographs on Tacitus and Euripides in the
Ancient Classics for English readers. 'Captain,' since
Colonel, 'Sterling' is John Sterling's brother, 'Geraldine'
is, of course, Miss Jewsbury, who contributed a paper to
No. 1 of *The Inspector*. Mrs. Carlyle's second surviving
letter will explain itself, with the exception, perhaps,
of the reference to 'Mr. Blomfield Rush.' Rush was a
noted murderer of those days, who had fired a series of
shots at the inmates of Stanfield, Hull, near Norwich,
killing two of them and severely wounding two more.
Nobody but Mrs. Carlyle would have thought of associat-
ing his homicidal persistence with the perseverance of
Bruce's spider. To proceed, however, with her letter—

' *Wednesday.*

'DEAR MR. ESPINASSE,—What on earth has taken *The
Inspector*, which we were hoping would go far in "the career
open to talent"? Pray, when you have half an hour's leisure
tell us the meaning of this sudden stop, and especially what you
mean by "a sulky mob"—both Mr. C. and I being puzzled with
the phrase.

'For the rest there is no harm done—the clever honest head
remaining on your shoulders all the same, to do work with some
other instrument, if not with this one first tried. Bless your
heart! think of Bruce's spider and of Mr. Blomfield Rush, and of
hundreds of other historical characters who have made even more
than *seven* trials before they got their thread to take hold.
Think, above all, of Mr. Thomas Carlyle (my husband and author
of various well-known works) who offered his *Sartor* to all the
booksellers in London, one after another, and the best answer he
got was from Fraser that he would print it on being payed (*sic*) a
hundred pounds! My "young friend" you *are* young, you must
remember (if tempted to fall back on misanthropy), and therein

you have an immense advantage over some of us ! It is absurd to hear a man of your years talk of people's good wishes for you having proved "unavailing." There has not been time yet for their availing. I suppose *no* man of talent—real talent, I mean —ever jumped into the right place for him until after a terrible deal of trying and struggling, if even then ; but, if he has the talent, he may still "thank God and write to his friends" (as we used to say at Haddington). Talent is talent, and "singular in itself there is nothing to compare with it—singular in itself there is nothing to equal it" [see the Duke of Buccleuch's speech on Sir Walter Scott]. So don't you be getting sour and bitter, and "all that sort of thing," which would please the Devil very much indeed, and very much vex your sincere friend,

'JANE CARLYLE.'

Unknown then to Mrs. Carlyle, something more disagreeable than the trivial collapse of *The Inspector* had thrown me into the despondent mood which she thus endeavoured to cheer. But enough of those

'Old unhappy far-off things
And battles long ago.'

V. GEORGE HENRY LEWES AND GEORGE ELIOT

CHAPTER I

EARLY CAREER OF LEWES

WHEN I first knew George Henry Lewes he was becoming a noticeable figure among London men of letters. Some years previously he had entered on what was to prove a long literary career. He began with an ample and varied stock-in-trade, so to speak, possessed by few professional authors of that generation. To a familiarity with the great writers of his own country he added a knowledge, more or less profound, of the languages and literature of ancient Greece and Rome,—he told me once that he read Greek for three hours every day,—of France and Germany, of Italy and Spain. An early love of physiology and kindred sciences allured him to medical studies, and recollections of his aspirations to become a biological discoverer possibly enrich the sketch of Lydgate's youth given in George Eliot's *Middlemarch*. Not long after he emerged from boyhood, he conjoined a strong taste for the drama with an eager desire to sound the depths of metaphysical speculation. He wrote plays, he took part in private theatricals (his grandfather, Charles Lee Lewes,

S

had been a comedian of considerable note),[1] and at nineteen he was one of a club of young tradesmen and others who met in the now dingy precincts of Red Lion Square, one of the subjects of their discussions being Spinoza and Spinozism.[2] What Lewes knew, and already he knew

---

[1] This grandfather was of Welsh origin, which may account for the Celtic-looking vivacity of the grandson. In none of the biographical notices of G. H. Lewes is there any mention made of his father. According to a memoir, prefixed to the *Comic Sketches* of his grandfather, the second wife of Charles Lee Lewes the actor was the daughter of 'a respectable innkeeper at Liverpool.' 'There are,' it is added, 'two sons alive who inherit from their mother a very considerable property.' One of these sons was probably G. H. Lewes's father, and certainly edited the *Memoirs* of the grandfather, subscribing himself, at the end of the preface, 'John Lee Lewes, Liverpool, 1805.' From G. H. Lewes's reference, in the note which follows this, to the ' social persecution ' which in youth he suffered from his rejection of 'accepted creeds,' it may be inferred that he and his father were not then on good terms. Lewes's early life was varied. He was at school in London, in Jersey, and in Brittany before being sent to Dr. Burney's once famous seminary at Green-wich. School-years over he was successively in a notary's office and a Russia merchant's counting-house, before, having walked the London hospitals for a time, he threw himself into London literature.

[2] When Lewes had become a prosperous and noted man, he was not ashamed of his early humble associates, and in an article on Spinoza, contributed to the *Fortnightly Review*, which he was editing, he gave an interesting account of this club, formed apparently a little before the beginning of Queen Victoria's reign. 'About thirty years ago,' thus wrote Lewes in 1866, 'a small club of students held weekly meetings in the parlour of a tavern in Red Lion Square, Holborn, where the varied questions of philosophy were discussed with earnestness, if not with insight. The club was extremely simple in its rules and quite informal in its proceedings. The members were men whose sole point of junction was the Saturday meeting, and whose sole object was the amicable collision of contending views on subjects which at one time or other perplex and stimulate all reflecting minds. On every other day in the week their paths were widely divergent. One kept a second-hand bookstall, rich in free-thinking literature ; another was a journeyman watch-maker ; a third lived on a moderate income ; a fourth was a bootmaker ; a fifth "penned a stanza when he should engross ; " a sixth '—doubtless Lewes himself—'studied anatomy and many other things, with vast aspirations and no very definite career before him. Although thus widely separated, those divergent paths converged every Saturday towards the little parlour in Red Lion Square, and the chimes of midnight were drowned in the pleasant noises of argument and laughter : argument sometimes loud and angry, but on

much, he could communicate in a lucid, flowing, and agreeable style. His industry was unflagging, and no discouragement daunted him. The criticisms and suggestions of the most exacting of editors he accepted not only with equanimity but with cheerfulness, and he once boasted to

these occasions always terminating in laughter which cleared the air with its explosions. Seated round the fire smoking their cigars and pipes, and drinking coffee, grog, or ale, without chairman or president, without fixed form of debate, and with a general tendency to talk all at once when the discussion grew animated, these philosophers did really strike out sparks which illuminated each other's minds; they permitted no displays of rhetoric such as generally make debating societies intolerable; they came for philosophic talk, and they talked.' Lewes mentions by name two only of the members of this club, then probably unique in London. One was James Pierrepoint Greaves, who became noted in certain circles as a mystic very far gone in theosophy. He came seldom and was ultimately driven away from it by a general explosion of laughter, which saluted his reply to an inquiry what he meant by speaking of himself as 'phenomenised,' a mysterious condition of which he was given to boasting. 'I am what I am,' quoth Greaves, 'and it is out of my "Iamity" that I am phenomenised.' *Solvuntur risu tabula.* A more fruitful person was one Cohn, or Kohn, a German Jew, to whom some permanent interest attaches since he is understood to have been the original Mordecai of *Daniel Deronda*. He was a member 'whom,' Lewes wrote, 'we all admired as a man of astonishing subtlety and logical force, no less than of great personal worth. He remains in my memory as a type of philosophic dignity. A calm, meditative, amiable man, by trade a journeyman watchmaker, very poor, with weak eyes and chest; grave and gentle in demeanour; incorruptible, even by the seductions of vanity. I habitually think of him in connection with Spinoza, almost as much on account of his personal characteristics as because to him I owe my first acquaintance with the Hebrew thinker. My admiration for him was of that enthusiastic temper which in youth we feel for our intellectual leaders. I loved his weak eyes and low voice: I venerated his great calm intellect. He was the only man I did not contradict in the impatience of argument. An immense pity and a fervid indignation filled me as I came away from his attic in one of the Holborn Courts, where I had seen him in the pinching poverty of his home, with his German wife and two little black-eyed children: indignantly I railed against society, which could allow so great an intellect to withdraw itself from nobler work and waste the precious hours in mending watches. But he was wiser in his resignation than I in my young indignation. Life was hard to him as to all of us; but he was content to earn a miserable pittance by handicraft and keep his soul serene. I learned to understand him better when I learned the story of Spinoza's life.' One day Cohn

me that there was scarcely any editor whom he wished to
cultivate to whom he could not supply just the article
that was wanted.　To say nothing of journalism, his work,
before he was thirty, was to be found almost everywhere
in the higher periodical literature of the day, in the
Edinburgh, the *London and Westminster*, the *British and
Foreign*, and the *Foreign Quarterly* Reviews.　Later, and
at a time when of serious and solid periodicals appearing
at intervals of three months there were several more than
now, he told me, with not unnatural glee, that he had
an article in every one of them, 'except the d—d old
Quarterly.'　The subjects which he dealt with covered an
extensive area.　His earlier articles in the *Edinburgh
Review* alone ranged from criticism on the *mise en scène* of
the London theatres to disquisitions on Arabian philosophy.

Of course, writing thus much and on such a great variety
of themes, Lewes was not always effective.　All along,
indeed, he contributed more to 'the literature of knowledge'

('Cohen'?) picked up at a book-stall a German work in which Spinoza's
system was expounded, and from time to time as he mastered, during intervals
of business, its leading doctrines, he retailed them to the club.　'It was,'
Lewes says, 'the more interesting to me because I happened to be hungering
for some knowledge of this theological pariah—partly, no doubt, because he
was an outcast, for as I was then suffering the social persecution which
embitters all departure from accepted creeds, I had a rebellious sympathy
with all outcasts, and partly because I had casually met with a passage,
quoted for reprobation, in which Spinoza maintained the subjective nature of
evil, a passage which, to my mind, lighted up that perplexed question.'　At
last Lewes lighted, in an old book-shop, on a small crown quarto, *Spinozæ
opera posthuma*, and mastered at first-hand the system the rudiments of which
he had learned from Cohn.　In 1843 (*ætat* 29) Lewes made Spinoza the
subject of an article which was the earliest modern attempt in England to
rehabilitate that profound and original thinker, whose system even David
Hume spoke of as 'infamous.'　Soon after this acquaintance with Spinoza,
and doubtless to study German philosophy in the land of its birth, he went
to Germany, acquiring a perfect knowledge of its language.　His early
residence in Brittany had made him a master of French.

than to 'the literature of power.' But whatever he wrote
displayed a certain originality of view. Whether he was
dealing with literature, philosophy, or science, he was never
an echo of his predecessors or contemporaries. Lewes
was no worshipper of great names, and had in a singular
degree the courage of his opinions. In his *Biographical
History of Philosophy*, the earliest of his books which
attracted notice, it was interesting to see the boldness of
its young author's trenchant criticism of the systems of the
most renowned sages, and the confidence with which he
announced that the positive results of philosophy (in its
restricted sense of metaphysical and ontological speculation) from Thales to Hegel amounted to absolutely nothing.
Lewes had a great contempt for cant of all kinds,
especially the cant of literary idolatry. Naturally in his
conversation, even more than in his writings, he said right
out what he thought and felt. The expression of his contempt for cant, had he been cynical, would have been bitter,
but in his case it took the form of levity, and thus exposed
him, with serious people, to the charge of flippancy.
After meeting him, for the first time, Margaret Fuller
described him as 'a witty French flippant sort of man.'
It was not until she had known him for more than a year
that George Eliot herself wrote of Lewes, 'he has quite
won my regard after having had a good deal of my
vituperation. Like a few other people in the world, he is
much better than he seems. A man of heart and
conscience wearing a mask of flippancy.'

Among the many and varied results of Lewes's early
literary ambition was the production of a work of fiction.
At twenty-five he wrote a novel, *Ranthorpe*, for which at
thirty he found a publisher. It was a crude performance,

but, so far as I know, was one of the first, if not the very first, of those novels, since so plentiful, which are mainly pictures of modern literary life in London : its struggles, failures, and triumphs. Though undeniably clever, *Ranthorpe* was not a success. The indefatigable Lewes set to work again, and, amid other and more pressing avocations, produced a three-volume novel, *Rose, Blanche, and Violet:* a history of the varied fortunes of three sisters. He had taken considerable pains with it ; but, for a book of Lewes's, it appeared to me absolutely tedious (though it has been praised by critics more competent than I can pretend to be), and was received with indifference by the public. It was one of the very slight results of the publication of this novel that through it indirectly I made the acquaintance of its author.

Mrs. Carlyle being on a visit to the Barings at Addiscombe, I was sitting alone with Carlyle one evening in the second week of April, 1848. I had given him an account of the scene presented by Kennington Common on the once famous 10th of April, a day or two before. Partly from 'professional' zeal, partly from a spirit of adventure, I had taken my seat, with other brethren of the press, in the roomy car which bore Feargus O'Connor and the Chartist delegates to the Common, where were assembled many thousands of his dupes, whom he disappointed by directing them, while he himself shook with terror, to disperse quietly. Carlyle was beginning to compute how many persons in the vast assembly could have heard the orator's voice, when Lewes entered the room. After George Eliot saw Lewes for the first time, she described him as 'a sort of miniature Mirabeau in appearance.' As in Mirabeau's case, the ugliness and the remains of the ravages of the smallpox were undoubtedly there, but Lewes had a fine eye and an expressive countenance, which when lighted up by a smile was far from disagreeable. However it was Lewes's plainness of visage that led the Carlyles, as will be seen further on, to speak of him, though only for a time, as 'The Ape.' Lewes was a man of no concealments, and the object of his visit was soon apparent. He had sent Carlyle a copy of *Rose, Blanche, and Violet*, just published, and he came not to talk about the then absorbing topic of Chartism and Kennington Common, but to find out what Carlyle thought of his novel. Carlyle had read it, but the adventures of Mesdemoiselles Rose, Blanche, and Violet were not, as chronicled by Lewes, of a kind to interest him, yet here was the author bent on discovering his opinion of it! It was amusing, at least to me, to see how Carlyle fenced with the anxious inquirer. The author could extract little more from the reluctant critic than that *Rose, Blanche, and Violet*, showed 'more breadth' than its predecessor, *Ranthorpe*. However, by way of soothing his visitor, Carlyle added that Mrs. Carlyle had taken the book with her to the country, to be read not only by herself, but by 'a very high lady,' the Lady Harriet Baring, who became soon afterwards Lady Ashburton. Carlyle commenting in a depreciatory way on the amount of love-making in modern novels, Lewes retorted by referring to the amatory episodes in *Wilhelm Meister*. Carlyle rejoined that there was no more of that sort of thing in *Meister* than 'the flirtation which goes on in ordinary life,' a very different verdict from Wordsworth's and De Quincey's. 'I would rather have written that book,' Carlyle said, 'than a cartload of others,' and he went on to speak of Goethe's

'Olympian silence' and other transcendent qualities.
With admirable persistence Lewes took advantage of a
pause to ask if some gaming-house scenes in *Rose,
Blanche, and Violet* were not to be commended. Instead
of answering the question, Carlyle launched into a description of a gaming-house in Paris, to pay a visit of curiosity
to which he had been taken, by the late Sir J. Emerson-
Tennent, I think, and said that he remembered the faces
of the players at the gaming-table so vividly that if he
were a painter he could reproduce them even after that
long lapse of years. Abandoning his fruitless quest, Lewes
spoke of a life of Robespierre, which, as well as his life of
Goethe, he had then on the anvil. Seeing that I was
surprised at the conjunction of two such tasks, Carlyle
said genially : 'Lewes is not afraid of any amount of work.'
My fellow-visitor and I walked together part of the way
towards our respective homes. The junior asked the senior
whom did he consider to be at the head of our literature, and received for reply, 'Macaulay, undoubtedly.'
Lewes talked to me, as an aspirant, of the difficulties of a
literary career, laying stress on the loss of several hundreds
a year which he had sustained by the discontinuance of the
British and Foreign Review, which, as formerly recorded
(*ante*, p. 106) was munificently supported for several years
by the late Mr. Wentworth Beaumont, the wealthy M.P.
Meanwhile Carlyle had sat down and, at eleven o'clock p.m.,
indited to his wife a half-plaintive, half-indignant epistle,
beginning, 'Oh, my dear, be sorry for me! I am nearly
out of my wits. From three o'clock till now I have been
in a tempest of twaddle.' After some uncomplimentary
remarks on previous visitors, of whose names Mr. Froude
prints only the initials, Carlyle proceeds : 'In the evening

came in'—the writer of these pages—'and shortly after
the Ape'—Lewes, to wit. 'May the devil confound it! I
feel as if I had got enough for one day. No wonder I am
surly at people.' (There was no trace of surliness in his
manner that evening.) 'The wonder is rather I do not
shoot them. You wretched people! You cannot help me,
you can only hinder me. Of you I must for ever petition
in vain that you would simply not mind me at all, but
fancy in your hearts I was a grey stone, and so leave me.'[1]
In her reply, which, fortunately for Lewes's feelings, was
not printed until after his death, Mrs. Carlyle tells what
both she and the 'very high lady' thought of *Rose,
Blanche, and Violet*: 'Execrable that is. I could not have
suspected even the Ape of writing anything so silly. Lady
H. read it all the way down, and decided it was "too vulgar
to go on with." I myself should have also laid it aside
in the first half volume if I had not felt a pitying interest
in the man'—struggling industriously to support with his
pen a wife and expanding family—'that makes me read
on in the hope of coming to something a little better.
Your marginal notes are the only real amusement I have
got out of it hitherto.' Evidently Lewes was not then a
favourite of the Carlyles, though there is, in this extract
from Mrs. Carlyle's letter, a touch of womanly sympathy
with him. The truth, I take it, was that Lewes, who was
no respecter of persons, sometimes made Carlyle wince—
and Carlyle was more than twenty years his senior—by

---

[1] At the close of his letter Carlyle did me the honour thus to report to his
wife my account of the Kennington Common fiasco : ' E. was in the car with
Feargus O'Connor and the other Chartists. Never,' he says, 'in the
world was there a more total irremediably ludicrous failure than that operation ; seldom a viler cowardly scoundrel (according to E.) than that same
Feargus as E. there read him.'

laughing at his prophetics when they were dining out together in cheerful society. To this were added some literary sins. For instance, Lewes at one time did not write nearly so appreciatively and respectfully of Goethe as on becoming his biographer. Almost 'Philistine' in tone an admirer of Lewes has called the article on Goethe, which early in his career he contributed to the *British and Foreign Review* (it was however translated at the time into French and German), and of which Carlyle said to me that it was 'wide of the mark.' There was an attack on Niebuhr, too, and before I met Lewes, Carlyle spoke of him to me as an assailant of 'established reputations.' Carlyle had not then read the *Biography of Philosophy*. ' I didn't think,' he said, ' that I could learn anything about philosophy from that body Lewes'—a Scottish expression of contempt. All this altered in the course of time, especially with the appearance of Lewes's *Life of Goethe*, the undeniable merits of which Carlyle appreciated none the less because it was dedicated to himself in language of cordial admiration. After the catastrophe which separated him from his wife, ' the Ape' of former years became with Mrs. Carlyle ' poor dear Lewes,' and, after the establishment of the *Leader*, Carlyle pronounced ' that body Lewes ' to be ' the Prince of Journalists.'

I met Lewes occasionally during the first year of my acquaintance with him, but I saw much more of him in the succeeding year, during which he visited Manchester, where I was then residing. But of Lewes's visits to Manchester and of the establishment of the *Leader*, which followed on them, something will fall to be said in another chapter.

CHAPTER II

LEWES IN MANCHESTER

EARLY in the year after my first meeting with Lewes he paid a visit of some duration to Manchester, of which city I was then for the second time a denizen. One of the objects which brought him thither was the delivery of a course of lectures on the history of speculative philosophy. Lewes's expositions were lucid and lively, his manner was animated, and his audiences, though not large, were distinctly appreciative. His contemptuous treatment of metaphysics and his exaltation of science were not unsuited to the inquiring intellects of that utilitarian city. It was pleasant to be told that though you had never troubled yourself about 'the problems of life and mind,' you were just as wise as any of the long series of sages who had wended their toilsome way on the 'high *priori* road,' which, according to Lewes, led nowhere. A new era, he proclaimed, had dawned on mankind with Comte's promulgation of the Positive philosophy. Of Lewes's hearers, among whom I was one, many, I doubt not, went home content to know nothing which could not be 'verified by experience,' since beyond that, the clever and erudite gentleman from London assured us, there was really nothing to be known.

But it was not merely to discourse on the futility of metaphysics and to glorify Auguste Comte that Lewes came to Manchester. He wished to make a figure on the stage as well as on the platform. It was the revival of a wish which had animated him in his earlier years; the histrionic and dramatic efforts of his youth have been already mentioned. Since then he had written a serious drama, *The Noble Heart*, which remained unacted. On the public stage he had played Sir Hugh Evans in *The Merry Wives of Windsor*, when performed by the amateur company of men of letters and artists which, under the management of Charles Dickens, went 'on tour' for the benefit of the veteran Leigh Hunt. Some vague aspiration to become both a successful dramatist and a successful actor flitted through Lewes's mind, and he had resolved to try his wings at Manchester in both these flights. Just when he was finishing his lectures on philosophy the advertisements of the 'Theatre Royal, Manchester,' announced that 'This evening Mr. G. H. Lewes, the popular author, will make his *début* in *The Merchant of Venice*, one of the plays,' the Manchester impresario actually deemed it desirable to add, 'selected by her Majesty at Windsor Castle. Shylock, Mr. G. H. Lewes;' Barry Sullivan playing Bassanio. There was originality in Lewes's conception of Shylock, whom he endeavoured to represent as the champion and avenger of a persecuted race, and his gabardine and three-pointed beard were praised as accurate reproductions of old reality. Sooth to say, however, Lewes's personation of the Jew that Shakespeare drew was palpably ineffective, and his best friends were obliged to admit that Nature had not intended him to be an actor. He tried another part, that of the elderly hero, in his own drama, *The Noble Heart*, a play in blank verse, with Elizabethan touches. But his personation of a Spanish hidalgo was as wanting in dignity as that of the Venetian Jew had been in power. *The Noble Heart* was performed in London afterwards, but with indifferent success. Lewes gave up all serious pretensions to be a dramatist, and pretensions of any kind to be an actor. His one dramatic hit, *The Game of Speculation*, was merely an adaptation (said to have been executed in twenty-four hours), though a very clever one, of Balzac's *Mercadet le Faiseur.* He was for the most part content to be a dramatic critic, and one of great acumen, as his little volume *On Actors and Acting* abundantly testifies.

In Manchester, Lewes went a good deal into society, was a frequent guest of the Jewsburys, and made himself generally agreeable. He was eminently sociable and convivial, and an admirable *raconteur*, especially of French anecdotes gathered in Paris, where he had been recently in quest of material for his life of Robespierre. His anecdotes were often of a kind that would not now bear reproduction. One of the least unpresentable of them was a significant story of a Paris editor, to whom a serious-minded aspirant brought for publication an elaborate essay on the existence of a deity. 'Dieu,' was the businesslike editor's polite but disappointing reply, 'Dieu—c'est bien, très bien—mais, mon cher Monsieur, la question de Dieu n'est pas une actualité!' At a jovial Manchester supper-party, I heard Lewes give the imaginary account, not printed until years afterwards, of the different ways in which a Frenchman, an Englishman, and a German, might respond to an invitation to describe the camel; the Frenchman, after an hour at the Jardin des Plantes, presenting a sketch of the ship of the desert, lively and admirably written, though very superficial; the Englishman proceeding to the East, and after long investigation returning with a great budget of valuable but undigested facts ; while the German, retiring to his study, constructed the idea of a camel out of the depths of his moral consciousness. This clever, and a good deal more than clever, *jeu d'esprit* was first published by Lewes in his life of Goethe, I think. In whole or in part, it has been reproduced throughout the English-writing world, in innumerable books and articles, but I doubt whether its authorship is generally known. One of Lewes's few notable acquaintances during this visit was the late Dr. Vaughan, then Principal of the Lancashire Independent College at or near Manchester, and editor of the *British Quarterly Review*, to which Lewes was a frequent and prominent contributor ; his articles in it on Macaulay and Disraeli may still be read with interest. Lewes, who had then his *Life of Goethe* on the stocks, told me with considerable satisfaction that the eminent Nonconformist had pronounced the 'Confessions of a Fair Saint' in *Wilhelm Meister's Apprenticeship* to be a singularly accurate transcript of pietistic spiritual experiences. During one of his visits to my own domicile, the company not being exclusively male, Lewes gave us most sympathetically—for with all his faults he was then an affectionate husband and always an affectionate father—nursery stories of his children, sent him from London by his wife, who, he said, wrote to him unfailingly every day—a statement which afterwards acquired a pathetic interest.

Towards the end of the same year Lewes reappeared in Manchester, coming on an errand very different from either of the two which had brought him there on his previous visit. His mission was to raise some of the capital required for a literary enterprise, in which he was very much interested, the establishment of a new weekly journal, to be the organ of 'advanced' opinions, political, religious, and, above all, social, at that time, it was thought, without an adequate exponent in the higher London journalism. In his *Life of Robespierre*, published about the same time, and dedicated to his father-in-law, Swynfen Jervis, then or previously an M.P., and, I believe, a banker, Lewes, while condemning Robespierre's sanguinary fanaticism, had shown a strong sympathy with the general objects of the great French Revolution. In promoting the newspaper, which he hoped was to lessen his dependence on the editors of reviews and magazines, he was aided and abetted by his friend Thornton Hunt, Leigh Hunt's eldest son, a journalist of considerable experience and much more of a serious politician than Lewes himself. Thornton Hunt, who rivalled Lewes in plainness of visage, was some seven years his senior. The first noticeable incident in his journalistic career was his appointment, at five-and-twenty or so, to be assistant editor of the *Constitutional*, an unsuccessful London daily newspaper, started by a company, the chairman of which was Major Carmichael Smyth, the second husband of Thackeray's mother. Thackeray, then rather a fierce Radical, was successively its correspondent in Paris and its foreign editor in London. He is said to have lost his little all by investing it in the *Constitutional*, and is also said to have met his loss with the pious ejaculation, 'Thank God we have our religion left!' After the failure of the *Constitutional*, Thornton Hunt became a busy journalist in town and country. When he and Lewes were projecting their new journal he was on the staff of the *Spectator*, and looked forward hopefully to the prospect of being allowed to say his say on social

questions more freely than was permissible in that
shrewdly-conducted but then rather prosaic journal. The
times, indeed, seemed somewhat favourable to Lewes's and
Hunt's enterprise. To what I have said on this subject in
a sketch of the state of things when Carlyle was preparing
his *Latter-Day Pamphlets*—and the publication of the
new journal followed closely on that of *Latter-Day
Pamphlets*, No. 1—I may add a mention of the rise of
new movements throughout the country for the extension
of the suffrage and for undenominational education, the
latter begun in Manchester. It was not without justification that Lewes boasted to me of the extreme appropriate-
ness of the name selected for the new organ. There was
something in the mere name of the *Leader* to commend it
to the party of 'progress.'

Lewes's financial mission to Manchester was not un-
attended by some success. One of the largest Lancashire
contributors to the capital with which the *Leader* was
started was a wealthy and philanthropic German owner of
calico-printing works near Manchester. At the house
of William Edward Forster, at Rawdon, there were communings, too, between the projectors of the new Journal
and sundry North of England sympathisers. But the
chief financial supporter of the new journal at its start
was understood to be a Lincolnshire rector, still surviving
in advanced years, and so very 'broad' a Churchman that
he assisted in the execution of an English translation of
George Sand's works, and appended to one of his published
sermons a sketch of Fourier's scheme of social reorganisation. At last, on the 30th March 1850, the happy Lewes
saw the *Leader* launched under what appeared to be
favourable auspices. Thornton Hunt was its political,

Lewes its literary, editor, and the general editorship was shared between them. One of the sub-editors was the late George Hooper, who, having learned in youth the A B C of journalism from the John Robertson noticed in one of my Carlyle papers, became a journalist of note, and was known latterly by several meritorious contributions to military history and biography. Among the outside contributors were Mazzini, Miss Martineau, Herbert Spencer, Walter Savage Landor, Charles Kingsley, and even Mr. Froude, whose *Cat's Pilgrimage* and *Political Fables* appeared (anonymously) in the earlier numbers, but who in reprinting them has taken care not to mention that they were first published in an organ of so 'advanced' a Liberalism. One of the contributors of verse was Gerald Massey, who, in the columns of the *Leader*, if I remember rightly, first became known to fame as a poet. A novel 'feature' of the *Leader* was its 'Open Council,' in which men of all opinions were invited to express them, thus carrying out a favourite notion of John Stuart Mill's. In 'Open Council' was published a series of remarkable letters on the *Droit au Travail* by William Edward Forster. Of one unremembered but striking contribution by Lewes to the earliest numbers of the *Leader*, more hereafter.

T

CHAPTER III

LEWES IN LATER YEARS: GEORGE ELIOT

LEWES'S contributions to the *Leader* greatly aided its successful start. Literature, domestic and foreign, the drama and the stage, science at home and abroad, he handled with a versatility, vivacity, and verve which in their combination were unique in the journalism of the day. If the intellectual independence which he exhibited exposed him to the charge of attacking established reputations, it helped him to urge the claims which gifted young authors, as yet unknown to fame, possessed to recognition. The *Life Drama* of Alexander Smith, then a young man of one-and-twenty, a pattern designer in Glasgow, had not even been published as a whole, but was appearing piecemeal in the columns of the *Critic*, when time after time, in one of those *causeries* on literature which he was the first to prefix to the ordinary reviews of books, Lewes drew attention, which it might not otherwise have received, to the beauties and felicities of its diction. Another but this time a metrical tribute paid to Alexander Smith, in the columns of the *Leader*, was by George Meredith, who saluted his sonnet on Fame as the 'mighty warning of a poet's birth.' James Hannay's earliest novel, *Singleton Fontenoy*, was by no critic welcomed so warmly as by the keen-sighted Lewes, who at once pronounced it to be a 'remarkable work,' displaying 'the exuberance of youth and the promise of a ripe maturity.'

The unremembered but striking contribution of Lewes to the *Leader*, spoken of in the preceding chapter, was a fragment of a novel which, had he finished it, might have been his one successful work of fiction. The desire to be original, generally perceptible in Lewes's writings of every kind, is rather conspicuous in *The Apprenticeship of Life*. In modern fiction, from Miss Jewsbury's *Zoe* to Mrs. Humphry Ward's *Robert Elsmere*, when the religious belief of the hero is transformed, he is usually made to pass from Faith to Doubt. Lewes's hero undergoes the reverse operation. Armand is a young Frenchman, whose father, a Baron of the Restoration, having been fed on Voltaire and the Encyclopædists, is a fanatical freethinker. Brought up in his father's creed, or no creed, Armand has zealously adopted it, when he is converted to Christianity, though of a somewhat vague kind. The chief agent in his conversion is a meditative, eloquent, and persuasive Greek. Lewes took his Stavros Frangipoli (σταυρός being old Greek for the Cross) from a deceased friend of his and mine, Stavros Dilberoglue, a young Greek merchant settled in Manchester at the time of Lewes's visit, and characterised in the account of Carlyle's visit to that city. There were obviously frequent references to him and to his friendship with Lewes in the originals of Miss Jewsbury's recently-published letters to Mrs. Carlyle. But the editress of those letters has, *more suo*, suppressed his name, and all that survives of him in them is a meaningless ——. The proceeding was unnecessary, not to say provoking, since Dilberoglue has long been dead, and was a most interesting as well as irreproachable member of the Jewsbury circle.

He deserved not obliteration, but notice from an editress who has also been a biographer of Mrs. Carlyle, in whose correspondence he is often referred to. In the series modestly entitled *Epistolæ Obscurorum Virorum* which appeared in the *Leader* was a letter by Lewes on 'Communism as an Ideal,'—to be struggled towards now and ever, but to be realised only in a very distant future,—addressed 'to Stavros Dilberoglue.' His Christian name, conjoined with an English surname, survives in his godson, Mr. Stavros Jewsbury, now the representative of the Jewsbury family, a nephew of Miss Jewsbury and son of her brother Frank.

To return, however, to the hero of Lewes's novel. On account of his conversion to Christianity, Armand is almost driven from his home. He finds accidentally a refuge in the house of a lady-cousin, a fascinating widow of means. They love each other and are married, but they do not 'live happy ever after.' In course of time Armand falls in love with some one else. Seeing with sorrow the painful struggle in his breast between duty and inclination, his wife considerately effaces herself by pretending to commit suicide in order to set him free, while in reality she becomes a Sister of Charity. In the chapter in which this episode is narrated there is broached a theory of wedlock the laxity of which perhaps indirectly elucidates the catastrophe in Lewes's domestic life not long after this fragment of a fiction was published.[1] Whether the hero committed

---

[1] One brief extract from this *plaidoyer* of Lewes's for 'Free Love' will suffice. Describing the decay of the hero's love for his once adored wife, the novelist moralises thus: 'We daily hear inconstancy stigmatised as a vice, forgetful that constancy and inconstancy are independent of the will. We do not will to love; nor do we will to cease to love. As love brings with it its own sufficient reason, so also does the change bring with it its sufficient reason. Every feeling justifies itself (!). If love could be commanded inconstancy would be a sin.'

unconscious bigamy by marrying again while his first wife, though supposed to be dead, was alive, remains uncertain. He migrates to Paris, anxious to play an active part in the anti-Bourbon movement which preceded the Revolution of 1830. There are some very striking descriptions of the plots and plotters of that eventful time. But the story ends abruptly just when it was beginning to be most interesting, and when 'The Apprenticeship of Life,' Lewes had announced, was about to be developed into 'The Initiation of Work.'

The *Leader* had a fair circulation, especially among the younger and more thoughtful members of the 'advanced' party in politics and religion. Thus and otherwise it might have become self-supporting, but this never happened, and it is remembered as one of the extinct possibilities of journalism. Lewes himself gave up his literary editorship of the *Leader*, though without ceasing to be a contributor to it, soon after the formation of that domestic partnership with George Eliot which continued until the close of his life. They went abroad together, and Lewes inspected Weimar and its neighbourhood, diligently hunting up traits and anecdotes of Goethe for his biography of the great German, which appeared in the following year, and very much strengthened his literary position. I was not in London when it appeared, but I wrote elsewhere a review of it which gratified him. On meeting him when I returned to town, I asked him what he was doing, and he replied, 'Investigating the cilia of the snail!' Then and for several years he was very much occupied with scientific pursuits, producing among other books his instructive and agreeable *Sea-side Studies* and *Studies in Animal Life*. The latter book was reprinted from the first six numbers of the *Cornhill*, its insertion in which appears to have gone rather against the grain with Thackeray, whose tastes lay not at all in that direction. Writing on science, whether for the many or the few, Lewes, as usual, aimed at being original, attacking other people's theories and broaching novelties of his own. Some of these seem to have been in time accepted by scientific experts. Certain it is that, in the last edition of the *Origin of Species*, Darwin quoted him with approval, and conceded to be 'possible' the truth of Lewes's hypothesis that at the first commencement of life on our planet many different forms of life were evolved.

I was again far from London when the *Fortnightly Review* was established, with Lewes for its first editor. The fame of the *Revue des Deux Mondes* had long inspired a wish for an English periodical of the same superior kind, and, like it, issued at intervals of a fortnight. Years before the appearance of the *Fortnightly*, Carlyle told me that John Forster had been to him to ask for his co-operation in a scheme for the establishment of a periodical on the plan of the French reviews, and had been told by Carlyle that he 'did not think much of the French reviews.' At last the experiment was to be tried, and under peculiar conditions. Anthony Trollope and a few others clubbed together some thousands of pounds, and with this the *Fortnightly* was started. The sequel may point a moral if not adorn a tale in these days of authors' protests against publishers. Lewes was an admirable editor.[1] The con-

---

[1] Lewes's own contributions to the *Fortnightly* were numerous and varied. The most generally interesting of them was an article on 'Dickens in relation to criticism,' in which the claim of Dickens to a place among the great novelists of the world was so severely contested as to elicit from John Forster, in his biography of Dickens, a rather elaborate protest against its tone and tenor. The following extract from Lewes's article speaks for itself:—

'Dickens sees and feels, but the logic of feeling seems the only logic he can

tributors included some of the ablest men in England. As the articles were signed, the Review had the benefit of the names of their writers. It took at once a foremost place among English periodicals. But the management of its finances was in the hands of authors exclusively. So the thousands of pounds subscribed by Anthony Trollope and his friends melted away, and the *Fortnightly*, becoming a monthly, was sold to its publishers for an old song.

After eighteen months or so Lewes resigned the editorship of the *Fortnightly*, partly to devote himself to the composition of his philosophical *opus maximum*, *The Problems of Life and Mind*, among these problems being some which in earlier years he had regarded as insoluble by the experimental method, but to which, at least in part, he was now determined to apply it. Returning to London just after he resigned his editorship, I saw him occasionally thenceforward until the close of his life. With advancing years he retained his old vivacity, and though he complained often of ill-health, to the last not only were his spirits unflagging, but his very gait had the rush of impetuous and vigorous youth. No young author, flushed with the success of a first effort, could have shown more elation

manage. Thought is strangely absent from his works. I do not suppose a single thoughtful remark on life or character could be found throughout the twenty volumes. Not only is there a marked absence of the reflective tendency, but one sees no indication of the past life of humanity having ever occupied him. Keenly as he observes the objects before him, he never connects his observations into a general expression, never seems interested in general relations of things. Compared with that of Fielding or Thackeray, his was merely an *animal* intelligence, *i.e.* restricted to perceptions. On this ground his early education was more fruitful and less injurious than it would have been to a nature constituted on a more reflective and intellectual type. It furnished him with rare and valuable experience, early developed his sympathies with the lowly and struggling, and did not starve any intellectual ambition. He never was, and never would have been, a student.'

than Lewes when, verging on sixty, he saw vol. i. of his
Problems of Life and Mind reach a second edition soon
after it was issued. At the time I suspected that this
success was due less to an appreciation of the philosophical
acumen displayed in the volume than to the attractiveness
of its sub-title, ' The Foundations of a Creed,' and that many
of its readers may have been disappointed on finding in it,
not a new religion, but abstruse discussions on the first
principles which the author intended to apply in the subsequent treatment of biological and physiological questions.
Lewes, however, thought, and not unnaturally, that his
success was due to the increased interest taken in the
subject-matter of his book. Next to the importance of
biology and physiology in philosophical inquiry, the topic,
it seemed to me, on which Lewes most delighted to enlarge
was George Eliot, ' my wife,' he always called her. Traits
and anecdotes of her were frequently on his lips. Two of
the many things which he told me of her impressed themselves on my memory. Among her numerous accomplishments was a knowledge of Hebrew, and, according to
Lewes, during their rambles in German woods and forests,
she taught it him, not that he might· be able to read the
Old Testament in the original, but that they might talk
to each other without being understood by the polyglot
landlords and waiters of Continental hotels ! In illustration of the versatile keenness of her observing faculty he
said that, having had an opportunity for inspecting a winner
of the Derby,—Kisber, I think, was its name,—George
Eliot, after a slight scrutiny, pointed out some physical
defect or blemish in the steed, the existence of which was
at once admitted by the groom-in-waiting, and great was
his astonishment, the proud and happy Lewes declared,

that a lady should have detected what had escaped the ken of male connoisseurs in horse-flesh. Readers of George Eliot's Life know that her affectionate admiration of Lewes did not fall far short of that which he felt for her. She did not survive him long enough to carry out her intention of collecting and republishing his scattered contributions to periodicals, nor, at this time of day, is any one likely to do for him what she was not allowed to do. But Lewes was a man of considerable mark—such a judge as Mr. Leslie Stephen speaks of his 'extraordinary versatility and acuteness'—and he was intimate with a very great number of notable people. His life and work deserve a more adequate literary memorial than any which they have as yet received in here and there a magazine article.

The sad episode in Lewes's domestic history which has been previously referred to would have been forgotten long ere this had it not led to the intimate connection with George Eliot, which proved of such importance to both of them. That episode and its sequel produced at the time a great deal of gossip, much of which was prurient, and none of which shall I retail. But in the volume of *Conversations with Carlyle*, recently published by Sir Charles Gavan Duffy, there is reported one which turned on the then contemporaneous junction of Lewes and George Eliot, and which seems worth reproducing. Carlyle had been denouncing, as was his wont, George Sand's erotics, when Mrs. Carlyle took up her parable thus—

' " We had small right," said the little lady, " to throw the first stone at George Sand, though she had been caught in the same predicament as the woman of old, if we considered what sort of literary ladies might be found in London at present. When one was first told that the strong woman of the *Westminster Review*,"

George Eliot, " had gone off with a man whom we all knew,"
Lewes, " it was as startling an announcement as if one heard
that a woman of your acquaintance had gone off with the strong
man at Astley's ; but that the partners in the adventure had set
up as moralists was a graver surprise. To renounce George Sand
as a teacher of morals was right enough, but it was scarcely con-
sistent with making so much of our own George in that capacity.
A marvellous teacher of morals, surely, and still more marvellous
in the other character, for which nature had not provided her with
the outfit supposed to be essential." '

Then Duffy strikes in—

' The gallant, I said, was as badly equipped for an Adonis and
conqueror of hearts. Yes, Carlyle replied, he was certainly
the ugliest little fellow you could anywhere meet, but he was
lively and pleasant. In this final adventure, it must be admitted,
he had escaped from worse, and might even be said to have
ranged himself. He had originally married a bright little woman,
daughter of Swynfen Jervis, a disreputable Welsh member ; but
every one knew how that adventure had turned out. Miss Evans
advised him to quit a household which had broken bounds in
every direction. His proceeding was not to be applauded, but
it could scarcely be said that he had gone from bad to worse.'

Carlyle was generally as severe to ethical laxity in living
men as Mrs. Carlyle has just been seen to be towards one
of her own sex. The excuses which, in the passage quoted,
Carlyle made for Lewes were partly due to his later liking
for the male delinquent, and partly, it is possible, to his
having heard only Lewes's version of the story. But some
of those who knew it at first-hand did not share Carlyle's
indulgence to Lewes, and since Sir C. G. Duffy has thought
it worth while to revive that old scandal, and to represent
Lewes's conduct as condoned by so stern a moralist as
Carlyle, it is but right that what has been urged on behalf
of Lewes's co-delinquent should be heard, and that Carlyle's

mercy to Lewes should be tempered by justice to Thornton Hunt. This has been done by Mrs. Lynn Linton, who evidently was cognisant of all the facts, and who gives what is clearly her version of them in the following passage of her interesting, though not very well known book, *The Autobiography of Christopher Kirkland* (i. 273):—

'Among others I fell in with that notorious group of Free Lovers, whose ultimate transaction was the most notable example of matrimony void of contract in our day. But though those who floated on the crest of the wave,'—Lewes and George Eliot,—'and whose informal union came to be regarded as a moral merit, even by the strait-laced, had the more genius and the better luck, he who made personal shipwreck,'—Thornton Hunt,—'and from whose permitted trespass the whole thing started, had the nobler nature, the most fruitful heart, the more constant mind, and was in every way the braver and the truer man. He whom society set itself to honour, partly because of the transcendent genius of his companion, partly because of his own brilliancy and facility, was less solid than specious. The other, whom all men, not knowing him, reviled, was a moral hero. The former betrayed his own principles when he made capital out of his 'desecrated hearth,' and bewildered society by setting forth ingenious stories of impossible ceremonies which had made his informal union in a certain sense sacramental, so that he might fill his rooms with "names," and make his Sundays days of illustrious reception. The latter accepted his position without explanation or complaint, and was faithful to his flag, indifferent to selfish gain or social loss. And whether that flag embodied a right principle or a wrong, his steadfastness was equally admirable, and the constancy, which could not be warped for loss or gain, was equally heroic.

'It must never be forgotten, too, that he who afterwards passed as the fond husband, betrayed by the trusted friend, was, in the days when I first knew them all, the most pronounced Free-lover of the group, and openly took for himself the liberty he expressly sanctioned for his wife. As little as he could go into the Divorce

Court for his personal relief, because of that condonation and his own unclean hands, so little did he deserve the sympathy of society for the transfer which afterwards he put forward as his own justification and that friend's condemnation.

'This I say, with absolute knowledge of the whole series of facts from the beginning. And I say it for sake of the truth and in the interests of justice—though it be but justice to the dead.'

Society was at first as stern to George Eliot after her domestic intimacy with Lewes as Mrs. Carlyle had been. I remember hearing an instance of this some years after that connection was formed. Lewes and George Eliot once thought of establishing a domicile in Kent, and a south-eastern semi-suburb of London, much tenanted by wealthy city-people. When news of the intention of the distinguished pair reached the denizens of the region a council of male and female heads of families was held to consider whether George Eliot should be 'received.' It was decided that she should not. As is well known, public opinion altered in course of time, and, ultimately, the lady rejected by London citizens was courted and caressed by daughters of Queen Victoria herself.

VI. JAMES HANNAY AND HIS FRIENDS

CHAPTER I

JAMES HANNAY

ONE of the cleverest and brightest of the many Scotchmen who during the last fifty years have gained distinction in authorship, James Hannay was only nineteen when, leaving the navy, or the navy leaving him, he flung himself into London journalism and literature. His were wit and scholarship in abundance; he had read far and wide in English literature and among the classics of the world. During five years spent as a midshipman he had enjoyed ample leisure for self-culture, which he turned to good account, making up for any early deficiencies by a great deal of hard reading at the British Museum, or, as he called it, 'the Mus.' Very useful to him at his start, too, was the knowledge of men and things naval, and of many-coloured life on the shores of the Mediterranean, which he acquired in the service of Her Majesty, passing as he did from vessel to vessel. He had a quick eye for character and great talent for sketching it, vivid sympathies and also vivid antipathies. Captain Marryat never portrayed a naval commander so happily as Hannay did when with a stroke of his pen he described in one of his novels (Admiral)

'Charley' Napier as 'Benbow with a dash of Grimaldi.' He threw off numerous sketches of life on shipboard, which being out of the common run were acceptable to the editors of the lighter periodicals of the day. From time to time he collected and republished them in little volumes, the titles of which, *Biscuits and Grog* for instance, smacked pleasantly of the sea. For his pungent wit and mordant satire there was generally a market. It was the hey-day of facetious literature of every kind—springing out of the success of *Punch*—from jocular halfpenny journalism to Comic Histories of England, so that a grim humourist of the old school was heard to put the question, 'When are we to have a Comic Bible?' In an article which late in his life he contributed to the *Cornhill*, 'Bohemia in London,' and in his unfinished novel, 'Bagot's Youth,' which appeared in the short-lived *Idler*, started by Mr. Edward Wilberforce some five-and-thirty years since, Hannay sketched several of those joyous though generally impecunious companions of his early days of authorship, their jovial tavern-life, with its flashes of merriment, their feasting alternating with fasting, their shifts for raising the wind, their occasional capture of a capitalist to be lured into floating a new journal when an old one had died of inanition. Hannay was the wittiest and not the least convivial of the band. They are almost all of them gone, those jesters of forty and forty-five years ago, who spent faster than they earned, and lived gaily from hand to mouth. As Hannay rather touchingly wrote of them in his account of that Bohemia which he knew so well : ' The worst of these clever and pleasant fellows is (and the cleverer they are the harder it often goes with them) that they have a way of dying off as they draw towards

forty. They may see people under the table,[1] but people
get their revenge by seeing them under the sod.' Hannay
himself died when he was only forty-seven. He and his
co-mates of those days have left no successors. The
Bohemia in which they disported themselves was annexed
long ago by the great Empire of Respectability.

Not merely as a wit, but as a scholar and a feudalist,
Hannay looked, like Saul the son of Kish, taller from the
shoulders upward than his allies of the comic pen. Nor
was he content with his natural altitude, but loved to
mount, metaphorically of course, on the table, and sound-
ing many a flourish of trumpets, unfold a banner with the
strange device, 'Blood and Culture.' Hannay's own pretensions to 'Blood' were founded mainly on his connection
with the Hannays of Sorbie, a Scottish family of whose
existence past or present I never found any one cognisant
but himself. A more notable claim of the kind was, that
among his ancestors, he said, was the Dean Hannay whose
reading of Laud's Scottish liturgy in the High Church of
Edinburgh provoked Jenny Geddes to fling at his head the
memorable stool, the flight of which through the air pre-
luded the great English revolution of the seventeenth
century. However this may have been, Hannay's admiration for the 'claims of long descent' became for him a
sort of religion. It led him to master the intricacies of
heraldry, and so much of the genealogies and history of

---

[1] An amusing feat of Hannay's in this way was told of him during that
sojourn of his in Edinburgh, which will be chronicled further on. He gave
a dinner-party, in honour of an English visitor, of some literary distinction.
All the other guests were countrymen of the host, and entered cheerfully with
him into a conspiracy to make the Southron tipsy. With the aid of some
potent whisky, presented in the form of toddy, this was easily effected,
and the Englishman was under the table. Then Hannay rose, and jubilantly
shouted, 'Gentlemen! we have avenged—Flodden!'

really old English families, that he could have passed an examination in Dugdale's Baronage, which comes down no later than the reign of Charles the Second. Hannay might have applied to himself, *mutatis mutandis*, what he wrote of one of his friends whose feudal tastes resembled his own : ' The ordinary Cockney witling looked with astonishment on a man who was as familiar with Matthew Paris and Froissart and the Paston letters as he himself with Dumas or Dickens, and who had a veneration for the Houses of Home and Stanley which the Cockney rarely retains for his grandfather and grandmother.' Bracketed with ' Blood ' in Hannay's estimation was ' Culture,' by which he meant chiefly classical scholarship. Most admirable of all was the union of both ' Blood and Culture,' and, in Hannay's eyes, was not that union consummated in the person of the fourteenth Earl of Derby (father of the lately deceased Earl), whose ancestor, the first Earl, turned the scale against Richard Crookback on Bosworth Field, while he himself translated the *Iliad* into English verse ? Hannay was never weary of insisting that many of our greatest writers, among them, Scott, Byron, and Shelley, were men of good family.

Of course it was not by such peculiarities, however interesting, but by his wit, intellectual insight, thoughtfulness, and depth of feeling, evidences of which were scattered broadcast even in his earlier writings, that Hannay attracted the attention and procured the regard of such of his seniors as Thackeray and Carlyle, the two of his contemporaries among men of letters whom he most admired. Thackeray came to have such confidence in him that when about to pay his first visit to America he gave Hannay the MS. of his Lectures on the Humorists to edit and annotate in his absence. ' *Tant soit peu,*' Hannay told me, was Thackeray's monition to him in regard to the annotations, which were excellently done and with due regard to Thackeray's wish for brevity. It was Hannay who congratulated Thackeray on that exquisite touch, in *Vanity Fair*, Becky admiring her husband while he is chastising her *cicisbeo*, Lord Steyne, congratulation which drew from Thackeray the often quoted and misquoted response, 'Well! when I wrote that sentence I slapped my fist on the table, and said, "*that* is a stroke of genius!"'[1] Carlyle was much struck by the varied talent displayed in Hannay's first novel, *Singleton Fontenoy, R.N.*, certainly a very remarkable book to have been written by a young man of twenty-three. He asked Hannay to call on him. Hannay told me that he was rather startled when, as soon as he was seated, Carlyle launched out into praises of the life of a sailor, 'battling with the winds and waves,' and characteristically half-reproached his young visitor with quitting the navy to betake himself to such a trade as literature. Afterwards Hannay completely won Carlyle's heart (though I do not think that they ever saw very much of each other) by a defence of him and of the *Latter-Day Pamphlets* from an attack made on both, and attributed to Sir Archibald Alison, in a ponderous article in *Blackwood's Magazine*. In ' Blackwood

[1] In the same newspaper-article, from which this anecdote is taken, and using the editorial ' we,' Hannay gave the following pleasant little reminiscences of Thackeray :—

'He once pointed out to us the very house in Russell Square, where his imaginary Sedleys lived—a curious proof of the reality his creations had for him.' And again, ' We remember in particular, one evening, after a dinner-party at his house, a fancy picture he drew of Shakespeare, during his last years at Stratford, sitting out in the summer afternoon watching the people,—which all who heard it, brief as it was, thought equal to the best things in his lectures.'

U

versus Carlyle: a Vindication by a Carlylian,' dedicated to Emerson, there was, among other striking things, an assertion of the value of the seer and the thinker to society as being much greater than that of the so-called 'practical man.' The passage may still be glanced at with profit and pleasure.[1]

Two or three years more and Hannay had become so well known to fame that he found a pretty numerous audience, of more than the average intelligence, listening to the series of lectures on 'Satire and Satirists,' which he delivered in the Portman Square Rooms. The satirists dealt with ranged from Horace and Juvenal to Byron and Moore, and in the following year the lectures were published

---

[1] Here is an extract from it :

' A notion is abroad that that only is 'practical' which can be measured or eaten. Show us its net result in a marketable form, the people say, and we will recognise it ! But what, if there be something prior to all such 'net results,' something higher than it ? For example, the writing of an old Hebrew Prophet was by no manner of means 'practical' in his own times ! The supply of figs to the Judean markets, the price of oil in the synagogue-lamps did not fluctuate with the breath of those inspired songs ! But in due time the prophet dies, stoned, perhaps, by the *Blackwood* critics of those days ! and in the course of ages, his words *do* have a 'practical' result by acting on the minds of the nations ! How different that result from what would have been the case, if he had been 'practical' in the vulgar sense, and had suggested alterations in the breadth of the phylacteries, or rules for the guidance of the money-changers . . . In England what has not happened from the fact that the Bible was translated ? We have seen the Puritans—we know what we owe to them—what the world owes to them ! A dozen or two of earnest men two centuries ago were stirred to the depths of their souls by the visions of earnest men many centuries before that : do you not see that that circumstance has its 'practical' influence in the cotton-markets at America at this hour ? Some men are primarily spiritual ; some practical. It is practical to build a ship— what more practical than sawing the timber and laying the plank ? But something comes before that—the divine desire to cross the ocean and carry life and religion to another land. It is practical to make a coffin, but I fancy that your ordinary undertaker is not such a man as the first saddened being, whose heart told him that tenderness and reverence were due to the lost one's ashes.'

in volume-form. It was on the whole a brilliant book, and specially interesting to some from the proofs given in the lectures on Horace and Juvenal that Hannay was fitted to grapple with a most desirable literary enterprise, which even now has been scarcely attempted in England, that of bringing before us as real, living, breathing, flesh-and-blood men several at least of those great Roman writers with whom, from Catullus to Tacitus, above all with Cicero, he had long been familiar.

The year after the publication of *Satire and Satirists*, my previously slight acquaintance with Hannay ripened into intimacy on the establishment of a clever but long extinct little paper, the *Illustrated Times*. The story of that journal has been told by Mr. Edmund Yates, in his *Reminiscences*,[1] where he avers, no doubt correctly, that, as 'The Lounger at the Clubs' of the *Illustrated Times*, he sowed the seed from which has sprung the tree of Society Journalism, a tree flourishing and wide-spreading, but one under whose branches little that is beautiful or useful can grow. Hannay was among its contributors (*quorum pars parva fui*); indeed, he was its chief political writer. One

---

[1] While carefully cataloguing the writers of light and airy contributions to the *Illustrated Times*, Mr. Yates omits mention of a series of articles of a rather weightier though still of a gossipping kind which did much to make the journal popular. They were entitled, 'The Inner Life of the House of Commons,' and were written by the late Mr. William White, who had certain special opportunities for knowing something of what he described. He was originally a bookseller at Bedford, where, being a Liberal, he assisted the Russells in the electioneering operations of their candidates for Parliament. In gratitude for his services Lord Charles Russell, when Serjeant-at-Arms, appointed him Principal Doorkeeper of the House of Commons. It was a position which, of course, made him thoroughly acquainted with the *personnel* of the House, and from his genial disposition he became a general favourite with the members. His lively personal sketches of the sayings and doings of the House of Commons were as popular in their way as Mr. Yates's miscellaneous gossippings, in which things political and Parliamentary were seldom or never touched on.

of the sub-editors was John George Edgar, who wrote some fifteen volumes of history and biography for boys, breathing a most chivalrous spirit. They had a very large sale both at home and in the United States. Edgar was in all respects an original, and became a friend of mine as well as of Hannay. A Berwickshire man, he loved to call himself 'a poor Scottish gentleman,' and claimed kinsmanship with some noble Border family. For Edgar, the Feudal Baron was the ideal type of manhood, and the brightest period of history was to be found in the so-called 'dark ages.' I remember him coming to me in a state of some excitement, and confiding to me as a profound secret his mournful discovery that his beloved Barons had been in the wrong in their struggle for Magna Charta! On another occasion, he described to me an interview with a damsel whom he had wooed without having won, her relatives not unnaturally disapproving of the match. He wound up, he told me, a passionate appeal to her by declaring that if she hesitated to plight her troth to him, he would set off for Palestine! like Schiller's Ritter Toggenburg. But he never married and he never went to Palestine. Many were the carouses which came out of the *I. T.*, as Hannay always called the *Illustrated Times*, and in them Edgar played his part not wisely, but too well. He died at thirty; peace be to his ashes! A sub-editorial colleague of Edgar's for a time was the now well-known Mr. Frederick Greenwood. With him Hannay formed an intimacy which had an important effect on Hannay's later career. But I am approaching the appointment of Hannay to be editor of the *Edinburgh Courant*, and what led up to it. His Edinburgh editorship, forming as it did a very curious episode both in his biography and in the history of Scottish journalism, must be reserved for another chapter.

CHAPTER II

HANNAY IN SCOTLAND AND AFTERWARDS

A FEUDALIST and a Carlylian when he first became a political journalist, Hannay was not at all attracted to the Manchester party, or to the Palmerstonian Liberalism which succeeded its supremacy, and he was repelled by the vulgarity, as it seemed to him then, of that metropolitan form of Radicalism with which chiefly he came into contact. He was drifting towards Conservatism, when he surprised his friends by suddenly presenting himself as a candidate for the Dumfriesshire Burghs at the General Election which followed the defeat of Lord Palmerston, on the China question, by a coalition of the Conservative, Peelite, and Manchester parties. The Hannays came from that part of Scotland, and Hannay's father had in the old days contested Dumfries as a Tory. It was not, however, as a Conservative that the son stood, but as James Hannay, man of letters and champion of 'social reform.' At public meetings of the electors he dilated on the desirability of increasing the man-of-letters element in the House of Commons, and instructed, if he did not convince, his hearers by telling them of the Parliamentary and official careers of the Queen Anne's men and others who had distinguished themselves in literature, even bringing into play so old a story as the diplomatic mission of Grotius to England.

The candidate whom he opposed was the late William Ewart, a commonplace man, but a zealous philanthropist. His championship of the abolition of capital punishment is forgotten, but he deserves to be remembered as the author of the first of those Free Public Library Acts the effects of which have been so very useful. Ewart had for sixteen years represented in an unexceptionable fashion the Dumfriesshire Burghs. The electors not unnaturally preferred their old Member to such a comparative stranger as the brilliant young gentleman from London. Ewart polled 321 votes to Hannay's 125. By a rather curious coincidence, only a few months after Hannay's courageous candidature his friend and senior Thackeray stood unsuccessfully, at a by-election, for Oxford city, against that highly-respectable Peelite statesman Mr. (afterwards Lord) Cardwell. These were Thackeray's and Hannay's first and last appearances in the electoral arena.

Though defeated, Hannay was not cast down. He plumed himself, indeed, on the number of votes which he had received, and as his supporters appear to have been chiefly Conservatives, his tendency to join that party was strengthened. With the true literary instinct, moreover, he proceeded at once to utilise his recent and often amusing experiences of canvassing in an article on 'Electioneering,' in the *Quarterly Review*, a connection with which he had formed some time previously. It was an instructive as well as agreeable article, for it contained lively sketches of some of the most notable contests in our electoral history. Some nine articles, biographical, historical, and literary, all of them interesting, thoughtful, and vivacious, which during these years he contributed to the *Quarterly*, he republished afterwards in a volume dedicated to Carlyle. I remember

the natural glee with which early in his connection with
that famous periodical he spoke of having 'led off the
Quarterly' thrice, his articles having received the place of
honour in three numbers consecutively. He did not write
in it expressly on politics, but his connection with the
great quarterly organ of Conservatism again drew him
closer to the Conservative party. Hannay became more
and more Conservative, and that at a time when it was
comparatively uncommon for clever young men to join
their fortunes to the depressed and defeated party, which
it then was. The wit, pungency, and vigour of the satire
which he heaped on Liberals and Radicals attracted the
admiring notice of the Lord Stanley afterwards Earl of
Derby, who died not many months ago, who was then one
of the younger leaders of the Conservative party, and who,
as Hannay told me, styled him 'the Douglas Jerrold of
Conservatism.'

This patrician appreciator of Hannay's rare satirical
powers was one of the Conservative leaders who recognised
the necessity for improving and developing their press,—
which at the time of the repeal of the Corn Laws had fallen
into deplorable ineptitude,—and for enlisting in its journalistic service men of mark and likelihood. Something had
been done in this direction in England when the Scottish
Conservatives, too, came to the conclusion that their cause
might be advanced by the establishment of a daily organ
in Edinburgh to confront the all-powerful *Scotsman*, edited
as it was by the late Alexander Russel, the ablest journalist
whom Scotland had then produced. They made the
arrangements needed to convert into a daily Conservative
organ the venerable *Edinburgh Courant*, which at that
time maintained a strict political neutrality. Its editor,

who had been recommended to the post by the late Sir Arthur Helps, resigned when this decision was formed. A Conservative editor was required, Lord Stanley was consulted and he recommended Hannay for the editorship of the transformed *Courant*. Hannay was both a husband and the father of a somewhat numerous family. The salary offered was, for those days and for Scotland, considerable. Hannay accepted the post, and held it for four years.

'Like his national symbol, the thistle, he had a prickly wit and a prickly temper,' Hannay once wrote of Smollett, and it was true of himself. Coming, moreover, from the headquarters of politics and literature, the admired of English Conservative chiefs and the friend of Thackeray and Carlyle, he looked down on the political and literary notabilities of Edinburgh, whether they belonged to his own party or not, and he never hesitated to make them know that he looked down on them. Not in the very least a tuft-hunter, and accustomed to lead an extremely free and easy life among his brethren of the pen in London, he eschewed in Edinburgh that society of the higher class which his editorial position, to say nothing of his talents, enabled him, and might have tempted others occupying it, to cultivate,[1] choosing for his associates boon companions who looked up to him, flattered him, and encouraged his

---

[1] One anecdote of Hannay in Edinburgh society, showing him to be as little a respecter of persons there as elsewhere, was told me by himself. The late John Blackwood, as then the head of the great Tory publishing firm which issued *Blackwood's Magazine*, was rather an important person in Edinburgh, especially to its Conservatives. Shirley Brooks happening to visit Edinburgh, Blackwood asked him and his old friend Hannay to dinner. In the conversation which followed the repast, with less than his usual tact, since both of his guests were journalists, the host remarked that he never cared to have men connected with the press as contributors to his magazine. 'Less jaw, Blackwood, and more claret!' was Hannay's retort.

imprudences, laughing approvingly when in doubt as
to the choice of a victim for his next leading article, he
would ask, 'Who is to be hoisted to-day?' Hannay's
aim was not to popularise Conservatism in Scotland,
but to preach his gospel of 'Blood and Culture,' and
to satirise those whom with or without reason he
disliked. He lashed the organs and oratory of the
Whig *Bourgeoisie* of Scotland as deficient in respect for
'Blood.' 'Culture' is, perhaps, more generally diffused
among Scotchmen than among Englishmen, but the educated and educating classes in Scotland are certainly
inferior to the Southron in classical scholarship, and this
Hannay chose to identify with culture. He seemed to lie
in wait for any misquotation from a classic or mispronunciation of a Greek or Latin word, and then came a castigation
which made Edinburgh ring with the wail of the delinquent and the protests of his indignant friends. Mrs.
Oliphant has filled whole pages of her biography of the
late Principal Tulloch with an account of the needlessly
painful effect produced on him by Hannay's satirical comments on some trivial misquotations and mispronunciations,
and she even hints that these aggravated the malady
under which Dr. Tulloch sank into the grave![1] (Edmund

[1] 'The *Edinburgh Courant*,' Mrs. Oliphant says, ' was not an eminent organ
of literary opinion like *Blackwood's Magazine* or the *Edinburgh Review*, but
it was at this period under the editorship of an exceptionally clever man of
letters, himself of the very essence of what has been called the Cockney school,
and out of his element in the northern capital. I have always heard that he
was a good scholar, with all the minutiæ of English classical training at his
finger-ends. This was a point upon which Principal Tulloch at all times
mourned and exaggerated his own deficiency. . . . The insignificance of the
organ, in the present instance, may be thought to lessen the responsibility, but
the organ was not insignificant to the Principal, in whose immediate circle it
was in full circulation. Certain errors of the press, unimportant slips of the
pen, or failures of memory, a quotation inaccurately rendered, or other literary
sin equally venial, were seized upon as the subjects of repeated articles, and

Burke was an irritable man, but with what presence of mind, good temper, and felicity did not he turn an orthoepic blunder to account when the House of Commons clamoured against his mispronunciation of *vectĭgal* as *vectīgal*!) And what was occasionally censurable in the tone and tenor of Hannay's contributions to the *Courant* was too often allowed to neutralise the much that was admirable in them. Many of them are models both in matter and manner, the products of a keen and vigorous intellect, and rich in felicitous illustration. Hannay always wrote, too, with the greatest care, and no slipshod sentence ever escaped from his later pen. I know of hardly any British journalist since Albany Fonblanque whose newspaper articles so well deserved republication as those which Hannay collected from the *Courant* and reissued in a volume of *Characters and Criticisms*. With other interesting matter, grave and gay, it contains what, so far as I am aware, is very much the ablest and most conclusive reply ever made to Buckle's shallow account of the history and working of Presbyterianism in Scotland.

Tulloch was then held up to his world—nay, to himself, which was worse—with just the kind of ridicule which was most adapted to make life intolerable to him. It would be vain to say that this was the cause of his illness; the real fact being that it was his illness which gave it so great a power to annoy, but it for the moment directed the course of the growing evil, and decided the peculiar instrument, which incipient disease, whether mental or physical, seized for his torture and dismay.' Mrs. Oliphant quotes a letter from Dr. Tulloch, written at the beginning of 1863, in which he says: 'I am a little freer from annoyance, and I hope I may get more elasticity of spirit.' His friends were indignant about the *Courant* and had discontinued it. 'Various respectable people,' Dr. Tulloch adds, 'have been doing so, which may make a change.' 'It gave him a little consolation to be thus looked up to by his friends, but the poisoned arrow had by this time struck home. On his return from Edinburgh the shadows kept growing darker and darker.' My only comment on this passage is that Mrs. Oliphant committed a grave error in describing Hannay as 'of the very essence of what has been called the Cockney school,' one which, as it happened, he was continually satirising.

Hannay's already weakened hold on his Edinburgh editorship received a final blow (at least so I was told) through the death of a wealthy Scotchman, who was not only one of his warmest admirers, but an important contributor to the funds of the *Courant.* This financial pillar of the paper was a prosperous whisky distiller, and many a jovial evening he and Hannay had passed together, imbibing in its purest and mellowest form, though of course with aqueous and saccharine adjuncts, the great national beverage of Scotland. Coincident, fortunately, with the decease of the worthy distiller, was the establishment of the *Pall Mall Gazette*, the projector and first editor of which, Hannay's old friend, Mr. Frederick Greenwood, offered him a substantial engagement on it, and this he accepted cheerfully. At the outset, and for some years afterwards, the *P.M.G.* was an organ of so-called Philosophical Liberalism, and Hannay hinted to me rather plaintively that he could find in it no expression for his Conservatism. In due season, however, he found expression for it in an able but not long-lived and now forgotten journal. This was the *Imperial Review* founded by Hannay's friend, with whom I, too, became pretty intimately acquainted, the late Henry Cecil Raikes, Postmaster-General in Lord Salisbury's Second Administration. Raikes, who had then turned forty, was a man of good family, his grandfather having been Chancellor of the Diocese of Chester. He had distinguished himself at Cambridge, and been called to the bar, but did not practise. Able and genial, a clever speaker and writer, he threw himself early into politics and became one of the most active and energetic of the younger Conservatives. He had unsuccessfully contested boroughs,

Chester one of them, when he bethought him of serving his party through journalism. The *Saturday Review*, then independent, was more Liberal than Conservative, and a junior admirer of his aiding him with capital and becoming nominal editor, Raikes founded the *Imperial Review*, as a weekly organ of advanced Conservatism, on the lines of the *Saturday*, like it containing only original articles, without news. The *Imperial* was well edited, very well written, Raikes himself being a frequent contributor, but its supporters were more select than numerous. Among Hannay's contributions was a series of incisive papers on 'Cads,' a worthy sequel to the *Snob* papers of his master, Thackeray, and rivalling them in pungency at least. Soon after their appearance, and a very creditable career of two years, the *Imperial* was discontinued partly from lack of support, partly because Raikes had attained the first object of his ambition, and been returned for Chester city. On becoming Prime Minister a second time Disraeli, with his usual eye for serviceable ability, made Raikes Chairman of Committees of the House of Commons, the duties of which office he discharged very satisfactorily, so long as his party remained in power. When Lord Salisbury became for the first time Prime Minister, Raikes was left out in the cold, although he had risen to be one of the Members for the University of Cambridge,[1] and had been an indefatigable

---

[1] The late Mr. Stephen ('J. K. S.') contributed to the *Pall Mall Gazette* an imaginary and satirical 'Election Address,' from Raikes to Cambridge University on the occasion of his candidature. The clever satirist knew nothing apparently of Raikes's connection with the *Imperial Review* and intimacy with Hannay among other men of letters. 'J. K. S.' very unjustly made Raikes say :

> I never quit, as others do,
>   Political intrigue, to seek
> The dingy literary crew,
>   Or hear the voice of science speak, etc.

worker and speaker for the Conservative cause. He might
have been similarly neglected on the formation of Lord
Salisbury's Second Ministry, and it was only (at least so I
heard at the time) in consequence of a memorial from
influential members of the Carlton urging his claims, that he
was appointed Postmaster-General, an office which he did
not find a bed of roses. He died in harness. He was very
tall; otherwise, in physique and physiognomy, Hannay bore
a certain resemblance to him. The *Imperial Review* was
never revived, though its revival had been contemplated.

Both before and after his return from Edinburgh to
London, Hannay contributed occasionally to the *North
British Review* and to *Temple Bar*. I remember a striking
article of his on George Buchanan in the *North British*, and
one on Béranger in *Temple Bar*, for Hannay's range of intellectual sympathy was wide. But it was in the *Cornhill* that
much of the best of his later literary work appeared. To
it belongs the article on London Bohemianism previously
quoted, with another full of acute and not ungenial
comment on Scotland and the Scotch during the sixth
decade of the nineteenth century, as well as an admirable
article on Martial, which enabled the reader, in Hannay's
own words, to ' realise the life that Martial led almost as
well as if he had now chambers in the Temple and published
his books in Piccadilly.' I saw a good deal of Hannay
during the later years of his final residence in London. He
was hospitable, social, witty, anecdotical as ever, but his circumstances were somewhat clouded, for Hannay never was
intimate with that Prudence whose presence, according to
one of his favourite Roman satirists, brings with it all the
deities beneficent to man. It was understood that if a
vacancy in the Chair of English Literature in Edinburgh

University occurred when the Conservatives were in office it would be given to Hannay. But when W. E. Aytoun died, Lord Palmerston was Prime Minister and Sir George Grey having, as Home Secretary, the selection of a successor to Aytoun, he appointed the able and accomplished biographer of Milton, Professor Masson, to the chair vacant through Aytoun's death. Had Aytoun lived for another year, with the return of the Conservatives to office, Hannay would very probably have been his successor. As it was, he was not forgotten by his early patron, who from Lord Stanley had become Earl of Derby and Foreign Secretary. Through his kindness Hannay received, just when he needed it most, a consulship, ultimately at Barcelona, with an income adequate and steady. The substance of the consular reports which he sent to the Foreign Office was probably furnished by his subordinates, but there were in them occasional Hannay-like touches, as when he indicated the superiority of this or that cheap vintage of Catalonia to the worse and dearer sherries vended in London. I heard from him now and then, his letters being full of longings for London, and of weariness with the sight of orange groves, of blue skies and sea. His greatest delight was to welcome the arrival of a British man-of-war, to board it, and to carouse with the officers of a service which he loved to the last. At Barcelona he wrote to the *Pall Mall Gazette* a series of lively and interesting letters from ‘ an Englishman in Spain.’ The night before he died, he corrected for the *Cornhill*, where it duly appeared, the proof of a characteristic article on ‘ Sea Novels : Captain Marryat,’ in which occurs the passage respecting Smollett previously quoted. It is worth noting that Hannay received his consulship from the late

Lord Derby exactly a hundred years after the invalid and work-worn Smollett sailed from England to die in Italy, having been refused by Lord Shelburne a similar appointment, although the kindly David Hume, then Under-Secretary of State, did his utmost to procure it for him.[1] During one of their latest colloquies, Sir Walter Scott and Wordsworth united in lamenting the Ministerial ill-treatment of the author of *Humphrey Clinker*. No future chronicler of the ' Calamities of Authors' will be able to complain that James Hannay met with the neglect which embittered the last years of Smollett.

[1] In a sympathetic letter (of September 1768) to Smollett, Hume attributed the failure of his good offices to ' the indifference of Ministers towards literature, which has been long, and indeed always, the case in England.'

CHAPTER III

A LIFE of Hannay was to have been written by one of
his surviving boon-companions of a literary turn,
who owed a great deal to him. But the project was never
executed, it being discovered, I suppose, that whatever may
have been made out of Hannay living, little or nothing
was to be made out of Hannay dead. If that life had
been written, the reader would have been spared much of
the miniature biography of Hannay which has been given
in the preceding chapters. Then, again, after Hannay's
death, there was some talk of collecting from the *Cornhill*
his often admirable contributions to it and republishing
them in volume-form, as he himself had done with the
articles which he contributed to the *Quarterly Review*.
But that project, too, and, I was told, for commercial
reasons, went no further than talk. Had it been executed
the reader would be spared what follows.

I shall confine myself to some account of, and extracts
from, two of Hannay's *Cornhill* articles already mentioned,
one of them 'Bohemia in London,' the other 'The Scot
at Home.' Hannay's acquaintance with the London
Bohemia was, as may have been already surmised, as
'extensive and peculiar' as Sam Weller's knowledge of
London in general. One object of his article was to

rehabilitate the Bohemian not of every type but of the best type, for although, he admitted, 'there are many blackguards who are Bohemians, it does not follow,' he maintained, 'that every Bohemian is a blackguard.' The Bohemian of that best type, specimens of which he proceeded to describe, is 'a gentleman who being no worse born or bred, or educated than other folks, is yet through some strong peculiarity of temperament in the first instance, acted on by circumstances in the second, alienated from society in its established, conventional, and certainly very convenient sense.' And 'what,' asked Hannay, dropping the apologetic, and waxing enthusiastic,

'What but the Bohemian element has made us a great maritime and colonial power? There were graver elements, I admit, too ; but without the careless, rollicking, unattached social outlaw of a fellow, you would never have got your rough work done. Some of your fine work, too, in the cause of the spread of British greatness, has been due to the same spirit. A dash of Bohemianism must be claimed as existing in your Spekes and Burtons, and many a good fellow, both officer and private, who fell before Sebastapol and Delhi, was there because he belonged to the brotherhood.'

Hannay's entertaining article portrays several kinds of Bohemians, especially the naval. But I shall limit myself to his sketches of literary Bohemians were it merely because in this case only can I generally identify the originals of his portraits. Of his many Bohemian brethren of the pen, there were three, I think, whom he liked best, and his friendship with them proved his genial catholicity of disposition. Two of them, Edward Whitty and Robert (commonly called 'Bob') Brough, were fierce, not to say ferocious, Radicals. They scoffed at Hannay's gospel of

X

'blood and culture,' at least the culture which he identified with classical scholarship. The other to whom reference has been already made, John George Edgar, was 'feudal and aristocratic to the bone.' He 'regarded all families as upstarts that had risen since the Reformation, which he looked upon as a plebeian and overrated movement.' Whitty came of a family well known in Liverpool journalism, and for a few years he blazed like a meteor in the firmament of that of London, contributing to the *Leader* singularly vivid and vigorous sketches of the proceedings and *personnel* of the House of Commons, with striking portraits of the public men of the day. Carlyle was rather taken by them. Some of them were republished in volume-form, and, if even now read or dipped into, will yield a certain satisfaction.[1] His solitary novel, *Friends of Bohemia*, was in my recollection of it, and despite its suggestive title, far less interesting than his dashing newspaper sketch-work. He disappeared somewhat suddenly, and the last one heard of him was that he had died at thirty-three, just after he landed in Australia. From the very little that I saw of him, I judged him to be a Bohemian of the Bohemians. He is the Ned Wexford of the following passage, which comes after one describing the 'classical Bohemian' (a type, not an individual), 'to whom humour seems to consist in ever new ways of putting the

---

[1] Though a vehement Radical, the quick-sighted and outspoken Whitty frankly criticised the Radical leaders of his day. This did not make him popular with his party, a fact which suggested to the friendly Hannay the following epigram :

'*A Radical mystery explained.*

Can you tell why it is that in country or city
The Rads never puff the productions of Whitty?
He's so sharp, shrewd and honest, the pitiful elves
Think he cannot be possibly one of themselves.'

fact that a man could not construe.' 'I should like to put him *on* in the *Pro Cluentio*, sir,' he would ·say, when Aniseed Potts of the *Mausoleum* was mentioned, the late Hepworth Dixon of the *Athenæum*, whom Hannay loved to ridicule :

'As every exaggeration breeds its opposite, so the classical Bohemians were succeeded by men like that arch-Bohemian, Ned Wexford, who, though one of the cleverest fellows of his time, used to ask whether Cicero had anything in him? and whether Aristophanes would, if alive now, be allowed to write in *Punch*? Ned's prejudice against the ancients was that they were generally respected by the established powers of the world, with which he was in perpetual war. He delighted to sow a little seed of revolution as he lounged for his pleasure through the streets. "Why beg of me, my good man?" he asked a mendicant. "Go to the Bishop of London, he's got twenty thousand a year!" And yet Ned was full of humanity, as he showed in one most remarkable instance which deserves recording. In a neighbour-hood where he once lived, a certain house was in a state of siege. So close was the blockade, that the bailiff, rather than leave his post, endured every extremity of cold and hunger. Wexford passing by saw the position, and immediately entering the nearest "public" ordered bread and cheese and a pot of porter—whose light white coronal of foam might have melted the heart of a teetotaller. "Send these," he nobly said, "to the man at the door-step there." "To *him*, sir!" exclaimed the land-lord, "why, he's a bailiff!" "And what then?" Wexford answered, "Is a bailiff to starve in the discharge of his duty?" "Well, sir, you *h'are* a Christian!" was the comment of Caupo. Nor was he far wrong. All Ned's natural sympathies as a man and a Bohemian were with the gentleman besieged. But there was a triumph of principle in feeding the natural foe of his order, beyond the Christianity of many writers of tracts. On another occasion, Ned Wexford kindly officiated at the stall of an old lady in Regent Street, and sold her oranges for her while she went and refreshed herself at his expense. He was once found dancing on the beach at that pleasant little Cockney Baiæ,

Southend, for the amusement of some children, among whom he distributed fourpenny pieces.   As a democratic writer, it was his duty to show sympathy with the people; and if his philanthropy had at such periods been artificially stimulated, whose business was that?'

My acquaintance with the literary Bohemians of Hannay's circle was slight, except in the case of John George Edgar.   Of the others, the one of whom I formed the highest opinion was Robert Brough.   My only conversations with him were not on politics but on literature and the drama, of the modern masterpieces of which this writer of innumerable and ephemeral burlesques had a thorough and keenly appreciative knowledge.   I found him a sensible, thoughtful, and well-informed man.   There is a genial account of his career and character in Mr. Edmund Yates's *Recollections* previously referred to. Robert Brough (his chief fiction was a novel, partly autobiographical, *Marston Lynch*) is the Bob Marston of the passage which is about to be quoted, and in which Hannay has not done justice to Brough's literary talent. He had conspicuous merits both as an original poet and a metrical translator, and he needed only more prudence in the conduct of life, with length of days—like so many of his Bohemian brethren he died early, at thirty-two—to have obtained enduring literary distinction:

'Wexford, it will be readily believed, was a great favourite in Bohemia, with the manly Stodger, who engaged in such terrific combats at nights, that he would send to you before breakfast begging you to come at once "bringing a sovereign and a surgeon"—with the roving Roribel, who used to put up at strange inns, and ring in the morning to ask the waiter where he was? with the playful Bob Marston,[1] who, when the porter at

---

[1] Brough dedicated to Whitty his *Songs of the Governing Classes*, a new edition of which, with other of his verses, was republished not long ago.

the British Museum demanded his reading-ticket, volunteered in
addition to show him his protection' (from arrest). 'Bob's
horror of the polite and conventional world was such that he
once gave it as a reason for leaving a place that "the clergyman
of the parish had called upon him." "By Jove," he went on,
"when it came to *that*, I thought it was time to be going back
to London." A dress-coat was a Nessus-shirt to him, and patent
leather boots a torture like the famous "boot" of the seventeenth
century. While Wexford was essentially political in his intellectual tastes, Marston belonged to the comic Bohemians proper.
He was pretty sure to be one of the promoters of the innumerable little facetious journals that came out—and went in again—
some dozen or fifteen years ago. He wielded the *Tomahawk*,
he glittered in the *Firefly*; the echo of his voice was heard in the
snap of the *Cracker*, and he helped to work the machinery which
set in motion the terrible *Rack*. Who so merry at the
preliminary supper with which such ventures were ushered into
the world? Who so philosophically calm when the sham
capitalist had levanted, owing a small balance to his contributors,
and a large one to his paper-maker? . . . How kind of thee,
Bob, after taking a house to say to an intimate friend, "I'm a
householder now, old boy, and always good to be bail!" How
cheerfully didst thou reflect, when circumstances forced thee to
drink the smallest of beer, that at least the stuff had the merit of
being *wet*! The law itself did not appal or humiliate thy
Aristophanic spirit, for when a cruelly sarcastic beak, in inflicting
a fine of five shillings, inquired whether certain fluids did not
impregnate thy writings, the answer was ready, "Yes, and they
sell in consequence."'

But the literary Bohemian most loved by Hannay, the
Jonathan of this David, was the Edgar whose acquaintance
the reader has already made, and who is the Jack Pringle
of my closing extract from Hannay's article:

'Few men in London (the Prague, or capital of the nation)
were better friends than the essentially democratic Bob Marston
and the great feudal Bohemian, Jack Pringle, the Lion of the

North. No double-distilled old Tory of the Winchilsea or New-castle breed ever surpassed Jack in devotion to the monarchy and nobility of these realms. . . . He added a certain romantic and pungent element to the London Bohemianism which is essentially of the town towny. A clear blue northern eye, a tall and manly figure, and a chivalresque politeness at once cordial and stately, conciliated to him the regard of men whose ways and thinking about life and books were altogether different. The Bohemian is profoundly tolerant, for he only wants to be amused; and Jack Pringle's aristocratic Toryism was invested with a humour and a jollity both extravagant but both real. He could have drunk fair with Rollo or Harold Blaatand. He would have opened a vein in his arm if there was no other way of paying for a brother Bohemian's beer. And he could sustain his opinions by a most excellent knowledge of the feudal and genealogical history of Great Britain—to read about which was his only study, as to write about it was his only profession. . . . For Hume, Scott, Clarendon, Comines, Jack would loudly express his admiration, but he ranked Tom Moore with fiddlers. His admiration, too, was always expressed in the lofty terms derived from the incessant perusal of books describing great historical crises. "'Tom Kilby, sir,' he said," ("Tom Kilby" thinly disguises the name of a now well-known Conservative publicist) "a common friend of ours, is one of Clarendon's heroes." In Jack's own books, if you open them at random, you are pretty sure to light on passages beginning "'Dog,' exclaimed the Grand Master fiercely," or "So saying, the great earl put spurs to his horse," etc. The present Earl of Derby' (the Prime Minister Earl, and Rupert of debate) 'was never spoken of by Jack except as "THE EARL." Many a bumper he drained to him, and many a Herts clodhopper' (Edgar's domicile was in the Barnet region) 'and London Cockney drank at Jack Pringle's expense by drinking the Earl's health. On festive rambles it was difficult to be with Jack without incurring personal risk. Once, when we were riding together in Sussex, he proposed that we should carry off a cow in the old Border fashion; but I felt sure the humour of the proceeding would not be appreciated at Lewes Assizes. At these times he was peculiarly characteristic. Nothing could exceed his courtesy to the common people, whom he thought it his duty, *en bon gentilhomme*, to protect. But, if accident brought him into collision with a prosperous middle-class man, he was severely and ironically polite, or haughtily contemptuous. . . . *Vale, Vale*, O good Jack Pringle. Thy grave shall not want thy favourite white rose—a plant which, in our Scottish history, always required much moisture.'

Is there anything of a similar kind, even in Charles Lamb's charming personal recollections, more playfully and pleasantly genial than these sketches of Hannay's vanished Bohemian friends?

'The Scot at Home,' the other *Cornhill* paper of Hannay's to which I wish to call attention, was written soon after his return from Edinburgh to London. It embodied the results of the knowledge of his countrymen acquired by him during a sojourn of several years in his fatherland, a sojourn longer than any which had fallen to his lot since his earliest years. One of the chief of these results was a conviction that Scotland to some extent, and the Scottish capital to a great extent, had been Anglicised. Nearly three decades have elapsed since 'The Scot at Home' was written, and to judge from the contemporary utterances of that most patriotic of Scotchmen, Professor Blackie, the transformation of Scotland which Hannay noticed has been proceeding ever since. The Professor regards it with indignant regret; Hannay viewed it with equanimity, and even as the inevitable result of causes which would have had the same effect many centuries ago but for the attempts of the Plantagenet kings to subjugate Scotland. Many Scotchmen and still more Englishmen may learn something from the following passage on 'the curious obscurity and error,' as Hannay opined, 'which long hung over Scottish History and is not yet,' even in 1893, 'by any means dispelled':

'The war of independence, followed as it was by incessant struggles, so isolated the Scotch from the South, that they threw back their present impressions of separation into the past, and substituted for real history a series of half-true traditions. They forgot, in fact, their own history, and it was nobody else's business to put them right. They talked of themselves as a homogeneous nation of immemorial antiquity, and looked upon Edward's attack on their independence as a Dutchman does upon Louis the Fourteenth's invasion of Holland. The Stuarts they regarded as descendants of Banquo; Bruce and Wallace as Scots in the sense in which Harold was an Englishman, or Tell a Swiss; and their "auld enemies" of England as a race differing from them like German from Slavonian or Frenchman from both. Indeed, notions of this kind are widely held in Scotland even now. Yet nothing can be more certain than that the governing part of Scotland—the Lowlands—the "southern or civil part of Scotland," to borrow the happy expression of an Elizabethan writer—was essentially Teutonic long before Edward was thought of. The language is there to speak for itself, in excellent Saxon, with a Scandinavian admixture; while, to complete the likeness between North and South Britain, even in the thirteenth century, if England had a Norman aristocracy by conquest, Scotland had one by colonisation. The Stuarts, or more properly Stewarts, came from Shropshire, bringing the ancestor of Wallace (*Le Waleys* was as much a Scotch as an English name) and of other Scotch gentlemen with them. The Bruces were Yorkshiremen of Norman descent; the Maxwells either Saxon or Norse; the Lindsays, Hays, Setons, Montgomeries, Maules, etc., all Norman to a man. We need not hold with Sir Francis Palgrave that Scotland was a mere part of the Saxon empire and that Edward had a just claim to its *suzeraineté*, though this view has been virtually accepted by so patriotic and accomplished a Scot as Lord Lindsay. It is not necessary to our present purpose to enter on that inquiry. What is necessary to point out is that the races were cognate through and through—*the Highlanders*

being as different from the Lowlanders as Welsh from English,
and this is the key at once to the Scottish character and the
Scottish history.   For, after all, the qualities even of the conventional Scot of English literature, his thrift, his mother-wit, his dry
reserve, his determination to get on, are only ugly exaggerations
of the known qualities of the English themselves.   A Celt thinks
them both cold and both slow, and the Scot only the colder and
slower of the two.   The fundamental resemblance between the
nations is much more seen by comparing the northern than the
southern Englishman with the Lowlander.   Indeed, in some
respects, a man of Cumberland is more like a man of Dumfriesshire, or a Northumbrian like a Berwickshire man, than either is
like his fellow-countryman of Sussex and Devonshire.   When a
Highlander was producing *Ossian*, a Lowlander was producing
the *Wealth of Nations*, which the English mind accepted at
once, and has since made the basis of its commercial policy.
And if the Union has proved so successful, it is not that the
Scotch have been quite without grievances. . . .   It is that the
natural ethnological affinity of the populations has told under the
influence of free intercourse, just as it would probably have told
even had Edward succeeded in prematurely uniting the two
kingdoms by the sword; in achieving that union by a rape which
Providence had decreed should be achieved by a marriage.'

'The Highlanders' are 'as different from the Lowlanders as Welsh from English,' as Celt is from Saxon—
how very obvious and familiar a fact! the reader may say.
Yes, but how often it is practically ignored.   Long after
the disappearance of the Druids, the Welsh had, I suppose,
a distinctive national costume, and Welsh women still
wear, if I am not mistaken, a peculiar head-gear.   Yet
what would be said if, on the occasion of a purely English
festivity, the guests were requested to appear in the old
national costume of Wales?   Is it a whit less absurd to
read, as one does in the advertisements of the annual
banquet in London of a purely Scottish, and not in the

least distinctively Highland, charity, that 'gentlemen are requested to appear in Highland costume'? The subordination, thus symbolised, of the Teutonic-Scandinavian Scotchman to the Celtic Highlander has been more or less prevalent in literature and life since the Scottish Celt was idealised by Sir Walter Scott, who, when George IV. visited Edinburgh, actually figured in Highland costume before the King. The late John Hill Burton, in his *History of Scotland*, makes these pertinent remarks on the subject:

'Neither in the representation nor the description of the great Highland leaders of early times do we find any trace of the modern Highland dress. At the time when there are indications of its use by the common people in its ruder form, it seems to have been no less out of the question as a dress for the great man than the concrete of glutinous rags now forming the national costume of the Irish peasant would be as the dress of his landlord. It may be safely pronounced that no genuine picture of a chief or gentleman dressed in tartan is producible of so early a date as the reign of Charles I. The Highland gentry of whom we possess representations—even the old marauder, Sir Ewan Cameron of Lochiel—are all attired in the fashionable costume of the period.'

Burton goes on to show that the modern form of the Highland dress dates from the period between the rebellions of 1715 and 1745, when Marshal Wade was laying down in the Highlands those roads, the value of which has been commemorated in a famous distich. The Highland costume, as we have it now, appears to have been then mainly the invention of a worthy and enterprising English Quaker, Thomas Rawlinson, who was owner or manager of some iron-smelting works at Invergarry. He was very fond of the costume, and wore it himself. 'Surely,' Burton adds, 'the Quaker in Highland costume would be an exceptional phenomenon, even in the age of the restoration of the "garb of old Gaul."' But this is a digression. To return to Hannay's article.

Hannay compares the present and the past of the professions in Scotland to illustrate his statement that 'the gradual decomposition of Scottish nationality, the steady, continuous transmutation of that nationality into provincialism is the one great movement which attracts the attention of observers of the Scot at Home.' There could be no more characteristic Scotchman of the old school than the Scottish Presbyterian minister :

'Usually an excellent specimen of the Scottish middle-class, taking the term in its widest sense. He is a shrewd, thoroughly moral, and respectable man, with a homely good-nature, and sometimes a genuine touch of humour about him. In his solid, comfortable manse you are always sure of his hospitality, of admirable Scotch mutton, and a glass of wine, or better still, an unimpeachable tumbler.'

But even among the ministers of the Kirk a new and half-Anglicised school is forming :

'The young Scotch Presbyterian minister is not what the man of the last generation was. There is a dash of jaunty Anglicanism about his waistcoat and tie, and he likes to be called "a parson." An odour of Maurice and Kingsley may be smelt in his sermons —like the scent on his handkerchief—and his elaborate extemporary prayers are streaked with phrases from the English Prayer-Book. He takes a walk on Sundays, and in moods of a sublimer daring smokes a cigar in public. What would he give—could we see his heart of hearts—to be an Oxford first-class man, and to hold a jolly living in some county, where he would be a magistrate, and have a good social position, and could even join the hounds without being instantly set down as having ridden straight off to the Old Gentleman ?'

What Hannay wrote of the decline of Scotch vernacular
poetry is probably as true now as it was then, but what
he said of the all but total absence of a national element
in contemporary Scottish literature has since become
inapplicable :

'Now-a-days a Scottish poet forms himself on Keats and
Tennyson much as he might do if he had been born at York or
Newcastle. There are imitations of the old Scots songs and
ballads written ; but they are only imitations, and they no longer
take a place in literature. . . . The vast impetus of Burns set
all the country off, as an earthquake sets the bells ringing ; and
there are little bells ringing from that mighty vibration yet. But
little of the poetry thus produced is ever good of its kind, much
less good enough to constitute a national poetry in a cultivated
and fastidious age. The historical school to which Mr. Hill
Burton belongs is at least national in its subject. But it addresses
itself only to a part of the population ; and the Scot at Home,
who writes to the reading public proper, writes insipid tales,
respectable reviews, or twaddling essays precisely similar in
character to those of Englishmen of the same calibre.'

Any one who has surveyed the literature produced in
Scotland or by Scotchmen since the appearance of Lord
Cockburn's *Memorials of his Own Time* (and that book,
surely 'national' enough, was published a good many
years before Hannay wrote of the Scot at Home) must have
been struck by the number of the contributions, many of
them both excellent and successful, to Scottish archæology,
history, and biography, quite independently of the operations of such great Scottish book-clubs as the Bannatyne,
the Maitland, and the Wodrow, and they, indeed, have
rather slackened in their activity. In fiction the popularity, both in Scotland and England, of Mr. Barrie's works
shows what interest can be aroused in contemporary Scottish

life, even the humblest, when it is delineated by sympathetic genius.

Turning to social life, though the passage which I am about to quote is descriptive of Edinburgh as Hannay knew it rather than of Scotland generally, he supports his favourite thesis thus :

'What is true in literature of the Scot at Home is true in life. No Scot of the cultivated class now talks Scots, though it was talked by such within the memory of men who are still alive. . . . So, too, throughout all social life. In Edinburgh a regular Scotch dinner may be ordered at a tavern, with cockaleekie, haggis, and sheep's head in order, and an admirable dinner the visitor will find it. But the regular Edinburgh dinner of private life differs in no respect from a dinner given in the same rank of society in London. . . . What is true of the dining-room is true of the drawing-room. You hear the same fashionable foreign music of the day which you hear in the metropolis—not the characteristic Scottish music of the soil. There are damsels to be met in Scotland, however, who sing the national songs charmingly; and a really good-looking Scottish damsel, with paly gold hair, fair complexion, and a figure inherited from a vigorous race, is one of the prettiest sights of a country, whose own beauty deserves to be adorned by living beauty.'

From the Scottish Venus Hannay passes to the Scottish Bacchus :

'The Scotch are gradually dropping their language and allowing a thousand little innovations in manners to creep into their land. But they are still true to the native beverage with a deep and enduring love. . . . It is not for the gin-and-brandy-consuming Cockneys of the middle-class to be hard on a nation which drinks a better spirit than either, and drinks it in the form of that toddy which, according to Lockhart, Sir Walter preferred to all the wine in the world. Besides, the amount of toddy consumed is exaggerated by popular rumour. Ten-tumbler men are now rare. A minister like that Dumfriesshire one, who, after his ten, observed that he was "mightily refreshed," could not now be found ; much less the Aberdeenshire one, who falling asleep after giving out the psalm, and being awakened by his precentor with the words "it 's dune," answered, " Na, na, there 's mair in the black pig yet," under the impression that they were carousing together in his manse. The Ten-Tumblers Club of Cupar, the chairman of which once went to bed on eight tumblers, and observed in the morning that he would not again tamper with his constitution, is extinct. And the old laird, who on seeing two friends enter his avenue, exclaimed, "Rax me doun the whisky bottle—we 'll start fair !" has long since laid his moist clay with that of his fathers.'

It is curious, yet not uncharacteristic of Hannay, that so convivial a man should have thus expressed a mild preference for the comparative temperance of the Scotland of his own time to the enormous toping of its past. But he was defending the later bibulous customs of his father-land, as he knew it, against the Cockney Bohemians who jeered very inappropriately at the whisky-drinking of Scotland. Hannay was not behind-hand in satirising the faults and defects of his countrymen, but he was ready to defend them from the assaults of Cockney witlings.

The hero of his unfinished novel, *Bagot's Youth*, was represented as having been brought up in Greece, in which classic country the father of Bagot (in the story of whose youth, Hannay occasionally adumbrated his own auto-biography) was supposed to hold a consular appointment of some kind. Bagot, being educated at Athens, naturally acquires a considerable proficiency in ancient and modern Greek. Of course, for Hannay wrote what there is of *Bagot's Youth*, long before he was invited to become the editor of the *Courant*, he had no thought then of making use of his hero to satirise denizens of Edinburgh. But in an exasperated mood, after he left the *Courant* and returned to London, he told me that he intended to bring Bagot to the Modern Athens, and make him an extra-mural Professor of Greek there, what the Germans call a *privat docent*. This migration of his hero would have enabled him to indulge in satirical remarks on that ignorance of Greek north of the Tweed with which, in season and out of season, he was constantly twitting scholars and clerics among his countrymen. There was, in Hannay's time, a Dr. Robert Lee, a prominent minister of the Kirk in Edinburgh, who was a Broad Churchman of the Presbyterian kind, and somewhat of a Presbyterian ritualist to boot, he having introduced a sort of liturgy into the worship which went on in his church. Hannay's own orthodoxy was by no means excessive, but he detested Broad Churchism, he said, as a despicable compromise by the aid of which its clerical votaries tried at once to salve their consciences and with complete success to retain their emoluments. This Dr. Lee and his allies, for their alleged ignorance of Greek among other delinquencies, Hannay assailed with the utmost pertinacity. One morning there appeared in the *Courant* an explanation of the passage in the Shorter Catechism, 'Works of Necessity and Mercy.' 'If Dr. Lee,' quoth Hannay editorially, ' had to read an easy bit of Greek, it would be a work of necessity for him to use a lexicon, and a work of mercy to give him one.' Fortunately for his peace of mind, Dr. Lee was not so sensitive as Dr. Tulloch, and being, moreover, in robust health, did not allow himself to be perturbed by Hannay's satire. But still more persistent was Hannay's persecution of Professor Blackie, a man whom it might have been thought nobody could dislike, and who, after having filled for many years the Chair of Greek in Edinburgh University, and executed a spirited translation of Æschylus (his metrical translation of Homer was after Hannay's day), must surely have known some Greek. Partly to torment Professor Blackie, Hannay set up, as greatly superior to him in Greek scholarship, an aged gentleman of the name of Veitch, whose knowledge of Greek was doubtless considerable, though Hannay, for his own ends, exaggerated it. This Veitch's reputation rested chiefly on a Manual of Irregular and Defective Greek Verbs, which the Clarendon Press at Oxford honoured by printing an edition of it. Another feather in the defunct Veitch's cap was that some continental scholar, when writing to him, addressed the letter ' Professor Veitch.' This gave Hannay occasion for a malicious epigram, the point of which was that the man who had the chair knew no Greek, while the man who knew much Greek had no chair. I had the pleasure of a slight convivial acquaintance with this thorn in Professor Blackie's side. Whether the veteran Hellenist knew Greek, or whether even he knew English, it was impossible for a fellow-guest to discover, since like Madame de Staël's neighbour at the London dinner-table, he had 'a great talent for silence.' But of his powers as an imbiber of whisky toddy there could not be the slightest doubt. He sat like a rock and he absorbed like a sponge, growing with every fresh tumbler more taciturn, if possible, than when he began. But what learned discourse would have flowed from his lips had Hannay brought to Edinburgh the hero of his novel ! How Bagot would have crowed over Professor Blackie and proclaimed the superiority in Greek scholarship of the Old 'un (as Veitch was familiarly called) to the

University Professor! Hannay, however, never carried out his intention of continuing *Bagot's Youth.* He took his revenge on the heads of the Conservative party, the managers of the *Courant,* and all and sundry in Edinburgh against whom he harboured a grudge, by satirising them in an article 'Recollections of a Provincial Editor,' which he contributed to *Temple Bar* not long before he was appointed consul at Barcelona. It would not repay much quotation. The only survivor of his satire—for this time Professor Blackie escaped—is a well-known Scotch essayist and cleric. A few words in the passage dealing with him must be suppressed as too savage, and perhaps too unjust to be reproduced. Here is the substance of it. Reekyborough, of course, means Edinburgh (Auld Reekie):

'I love,' Hannay wrote, 'to meditate on Binks, and to read him in the *Goody Two Shoes Magazine*—that periodical which now represents the literature of the Church of Robertson and Reid and Campbell and Blair. The fatuous vanity disguising itself for a moment under sentimental self-depreciation, but reappearing at once in the smirk which accompanies pointless detraction—the airy toadyism of the vulgar Reekyborough fast man, which can make a clergyman stoop to talk of his church as 'our shop,' these are the traits which, in hours of satirical reverie bring before me, the image of my quondam acquaintance, Binks.'

The Scotch Conservative leaders, the 'Patter' and 'Foxy' of this prose satire of Hannay's, are not only in their graves (one of them had a very tragical end), but forgotten, great men though they once were in the Parliament House of Edinburgh as Lord Advocates and so forth. Hannay, too, is in his grave. *Requiescat: Requiescant.*

Y

VII. LEIGH HUNT AND HIS SECOND JOURNAL

WHEN I first knew Leigh Hunt he was verging on fifty-five, and resided in Edwardes Square, Kensington, the region which furnished him with material for one of the most agreeable of his books, *The Old Court Suburb*. From the airy, lightsome cheeriness of so many of his writings, I had expected to find him all briskness and vivacity. On the contrary, as he sat and talked among his books, busts, and engravings, tall, dark-complexioned, with thoughtful brow and expressive hazel eyes, his greyish-black hair flowing down to his shoulders, he gave you the impression of courteous dignity and repose. In a grave, sweet voice, he spoke frankly, but always kindly, of the notable men with whom he had been intimate, and of whom a junior as I was might wish to hear, Shelley and Keats, Hazlitt and Charles Lamb. Of his later and then living contemporaries it was Thackeray about whom he showed most enthusiasm, saying that since *Tom Jones* there had been no novel at all equal to *Vanity Fair*. Hunt's household at that time included his wife, a confirmed invalid, always confined to her room, to whom he was unweariedly attentive, two dark-eyed, youthful daughters, and an affectionate son, Vincent, whose death a few years afterwards was a very heavy blow to him. He liked his domicile and its surroundings. Edwardes Square, with its pretty houses, large enclosure, gardens behind, and spacious grass-plots in front, had been 'invented,' as he phrased it, by a Frenchman, and Hunt has recorded his inability, when he first saw it, to reconcile it with 'English principles' of housebuilding and street-construction. It was quite a *rus in urbe*, just suited for a poet who, while delighting in trees and flowers and verdure, loved also to hear the busy hum of men. One defect in the house which I could not but observe was of the sanitary kind. Whether the painful fact was due to the nationality of the builder, or whether the drains had gone permanently wrong, Hunt's domicile was disagreeably malodorous. I was never more unpleasantly conscious of this state of things than once when Leigh Hunt was warmly expatiating on the merits of his friend Dr. Southwood Smith as a sanitary reformer, and expressing a hope that, for his services in that way, the Government would do something for him. I thought to myself that Hunt's zeal for sanitary reform might have been usefully directed to effect an improvement in the same direction at home. But, with all his love for the fragrance of flowers, shrubs, and newly-tedded hay, Leigh Hunt did not seem in the least disturbed by what was painfully unfragrant under his own nose, and for I know not how long no effort appeared to be made to abate the nuisance. By a visitor who like myself knew nothing of the financial difficulties which then, as almost always, embarrassed him, but which never disturbed his outward serenity, Leigh Hunt might have been pronounced a happy old gentleman. Afterwards, when I learned that at the time of those first visits of mine his financial embarrass-

ments were very serious, I remembered a little incident
which did somewhat impress me at the moment, but not
so much as when it seemed to connect itself with the care-
lessness in money matters which must have aggravated, if
it did not cause, his constant pecuniary difficulties. One
fine summer evening we were sitting by the open window
of the little front parlour, which was flush with the roadway, where an organ-grinder was evoking from his instrument strains of the usual kind. During a pause in the
music the operator made the customary pantomimic appeal
for a gratuity. Hunt felt in his pocket and found in it a
sovereign, but no small change. He turned to one of his
daughters, who was in the room, and handing her the
sovereign bade her go and get it changed, and then give
the organ-grinder a shilling! The incident was a trivial
one, but it became to me on remembrance, as Carlyle was
wont to say, ' significant of much.' The Carlylian story
of Leigh Hunt's sovereigns placed on the mantelpiece in
readiness to meet the inevitable demand for a loan is well
known, and very probably the sovereign to be changed for
the organ-grinder's shilling had been borrowed. Hunt's
own way of life was extremely simple, and his personal
expenditure could not have been other than slight. There
must have been great mismanagement somewhere in his
household, and Hunt was not the man to check it. I
once heard Carlyle express surprise that ' a man of Leigh
Hunt's sense ' did not manage his economics better, and
then suggest that it was because Hunt had never watched
a ploughman at work, toiling and moiling all day for a
scanty wage. But, without having been brought up, like
Carlyle, in the country, Hunt must have seen, in the course
of his life, a great deal of manual work done. The very

compositors who set up the type of the *Examiner* worked, in their way, as hard as any ploughmen.

After an absence of a year or two from London, I revisited Leigh Hunt in Edwardes Square, and found him in excellent spirits. His charming autobiography was being received with a chorus of approval, which gladdened the veteran's heart and brought him again very prominently into notice. He was considering a literary project, of the inception and execution of which the story is now to be told for the first time, since his reference to it in the Autobiography is of the slightest, and both the son who edited his correspondence and his formal biographers have dismissed it in still fewer than his own words. The project was broached to him not by any of his London friends, in or out of the publishing world, but most unexpectedly by a stranger, a young Manchester man. This was a certain John Stores Smith, who, while under twenty, and engaged in the Manchester cotton-trade, had written, in the purest Carlylese, a biography of Mirabeau, the only one, so far as I know, of any mark as yet produced in England. From his diminutive stature he was known to his friends as 'little Smith,' but he was clever, fairly accomplished, and remarkably fluent, both as a writer and a speaker. He was ambitious withal, and his ambition not unnaturally was directed towards literary life in London. Circumstances enabled him in some measure to gratify his aspiration. On attaining his majority he sold a piece of agricultural land which he had inherited, and with the proceeds he migrated to London. His life of Mirabeau had brought him into correspondence with Carlyle. On knowing him personally, Carlyle came to like the little man, whom, however, from his over-readiness to flare up about anything or nothing, the Sage compared to 'turpentine.' Soon after his arrival in London, Smith published, at his own charges, a striking volume, *Social Aspects*, which might have had for its epigraph, 'Whatever is is wrong.' The public, which listened with impatience to the jeremiads of Carlyle in the *Latter-Day Pamphlets*, did not care much for the denunciations of this little-known young gentleman of one-and-twenty. Nevertheless, the seeming sincerity of his fervid protests against the manifold iniquities of the age procured him the regard of Charles Kingsley.

Social Aspects not having set the Thames on fire, its author bethought him of devoting the remainder of his capital to the establishment of a periodical in which he could flourish his own pen to his heart's content, and from which, if successful, a permanent return might be obtained. Somehow or other he was brought into communication with Leigh Hunt. The result was an agreement between the youth and the veteran for literary co-operation. Sixteen years previously had been founded *Leigh Hunt's London Journal*, for editing which he received eight guineas a week ; Carlyle, then engaged in a dire struggle with poverty, thinking, as he recorded in one of his letters at the time, what wealth such an income would be to his frugal self. The *London Journal*, though popular as it deserved to be, for it was brimful of Leigh Hunt, after a cheerful existence of two years, collapsed from a failure of the needful supplies. It was now decided to revive it, with the omission of 'London' from the title. Leigh Hunt gave his name to the new venture ; Smith supplied the capital. Both were to contribute. The editorship was to be a duumvirate ; the junior at first, however, giving a pretty free hand to the senior, whose name and connections were, he hoped, to attract distinguished contributors. Hunt at once exerted himself to beat them up. Among the first to whom he applied were his old friends Carlyle[1] and Walter Savage Landor certainly, and Tennyson probably. If an application was made to Tennyson nothing came of it. With Carlyle and Landor, Hunt was successful. His personal intercourse with Carlyle had ceased for some years, but Carlyle retained an affectionate regard for his old friend.[2] He promised to contribute to the earlier numbers, and he

[1] Leigh Hunt had been first attracted to Carlyle by his remarkable essay 'Characteristics' (*ante*, p. 57), from which have flowed many contributions to the 'Philosophy of the Unconscious,' and concerning which Macvey Napier, when inserting it in the *Edinburgh Review*,—he succeeded Jeffrey in the editorship,—wrote to Carlyle : 'I do not understand it, but it has the stamp of genius.' I have heard that Lord Brougham was so disgusted by the essay that he threatened if anything more by 'that man,' Carlyle, appeared in the *Edinburgh Review*, he himself would cease to contribute to it. Hunt's admiration for the 'Characteristics' led to a friendly correspondence with Carlyle. On hearing of the establishment of Hunt's *London Journal*, Carlyle wrote him a letter (Craigenputtock, 18 April 1834) which has not hitherto been published, and from which the following is an extract :

'The starting of your Journal was a glad event for me : it seemed one of the hopefullest projects in these days ; and surely it must be a strange public, one would think, in which Robert Chambers (a very silly kind of man) prospers and Leigh Hunt fails. You must bear up steadily at first ; it is then in this, as in all things, that the grand difficulties lie.'

Robert Chambers's prosperity was the success of *Chambers's Edinburgh Journal*. He may have been, in Carlyle's estimation, 'a very silly man,' but he was at least a man of business, which Leigh Hunt was not. Some two months after this letter was written, Carlyle settled in London with Leigh Hunt for his near neighbour. Of Carlyle's feeling towards Hunt, his liking for the man and the writer, mingled with weariness of his optimism, and of the 'hugger-mugger' dominant in his household, there are abundant illustrations in Carlyle's Reminiscences, Journals, and Letters.

[2] At this time I was in the habit of visiting both Carlyle and Leigh Hunt, and once or twice was the bearer of friendly messages from each to the other. Carlyle saying to me that he thought of 'making a pilgrimage' to Kensington and Hunt, I told this to Hunt, and it was in a tone of proud dignity, which impressed me, that he replied, 'I shall be very happy to see Mr. Carlyle.' I do not think that the pilgrimage was ever made, but Hunt paid

kept his promise. Through the courtesy of Leigh Hunt's grandson I am enabled to give the veteran's hitherto unpublished and delightfully characteristic appeal to Landor for contributions, which he headed

SOLILOQUY.

'I wonder (beautiful, absurd word!) if Landor has seen the announcement of a certain *Leigh Hunt's Journal*, and I wonder still more if he could find among his papers some epigram or thought, or least fragment not polemical, something on the sunny and dulcet side of him (for the Journal, though

the one visit to the Carlyles, his intimation of an intention to which effect is the chief subject-matter of another hitherto unpublished letter of Carlyle to Hunt about to be quoted. I think it very probable that he went to Chelsea to make inquiries about John Stores Smith, who was much better known to Carlyle than to Hunt. The letter is undated as regards the year, an exception to Carlyle's usual practice, of which his wife's was the reverse. 'Vincent' was Leigh Hunt's faithful son, previously referred to. The 'book' was doubtless Leigh Hunt's Autobiography. Doubtless, also, the 'Mr. Story' mentioned was the American sculptor afterwards known as the author of *Roba di Roma* and *Graffiti d'Italia*. It was in the dusk of a summer evening that Vincent Hunt arrived, and what with the gloaming, what with a crowd of visitors, Carlyle had not observed that a letter from Hunt accompanied the book:

'*Chelsea*, 21 *June* (*Friday Evening*).

'DEAR HUNT,—Many kind thanks! I saw the book, and sent thanks for it by Vincent; but I did not know, till this minute, what other pleasant thing lay in the letter itself, which the dusk and the hurry would not suffer me to read at the moment. By all means, yes, yes! My wife is overjoyed at the prospect of seeing you again in the old good style, courage and do not disappoint us. We are here, quite disengaged, and shall be right glad to see you.

'I hope Vincent explained what a miscellaneous uproar had incidentally got about me to-night, and how for want of light, as well as of time, I missed the touch of the letter altogether. Tuesday, remember! We dine about five and tea comes naturally about seven,—sooner, if you will come sooner.

'One of my people to-night, an accomplished kind of American, has begged a card of introduction to you; he is a son of a certain Judge Story; is himself, I believe, a kind of sculptor and artist as well as lawyer: pray receive him if he call; you will find him a friendly and entertainable and entertaining man.

'And so—till Tuesday evening—Yours with all regard,

'T. CARLYLE.'

expressing itself pretty freely too as far as it goes, means on
the whole to be a sweet, all-embracing kind of phenomenon),
and so manifest his good wishes for the new adventure. Something of Carlyle will be in the first number, and (I hope) of
Tennyson. Also much announcement of all sorts of agree-
ments to differ on the part of its correspondents.

'But Landor must not be offended if I add that we receive
no contributions, even from the wealthiest genius (in any sense
of that epithet), without paying for them, and by the hand-
somest standards of payment.'

Landor's assenting reply, now also published for the
first time, was prompt and cordial:

'DEAR LEIGH HUNT,—Success to you in all your undertak-
ings! You see I do not defer my answer one single post.
The only poem worth your notice is one I sent to Forster'
(John Forster, then Editor of the *Examiner*) 'some months
ago—and it was expressly for money, which a poor family
much wanted. Luckily I have had, what I never thought I should
have at the close of the year, enough for that purpose: and
whatever I can fairly gain now, I will give to the patriots
in Germany.

'I will now write to Forster, who will send you some dramatic
scenes, if he has not yet disposed of them.—Believe me
sincerely yours,   'W. S. LANDOR.'

Forster did *not* send the 'Dramatic Scenes,' and Landor
substituted for them some versicles, which Hunt entitled
Poemetti.

No. 1 of '*Leigh Hunt's Journal*: a Miscellany for the
cultivation of the Memorable, the Progressive, and the
Beautiful,' contained those versicles by Landor, which, like
others contributed by him to subsequent numbers, were of
the slightest possible value. Hunt began in it, and for
several weeks continued, a series of papers, 'The Town'—
a supplement to his very pleasant volume with the same

title on the historical and biographical associations connected with the streets of London. Carlyle's name was a
tower of strength, and the sale of the first three numbers
of the Journal was much aided by his three articles, 'Two
Hundred and Fifty Years Ago,' picturesque and vivid
sketches of some English duels fought in the reign of
James I. They were partly derived from material which
he had collected for his never-finished history of the
Scottish Solomon. And he took some pains with them,
though they appeared as merely extricated 'From T.
Carlyle's Waste-Paper Bag,' for he was rather given to
showing himself a little contemptuous even when he was
doing a kindly action. The usual love of the public for
novelty, along with the names of Leigh Hunt and Carlyle,
the one as editor, the other as contributor, did so much for
the Journal at its start that, after the issue of the third
number, Hunt wrote thus cheerfully, in another unpublished
letter, to Landor : 'The Journal promises beautifully, and
hope gives me new strength.' Alas! the source of the
strength thus derived was not long in drying up. The
London Journal, whether in its original matter or its
extracts, had been pervaded throughout by Leigh Hunt,
whose connection with the new Journal was limited to
such papers as those on 'The Town' and to a few occasional tales and dramatic sketches. Smith's contributions,
chiefly comments on the incidents of the day, were not
particularly effective. The sub-editing was indifferent,
and the business management worse than indifferent.
As the circulation dwindled, Smith asserted his proprie-
torial and co-editorial claims, which clashed with those of
Hunt, and not less true of the conduct of a periodical than
of a campaign is Napoleon's saying : 'One bad general is

better than two good ones.' A bone of contention
between the Duumvirs of the Journal was the remuneration 'by the highest standards of payment' which in his
large-handed but unpractical way Leigh Hunt assigned
to the contributors whom he favoured. I remember
Smith grumbling to me (I was one of the contributors)
about the magnitude of the sums paid to Walter Savage
Landor (and to benefit 'the patriots of Germany') for
his mostly rather trivial *Poemetti.* As the contents of
Smith's exchequer, never amply filled, were gradually
drained away, the relations between him and Leigh Hunt
became more and more strained. It was said at the time,
on the authority of Leigh Hunt himself, and the statement has been recently revived, that the end was hastened
by something which appeared in the Journal reflecting on
Lord John Russell, whom Leigh Hunt admired as a
politician, and to whom he was deeply grateful for his
pension. I heard Smith, who was a very satirical young
gentleman, describe Leigh Hunt sallying forth, with an
enormously high shirt - collar, to attend Lady John
Russell's receptions as a duty which he owed to his benefactor. But the real cause of the catastrophe was a
financial one. It was when the capital which started it
had disappeared that, after a troubled existence of not
quite four months, *Leigh Hunt's Journal* died, simply of
inanition. Among the occasional contributors who could
not avert this catastrophe were R. H. Horne, William
Allingham, and 'Parson Frank,' the *nom de plume* of the
Rev. Francis Jacox, since known by several meritorious
contributions to literature. He and I are, with one
exception, the sole survivors of the contributors to *Leigh
Hunt's Journal.* The one exception is Mr. James Payn,

whose name—he was then a young man of twenty—is suffixed to some pathetic verses, *A Poet's Death*, which appeared in one of the later numbers of the Journal, and which Smith boasted, I know not with what truth, was the first introduction, by name, of Mr. Payn to the reading world.

Smith himself returned to Manchester, whether or not a sadder and a wiser, certainly a poorer man. He re-entered, though in a modest way, the Manchester cotton-trade, and, having earlier gone through various phases of religious belief, became a Roman Catholic. This change, and his reputation as a man of literary promise, procured him the favour of several great people, among the English Roman Catholics, and I suppose led to the acquaintance with the Tichborne family, which enabled him to give some telling evidence against 'The Claimant' during the trial of the most protracted *cause célèbre* of our time. Much more conducive to his worldly prosperity was his appointment by a beneficent Manchester capitalist to be the manager of certain coal and iron mines in Derbyshire. His success in this position was a conspicuous contrast to his failure as proprietor of Leigh Hunt's Second Journal, and he amassed considerable wealth. In the intervals of business he contributed to the Manchester press, and published a volume of translations from Heine. He died not long ago, in Derbyshire, having in his early career afforded another proof of the risks run by men of letters when they engage in the commerce of literature. I learned his decease by seeing it announced in an 'Evangelical' organ, which noticed the event in order to add the intimation, that before dying he had expressed a wish to be buried according to the rites of the Church of England.

VIII. MANCHESTER MEMORIES:
Edwin Waugh

O N the first Saturday of May 1890, not much more
than three years ago, toiling and money-making
Manchester presented an unusual spectacle. For two and
a half miles from the railway station named after that
busiest of human beehives, the Exchange of Manchester,
onwards and upwards towards Kersal Moor, from which
there is a panoramic view of the great industrial city,
with its church-steeples and mill-chimneys looming ath-
wart a canopy of smoke, there stood on either side the
roadway thousands of spectators reverently doffing their
hats and caps as a hearse with the coffined remains of one
well known and endeared to them wended on its way
towards Kersal Church and graveyard. As the hearse
passed them the spectators fell in behind it to swell the
funeral *cortége*, in which were the Mayors of Manchester
and Salford in their carriages, with other representatives
of local municipal officialism, and with deputations from
most of the populous towns by which Manchester is
belted. There had been in Manchester no public and
civic demonstration on the death of a townsman so
striking as this since, more than forty-five years before,
the remains of the originator of the atomic theory, John
Dalton, were borne to their last resting-place, past great

crowds of onlookers, and followed by a funeral train a mile long. By the death of Dalton, his chief biographer says, rather mournfully, 'the first proof was furnished to many that he was once alive.' This could not be said of him to whom Manchester and Lancashire paid the last honours in the May of 1890. Edwin Waugh was not, like John Dalton, a great man of science, but his name was a household word throughout his native county, and in many a home which had never been visited by a glimpse of the atomic theory. Probably not one of the multitude of witnesses of his obsequies—operatives and artisans being conspicuous by their presence—but was familiar with the song which first conferred fame on the Lancashire Burns, as Edwin Waugh has been fondly called.

When I first made Waugh's acquaintance, he no more than myself surmised that he was to become a Lancashire celebrity. He was thirty, but had not said or done anything that gave the promise of future distinction. Of humble birth and self-educated, he had been for years a journeyman printer when he became assistant-secretary of the Lancashire Public School Association, an episode in his career of which his biographers could say next to nothing because they knew next to nothing. He was acting in that capacity when I was appointed Secretary of the Association. Its most strenuous promoter was Samuel Lucas, who is not to be confounded with a bearer of the same name, for some years literary critic of the *Times*. Waugh's, and afterwards my, Lucas was of Quaker origin. He was a brother of Frederick Lucas, who, being converted from Quakerism to Romanism, became editor of the *Tablet* and an M.P. Samuel Lucas married a sister

of John Bright, an angelic-looking lady; both husband
and wife are in their graves.   During her widowhood, and
much to my surprise, she figured frequently on the platform as an advocate of temperance, woman's rights, and
so forth.   When Lucas aided in founding the Lancashire
Public School Association, he was settled in Manchester
as manager of a cotton-mill; several years afterwards
he removed to London on being appointed first editor
of the *Morning Star* (that *bright* particular star, some
would-be wit called it), a journal which was established
with Manchester money, as the organ of the Manchester
party, and which expired in the arms of the last of its
editors, Mr. John Morley.   Lucas was an amiable man of
fair intelligence, with a good deal of quiet energy, and
whatever of this he could spare from the management of
his cotton-mill, he devoted to the Lancashire Public
School Association.   Its object was to establish throughout Lancashire (and. when it became afterwards the
National Public School Association, throughout the
country as well as the county) schools supported by
local rates and locally administered (*ante*, p. 201).   Dogmatic theology was to be excluded from the instruction
given in them, but the chief principles of Natural Religion
and of ethics were to be taught, and Scripture extracts,
like those in use in the Irish National Schools, were to be
read for edification.   When the Association emerged from
its infancy into something like vigorous youth, it met
with formidable opposition.   The clergy, for obvious
reasons, were hostile to it, but to this there were a few
welcome exceptions, though chiefly out of Lancashire,
not in it.   One of these was the then famous Dr. Hook,
the High Church Vicar of Leeds, afterwards Dean of

Chichester.[1]   The Parliamentary Grants in aid of popular
education were given only to supplement local subscriptions,
and in proportion to the amount of these.   The consequence was that the poorest districts, in which the local
subscriptions were naturally least, but which needed the
grants most, received the smallest amounts.   Working
energetically in such a parish as Leeds, Dr. Hook saw the
glaring insufficiency of the system then in vogue, and was
attracted by the scheme of the Association.   Its bitterest
opponents were the Nonconformist champions of purely
voluntary education (a Voluntaryism run mad, and now
quite extinct), led by the late Edward Baines of Leeds.
He was fiercely hostile to the system of Parliamentary
Grants in aid of popular education because they were
awarded only to schools in which religious instruction was
given, and this he considered to be neither more nor less

---

[1] This large-hearted and, though a strenuous High-Churchman, this
broad-minded ecclesiastic was indeed the first prominent advocate of State-
education of a purely secular kind.   In his pamphlet, published so long ago
as 1846, *On the means of rendering more effective the Education of the People,*
Dr. Hook, at that time Vicar of Leeds, began by showing the utter inadequacy
of the then established system of voluntary effort, aided by Parliamentary
Grants, to cope with the educational destitution of the country.   He proposed
therefore the levy of a rate in each county for the establishment and support
of public schools within its borders.   The rate was to be levied by the
County Magistrates, who were to choose for each school-district an administrative School Board, without regard to the religious opinions of its members.
This preference of selection by the Magistrates to popular election by the
ratepayers sprang, of course, from Dr. Hook's Toryism.   Next he contended
that, as the ratepayers included Dissenters as well as Churchmen, it was
impossible to frame a programme of religious instruction which would be
acceptable to all.   Theological instruction was consequently to be rigidly
excluded from the schools.   The province of the school-teacher was to be
strictly confined to secular education.   The religious instruction of the school-
children was to be left to the clergy and to the Nonconformist ministers, in
accordance with the creeds and wishes of the parents.   The daring, as it was
then, of Dr. Hook's proposals led to numerous hostile criticisms on them by
his brethren of the Church of England.

than a State-endowment of religion, in direct contravention
of the cherished principles of Nonconformist Voluntaryism.
To the scheme of the Lancashire Public School Association he, as an Evangelical Nonconformist, was quite as hostile, because it excluded from its proposed schools dogmatic
theology, and aimed, in Baines's opinion, at what he
regarded as transcendently pernicious—a gigantic State-
endowment of Secularism.   From the Lancashire Liberal
leaders the Association received either half-hearted support
or none at all.   Before I became its Secretary, Cobden
made a speech to it, in which, after bidding it go on and
prosper, he said good-bye to it, and went his way to
promote agitations (for Financial Reform, Reduction of
Armaments, etc. etc.), more attractive to him, but, as it
proved, much more sterile.[1]   Just after I became its Secretary, John Bright told me frankly and bluntly that to stir
up the education question anew was 'like flogging a dead
horse:' though his younger brother Jacob was a staunch
supporter of the Association.   The only sympathiser with
the objects of the Association who became afterwards a
notable public man was William Edward Forster, whom I
had known previously in London, and whose tall ungainly
figure and rasping voice I well remember.   He came over
to Manchester occasionally, partly to visit his friend Miss

---

[1] Not long after the delivery of the speech referred to, Cobden indited to
George Combe, in connection with it and with Baines's belligerent attitude,
the following *apologia* : ' I hope you will not think there is any inconsistency
in the strong declaration I made at the meeting of the paramount importance
of the question of education, and my apparent present inactivity in the
matter.   Owing to the split in the Liberal party, caused by Baines, it
would be impossible for me to make it the leading political subject at this
moment.   Time is absolutely necessary to ripen it,' etc. etc. (Morley's *Life
of Richard Cobden*, ii. 41).   The reader will perhaps see in this deliverance
a confirmation of the truth of Emerson's estimate of Cobden (*ante*, p. 158) as
the 'embodiment of English discretion.'

Jewsbury (*ante*, p. 140), and showed considerable interest in our movement. But sympathy more than active support was all that he could give us, for he was in Yorkshire, and had enough to do there fighting Baines and the other champions of voluntary education pure and simple. More than twenty years had to elapse before, through his Education Act of 1870, Board Schools were established very much on the plan of the Lancashire Public School Association.[1] But such a result, though it might be struggled for, could not fail to appear distant, even long after the establishment of the Association. However, there are some who prefer volunteering on a forlorn hope, while others abide watchfully among the stuff, waiting until the assault has been successful, when those can join in the cry of 'Victory,' who have not stirred a finger to help in achieving it.

Oratory was needed for the public meetings · of the Association in town and country, but orators were scarce. To declaim against an obnoxious tax was the task, comparatively an easy one, of the speakers at the meetings of the Anti-Corn-Law League. Here a new tax was to be imposed, with benefits far less palpable than those which could be made clear to the meanest capacity by the exhibition of the big loaf, said to be procurable through Free Trade at the price paid, while the Corn Laws were unrepealed, for a very little one. The Anti-Corn-Law League, moreover, had at its command an

[1] A few figures show the enormous expansion of the national pecuniary aid given to popular education during the last forty years or so. In 1852 that aid, given solely by a Parliamentary Grant, was £166,483. According to the latest returns which I have been able to inspect, the Government Grant in a recent year was £3,287,285, while the School Board rates amounted to £1,320,486—together, £4,607,771, or more than twenty-four times the amount from taxation paid in 1852 to aid popular education.

organised staff of paid and fluent lecturers, but such aid
was far beyond the slender resources of the Lancashire
Public School Association. When, as occasionally happened, the supply of amateur-oratory fell short of the
demand, the unfortunate Secretary had to work with his
tongue as well as his pen and mount the stump, quite
'unaccustomed to public speaking' though he was.
Sometimes the scene was a Manchester Nonconformist
chapel, the congregation of which was sure to swell the
audience. I remember vividly one great roomy edifice
of the kind, pulpited and pewed, the pastor of which was
not connected with any known religious denomination,
but had evolved a queer kind of quasi-Christian doctrine
and added to his cure of souls the care of the bodies
of his congregation, to whom when they required it, he
gave medical advice, and dispensed medicines made up
according to eccentric prescriptions of his own! Sometimes the scene changed from Manchester to an outlying
hamlet, where a friendly mill-owner was monarch of all he
surveyed, and the whole of the little population worked
in his factory and lived in his cottages. They would
supply the audience and he, taking the chair of course,
the mill school-room for the oratory, bestowing on the
orator, if unaccompanied, kindly hospitality for the night.
The audiences were generally sympathetic, especially when
the oratory was militant as it occasionally became, and the
hearers were Manchester operatives. I have still in my
mind's eye their eager up-turned grimy faces as they drank
in denunciations of those who kept their children ignorant.
There never was any display of opposition to the scheme
of the Association, such as was exhibited in Yorkshire
to a somewhat similar movement. At one Yorkshire

meeting, indeed, the audience at which had fallen under the influence of Edward Baines's propagandism, a speaker on the blessings of education and the insufficiency of voluntary effort for its extension, was interrupted by a zealous obscurantist of humble life, who, going far beyond Baines himself, shouted, at the top of his voice, the protest, 'we wunna be tite!' (we will not be taught).[1] The Lancashire workers were very willing to see their children 'tite.'

That in time the Lancashire Public School Association had made sufficient way to enable it to organise, after the manner of the Anti-Corn-Law League, a great public meeting in the Free Trade Hall of Manchester, a meeting at which Carlyle himself, contrary to his wont, showed himself inclined to be present and to speak, has been already recorded (*ante*, p. 201-2). But so little at first was the success of our enterprise deemed probable, that Waugh's immediate chief and Waugh himself were dubbed Don Quixote and Sancho Panza, names partly suggested, no doubt, by contrasting peculiarities of *physique*. Otherwise and except in so far as Waugh, with his rustic upbringing, was full of remark homely as well as shrewd and racy, the *sobriquet* was unjust to him. His zeal in the cause of popular education was quite as great as his chief's, and he had a genuine desire to see children of the class from which he had sprung receive the instruction denied by circumstances to himself. His, moreover, was a temperament as poetic as that of the real Don Quixote's delightful henchman was prosaic. In the intervals of business *my* Sancho, seated at an opposite desk, would conn Spenser's 'Faerie Queene' or some other

---

[1] I tell the story as it was told to me, though a West Riding friend objects that 'we wunna be tite' is not true Yorkshire vernacular.

favourite poem, and now and then call my attention to a
stanza or passage which he thought peculiarly striking or
musical. He had begun to scribble verse, but his flowers
of poesy were for the most part born to blush unseen. If
a Manchester paper inserted any of his metrical compositions, he was taken to task, not, of course, by his immediate
chief, but by Lucas, who prohibited him from so much as
inditing letters to the newspapers, though intended to further the objects of the association. Poor Waugh's official
functions were of a subordinate and far from congenial kind.
Among his duties was that of making arrangements for the
holding of public meetings in Manchester and neighbourhood, of attending them when held, of distributing at the
close of the proceedings pamphlets and fly-sheets, and of
receiving the names of new subscribers if any were forthcoming. On one occasion Waugh was reporting to the
Committee his operations at one of these meetings. He
was asked whether he had received any promises of subscriptions. 'No,' said Waugh, but he added, in a cheerful
and encouraging tone, 'they would take any quantity of
paper!'—a statement which elicited a laugh from a usually
sedate conclave. Sometimes Waugh and I had to realise
personally the contrast between the readiness to applaud
speeches and 'take any quantity of paper' on the one
hand, and the disinclination to subscribe on the other.
The Lancashire Public School Association was, as is the
appealing boast of many hospitals and philanthropic
institutions, 'supported wholly by voluntary contributions.'
Sometimes at the week's end the exchequer was empty
and Waugh and I had to consider how the payment of our
very modest salaries was to be effected. If, as would happen, there were no annual subscriptions just due, nothing

was left but for Waugh to hunt up some supporters of the
Association whose subscriptions were in arrear.   Many a
joke we indulged in when scanning the list of subscribers,
and deciding who were the most likely to furnish the small
sum required.   We were comparatively young—I was
some years Waugh's junior—and we made a jest of our
little perplexities.   On these occasions there was often
on my lips, for Waugh's behoof, a vernacular rendering
of the Virgilian *Hæc olim meminisse juvabit.*

The consolatory prediction came true for Waugh at
last.   After an absence of some years in London, I returned to Manchester as the editor of a newspaper there,
and found him plodding wearily on as traveller to a printing firm.   I saw a great deal of Waugh during this my
third and final sojourn in Manchester.   He was one of
the original members of a little social and literary club
which I founded, and which, from an old affection for
Sterne, I christened 'the Shandeans.'   We dined and.
supped together almost daily.   Our talk was of literature
and art, and many a pleasant hour we passed together.
There was nothing else of the kind in the Manchester of
those days.[1]   Manchester has now two literary and art

---

[1] Several literary Londoners visiting Manchester received the Bohemian
hospitality of the Shandeans.   But by far their most distinguished visitor was
the late Laureate.   Tennyson, accompanied by his friend Woolner the sculptor,
now also deceased, was in Manchester at the time of the great Art Exhibition
of 1857, and pitched his tent in semi-incognito at a quiet old hostelry where
his expressed wish to be free from visitors prevented intrusion.   Woolner was
a friend of the late Frank Jewsbury (*ante*, p. 133), brother of Miss Jewsbury
the novelist and a leading Shandean, who came upon him and Tennyson in
the galleries of the Exhibition, and invited both of them to spend the evening
at his house in Ardwick.   Tennyson inquired rather gruffly what he was to do
when they got there, but, on learning that the invitation came from a brother
of Miss Jewsbury, whom he had known in London, he accepted it.   Word was
sent round to the Shandeans to muster for the reception of the poet.   Tenny-

clubs each with a club-house of the London pattern, which the Shandeans had not, and there is besides a Manchester Literary Club, not so much social as intellectual, which holds its meetings monthly, and has papers read before it, afterwards published formally as 'Transactions.'   Waugh had a fine voice, powerful and sweet, and was the chief vocalist of the Shandeans ; at whose meetings he was one of the most constant attendants, and whose companion-ship and sympathy were a great solace to him in his daily drudgery.   He was now, however, composing a series of sketches of life and manners in his native county, chiefly its nooks and corners, where nothing but the unadulterated Lancashire dialect was spoken, where the manners were primitive, where old traditions and legends lingered, and a popular oath was 'by the mass,' as in the centuries before the Pilgrimage of Grace.   The question was how to find a local publisher for a purely local book.   Publishing in Manchester was then of the meagrest and humblest kind. When Samuel Bamford, Waugh's senior contemporary, produced his *Passages in the Life of a Radical* (*ante*, p. 152), the most notable Lancashire book of that generation anterior to Waugh's, he was forced to be both his own

---

son said little during the evening, but smoked a great deal, with his feet on the chimney-piece, and listened with apparent interest to the conversation. Among the Shandeans present was the late John Stores Smith (*ante*, pp. 341·2), who not only regaled the Laureate and his fellow-guests with a characteristic jeremiad on the wickedness of the times but suggested a correction of the punctuation in a line of 'Locksley Hall,' the substitution of a comma for a semi-colon, or *vice versâ*, a correction which the Laureate graciously accepted. The cabman who came at the hour appointed by his illustrious fare was bribed by the host to wait until summoned, and Tennyson was so little weary of the company in which he found himself, that it was two or three in the morning before he departed, declaring that he had never in his life met with such an odd set of fellows.   This, of course, the Shandeans took as a compli-ment to their powers as entertainers.

publisher and his own retail bookseller.[1] He had the book printed in sheets, which he folded and his wife covered. Then he hawked them about, a mode of distribution which he continued with that and his other books for many a year. There must be denizens of the Manchester of to-day who remember the figure of the sturdy and stalwart Bamford trudging along highway and byway with his wallet full of specimens of his publications, in search of friendly purchasers. To procure a local publisher, for an unknown author like Waugh, was not then or at any time an easy matter. Circumstances favouring me, however, I found him a Manchester publisher, and I have the satisfaction of thinking that I was of use to my ex-Sancho, and helped him to take his first step towards fame. That earliest book of his, prose *Sketches of Lancashire Life and Localities*, contained some of the best and freshest writing that ever came from his pen, and was conspicuously marked by his most characteristic qualities, a love of nature under all her aspects, a deep sympathy with humble Lancashire folk, a quick eye for the humorous in their ways and speech, and for the pathetic in their lot, with great skill in reproducing dramatically their talk in the homely but expressive Lancashire dialect.

Good judges recognised the varied merits of the volume, and Carlyle pronounced its author 'a man of decided mark.' It was not much of a financial success, but it made Waugh known. Fame came to him suddenly and unexpectedly only a year after its publication. In a fit of the happiest poetic inspiration he threw off the touching lyric, 'Come whoam to thi childer and me,' and, printed as a

---

[1] There is a tolerably copious memoir of Bamford (whom I knew well) in my *Lancashire Worthies* (second series, 1877).

single sheet, it leapt at once into a popularity unparalleled
in the annals of modern song. It was sold literally by the
million, not only in Lancashire, but throughout England
and in the colonies. The Baroness Burdett Coutts ordered
some twenty thousand copies of it for gratuitous distribution in humble homes. The fastidious *Saturday Review*
called it 'one of the most delicious idyls in the world, so
full of colouring, yet so delicate, so tender, and so profoundly free from artifice.' Waugh had no longer to
travel for a printing firm, and could live reputably
by his pen. Manchester newspapers and publishers
welcomed whatever came from it, prose and verse in
the Lancashire dialect as well as purely English, Lancashire sketches and tales, and accounts of tours and trips
in many regions of England and Scotland with at least
one libretto for the Christmas pantomime in a Manchester
theatre. Occasionally I saw him, prosperous and happy,
when a flying visit was paid by me to Manchester, or by
him to London, and many a laugh we had over the old
days, and those Saturday mornings on which we had to
go together into Committee of Ways and Means to provide
for the day passing over us.

When at last old age and infirmities overtook him,
Waugh was generously dealt with. Influential Lancashire
M.P.'s, supported by the influential among their consti-
tuents, urged his claims on successive Governments. I remember taking to the House of Commons, to be signed by
Members for Manchester and Salford, a memorial to the
Premier on behalf of Waugh, to which were attached the
signatures of several hundreds of Lancashire men of some
position in the county, probably the most numerously-
signed memorial of the kind ever presented to the head

of a British Government.   These efforts bore fruit.   One
Prime Minister gave him £150 from the Royal Bounty
Fund, payable during three years.   Another Prime
Minister conferred on him a Civil List Pension of £90 a
year.   His Lancashire friends and admirers raised for him
during some ten years an annual £200.   In order to save
his self-respect it was called the Waugh Copyright Fund.[1]
The lately deceased Lord Derby contributed to it liber-
ally, and the subscribers were supposed to be the owners
of Waugh's copyrights, though when he could dispose of
them to his own advantage they raised no objection, and
went on contributing to his support as before.   Pleasant
for Lancashire men, but painful for Scotchmen, is the
inevitable contrast between the closing years of Edwin
Waugh and those of Robert Burns.

The programme, daring it was thought to be, of the
Lancashire Public School Association excited, as has been
partly seen, during my and Waugh's Secretariat, some
attention among thoughtful men unconnected with politics.
One of them—he paid us a visit from Liverpool where his
mother resided—was Arthur Clough, whose poems have
found enthusiastic admirers among cultivated readers.   A
twofold interest then attached to him as the author of a
spirited poem in English hexameters, the Bothie of Toper-
na-Fuosich, describing the sayings and doings of an
Oxford reading party in the Scottish Highlands, and as a

---

[1] The Honorary Secretary of the Fund, like Waugh, an old Shandean,
was Mr. J. H. Nodal of Manchester, the editor of an interesting local paper,
the *Manchester Weekly News*, President of the Arts Club of Manchester, and
for the last eighteen years Honorary Secretary and Director of the English
Dialect Society.   On the removal of its headquarters from Manchester to
Oxford, Mr. Nodal has just been succeeded in these offices by Dr. Joseph
Wright, Deputy Professor of Comparative Philology in Oxford University.

courageous man who, from doubts of the truth of orthodox theology, had resigned his Oriel fellowship and tutorship, with all their academic promise for his future. I remember him well with his fresh-coloured face, boyish-looking yet anxious, his rather stalwart Lancashire figure, encased in a loosely-buttoned black frock coat, and altogether with an aspect partly that of a cleric, partly of an athlete. ·He came to Manchester to see and to hear, rather than to talk, and the state of painful transition both of mind and circumstances, in which he then found himself, predisposed him to even more than his constitutional taciturnity. I convoyed him on the usual visit to Mr Jacob Bright's, at Rochdale, where he received the welcome and hospitality usually bestowed there on interesting strangers.[1] Our host, I remember, explained to Clough with hopeful enthusiasm a scheme much favoured at that time by advanced Liberals in and out of Lancashire, to substitute elective County Boards for the Quarter Sessions rule of the squirearchy. The scheme came to nothing at that time, or for a long time afterwards, until in 1888 the Act of Parliament establishing County Councils was passed, but not under the auspices of Mr. Jacob Bright's political allies. I saw Clough afterwards in London. He had not recovered from the painful wrench of quitting Oxford and was quite as taciturn as in Manchester. Even Carlyle (who admired the man more than the poet) complained that Clough was 'very stingy of his speech,' a

---

[1] After this visit to Manchester and Rochdale, Clough wrote thus to a friend: ' I like the Manchester people, of whom I have been seeing a little, better than the Liverpudlians. They are more provincial perhaps, but have more character, are less men of the world, but more men of themselves. Your sanguine friend still puts his trust in master-manufacturers as in those olden foolish days, etc.'

seemingly strange complaint to come from the great apostle of silence. Clough had then entered on the duties of an office, to which he was appointed not long after leaving Oxford, the Principalship of University Hall, London, now the headquarters of Robert Elsmere propagandism, then a sort of educational hostelry in which young Unitarians attending University College were boarded and coached. Mr. Froude therefore considerably exaggerates when he describes Clough's integrity as having led him not only 'to sacrifice a distinguished position and brilliant prospects' at Oxford, which is perfectly true, but as having 'brought him to London to gather a living as he could from under the hoofs of the horses in the streets.' By the utmost stretch of metaphor the holder of the Principalship, tolerably remunerative, of University Hall, cannot be said to have doomed himself 'to gather a living as he could under the hoofs of the horses in the streets.' After a few years, Clough resigned the Principalship of University Hall, because he had become a candidate, with what he thought a moral certainty of success, for some better paid or more congenial academic position in Australia. His candidature was unsuccessful. Upon this he migrated to Massachusetts to enjoy the society of his friend Emerson, and to teach Greek to young New Englanders, contributing at the same time to American periodicals, and revising the spirited but inaccurate translation of *Plutarch's Lives* which appeared as the handiwork of Dryden. From these transatlantic occupations he was recalled to England to be an Examiner in the Education Office. To this appointment a good salary was attached; its duties were of a purely routine kind, and he held it until his death.

'Carlyle led me out into the wilderness and left me there'
is a saying attributed to Clough and sometimes reproduced by his admirers when writing about him. It may
be true enough of the spiritual relations between Clough
and Carlyle. Carlyle did not furnish Clough with a new
religion in exchange for that which he had abandoned, and
for the simple reason that Carlyle, who had also abandoned
the old religion, had not found a new one for himself. But
it was always understood that Carlyle was mainly instru-
mental in procuring for Clough the appointment in the
Education Office which restored him to his country and
rescued him from unsatisfactory drudgery in New England. If this be so, it was the most substantial benefit
ever conferred by Carlyle on any of his friends, whether
pacing the streets contentedly or seeking a living under
the horses' hoofs of Mr. Froude's—in the case of Clough—
most inappropriate metaphor.

THE 'CRITIC': HISTORIES OF PUBLISHING HOUSES

MORE than ten years before I became connected with it, the *Critic*, a literary journal, was founded by the late Mr. Serjeant Cox, then the proprietor of the *Law Times*, and long afterwards of the *Field* and the *Queen*, among other periodicals. Towards the close of the first decade of its existence, the *Critic* had among its contributors the late William Maccall (*ante*, p. 250). Under the signature of 'Kenneth Morency,' afterwards exchanged for that of 'Atticus,' which became pretty well known, he preached from this new pulpit a series of vehement and eloquent lay-sermons. Among his purely literary articles of that time may be mentioned several on De Senancour and his *Obermann*,[1] the melancholy book, which was

---

[1] In his 'Stanzas in memory of the author of *Obermann*, November 1857,' Matthew Arnold went the length of placing De Senancour in the same rank with Goethe and Wordsworth :

> ' Yet of the spirits who have reign'd
> In this our troubled day,
> I know but two who have attain'd
> Save thee, to see their way.
>
> In England's lakes in grey old age,
> His quiet home one keeps ;
> And one, the strong much-toiling sage,
> In German Weimar sleeps.'

unnoticed, so far as I am aware, by any English writer before Maccall, and, only later, made by Matthew Arnold the theme of some of his melodious pule.

Not long after the formation of Maccall's connection with the *Critic*, I made his acquaintance (*ante*, p. 250), and he introduced me to it. It was then, and for years continued to be, both issued fortnightly and edited by its proprietor. One of my first contributions was a biographical sketch of Carlyle, for which I translated into English Goethe's German version of the English original of the very interesting letter to the poet-Sage of Weimar, in which Carlyle gave an account of his life and literary work at Craigenputtock. That translation of mine has been copied into numerous biographies of Carlyle without correction of a glaring error of the press committed in it, and previously pointed out (*ante*, p. 62). My knowledge of Carlyle's early life, or rather such knowledge of it as I then communicated to the readers of the *Critic*, was derived from recollections of his letters written during boyhood and youth to his old school-fellow Mitchell, who became one of the masters of the Edinburgh Academy. These letters had been carefully preserved by Mitchell, and for years after his death the originals were handed about in Edinburgh among Carlyle's admirers there, to be perused, on the understanding that they were not to be copied.[1] When my sketch of Carlyle appeared in the *Critic* I wrote to him to explain that none of the information which it contained respecting him had been derived from anything told me either by himself or by any of his relatives. He took no direct notice either of this

[1] Selections from them have been published by the American Professor Norton in his edition of *The Early Letters of Thomas Carlyle*.

intimation or of the sketch itself, but I could see that he was not displeased with either.

The connection thus begun with the *Critic* speedily expanded. Taking a hint from George Henry Lewes's agreeable literary *causeries* in the *Leader*, I wrote in every number of the *Critic* for years, under the signature of 'Frank Grave,' an article entitled 'The Literary World: its Sayings and Doings.' Though occasionally, I fear, disfigured by something verging on flippancy, it was relished by those who were more ignorant than myself of current English literature, and of the authors who were producing it. To that article I added one in which 'The Critic Abroad' summarised as fully as he could the Continental literature of the fortnight. But the most salient of my earlier contributions to the *Critic* consisted of a series of articles (signed 'Herodotus Smith') then novel of their kind. They were sketches of the periodical and newspaper press, from the *Edinburgh* and *Quarterly* to *Blackwood's Magazine*; from the *Times* to the *Examiner*. In these biographies, so to speak, of noted reviews, magazines, and newspapers, accounts were given of their origin and progress, with sketches, better or worse, of their more notable contributors both in the past and in that particular present to which my articles belonged. Since then there have been several elaborate histories of the British newspaper press, but of our chief periodicals I do not know of any history since my sketches of them appeared in the *Critic*. In writing them I had no assistance worth speaking of, except in the case of *Fraser's Magazine*. Through a common friend, information respecting that once famous magazine was offered me by an old and conspicuous Fraserian, who had at his fingers' ends the story of its origin, and had been the familiar friend of its originators. This was the 'Reverend' Frank Mahony, better known, and once very well known, as a scholar, a wit, and a versifier by his *nom de plume*, 'Father Prout.' Father Prout's *Reliques* contain scholarly and felicitous Latin versions of such familiar lyrics as Nora Creina, Lesbia of the beaming eye, and so forth. These Latin versions, with a gravity almost worthy of Swift, Father Prout declared to be the true originals, English translations of which 'Tom' Moore and others had palmed off, as original verse of their own, on the British public! The Father had not only been educated by the Jesuits, but became a member of the order, and was in his younger years a zealous one. When I knew him there was still a touch of the clerical in his costume, as he was always in black, but he had ceased to be a Jesuit in anything but name. He could not be called a denizen of the London Bohemia, but was domiciled in its outskirts, visiting occasionally the haunts of the more reputable of its inhabitants, for even the Bohemia of those days had its class distinctions. He invited me to have a chat with him in the old office of the *Globe*, then a Liberal organ, to the staff of which he was attached, and for which the malicious averred he wrote, without stirring from the Strand, what professed to be correspondence from Rome. He was a genial kindly little man, whose blue eyes looked at you over his spectacles, and who spoke in an undertone with a slightly Milesian accent. In a dark and dingy room of the *Globe* office he poured into my willing ears the early story of *Fraser's Magazine*, with racy anecdotes of its founders, all of which were reproduced in the *Critic*. In his last years he was Paris correspondent of the *Globe*, and did really write his letters

2 A

in Paris, where he died. They buried him in his native Cork, within earshot of those 'bells of Shandon' of which he sang in still-remembered rhymes.

Besides these varied contributions to the chronicles of literature at home and abroad, present and past, some of which required more or less research, I did a good deal of reviewing for the *Critic*. It would be affected modesty if I were to pretend that my work on the *Critic* did not contribute to make it, as in those years it at last became, a successful periodical. It had before very long 7000 subscribers, its nominal price being sixpence, and if an allowance off this price was made to them, on the other hand, as the *Critic* was sent direct from the office to the great majority of its purchasers, there were not to be deducted from the proceeds the discounts which must have been given to 'the trade' if it had been circulated in the usual way. My contributions were anonymous, or at most pseudonymous. Once, and once only during my connection of many years with the *Critic*, was my name suffixed to a series of articles, entitled 'Two Centuries Ago,' which, had I been permitted to continue them, might have possessed a slight permanent value. They were based on researches in those King's Pamphlets, in the Library of the British Museum, on the importance as materials for English history during the Commonwealth and Protectorate periods Carlyle laid great stress (*ante*, p. 86). I intended to chronicle in them not only the political, literary, and religious history of England during the corresponding fortnight of 200 years before; but also its social and industrial life, any account of which is conspicuous by its absence from Professor Masson's otherwise comprehensive work, his monumental *Life of Milton*. Their discontinuance rather nettled me, and one of my favourite subjects for treatment in the columns of the *Critic* was the injustice done to young authors by the anonymous system. Since then great breaches have been made in that system. Some of our foremost periodicals regularly publish the names of their contributors ; so do, in many cases, the chief illustrated journals. But the change has not been nearly so favourable to the young author as I then fancied that it would be. ' It has led some editors to seek before all things in their contributors, not sterling work, but great or high-sounding names. That the contributions of writers of proved literary distinction should be acceptable to editors of periodicals is in the nature of things. But, since the anonymous system has been relaxed, editors welcome with eagerness commonplace, which they would reject unless they could parade it as contributed by a peer or peeress, a Bishop or a Dean, a well-known politician or M.P., the proper arena for platitudes of these last being the House of Commons, the platform, or the waste-paper basket. What editor in his senses, would, under the anonymous system, have admitted into the pages of his periodical Mr. Gladstone's dreary disquisitions on the Gods of Olympus ? And the space devoted to the gratification of the vanity of these amateurs is, of course, so much taken away from the legitimate domain of men and women who have something to say which would be worth reading. In the old days the ladies and gentlemen who now occupy, most undeservedly, foremost places even in the better class of periodicals, had their vanity innocently gratified by contributing to the now extinct annuals : the *Keepsakes* and *Amulets*, the *Literary Souvenirs*, and *Books of Beauty*. ' Persons of quality ' had a literature of their own, written

solely and read solely by themselves. Its gradual extinction is, from one point of view, very much to be regretted
in the interest both of the reading public and of the
promising young author.

Not long after I had made way in the *Critic* and become
its chief, or at least its most copious contributor, George
Gilfillan said, in a letter to his friend Sydney Dobell, 'I am
asked to write for the *Critic*, which has got into new and
able hands.' This was inaccurate. One new and copious
contributor might be engaged on it, but it was still edited
by the proprietor. 'My reason,' Gilfillan continued, 'for
accepting the request is, I don't disguise it, to do all that in
me lies to destroy the *Athenæum*, that *Times* of literature,
only without its thunder'—an attempt which has been
made several times since then, but has generally ended in
disaster to those who made it. Among the good George's
earlier contributions to the *Critic* was a notice of Alexander
Smith—'in whom he had discovered, he fancied,' a Scottish
Keats—with extracts from Smith's unpublished poem, 'A
Life Drama,' his first conspicuous appearance on any
literary stage. Of Alexander Smith something has been
already said (*ante*, p. 290), and more will be said hereafter.
Subsequently the kindly Gilfillan introduced in similar
fashion to the *Critic* and its readers another 'new poet,' a
Mr. Stanyan Bigg, of Ulverstone, in whom George discerned,
he said, 'much more culture than Smith, and a subtler if
not so strong a genius.' Mr. Bigg's 'Night and the Soul,'
however, was not a success. During nearly each of six
or seven successive years, Gilfillan contributed to the
Critic several papers, among them some of the best and
most striking which he ever wrote; notably those on De
Quincey. They were signed 'Apollodorus,' by which

nom de plume W. E. Aytoun held up Gilfillan to undeserved ridicule in *Firmilian.* Gilfillan's glowing papers, always eloquent while not undiscriminating, excited considerable attention in their contrast to the general tameness (occasionally flavoured by cynicism) of English criticism.

After some years of labour on the *Critic*, I was offered, and I accepted, the editorship of a Manchester newspaper. Returning from Manchester to London, after an absence of several years, I resumed my connection with the *Critic*, which, during the interval, had been completely transformed. It was now issued fortnightly instead of weekly, and it had a new editor. As a consequence of this change, there was an abandonment of the former plan by which the greater part of the impression of each number was supplied from the office direct to subscribers. 'The trade' was now, as in the case of most other journals and periodicals, invited to sell the *Critic*. It had a much more businesslike look, and was much better organised than in the days of 'Frank Grave' and 'Herodotus Smith.' But there was nothing in its contents sufficiently striking to make the general public prefer it to the long-established and carefully-conducted *Athenæum*, while many of the old subscribers, who did not grudge paying for a fortnightly literary journal, grudged paying for a weekly one. George Gilfillan's contributions, too, ceased, and the vehemence becoming more and more aggressive of William Maccall's 'Atticus' papers repelled as many readers as they attracted. In the old days the proprietor had been a gainer by the fortnightly *Critic*, he was losing by the weekly *Critic* when I joined it.

After this renewal of my connection with the *Critic*, I was asked to write for it a series of histories of the chief publishing houses of London and Edinburgh. Carlyle had said that a good history of booksellers would be much more valuable than most histories of kings, so I went to work pretty cheerfully and very industriously. I wrote, and there duly appeared, three Histories of Publishing Houses, being the only contributions of mine to the *Critic* during my second and final connection with it, which possessed any general interest. The publishing houses of which I was the historian were those of the three successive John Murrays, since 1812, of Albemarle Street, the firm of Longmans, and the Blackwoods of Edinburgh. That of the three John Murrays was the first published and the only one which I wrote, not merely without the slenderest aid of any kind from the House, but without even the cognisance of its head, or of any one connected with it. I reserve, for the moment, further reference to my history of it.

After the appearance of the history of the House of Murray, the Messrs. Longman aided me so far, and so far only, as the history of their firm during the eighteenth century was concerned, and they saw the proofs before publication. Their accounts and some other documents illustrating their publishing and bookselling operations (for they were booksellers as well as publishers) during the eighteenth century were often very curious, showing the strange use, as it now seems, which country customers made of the bookselling firms in London with which they had dealings.[1] Instructive, too, was the light thrown on

[1] The following is an extract from Chapter i. of my history of the ' House of Longman:'—

'A great wholesale house in London would be rather surprised now if it received from a country bookseller instructions to forward in next parcel, with the magazines and books ordered, " 1 sliding Gunter from some of the instru-

the share-system prevalent among publishers in the last century. In the then comparative dearth of publishing capital, the copyright of a book, or the expense of publication and the profit or loss attending on it, was shared among a greater or smaller number of publishers, or 'booksellers' as they were then called, and, indeed, as they then were. Thus there was established in 'the trade,' a sort of fraternity very different from the isolation in which each member of it now finds himself.[1] Of my history of the House of Blackwood, the proofs were seen by the late John Blackwood, who was then the acting head of the firm.

Executed, as already stated, without the slightest extraneous aid of any kind, was my history of the House of Murray, onwards to 1860, from its establishment in 1768, by Lieutenant McMurray of the Marines, who, from the prejudice then existing in London against the Scotch, had to drop the 'Mc' when starting as a bookseller in Fleet Street, and who had hoped to have for a partner in his new venture, his friend and countryman,

ment makers," or "1 box of Eddowe's aperient pills," or "2-eighths share of lottery ticket," or "1 oz. of cobalt as advertised in the covers of the *Gentleman's Magazine*," or such a direction as "Please send as above on Saturday, and pay Mr. Barratt, Parliament Place, Palace Yard, Westminster, £1, 6s., king's rent, due 10th October last, for the Vicarage of Holycross, Shrewsbury." Yet the very items quoted turn up in bookselling records, late on into the eighteenth century.' I am not sure, but I think it probable, that these items were derived by me from some of those eighteenth century documents in the archives of the Messrs. Longman, which I was allowed to inspect and to utilise.

[1] A final survival of this share-system was exhibited in the case of Dr. Latham's edition of *Johnson's Dictionary*, the first instalment of which was issued in 1860, with no fewer than twenty-four London firms enumerated on the title-page as its publishers. The edition was far from being a financial success. Five London firms united to publish the original edition of *Johnson's Dictionary* issued in 1755. Of these five, the Messrs. Longman are the sole survivors.

the ill-fated Falconer, the poet of the *Shipwreck*. Great, very great was the amount of time and labour which I spent on that comparatively thankless task. The result was as elaborate and exhaustive a history as the most diligent and persevering research could make it. Its quantity—it is not for me to speak of its quality—was considerable; if printed in the same type as that on which the reader's eye is now resting, it would fill a space not far short of a hundred pages such as those contained in this volume. This history of the House of Murray excited a good deal of attention in and out of what are called 'literary circles.'

Many years subsequently it was resolved in Albemarle Street to carry out the suggestion with which my history of the House of Murray closed. 'If it be true,' I wrote, 'as Mr. Carlyle has said, that a good history of booksellers would be much more valuable than most histories of kings, then there are monarchs with whose elaborate biographies we would cheerfully dispense to receive in exchange a Life and Correspondence of the late John Murray of Albemarle Street.' The necessary materials were hunted up in the archives of the House and placed in the competent hands of Dr. Smiles. Thirty years after my suggestion was printed appeared Dr. Smiles's history of the House of Murray, *A Publisher and his Friends*, the second John Murray, with an account of his father the Lieutenant of Marines. It was some satisfaction to me to learn that, when Dr. Smiles received the commission, my history of the House of Murray, which had been carefully preserved in Albemarle Street, was placed in his hands as an excellent ground-plan for him in the composition of his work.

Before the publication of Dr. Smiles's volumes I became a second time the historian of the House of Murray, and this time not only at the instance of the late Mr. Murray, but to some extent with his co-operation. More than twenty years after my elaborate history of the House of Murray appeared, and I had quite forgotten that I had ever written it, I received one morning a note in which a correspondent, whose name was unknown to me, asked if I had any objection to write a history of that publishing house. It turned out that the note came from the London representative of the New York publishing firm of Harper, whose *Harper's Magazine* is as well known in this country as many of our native periodicals. The origin of the inquiry made to me, on the part of the Messrs. Harper, was the following : A scion of the House of Murray, visiting New York, had received from the House of Harper a hospitable welcome, and when a scion of the House of Harper afterwards visited London, he in his turn received a hospitable welcome from the House of Murray. The American visitor was shown, among other things, the famous drawing-room in Albemarle Street, redolent of the memories of many literary celebrities. There Sir Walter Scott held his first colloquy with Lord Byron. The cremation of Byron's memoirs, bequeathed to and surrendered by 'Tom' Moore, was performed in the fireplace of that room. On its walls are the portraits for which, to be presented by them to the second John Murray, sat Byron, Moore, Campbell, Southey, Gifford, Hallam, Lockhart, Washington Irving, and Mrs. Somerville among others. Surveying them, as he stood in the middle of the room, the scion of the House of Harper exclaimed, 'What a capital subject for an article!' The late Mr. Murray consented to allow copies to be taken of the portraits in his possession, and drawings to be made illustrative of the history of his House, for reproduction in *Harper's Magazine*. But who was to write the letter-press accompanying the illustrations? Mr. Murray bethought him of the writer of these pages, who twenty years or so before had been the historian of his house. A common friend furnished him with my address; hence the unexpected question put to me by the London representative of the Messrs. Harper. They offered me most liberal terms for an article to produce which, with my former history of the house before me (Mr. Murray lent me his copy, I had none of my own) was comparatively an easy task. It had only to be condensed and briefly continued 'up to date.' While engaged on this second history I had occasional consultations with the late Mr. Murray,[1] and with his partner, the late Mr. John Cook (a descendant of the founder of the house, Lieutenant McMurray), a genial old gentleman, but afflicted with a deafness which rather obstructed conversation. Murray went carefully over my first history of his House, suggesting a few emendations and additions, and giving me some hints for continuing the account of the publishing operations in

---

[1] The perpetuation of 'John' as the Christian name of the successive heads of the publishing house of Murray may confuse the reader. The chronology of the Murrays is the following : The first John Murray, previously Lieutenant McMurray, founded the house in 1768, and died in 1793. He was succeeded by his son, the second John Murray, the publisher and friend of Lord Byron and founder of the *Quarterly Review*, who died in 1843. His son and successor, the third John Murray, spoken of in the text as 'the late Mr. Murray,' died in 1892, and was succeeded by his son the present Mr. John Murray, fourth of the name.

Albemarle Street down to the time at which I was writing. The only at once noticeable and novel information which I received from him was rather curious and interesting. He unearthed and presented to me, in its original grey pasteboard binding, a thin octavo volume the title of which ran thus: 'The Life of Paul Jones, from original documents in the possession of John Henry Sherburne, Esq., Registrar of the United States. London, John Murray, Albemarle Street, 1825.' 1825 was both the year of the appearance of the first instalment of *Vivian Grey*, and the year preceding that of the appearance of the ill-fated *Representative*, of which, and of Disraeli's connection with it, more hereafter in the section of this volume entitled 'Lord Beaconsfield and his Minor Biographer.' That life of Paul Jones was seen through the press, and furnished with a preface by no other a person than the young Benjamin Disraeli, who had not then attained his majority, and in his preface, especially if you know beforehand who was its author, there may seem to be discoverable here and there Disraelitish touches. In due course the article appeared, copiously illustrated, in *Harper's Magazine*, and, though I wished it to be anonymous, with my name attached to it. On the other hand,—I take this opportunity of publicly acknowledging it,—the Messrs. Harper behaved to me with a liberality even exceeding that of their original proposal. I had contracted to write a certain number of pages —I forget the exact number—at a very handsome rate of remuneration *per* page. With such ample material at my command I supplied something like twice the number of pages agreed on. I wrote to the Messrs. Harper to say, as it was only right to say, that if they chose to print the overplus, I should expect no more remuneration than that which they had promised for the smaller number of pages contracted for. I was then given to understand that the editor of *Harper* hoped to print all the 'copy' which I had sent. Exigencies of space forbade the fulfilment of this hope, and the article, as it was printed in *Harper*, contained only about half of the matter which the firm had originally asked for. Not only, however, did they pay me for the number of pages which they had asked me to write,—this, I suppose, they were bound in honour to do,—but they paid me spontaneously, and much to my surprise, no trifling additional sum, in consideration of the superfluous pages which they had not contracted for, which of course they did not use, and which neither in honour, nor on any other ground, were they in the slightest degree bound to pay for. When I hear American publishers reviled for their alleged ill-treatment of cis-Atlantic authors, I always cite, in illustration of a very different mode of proceeding, the conduct of the Messrs. Harper to myself.

The proprietor of the *Critic* gave receptions and dinner-parties at his house in Russell Square. At one of these receptions, I remember meeting John Martin, the painter of the grandiose works which were once conspicuous in the world of art, and which, especially Belshazzar's Feast, were so acutely criticised by Charles Lamb. Martin was a quiet rather nervous little man who talked less of art than of his soaring schemes for the sanitary and other improvement of London. Of the dinner-parties, I recollect one among the guests at which were some notable people, for instance, Eothen-Kinglake, Robert Chambers, his son-in-law, W. H. Wills, the working editor of Dickens's

Household Words, a very acute gentleman ; Charles Knight, the publisher, genial and rather dignified ; and that professional diner-out, Henry Crabb Robinson, who had rubbed shoulders with a good many distinguished people, had been intimate with Wordsworth, accompanying him on a Continental tour, and had read 'Samson Agonistes' with Goethe at Weimar. Robinson's posthumous *Diary*, with its generally vapid and inane gossip, had some vogue at the time of its publication. There was very little general conversation. Eothen-Kinglake was reputed to be a vivid talker, but, if he spoke at all, it was to his immediate neighbours. I had a little chat about Shakespeare with Charles Knight, and was surprised to find that so accomplished a Shakespearian editor knew nothing of Ludwig Tieck's interesting novel, the *Dichter-leben*, in which he introduced Shakespeare himself with Marlowe, Greene, and others of their contemporaries. The post-prandial talk was monopolised by Crabb Robinson almost altogether. His monologue consisted mainly of anecdotes of small German poets, the *Dii minimarum gentium* of Teutonic literature, and was not only uninteresting but wearisome. He knew Carlyle in early days (since then their acquaintance had long ceased), and I asked him whether the Sage of Chelsea was modest when he was young. 'Well, you know,' was the reply, 'Mr. Carlyle could *never* have been modest.' I told this to Carlyle, who laughed heartily, and gave an account of his meeting, at Crabb Robinson's, a Mr. Sothern, who was a contributor to the *Westminster Review*, and afterwards held a diplomatic appointment in South America. Carlyle must have been on that occasion in an even more than usually contradictory mood. He told me as a good joke that, when next Sothern met 'Crabb,' he complained of the snubbing which he had received from Carlyle, adding with a certain pathetic modesty, 'Why, I couldn't have been always in the wrong!'

Of the acquaintances whom I made through my connection with the *Critic*, only two figure in my memory, Alexander Gilchrist and Charles Wycliffe Goodwin. During the later years of the *Critic's* existence, the art department was assigned to Gilchrist, who had already acquired a reputation by his *Life of William Etty*. The story of Gilchrist's father is a singular one. Originally a pastor in a dissenting communion, the General Baptists, in time he began to doubt the truth of the doctrines which he was preaching. He wrestled with his doubts, but the doubts gained the day. Thereupon he resigned his pastorate and betook himself to what was for him, after such a career, one of the strangest of all possible occupations. He rented a picturesque old flour-mill, embosomed in rich foliage, at Mapledurham, on the Thames (near Reading), famous in our poetic annals as the seat of the Blounts and associated with memorable passages in the biography of Pope. In the midst of some of the prettiest scenery on the banks of the Thames, the young Gilchrist imbibed a love of the beautiful in nature, and developed a taste for poetry and art. The mill, as may be easily imagined, proved a failure in the hands of the ex-dissenting pastor, who was removed to another and a better world, when his son was a boy. Somehow, through the generosity of relatives, I suppose, the young Gilchrist received a fair education at University College School, and was even enabled to be called to the bar. But

making no way as a barrister, he began contributing art
criticism and miscellaneous literary matter to the *Eclectic
Review* and other periodicals. At last his *Life of Etty*
procured him a reputation. The biographical workmanship
and knowledge of art displayed in it were far above the
average, and it attracted the favourable notice of Carlyle,
on whose *Life of John Sterling* indeed it appeared to me
to have been considerably modelled. With position, or at
least prospects, improved by the success of the *Life of
Etty*, Gilchrist married a very amiable and clever lady,
who herself became reputably known in literature, and
an interesting biography of whom has had many readers.
The first time I dined with Gilchrist, he made some
reference to his desertion of the bar, on which I remarked,
of course jocularly, 'you ought to have married a solicitor's
daughter.' 'That,' Gilchrist replied, looking at his wife,
'is exactly what I did.' Mr. and Mrs. Gilchrist became
intimate with the Carlyles, next door to whom in Cheyne
Row they were ultimately domiciled, and by whom they
were welcomed not only as agreeable and intelligent, but
as quiet neighbours, averse from permitting any of those
noises of cock-crowing, dog-barking, and the like, so
dreaded by the Sage, and so painful to his shattered
nerves. In the biography of Mrs. Gilchrist there are several
interesting notices of the Carlyles, with letters from Mrs.
Carlyle and reports of the Sage's Table-Talk. Gilchrist
was a middle-sized, good-looking man, with a florid complexion, a face beaming with good-nature, as well as
intelligence, a pleasant companion, and with always a touch
of the æsthetic in his costume. He made a very decided
hit by the first instalment of his life of William Blake,
with illustrations from his pictures and drawings and

selections from his poems and prose writings. Blake, as a painter and a poet, was neglected in his own day and generation, so that he was styled *Pictor Ignotus* on the title-page of Gilchrist's book. Since its appearance, the mystical painter has been *notus* and even *notissimus* to the present generation. Just as Gilchrist had become a prominent man, he died, at the early age of thirty-three, of a fever, which had attacked his children, and which he caught while nursing them. His unfinished biography of Blake was very ably completed by his accomplished widow since deceased. As the joint author of what is known as the Thomas-Gilchrist and 'basic' process for the dephosphorisation of molten iron, one of their sons, Mr. Herbert Gilchrist, has reaped fame and fortune in a department of things very different from that in which his father won his reputation.

The father of my friend, the late Charles Wycliffe Goodwin, was the head of a very eminent firm of solicitors at King's Lynn, Norfolk. One of his sons, an elder brother of Charles, took orders, and as Dr. Harvey Goodwin preceded, in the see of Carlisle, the present Bishop. Bishop Harvey Goodwin was a prolific author. Many of his volumes of sermons and other devotional works were very popular. He was also a copious contributor to periodicals, in which, though he was what might be called a Broad Churchman, he delighted to impugn the Darwinian theory of evolution. Charles, too, when entered at Catherine Hall, Cambridge, of which, in time he became a fellow, was intended for the Church. But his spiritual development and that of his brother, the late Bishop, were as different as in the case of the brothers John Henry and Francis Newman, and of two other noted brothers, Hurrell and James Anthony Froude. In point of fact, Charles Goodwin became an agnostic. His was a fellowship which, after a fixed number of years, he could retain only by taking orders. His views on religious matters having been transformed, when the time came for him either to resign his fellowship, or to take orders, he honourably chose the first of these alternatives. The act was the more honourable, since some misconduct, on the part of a member of the King's Lynn firm, had effected the impoverishment of his father and of Charles himself. Only a very moderate income was left him, and this he eked out occasionally by his pen. He was called to the Bar, but that was an uncongenial vocation. He never practised. The chief result of his legal studies was that he edited a law-book or two for the proprietor of the *Critic*, and this connection procured me an acquaintance with Goodwin which in time became friendship. Later in his career he edited the *Parthenon*, the short-lived offspring of the *Literary Gazette* which had been resuscitated under Shirley Brooks to be a competitor of the *Athenæum*, and had, if I remember rightly, Mr. John Morley for its last editor. In spite of Goodwin's scholarly editorship, the *Parthenon*, like the revived *Literary Gazette*, added another to the failures of attempts to shake the supremacy of the *Athenæum*. Goodwin also contributed remarkable papers on Egyptological subjects to *Fraser's Magazine*, to the *Cambridge Essays*, and to the transactions of learned societies. But the one literary achievement, which brought him conspicuously before the reading world, was his contribution of a paper on the ' Mosaic Cosmogony ' to the once famous *Essays and Reviews*, the seven contributors to which were dubbed by some orthodox assailant the *Septem contra Christum*, although among them was the present Bishop of London, then the Rev. Frederick Temple, Head Master of Rugby.[1]   Goodwin, being quite estranged from the Church of England, was the only layman among the Essayists and Reviewers, and, having no ecclesiastical pains and penalties to fear, he spoke out very freely the truth as it was in him.   He not only assailed very effectively the cosmogony ascribed to Moses, but all those questionably ingenious theories broached by Dr. Chalmers, Dean Buckland, and other champions of orthodoxy, to reconcile things so irreconcilable as the facts of science and the letter of the Bible.   Goodwin's essay produced a considerable sensation, and educed from angry orthodoxy a number of replies, to none of which did he deign to make any rejoinder.   His erudition was as extensive as it was deep, in proof of which it may suffice to say that besides being a good classical, Hebrew, and German scholar, he was both one of the most accomplished Anglo-Saxon scholars, and one of the profoundest Egyptologists of his time.   When I knew him he was devoted to Egyptology, which, in his case, included a thorough knowledge of

---

[1] Bishop Temple was the first member of the Broad Church party whom Mr. Gladstone elevated to the Episcopate. His appointment to the see of Exeter was, however, it may be surmised, mainly due to his having harangued the townsmen of Rugby in favour of Mr. Gladstone's successful scheme for the disestablishment of the Irish Protestant Church. Since he has been seated on the Episcopal Bench, Bishop Temple has once, at least, spoken his mind freely on some delicate and much-debated matters. He was Bishop of Exeter when he delivered, in 1884, the Bampton Lectures, taking for his subject 'The Relations between Religion and Science.' In one of these lectures he spoke of 'the allegory of the garden of Eden,' while in another he declared that he cheerfully accepted the Darwinian theory of evolution as redounding more to the glory of God, than did the old theory of special creations.

Coptic. Of the origin of his Egyptological studies more hereafter. Though not at all unsocial, he lived a secluded bachelor-life as a tenant of chambers in the Temple, where his only companion was a favourite cat, the plumpness of which testified to its owner's fond care of it. His chief relaxation was music ; he played on more than one instrument, and was, I believe, for several years musical critic of the *Guardian*. Surrounded by his books, con-spicuous among them volumes full of reproductions of hieroglyphics and hieratic papyri, he would talk to me by the hour on the results of the latest Egyptological researches, and the influence exerted by Egypt on the earliest intellectual development of ancient Greece : a theme on which he delighted to dilate. Although an agnostic, he contributed to the *Speaker's Bible* some notes on the presence of Egyptian words in the Pentateuch, which, with others from Egyptological experts, were regarded by the editor as strongly militating against one modern theory, that the books ascribed to Moses were wholly composed at a very much later time than his. With all his learning, Goodwin was one of the most unpretending and modest of men, and, though fortune had not thus far smiled on him, he was always contented and cheerful. Absorbed in those abstruse and beloved studies of his, Goodwin seemed to me a very happy man. What a contrast between his tranquil and studious existence in the Temple and the rackety tavern-life of those London Bohemians, Hannay's genial descriptions of which and whom have been previously quoted ! But Goodwin, too, had his ambition. It was to obtain some consular or other official appointment in Egypt, which would enable him to prosecute his researches in the land the ancient literary monuments and memorials of which formed the principal subject of his studies.   Lord John Russell, with whom Goodwin's friends had some influence, could, or would not, do this for him.   He was offered, however, and he accepted, an assistant-judgeship in the newly-created Supreme Court of China and Japan.   Marrying before he left England to enter on his duties at Shanghai, he sailed quite contentedly for China, taking with him the monumental work of Lepsius, the *Denkmäler Egyptiens*, which had been sent him from the then German Emperor, grandfather of the present one.   During the one holiday-visit which he paid to England, I saw him, and found him well pleased with his position at Shanghai, and with the society of the cultivated and agreeable members of the English colony there.   Soon afterwards I heard of his death, which was very much regretted by all who knew him at home and abroad.

I wrote the memoir of Goodwin for the *Dictionary of National Biography*. A trifling incident in its preparation is worth chronicling, as showing how in literary matters, when the memory alone is relied on, the testimony of a man of the highest character, and the most unimpeachable integrity and truthfulness, may be found not quite flawless.   In writing of Goodwin's early life before I made his acquaintance, I naturally made use of an obituary notice of him, which his brother Bishop Harvey Goodwin had contributed to a literary periodical.   In his fraternally sympathetic memoir, the Bishop ascribed his brother's early-developed love of Egyptology to having read, when very young, an article on the subject in the *Quarterly Review*, on one of the pages of which, Dr. Harvey

Goodwin added, a number of hieroglyphics were reproduced. I searched the volumes of the *Quarterly*, of the dates suggested by the Bishop's statement, but could find no article that answered his description.   But I found one that exactly coincided with it in a number of the *Edinburgh Review*, the date of which was satisfactory for my purpose, and the article contains just such a page of reproduced hieroglyphics as those mentioned by the Bishop. When sending to the Bishop a proof of my memoir of his brother, I hinted to him that he must have been mistaken, and that he had assigned to an article in the *Quarterly Review*, an effect on the mind of Charles, which was due to an article in the *Edinburgh*.   In the correspondence which ensued, the good bishop firmly, and even emphatically, asserted the accuracy of his original statement.   He could not, he said, have been mistaken.   His remembrance of the incident was perfect, and to clench the matter, he said that the *Edinburgh Review* never entered his father's house.   Before, however, the proof was returned to the editor of the *Dictionary of National Biography*, the bishop came to town, and, having consulted and searched the volumes of the two reviews, he wrote to me admitting that he was in the wrong, and that I was in the right. Upon this I offered—while putting the matter correctly in the proof—to avoid a reference to his authorship of the error.   In a final letter to me, that of a Christian and a gentleman, the excellent bishop declined my offer, requesting me to indicate him as the author of the mistake, and winding up with the familiar declaration : *Magna est veritas et prævalebit !*

X. LATER EDINBURGH MEMORIES

DURING the closing years of James Hannay's editor-ship of the *Edinburgh Courant*, I contributed to it regularly from London, and on his resignation (*ante*, p. 315) I became his successor. It was pleasant to return after the lapse of decades to one's native country and native city as the editor of the oldest newspaper in both. The finances of the *Courant* were in a deplorable state when I was appointed its editor. But with its finances I had from first to last neither right nor wish to interfere, and thus I was free to devote my time and attention to my editorial duties. During the whole period of my editor-ship, Hannay contributed to the *Courant* regularly from London, for the most part in a generally quieter style than when he wielded the editorial tomahawk in Edin-burgh.

The managers of the *Courant* left me very much to my own devices, and I was enabled to attempt to do some-thing for two deserving classes of the Scottish community and for one unfortunate section of the population of Edin-burgh. In the *Courant* were championed the claims of the Scottish schoolmasters, the Jedediah Cleishbothams of a new generation, to an increase of their too often scanty incomes. The columns of the paper were thrown open to the ministers of the Established Church for a statement of the grievances of those of them whose stipends, at that time, were sadly inadequate. As regarded my native city I seconded to the best of my ability the much-needed suggestions for the improvement of its sanitary condition put forth by its excellent and zealous Medical Officer of Health. Last not least, I instituted a not unfruitful inquiry into the condition of the poor of Edinburgh. A representative of the *Courant* was sent into the closes and wynds of the Old Town to report on the economics of the poorest of its inhabitants, and the structural and sanitary shortcomings of their over-crowded dwellings. From time to time there were published in the *Courant* his disclosures of the misery and pestiferous squalor which he had seen in the course of his peregrinations, misery often due to misfortune not to misconduct, and squalor caused not merely by extreme poverty but by the sordid neglect of too many of the owners of the lowest class of tenements, who wrung exorbitant rents from their tenants, and who, keenly alive to the rights of property, seemed to know nothing of its duties. These revelations produced a very great impression on the more favoured denizens of Edinburgh, and a result very creditable to many of them, especially to those of the gentler sex. Money, to an amount which surprised me, poured in, unsolicited, to the *Courant* Office, to be applied in the relief both of general destitution and of specific cases of distress which had been pointed out in the columns of the paper. The Scotch Poor Law was very much harsher than that of England, though it was not quite so bad as when its provisions were pithily summarised in the words, 'Take nothing from the rich, and give *that* to the poor.' The effect of these revelations in the *Courant* lasted beyond the time during which they were set forth in type.[1] Subsequently there were Conferences of Ministers of Religion, and some sort of philanthropic organisation was established to supplement the utterly insufficient resources provided by the Scotch Poor Law for the relief of destitution. A permanent *Courant* fund was instituted, and ceased to be usefully operative only with the death of the *Courant*. For my own part I saw all along that, admirable in itself and in its results as was the charity evoked by the disclosures in the *Courant*, the relief thus given was a mere anodyne, the administration of which, however imperatively called for, was not a cure for the wide-spread and deep-seated evil. But prompt and ample as was the munificence with which Edinburgh gave money to be applied in relieving distress and destitution, a deaf ear was turned to all and any editorial attempts to convince the philanthropic that the one permanently effective remedy for the social malady was the reproductive and adequate employment, municipal or other, of the wholly unemployed, and of the already employed, but at starvation wages.

The *Courant* was jogging on satisfactorily, when Lord Derby and Mr. Disraeli found themselves, after a considerable interval, once more in office. Stimulated by this unexpected triumph, sundry wealthy and zealous members of the Conservative party in Scotland were encouraged to put their hands into their pockets, with the hope of enabling the *Courant* to compete in the London-news department with the *Scotsman*, which, having a 'special wire' at its

---

[1] The substance of these articles was published in volume-form, with a dedication to the Ladies of the Modern Athens in a tiny tome, entitled *The Poor of Edinburgh and their Homes*, by William Anderson, reporter of the *Courant*; with a prefatory letter by the Rev. Dr. Guthrie.

command, gave every morning full reports of the Parliamentary proceedings, and other metropolitan intelligence of the preceding day. The concern, moreover, freed from debt, was to be placed in the hands of a new proprietor, who, on his installation, was to be started with a considerable sum 'down' provided by the munificence of Scottish Conservatism. Certain faint, very faint, overtures were made to me to conjoin the financial with the editorial control of the *Courant*, but for such twofold responsibility I felt myself utterly unfitted. As will be seen further on, the one Scotchman best fitted to undertake the general administration of the *Courant* fought shy of the enterprise. There were other Scotchmen, however, on both sides of the Border, competent to undertake it. But, before these persons could be inquired for, a Southron appeared upon the scene, to whose overtures, unfortunately for themselves, and for their purses, the Scottish Conservatives lent too favourable an ear. This was the Mayor or ex-Mayor of a town in the west of England who had become prominent in his district by a display of local electioneering zeal for the Conservative cause. Ambitious of shining in a more extensive sphere he had bought the old-established London evening paper, the *Globe*, long a staunch Liberal organ, and he turned it into a staunch Conservative organ. The Scottish Conservatives thought that they had made a lucky hit when the new proprietor of the *Globe* became the new proprietor of the *Courant*. But they had mistaken their man. He brought with him a youthful son even more objectionable than himself, who was to remain in Edinburgh to 'manage' the *Courant*, while the father, making London his head-quarters, 'managed' the *Globe*.

As proprietor both of the *Globe* and of the *Courant* he had dealings with Hannay, who portrayed father and son in his 'Recollections of a Provincial Editor,' previously referred to (*ante*, p. 337). These profess to be the handiwork of a certain imaginary Uchtred M'Guffog, whose autobiographical remains Hannay represents himself as editing. M'Guffog comes to 'Reekyborough' to edit a paper there in order that Hannay might give a version of his own experiences as the editor of the *Courant*. In the following passage, purporting to be M'Guffog's account of his editorship of an English west-country paper, Hannay not only sketches the aforesaid proprietor of *Globe* and *Courant* with his hopeful son, but adumbrates the facts of their connection with the writer of these pages :—

'A new appointment,' says M'Guffog, 'turned up, and I found myself in charge of a paper in a large west-country town. The proprietor an energetic, bandy-legged little man, had begun life as a hedge schoolmaster, had speculated successfully in railways, and was now keen after newspaper property, by which he hoped to gain influence and importance. He was one of a breed not uncommon now, a sham-genial Cad. He slapped you on the back : made a great splutter about the wines at his dinners, crying 'Lay into that 'ock, Mr. M'G ;' 'No 'eel-taps,' and so forth ; but never paid a shilling more than he could help, nor an hour earlier than he could avoid paying it. The social ambition of Weggles (that was his name) was a good deal interfered with by the state of his 'h's' and his nails. But I did not serve with him long. There was a young Weggles put into the office as a kind of 'manager,' and I soon found that the secret object of this was that I should educate him—till he was fit to supersede me ! The M'Guffogs sometimes coach gentlemen, but not these sort of people, and I did not like the prospect. At last Weggles junior took to opening my letters, and when remonstrated with became insolent. I kicked him down-stairs, and started for London by the first train, leaving the pair to bring out the next number of the *Western Monitor* between them.'

The misconduct of 'Weggles' junior (I shall retain the name given by Hannay to the pair of worthies) was the more aggravating that he opened and read not only letters to the editor, but private letters addressed to me by name and surname. To make the story of the M'Guffogs' finale more effective, Hannay has considerably exaggerated what happened in my case. The 'kicking down-stairs' must be understood in a purely figurative sense. Of course I resigned the editorship, but giving the notice stipulated for at the beginning of my editorial connection with the *Courant*. I worked out the remainder of my engagement in comparative peace and quietness, and, on leaving my native city, received from well-wishers and the staff of the paper the usual valedictory banquets, with the usual complimentary orations. The new *régime* did not last long, and greatly disappointed the Scottish Conservative patrons and dupes of Weggles. The money which they lavished on him was absorbed, but, in spite of the 'special wire,' they found the *prestige* of their organ diminish rather than increase. Weggles junior had disappeared suddenly into space before Weggles senior disappeared, also suddenly, into the grave. Disclosures made after his death, I heard, involved the ruin of widows and orphans, and others in the west of England, who and whose representatives had put their trust in him. This spoiling of the innocents was of course very regrettable, but I must confess that remembering what the patronage bestowed on Weggles had cost me, I chuckled a little on being told that an unknown quantity of the money subscribed for the *Courant*, by the severely respectable Conservatism of Scotland, had been devoted by Weggles to the support of a very questionable establishment in St. John's Wood. The Scottish Conservatives had anew to put their hands in their pockets, and the *Courant* was worked by a Limited Liability Company. Under this final *régime* I became once more a regular contributor from London, and as such was 'in at the death,' so to speak, of the venerable *Doyen* of the Scottish newspaper-press. It was suddenly slain by its own, as among some savage tribes, the aged as useless burdens are killed off by unfeeling kinsfolk. The *Scotsman* dropped a generous tear on the grave of its slaughtered foe, as one whose disappearance destroyed a link with a Scottish past of more than 150 years, and its obituary notice even contained an amiable intimation that the *Courant* had suffered by the loss of my editorial services. Certainly, too, a good deal of indignation had been felt and expressed by the rank and file of Scottish Conservatism when the *Courant* was transferred to a Southron, and such a Southron as Weggles. After his death, the *Globe*, remaining Conservative, passed into other and better hands, and has prospered ever since.

During that editorial sojourn of mine in Edinburgh, among the chief representatives of literature—apart from those who are still living, and to speak of whom might not be becoming—were Alexander Smith and his satirist in *Firmilian*, W. E. Aytoun. Of Smith's early career something has been already said (*ante*, p. 290). I had witnessed the dawn of his poetic genius in the *Critic*, when the advent of a 'new poet' was hailed by many, from Tennyson downwards, whose praise was well worth having.[1] My acquaintance with him in Edinburgh soon became friendship, among the results of which was that during my editorship, Smith for the first time contributed occasionally to the *Courant.* I found him one of the most likeable of men, so unaffected, so modest, so quiet, so distinguished among his Edinburgh compeers by his abstention from that 'arglebargling,' with the love of which even the patriotic Duke of Argyll has reproached his countrymen. After his first poem had made him famous, Smith was rescued from his original vocation as a pattern-drawer in Glasgow by being appointed to the Secretaryship of Edinburgh University (a post previously filled by the son of Christopher North) mainly through influence exerted on his behalf by the late Duncan M'Laren, then Lord Provost of Edinburgh. To Smith's income of £150 from his Secretaryship was added in time £50 a year as Registrar of the University Court, and both avocations left him, especially during summer, a fair amount of leisure. He had married a high-spirited Highland lady, who was a kinswoman of the Flora Macdonald of famous memory. She was known as 'The Chieftainess.' This designation was conferred on her by Aytoun, who, in spite of, perhaps a little because of, *Firmilian*, became very friendly to Smith, and introduced him to *Blackwood's Magazine*, in which he wrote a few articles. As children arrived, Smith found it more and more incumbent on him to eke out his income by his pen. His later were not so successful as

---

[1] One of them, it seems, was Mr. Herbert Spencer, who is rather unexpectedly found among Alexander Smith's admirers. That he was one is vouched for by the writer of an article which soon after the poet's death appeared in *Macmillan's Magazine* (for February 1867). The article was anonymous; but it is unmistakably from the pen of Alexander Smith's friend, Professor Masson.

his earlier poems, less through any lack of merit than
from the effect produced on the public by severe and
unjust charges of plagiarism perseveringly brought against
him in a London literary journal, and in part at least
ascribed, I know not with what truth, to the late William
Allingham, also a poet. The satire of *Firmilian*, too, had
its effect. Like a much greater man, Sir Walter Scott,
when Smith found that his poetic vein could no longer be
profitably worked he turned to prose. He contributed to
periodicals essays of sterling merit. He wrote a tale,
partly autobiographical, and above all, *A Summer in
Skye*, the picturesqueness and poetry of which have sent
many a Southron as well as many a Scotchman to con-
template the savage grandeur of the misty Cuchullins.
The poet's wife came from Skye, which she and her
husband visited yearly as the guests of one of her near
kinsmen, an important denizen of the island. It seems
that latterly, rather wearied of the drudgery of his academic registrarship, the poet thought of taking up his abode
in Skye to be tenant of a sheep farm, though, as one of
his friends remarked, his only knowledge of the sheep was
when it appeared on the table as mutton ! Whatever the
financial results of this scheme, had it been carried out,
and it was not, it would doubtless have led to the production of fine pastoral and other poetry. Among
the miscellaneous verses for which Alexander Smith
made those Skye volumes a vehicle of publication were
some lines written at Peebles which struck me much,
and which were favourites of his own. I seldom knew
him so pleasantly excited—he never talked of his prose
or verse—as when I told him that I had read aloud
those lines to a party of friends during an excursion to

Tweeddale, and that they had been listened to with delight.[1] As alternately host and guest, we saw much of each other. Silent as he was in general company, there fell from him, when the hearers were both fit and few, many a quietly incisive remark on Nature and on books—political and theological discussion he eschewed. He was a middle-sized, brown-locked man, with a squint, which gave a certain *espiègle* look to one of the honestest of faces. He lived at Wardie, a northern suburb of Edinburgh, within sight and hearing of the sea. One of his

[1] The whole poem is too long for quotation here. But the opening and closing verses afford a fair notion of what for many readers gave it a charm :—

> 'I lay in my bed at Peebles
>   With my window-curtains drawn,
> While there stole over hill of pasture and pine,
>   The unresplendent dawn.
>
> And through the deep silence I listened
>   With a pleasant half-waking heed
> To the sound which ran through the ancient town
>   The shallow-brawling Tweed.
>
> * * * *
>
> Was it absolute truth or a dreaming
>   Which the wakeful day disowns
> That I heard something more in the stream as it ran
>   Than the water breaking on stones?
>
> Now the hoofs of a flying moss-trooper,
>   Now a blood-hound's bay half-caught,
> The sudden blast of a hunting-horn,
>   The burr of Walter Scott.
>
> Who knows? But of this I am certain
>   That but for the ballads and wails,
> Which make passionate dead things, stocks and stones
>   Make piteous woods and dales,
>
> The Tweed were as poor as the Amazon
>   That, for all the years it has rolled,
> Can tell but how fair is the morning-red
>   How sweet the evening-gold.'

chief cronies was John (commonly called Jack) M'Lennan,
then known mainly by his curious disquisition on
'Primitive Marriage,' the primeval solemnisation of matri-
· mony by the bridegroom's physical-force capture of the
bride.　Jack (a *protégé* of the late Lord Houghton's) was
lively, clever, and erudite, an Edinburgh advocate with
little or no practice, somewhat cynical withal, and a
Radical, in so far at least as he was frequently complain-
ing of the political prominence and importance which fell to
the lot of men undistinguished, save through the accident
of rank or station.　At the comparatively early age of
thirty-eight Alexander Smith died while I was in Edinburgh, to the great regret of his many friends : personal
foe he never had.

During his last and lingering illness, only less than the
affectionate care bestowed on him by his wife, was that of
a cynic of cynics, his *fidus Achates*, Patrick (commonly
called Pat) Alexander, who edited the poet's prose-remains,
and prefixed to them an interesting memoir of their author.
Pat's father had been a well-known Professor at St.
Andrews ; and Pat himself was for a time in business at
Glasgow, but did not succeed in it, a failure not to be
wondered at.　He lived a free and easy life in Edinburgh,
the freedom, I fear, predominating over the ease, and in
intervals of conviviality wrote a good deal both of prose
and verse.　He was a great admirer of Carlyle ; but his
admiration was tinged by his usual cynicism, as was
shown in his 'Occasional Discourse by Smelfungus,' a
clever but rather coarse parody of Carlyle's style.　Pat's
intellectual speciality was the cultivation of what he called
'the higher philosophies,' with my alleged indifference to
which he was wont to reproach me, when it was only reluc-

tantly that I admitted occasionally into the *Courant*,—for which or for any daily newspaper they were little suited— his disquisitions on metaphysics and ethics. One of these was an able and searching, although not always dignified, criticism on that section of John Stuart Mill's Examination of Sir William Hamilton's Philosophy, in which Mill endeavoured to reconcile moral responsibility with the doctrine of necessity, a reconciliation considered impossible by his Edinburgh critic. Pat enlarged this essay, and, prefixing it to the 'Occasional Discourse by Smelfungus,' produced a little volume with the title *Mill and Carlyle*. In a subsequent edition of his Examination, Mill thought it worth while to reply in detail to Pat's rather trenchant attack on him, the irritating frankness of some passages in which Mill good-naturedly excused as merely in accordance with what he called 'Mr. Alexander's rollicking style.' Pat rejoined, and, in my humble opinion, had the best of the argument. It was his attack on Mill which procured him the appointment of Examiner in Moral Philosophy at St. Andrews. Since then he has followed his friend Alexander Smith to the grave.

I met occasionally in Edinburgh society that very clever and versatile gentleman, W. E. Aytoun, who, as already intimated, made amends to Alexander Smith for having satirised him in *Firmilian*. In Aytoun, too, there was a dash of cynicism, but a not ungenial pleasantry predominated in such conversation as I had with him. One remark which he made to me illustrated, I thought, the change which had come over Edinburgh since the days of Scott, Jeffrey, and Aytoun's own father-in-law, John Wilson. Then the literature produced in Scotland made the distinguished Scottish author a person of more or less distinction in London. His reputation in his own country was not affected by his reception in England and its capital. Aytoun, however, told me, and with complacency, of the success of the lectures on ballad poetry which he had delivered in London not only as pleasant in itself, but as peculiarly acceptable to him, because 'people here,' that is, in Edinburgh, began to think much of him after his London success. Though a staunch Tory, and understood to support the cause in *Blackwood*, of which he was one of the literary pillars, he did not take any personal part, so far as I observed, in Scottish political life. He told me, however, that he attended the meetings of the Royal Convention of Scottish Burghs, a curious quasi-parliamentary survival of the old days of Scottish independence, and that he found it great fun in what, I fancy, were little more than academic discussions to badger the late Duncan M'Laren. Aytoun died before I had been long in Edinburgh.

Having written, in the early days of my connection with the *Critic*, a biography of *Blackwood's Magazine*, and in later days a history of the publishing house of Blackwood, I had, before editing the *Courant*, been brought into communication, personal and epistolary, with John Blackwood, who was then the virtual head of the firm. He gave me a cordial welcome to Edinburgh, and during my stay there I had opportunities for testing the soundness of his judgment and the helpfulness of his disposition. He was rather small of stature, and spoke very slowly and deliberately, filling up his conversational pauses with pinches of snuff. As a publisher, he much preferred quality to quantity. To the management of an important publishing business, he added the editorship of *Blackwood's Magazine*, and, with the exception perhaps of the

Quarterly Review under Lockhart, no periodical of the time had so competent and vigilant an editor. In the conduct of the magazine he adhered closely to the anonymous system, and could thus utilise and develop the abilities of young men of promise but unknown to fame. One such, whom I came to know well, was the late R. H. Patterson. If I remember righly, John Blackwood told me that Patterson, while occupying some subordinate post in the Blackwood establishment, used to lay on his chief's table, time after time, manuscript verses which, as regularly, the chief threw into the waste-paper basket. At last, struck by the young man's perseverance, John Blackwood tested his capacity in some other than the metrical way, and was convinced of his literary promise. He encouraged Patterson, who became a more or less frequent contributor to *Blackwood*, and wrote sundry books, certain of which made even the currency question interesting. In time he became editor of the *Press*, a journal understood to be inspired by Mr. Disraeli and the late Lord Derby, and he long remained a conspicuous figure in Conservative journalism.

Another unknown man whom John Blackwood befriended, and of whom, in conversation, he once spoke to me as a man of genius, though one whom it was difficult to help, was a wayward if gifted individual, Andrew Wilson. He was the son of the eminent Free Church missionary, the Rev. Dr. Wilson of Bombay; but he did not follow in his father's footsteps. He spent part of his early life in Anglo-Chinese and Anglo-Indian journalism. He had distinguished himself in the former, when the heroic Gordon, afterwards the victim of the Mahdi at Khartoum, put his papers into the hands of Andrew

Wilson, who evolved from them his very able book, *The Ever-Victorious Army*, a narrative of Gordon's achievements in the suppression of the Tai-ping rebellion; supplemented by interesting remarks of Wilson's own on China and the Chinese, suggested by his personal observation of men and things in the Celestial Empire. A considerable section of the book was wisely published by John Blackwood in the *Magazine*, and his firm afterwards published the completed work. Andrew had some disease of the heart, or of the lungs, which made it desirable for him to breathe the air of Alpine regions. Hence his exploration of the Himalayas and adjacent regions—a series of vivid sketches of which were published in *Blackwood's Magazine*, and afterwards in volume-form by the Blackwoods as *The Abode of Snow*; it met with the very favourable reception which it deserved. I had no personal knowledge of Andrew Wilson, but he was well known to friends of mine who were fond of telling ancedotes of him as one of the most singular of beings, with a career of ups and downs. Among the most characteristic of the anecdotes told of him was the following :—When his fortunes were at their *nadir*, he applied for the editorship of an obscure weekly newspaper in a small town in the extreme south of Scotland. It belonged to an elderly and devout Presbyterian spinster, who asked him for a preliminary interview. Andrew having presented himself, the lady began by putting the leading question, 'And what, Maister Wilson, may your rel*ee*gion be?' With the greatest gravity, Andrew replied forthwith, 'Madam, I am a——Buddhist!' The collapse of his candidature was instantaneous.

The names of the distinguished people whom John

Blackwood secured as contributors to his magazine, and whose books he published, are as legion. Generally known among the incidents of his publishing career is his recognition of the genius of George Eliot. His correspondence with her was that of a friend as well as a publisher, and through its appearance in her biography, numbers of readers have become more familiar with the personality of John Blackwood than with that of any of the British publishers his contemporaries. That he did not cultivate, merely with an eye to business, the society of eminent authors, is proved by his intimacy with Thackeray, who was frequently his guest, but who never wrote a line in *Blackwood's Magazine*, and not one of whose books was published by the Blackwoods. Thackeray happened to be a guest of John Blackwood when he received from George Henry Lewes the MS. of the first instalment of George Eliot's earliest fiction, *The Scenes of Clerical Life*, whose sex, much less her name, was undisclosed. According to the obituary notice of John Blackwood in the *Times*, 'before the first instalment appeared in the magazine, he warned Thackeray, who was then his guest, that a new and more dangerous competitor in the domain of fiction than he had yet had to encounter was about to appear in the field.' The story looks on the face of it improbable, but it may be true. I can say, however, on very good authority, that Thackeray, instead of depreciating this 'dangerous competitor,' spoke with the highest approval of the chapters of 'Amos Barton' which were given him by his host to read, and at once detected, which John Blackwood and most other people did not, the writer of them to be a woman.

. One of my later colloquies with John Blackwood

turned on a subject interesting to both of us. It was at the time when, as already mentioned, the *Courant* was in a state of transition from an old proprietary to a new. John' Blackwood had a certain hankering for the ownership of the oldest newspaper in Scotland, and the chief organ of Scottish Conservatism. At his request, I brought for his inspection a list as accurate as I could procure of the liabilities of the *Courant*, most of them of ancient date. Of themselves they did not daunt him, and doubtless the Scottish Conservatives would have been only too glad to clear them off, and hand over to him the *Courant* free of debt. But after carefully considering his personal relations and manifold business engagements, John Blackwood decided not to stir in the matter. The result of this disappointing decision was—Weggles !

XI. LORD BEACONSFIELD AND HIS MINOR BIOGRAPHER

CHAPTER I

MY slight personal knowledge of Lord Beaconsfield arose out of one of very many contributions of mine to a well-known, an elaborate, and a bulky work of reference, the *Imperial Dictionary of Universal Biography*. These contributions were multifarious, ranging from the letter B to the letter Z, from Baber the founder of the so-called Mogul empire in Hindustan, to Zaleucus the legislator of the Locrians, and the congenial employment made the years devoted to it some of the pleasantest of my literary life.

The list of contributors contained the usual array of well-known names, but the owners of some of them, as is also usual, failed to furnish by the appointed time the memoirs assigned to them, and I was often called on to supply the deficiency. I remember having in this way to write, in a distressingly short space of time, a biography of Columbus, which had been expected from the late Sir Archibald Alison the historian. I began to contribute to the Dictionary under its first editor, my friend the late Patrick Edward Dove, an ill-fated man of great and varied ability and high character, who was struck down by a lingering disease which rendered him incapable of mental exertion, and which carried him to the grave before his time. I was happy to see ample justice done to his merits in the sketch of him which appeared in the *Dictionary of National Biography* when edited by Mr. Leslie Stephen.[1] That *Imperial Dictionary of Universal Biography* did really supply a want, and at one time its publisher was so satisfied with its success that he projected the issue of a Dictionary of British Biography, for which I drew up, at his request, a list of names in letter A. The project was perhaps suggested by an announcement of the late John Murray, made conspicuously year after year, without any result, that he intended to publish a 'New Biographia Britannica,' not a very felicitous title. He carried out his intention no further than to have a list of names drawn up. I once asked him why he did not go on with so much-needed a work. 'I funked,' was his concise and expressively idiomatic reply to my question. Meanwhile his standing announcement prevented at least one great London firm from undertaking a work of the kind. I remember being told by the late William Longman that if Mr. Murray abandoned the project it would probably

---

[1] As editor Dove was succeeded by Dr. J. F. Waller, but the working editor was the late Rev. John Service, who became rather a conspicuous minister of the Kirk. His father was a clerk in the employment of the late Mr. Dalgleish, for many years an M.P. for Glasgow, who took an interest in the clever son, and effectively aided him. After a varied ministerial career at home and in Australia, Service was ultimately settled in charge of a Glasgow church. The principal of his purely literary productions was a romance, 'Novantia,' published in *Good Words*, and republished as *Lady Hetty*. It was as a preacher, however, that Service chiefly attained distinction. He was one of the boldest of the Broad Church School which has sprung up in the Scottish Establishment, and two published volumes of his sermons testify to his courage and originality as a preacher. He is described as not only a striking preacher but a 'model pastor.'

be taken in hand by the firm of Longman. The publisher of the *Imperial Dictionary of Universal Biography* gave up, for reasons unconnected with the London etiquette of ' the trade,' his intention of issuing a Dictionary of British Biography. Had he carried out his intention, Glasgow, not London, would have had the honour of first producing a ' New Biographia Britannica.'

The *Imperial Dictionary of Universal Biography* included notices of living persons. These notices were so manipulated as to preclude the necessity for a supplement containing the biographies of the living persons who had been dealt with while the work was in progress, but who died before and after it was completed. The Dictionary was published in parts, the contents of which were brought up to date by additions to the sketches of living persons, and of those of them who died off from time to time. These explanations are needed to make intelligible some things in what follows. The names of many public men were among those assigned to me. The notices of living contemporaries which I wrote were as far as possible politically and personally colourless, and contained facts, with little or nothing of comment. When a proof reached me of any such notice of mine, I forwarded it to the person or personage concerned, and requested a correction of any errors in matters of fact which he (or she) might observe.[1] Among the personages

---

[1] A sample of their replies, a very characteristic one, from the late Harriet Martineau, may be given :—

' AMBLESIDE, *Jan.* 22/62.

' SIR,—You will see in the margin of the proof the few points in which I demur to your account of me. The most important is about my becoming an abolitionist in America. It was *because* of my abolition story, *Demerara* (1832), that I was invited all through the Southern States. I never remember

of whom I thus wrote biographical notices were Mr. Gladstone, who was then Chancellor of the Exchequer, and the late Lord Beaconsfield, who was then Mr. Disraeli, and who not long before had ceased for the second time to be Chancellor of the Exchequer through the fall of the Second Administration of the Earl of Derby, father of the Lord Derby lately deceased. To the best of my recollection Mr. Gladstone did not return the proof, but in a few lines of courteous acknowledgment said that he would retain it 'as a record,' thus implying, as I understood him, that the sketch needed no correction. Until very lately, when the preparation of these two chapters required an inspection of some of my contributions to the Dictionary, and a comparison of them as they were first printed with what they sometimes became, in consequence of additions and alterations, I had not for many years looked into it. In one of those later redactions, and a little to my surprise, I saw at the end of the notice of Mr. Gladstone not my initials, which were originally suffixed to it, but those of a contributor, who was employed by the publisher, after the printing of letter Z was finished, to revise the whole work, and to keep it, as previously mentioned, up to date. An inspection of the sketch

the time when I and all my family were not as heartily anti-slavery as we are at this hour.

'The Martineaus in Norwich were from father to son *Surgeons*, the last being the eminent operator of that name—my eldest uncle. My father was the first manufacturer in the family.

'I don't know whether it is of use to mention that I have been closely confined for seven years from heart-disease (like Florence Nightingale).

'There is one benefit from its being known—that it keeps away intrusive strangers, who are the plague of "life at the lakes." I need not add that the case (enlargement of the heart) is a hopeless one.

'It is for you to judge what to say or to omit,—I am, Sir, your obedt. servant HARRIET MARTINEAU.'

of Mr. Gladstone disclosed the fact that it contained all that I had chronicled of his career up to 1860, in which year it was written. The reviser had added a few years more of Mr. Gladstone's political biography to bring the sketch up to date, and he suffixed to it his initials 'R. H.,' as if he had been the writer of the whole article. I do not in the least make this statement by way of protest or complaint. Doubtless it would have been awkward to break up what was not a very long or elaborate article into two sections, with two sets of initials to denote their separate authorship. The sketch was a commonplace compilation, one neither to be proud of nor ashamed of. But if any idolater of Mr. Gladstone, desirous of seeing the biographical notice of him which he spoke of keeping 'as a record,' should turn to an edition of the Dictionary later than the first he might very naturally, without this explanation, draw, from the initials 'R. H.' at the end of the article, a conclusion which would be unjust to me.

I cannot now recollect whether, intentionally or not, I neglected to send the usual proof to Mr. Disraeli, or whether I did send one and, by some mischance, it failed to reach him. However this may have been, it was from headquarters that I first received the intimation that Mr. Disraeli had notified his discovery of mis-statements in my sketch of him. On learning this, I wrote to him to say that I pretended to no special knowledge of his career, that I had taken most of my purely biographical facts from previous sketches of him, and that I should be happy to correct any errors which he would point out to have been committed by me. In reply to what he styled my 'gentlemanlike letter,' he asked me to call on him, naming a day and hour for my visit. Very soon afterwards he wrote to me naming another day, excusing himself for the delay by saying that for that previously appointed he had received a summons to attend the King of the Belgians—certainly a very valid excuse from an ex-Chancellor of the Exchequer to a denizen of Grub Street. On the new-appointed day and hour, I presented myself at Grosvenor Gate. After receiving me, Mr. Disraeli conducted me to what he called his 'den,' at the top of the house, a very plainly furnished room. The immediate subject of my visit having been briefly discussed, he promised me some autobiographical notes, and then the dialogue, if dialogue it can be called, became general. He talked to me on men and things political with great frankness, considering how much of a stranger I was to him. I remarked particularly that when he spoke of his Conservative colleagues and followers he always said 'they,' not 'we,' as if he regarded himself as with them, not of them. 'They,' he said, were urging him to make an effort for restoration to office, but he had had enough of office with a majority against him in the House of Commons. He spoke cheerfully, however, of the existence of members of the Conservative party who had shown themselves, and hopefully of others who were to show themselves, possessed of the administrative ability required for office. The Peelites, the part played by whom in politics he compared to that of the Grenvilles of a former generation, were ceasing, he thought, to act as a compact and united body, and were being distributed among the two great parties in the State. Being myself from time to time engaged in journalism, I was naturally struck by the remark that ever since he had been connected with 'them,' the Conservatives, he had pointed

out to the party the great advantage which the Liberals
had over them in possessing an ' organised press.' Of his
chief rival, Mr. Gladstone, he spoke with what I thought
to be generosity, calling him ' a man of splendid abilities,'
adding, ' but hampered by his Church *liaisons*,' surely one
of the happiest of expressions (Mr. Gladstone was at that
time still a member for Oxford University). Towards the
close of the conversation, *apropos* of something or other, I
referred to an impression in the public mind that the
diplomatic action of the late Conservative Government
during the crisis which preceded the Italo-Austrian War
of 1859 showed hostility to Italy. ' *That*,' said Disraeli
curtly, ' was not borne out by the correspondence in the
Blue-books,' and the interview ended.

Soon after this first interview, I duly received Disraeli's
autobiographical and autograph notes. I found that they
corrected only two errors of fact in my notice of him.
One of these errors regarded the name of the firm of
solicitors to whom he had been articled. The other was
my statement that he had ' aided ' not only ' in founding '
but in ' conducting ' the once much-talked-of *Representative*, but this was an error universally prevalent at the
time, and not extinguished until years after Disraeli's
death, when extracts from the correspondence relating to
the second John Murray's solitary and disastrous newspaper
venture were published in Dr. Smiles's history of the House
of Murray, *A Publisher and his Friends*. Of Disraeli in
the solicitor's office, and of the story of the *Representative*,
more in my second and concluding chapter. Most of
Disraeli's notes related to his earlier years. Among the
exceptions were two, both of them more or less statements of fact. The first was one unknown to any of his

former biographers, namely, that in his second candidature for High Wycombe in 1835, he was supported by Sir Robert Peel, a disclosure which one would have hardly expected from him who made it. The other was that his becoming both Chancellor of the Exchequer and leader of the House of Commons without having held office previously was a twofold event which had never happened before, except in the case of Mr. Pitt during Lord Shelburne's Administration of 1782-83. Some of the autobiographical notes relating to his earlier years were curious and interesting, but further references to them must also be held over to another chapter.

CHAPTER II

MR. FROUDE'S biography (in the series entitled 'The Prime Ministers of Queen Victoria') is not only the latest but in some respects both the most complete synopsis and the most authentic account of Lord Beaconsfield's career. Not only had Mr. Froude many previous biographies to aid him, but he appears to have received from some one or other a few scraps of what is called 'exclusive information' respecting both the earlier and later years of Disraeli's life. It may suffice, therefore, in dealing with the autobiographical notes furnished me by Lord Beaconsfield, as mentioned in the preceding chapter, to compare his own statements respecting his boyhood, youth, and early manhood with those of Mr. Froude. Of Mr. Poticary's school at Blackheath Disraeli said nothing in those notes. But he did ample justice to the Greek scholarship of Dr. Cogan, the Unitarian principal of the school at Walthamstow, to which he was sent after learning little at Blackheath, and at which he remained for several years. Mr. Froude has a page or two about the Walthamstow school, but he has omitted to reproduce the well-authenticated anecdote that Dr. Cogan said of the one of his pupils who was to become the most distinguished of them all : 'I don't like Disraeli ; I never could get him to understand the subjunctive !' Between his departure from the school at Walthamstow and his entering a solicitor's office there is a blank in

Mr. Froude's narrative which the notes supply, and in an interesting way. On leaving Dr. Cogan's establishment, Disraeli was placed, he wrote, with a private tutor in Buckinghamshire, his father's adopted county, and there his education was 'severely classical,' so that, it may be hoped, he learned at last to understand the subjunctive! Nay, according to his own account, the 'severely classical' education which he now received gave shape to his first literary effort, one unknown to any of his biographers, Mr. Froude included. The young Disraeli actually produced and printed for private circulation an edition of what he called in those notes the 'Adonisian eclogue of Theocritus,' that charming fifteenth idyl, in which the two Syracusan women domiciled in Alexandria (Theocritus himself hailed from Syracuse), Gorgo and Praxinoe, visiting the festival of the resurrection of Adonis, chatter just as a thousand years later two London middle-class dames might chatter when pushing their way through a crowd assembled to witness a Lord Mayor's show or a Royal procession. ·If there survives a copy of the young Disraeli's edition of the fifteenth idyl of Theocritus, its possessor may boast himself the owner of a greater than any of the 'Curiosities of Literature' chronicled by Disraeli's father, and he should make haste to inform the world of his possession of it.

So far, Disraeli's autobiographical notes add to, but do not contradict, the statements in Mr. Froude's biography. But when we come to the circumstances connected with the young Disraeli's entrance into and departure from the solicitor's office in the Old Jewry, there is a decided conflict between Mr. Froude's statements and those of the autobiographer. Mr. Froude, speaking of the young

Disraeli's early ambition, simply says: 'He saw that to advance he must depend on himself and must make his way into some financially independent position. While chafing at the necessity he rationally folded his wings, and on November 18, 1821, when just seventeen, he was introduced into a solicitor's office in the Old Jewry.' Surely this is a very inadequate mode of accounting for the singular fact that a father in Isaac Disraeli's position should have placed his eldest and promising son in a solicitor's office. According to Mr. Froude, Disraeli remained at the desk for three years. Mr. Froude even gives, between quotation-marks, the testimony borne by one of the partners in the firm, who described the young Disraeli as 'most assiduous in his attention to business and showing great ability in the transaction of it' (here the quotation-marks end), and as likely, if allowed to go to the Bar, to attain to eminence there. Again, according to Mr. Froude, 'Ben,' as he familiarly calls him, 'acquiesced in his father's wishes,' which are taken for granted, and he was entered at Lincoln's Inn, 'apparently intending to pursue a legal career, but the fates or his own adventurousness ordered his fortune otherwise.' In view of Disraeli's possible career in wig and gown, Mr. Froude indulges, moreover, in the usual speculations of the 'what might have happened' kind. Now Disraeli's own statement was quite different from this, and explains satisfactorily, which Mr. Froude's does not, why he was placed in a solicitor's office. Very soon after receiving it I incorporated it with other of his statements in a second edition, so to speak, of my memoir of him in the *Dictionary of Universal Biography*. A proof of this second edition was sent immediately to Mr. Disraeli, who by returning it unaltered 'with thanks,' indorsed its accuracy. I used, as far as possible, Disraeli's own words, and I now transcribe from my memoir, re-edited from information given by himself, what may unquestionably be regarded as his version of the episode of the solicitor's office :—

'The elder Disraeli' (I wrote), 'who always lived in seclusion, and during the last years of his life almost uninterruptedly in Bucks, had a powerful friend who offered to provide for his promising son in one of the offices of the Court of Chancery. The post offered was one the tenure of which would in the usual course have led to some of the highest prizes of the profession. To be admitted as a solicitor was a necessary preliminary, and hence the myth that Mr. Disraeli was once, as has been often published, "an attorney's clerk." Although the legal life thus commenced was little more than a form, Mr. Disraeli soon relinquished it from a youthful restlessness of head and heart. In due course a younger brother, Mr. Ralph Disraeli, was offered and embraced the same opportunity, and that gentleman has now risen to the post of Registrar of the Court of Chancery, one of responsibility and emolument.'

There may not be an irreconcilable conflict between this statement of Disraeli's and Mr. Froude's, but they are certainly discrepant, and, as already indicated, Disraeli's explains what Mr. Froude's leaves unexplained. That the young Disraeli meditated a forensic career, because he was entered at Lincoln's Inn, is an unwarranted inference. It was by no means uncommon in those days for young men of a certain social position to be entered at an Inn of Court, and even to be called to the Bar, without the slightest intention of practising. A friend, a member of

Lincoln's Inn, who, to aid me in the preparation of this chapter, has kindly had searches made in the records of that Honourable Society, informs me that not only was Disraeli entered on its books on the 11th November 1824, leaving it on the 25th November 1831, but that Mr. Gladstone—a fact in the right honourable gentleman's career not, I think, generally known—was entered on the books of the same society on the 18th November 1827, leaving it on 25th November 1831. Yet one never heard or read that Mr. Gladstone thought of practising at the Bar.

The next salient statement in Disraeli's autobiographical notes related to his alleged connection with the second John Murray's ill-fated newspaper, the *Representative*, referred to in the preceding chapter. It is not wonderful that Disraeli showed himself annoyed by my assertion, in what was intended to be a permanent work of reference, that he had anything to do with 'conducting' the *Representative*. Until then he had allowed all sorts of idle tales on that subject to pass current, but now he thought it time to have the true story of his connection with the journal told. Absurd and malicious indeed had been some of these reports, and all of them testify to the ease with which an elaborate myth, not having the slightest basis in fact, may be evolved and believed respecting a distinguished man, even in his lifetime. One of these was that a leading article of Disraeli's in the *Representative* began thus: 'As we were sitting yesterday in our opera-box,' etc., etc. Even so late as 1871, that *gobemouche*, the late James Grant, many years editor of the *Morning Advertiser*, gave, in his history of the newspaper press, what professed to be a full, true, and particular account of the gorgeous furniture and fittings of the editorial rooms at the office of the *Representative*, in which the young Disraeli received his aristocratic friends and contributors. In his autobiographical notes, Disraeli admitted that he had something to do with the preliminary arrangements, but he assured me that, far from having edited the *Representative*, he had never written a line, or been asked to write a line, in it. The perfect accuracy of this statement has been proved from documents in the archives of the publishing house of Murray, printed by Dr. Smiles in his history of that house up to the death of the second John Murray, the well-known work, *A Publisher and his Friends*. In point of fact, and to speak a little in the Irish manner, Disraeli's connection with the *Representative* ceased before it actually existed. How it came about that after he had worked hard for the establishment of the *Representative*, the very name of which was given it by him, he ceased before No. 1 was issued to co-operate in its production, is partly explained in Dr. Smiles's book. Disraeli's version of the early history of the *Representative*, as given in the notes, was that John Gibson Lockhart undertook, with the countenance of Canning, at that time Secretary for Foreign Affairs, to edit the ill-fated newspaper, and that after its failure Lockhart (then editor of John Murray's *Quarterly Review*) set on foot the report that it had been edited by Disraeli. The statement that Lockhart edited the *Representative* may not have been literally accurate, but from the admissions made, and the documents printed by Dr. Smiles, it is clear that Lockhart's connection with the *Representative* was very intimate. 'The first number,' Dr. Smiles says, 'contained an article by Lockhart, four columns in length, on the affairs of Europe'—an article

very probably 'inspired' by Canning. Then, again, a fortnight after the issue of No. 1 of the *Representative*, when its
undoubted failure was distressing its proprietor, Lockhart is
found writing thus to John Murray (in a letter quoted by
Dr. Smiles): 'That I should have been in any measure
accessory to bringing you into the present situation
weighs, I assure you, more heavily on my spirits than
even the mass of domestic melancholy with which I am
at present surrounded'—the reference here is to the
failure of Constable, followed by that of the Ballantynes,
involving the financial ruin of Sir Walter Scott—'What I
can do in any way is always at your service, but even
the depression is proof enough that I have not the iron
nerves of the man fitted for daily collision with the world.'
Whatever had been, was, or became Lockhart's connection
with the *Representative*, Disraeli's account of his own
connection with that journal (a subject to which, strange
to say, Mr. Froude makes not the slightest reference) has
been proved to be perfectly accurate.

Those autobiographical notes of Disraeli having served
the purpose for which he gave them to me, I laid them
aside, and did not see them again for many years. I had
not shown them to any one, except that nearest and
dearest of relatives from whom no secrets (save those
pertaining to Freemasonry) ought to be hid by a husband.
On becoming a widower, I found that she had preserved
the notes, which I half-fancied had been destroyed. I
glanced through them, and again laid them on one side.
Not long afterwards—it has been seen (*ante*, p. 377) that I,
too, had (twice) been the historiographer of the publishing
house of Murray—when Dr. Smiles was engaged in the
composition of his history of this house, he said to me

incidentally in the course of conversation that he would be able to throw a good deal of light on the story of the *Representative*, but without dropping the slightest hint as to what would be disclosed. On this I remarked that I had in my possession a version of the story given me by Lord Beaconsfield, as Mr. Disraeli had then become. Dr. Smiles said in a casual way that he would like to see it. I replied that I should be very happy to comply with his wish provided I received permission from Lord Beaconsfield. Accordingly I wrote to him explaining the circumstances under which I desired, with his leave, to show Dr. Smiles that portion, and that portion only, of his autobiographical notes which related to the *Representative*. Very promptly, and apparently in haste, Lord Beaconsfield wrote the following reply, in the first paragraph of which I have ventured to interpolate, between brackets, a word or two which, or their equivalents, are obviously required to make the hurriedly-written sentence complete :—

'19 CURZON STREET, W.,
Feb. 9, 1881.

'DEAR SIR,—What I communicated to you was in confidence, and I have observed with satisfaction that you have always respected that confidence [*in the way*] which, became you as a gentleman and a man of letters.

'If you will do me the honour of calling on me to-morrow morning, or any other morning more convenient to you, I will speak to you on the subject of your letter.

'Half-past eleven is a time when you will generally find me disengaged.—Yours truly,   'BEACONSFIELD.'

On reading this brief epistle, I saw at once that its writer was a little nervous about his autobiographical notes. Accordingly I wrote forthwith to Lord Beaconsfield narrating their history since they came into my possession, and adding that, when I had the pleasure of calling on him, I would return them to him, without keeping a copy of them. Very soon afterwards I called on Lord Beaconsfield in Curzon Street. More than twenty years had passed since I last sat face to face with him at Grosvenor Gate. In the interval my head had considerably whitened, but though he was very much older than myself, there were only a few grey streaks in his raven locks, and after his death it was ascertained that, in contradiction to an ill-natured report, his hair had not been dyed. The interview was brief, and nothing was said about politics. One of the remarks with which he opened the conversation rather amused me. It was to the effect that he greatly enjoyed the transition from the fogs of Westminster to Mayfair. As his migration northwards had been caused by the fall of his Administration compelling him to leave the residence in Downing Street which he had occupied as Prime Minister, the remark reminded me a little of the saying about making a virtue of necessity. He asked how it was that so much was made of the *Representative* and his connection with it. In reply, I said something about the interest that attached to such an episode in the early career of a distinguished man. In the morning-room into which I was first ushered, and in the drawing-room in which I had the interview, everything wore a look of spick-and-span newness. I observed that in neither were there visible any pictures, or engravings, or busts. The only object in the shape of a work of art was in the drawing-room, and was pointed out to me by Lord Beaconsfield with some pride. It was a very elaborate and costly-looking construction in Dresden china, presented to him by Baron Tauchnitz in recognition of the profit which he had reaped from the production of his continental edition of *Endymion*, the last and to my mind one of the weakest of Lord Beaconsfield's fictions. But it was published after he became Prime Minister, and it had, therefore, an enormous, though a transitory, success. He explained to me that Baron Tauchnitz, having made with the London publishers of *Endymion* all the financial arrangements connected with its sale on the Continent, he was debarred from giving any share of the profits to the author; hence the present of the Dresden china construction. Having brought with me, according to promise, the autobiographical notes so often referred to, I returned them to him with the reiterated assurance that I had kept no copy of them, and he was evidently pleased. If the reader asks how it is that I have been able to reproduce so much of them for his benefit, the answer is simple. I have consulted my reproduction of them, given with Lord Beaconsfield's approval, in the second edition of my memoir of him in the *Dictionary of Universal Biography*, where what he meant for the public eye lies buried without any intimation that it was furnished by him. In reproducing in the *Dictionary* a portion of his autobiographical notes, I softened the passage which contained rather a serious charge against Lockhart, who was not alive to answer it. That was one of the reasons why, instead of referring Dr. Smiles to the second edition of my memoir, of which in truth I had not kept a copy, I was desirous that he should see the text itself of the passage concerning Lockhart. There linger, indeed, in my memory a few striking statements in those autobiographical notes, which clearly were not meant for the public eye. Therefore, I did not reproduce them in the re-edited memoir, and do not reproduce them now.

Probably I received one or more communications from Lord Beaconsfield anterior to that which I am about to give. If so, they have gone astray or have been destroyed, and I do not, with any exactitude, remember their purport. The two which survive were asked from me as autographs by friends who preserved them carefully, and have furnished me with them for the purposes of this chapter. The letters in the *Times* referred to in the following note of Lord Beaconsfield's to me were contradictions and refutations of various mis-statements respecting his connection with the *Representative* and his early literary career.[1] Lord Beaconsfield sent me copies of them,

---

[1] The letter to the editor of the *Times* from Lord Beaconsfield's solicitors, Messrs. Baxter, Rose, and Norton, contained the following passage, in contradiction of James Grant's absurd statement, referred to in the text, and of others equally absurd: 'Mr. Disraeli has never at any time edited any newspaper review, magazine, or other periodical publication, and rarely contributed to any, nor has he at any time received or required any remuneration for anything he has ever written, except for those works which bear his name.' To this letter was subjoined one from Sir Philip Rose, addressed to the editor of the *Leisure Hour*. To make the extracts from Sir Philip Rose's letter intelligible, I transcribe the following passage from a chapter, in the *Leisure Hour* sometime in 1871, of the autobiography of the late John Timbs, an industrious and, in a general way, a not unveracious compiler. 'In the autumn of that year, 1830,' said the veteran *Timbs*, 'I completed a *Handbook on Wines* for Marsh and Miller, publishers, Oxford Street. In visits to their shop, I inquired, "Who is that gentleman with a profusion of hair, and whom I often see here?" "That is young Disraeli," was the publishers' reply; "and he will be glad to execute any literary work for a guinea or two."' (!!) He had recently published a *Key to Almack's*, and a piece of more piquant satire, entitled 'A Geographical and Historical Account of the Great World,' to which is added 'A Voyage to its Several Islands, with a vocabulary of the language and a map,' etc. On the part of Mr. Disraeli (as he still was in 1871) Sir Philip Rose denied that his principal had ever, to his knowledge, entered the shop of Messrs. Marsh and Miller, or was the author of any of the publications enumerated. Sir Philip proceeded thus to demolish Timbs's reminiscences of 1830: 'At the very period, 1830, when

thinking, I suppose, that I might utilise them, somehow and somewhere, with the same object :—

> '19 CURZON STREET, W.,
> *Feb.* 14, 1881.

'DEAR SIR,—Lord Barrington was so kind as to make the necessary research in the *Times* (Nov. 3, 1871), and to copy the two letters. They give all the information which we desired on the particular subject, and a great deal more which I had forgotten.

'Lord Barrington's handwriting is not so clear as yours, but I trust you will decypher it without much difficulty.

'The letter to the *Times* is from my lawyers, that to the *Leisure Hour* is from Sir Philip Rose at my dictation.

'Let me hope that our acquaintance will not cease with this matter, which has cost you, I fear, much trouble, and in which you have shown so much courtesy.—Faithfully yours,

> 'BEACONSFIELD.'

Whether this expression of a wish for the continuance of our acquaintance was or was not mere politeness, neither time nor opportunity was given me to discover. In two months and a few days after he penned that note, Lord Beaconsfield was in his grave.

the autobiographer describes himself as often seeing Mr. Disraeli in Messrs. Marsh and Miller's shop, Mr. Disraeli was in Greece, and did not return from his travels, as I personally well remember, until just previous to the general election of 1831, when he returned to his father's residence in Buckingham-shire to stand for the borough of High Wycombe.'

THE END.

Printed by T. and A. CONSTABLE, Printers to Her Majesty, at the Edinburgh University Press.